Civil Remedies and Crime Prevention

Lorraine Green Mazerolle
and
Jan Roehl

Editors

CRIME PREVENTION STUDIES
Volume 9

Criminal Justice Press

Monsey, New York, U.S.A.

1998

CRIME PREVENTION STUDIES

Ronald V. Clarke, Series Editor

© Copyright 1998 by
Willow Tree Press, Inc.
All rights reserved.

ISSN (series): 1065-7029

ISBN: 1-881798-12-7

Contents

continued

PART III: COMMUNITY PERSPECTIVES

PART IV: CIVIL REMEDIES IN PUBLIC HOUSING

CIVIL REMEDIES AND CRIME PREVENTION: AN INTRODUCTION

by

Lorraine Green Mazerolle
University of Cincinnati

and

Jan Roehl
Justice Research Center

Civil remedies are procedures and sanctions, specified by civil statutes and regulations, used to prevent or reduce criminal problems and incivilities. Civil remedies generally aim to persuade or coerce non-offending third parties to take responsibility and action to prevent or end criminal or nuisance behavior. Early examples of civil remedy approaches typically targeted non-offending third parties (e.g., landlords, property owners) and used nuisance and drug abatement statutes to control problems. The penalties of these abatement statutes included repair requirements, fines, padlocks/closing, and property forfeiture, and sought to make owners and landlords maintain drug- and nuisance-free properties.

In recent years, the scope of civil remedies has expanded beyond non-offending third parties to specifically and directly target offending parties such as batterers, gangs, and delinquent youths. Civil remedies that directly target offenders (e.g., restraining orders, injunctions against loitering and gang member congregations) are oftentimes intermediate steps ultimately enforced by criminal sanctions (arrest, prosecution and incarceration of offenders).

Growth in the use of civil remedies as a crime control tactic is attributable to several factors. First, increasing use of civil remedies came at a time when communities and law enforcement officials recognized that criminal remedies were neither effective nor desirable for a wide range of problems. Second, the growth of civil remedy approaches to crime control coincided with increasing societal emphasis on prevention. Third, the accessibility of civil remedy tools provided alternative avenues to reverse the spiral of decline in many frustrated and disadvantaged communities.

These days, civil remedy solutions are the norm rather than the exception. Pressures on property owners and managers often result in the correction of health and safety violations, enforced clean-up and upkeep of blighted properties, eviction of problem tenants, and improved property management. Bans on drug paraphernalia, alcohol-related billboard advertising, spray paint, and cigarette machines in high-crime areas are used to prevent and reduce many problems. Injunctions against gangs, youth curfews and domestic violence restraining orders are used to prevent and deter potential perpetrators from engaging in criminal behavior. Many Crime Prevention Through Environmental Design (CPTED) initiatives and other prevention strategies (e.g., removing pay phones from drug market areas) are viewed as civil remedies. When useful civil statutes are absent, community forces, legislators, and policy makers often work together to enact new legislation.

This volume, *Civil Remedies and Crime Prevention*, explores the theory and practice of civil remedies. We offer a collection of papers that examine the social, legal and political issues raised by the use of civil remedies as well as a series of evaluative reports covering current civil remedy practices in the U.S., England and Australia. The contributors offer a critical snapshot of civil remedies in the mid-1990s, and point to the work to be done in the years ahead.

Our introduction has several goals: first, we explore some of the reasons behind the rapid development and acceptance of civil remedies for crime control purposes; second, we examine some of the linkages of civil remedy practices to theories underlying many other crime prevention and control initiatives; third, we outline the critical dimensions of civil remedy tactics and provide some supporting examples; and finally, we discuss the papers that are included in this volume and identify how they contribute to our understanding of civil remedies as an emerging and important area of crime control.

THE GROWING USE OF CIVIL REMEDIES

The proliferation of civil remedies used to control crime problems began in the mid-1980s. Several early civil remedy cases captured the attention of the public and law enforcement community, and catapulted the use of civil remedies from relative obscurity to mainstream crime prevention practices. One early test case involved the Westside Crime Prevention Association, a group of neighbors in New York City that in 1986 had exhausted all traditional avenues to eliminate drug activity at a local crack house. A private attorney, working pro bono on the association's behalf, filed a lawsuit against the property owner based on a 125-year-old state statute originally enacted to control "bawdy houses" (i.e., prostitution establishments). The statute defined a nuisance property as any real property used for "illegal trade, business, or manufacture," and outlined civil sanctions (up to a $5,000 penalty) that a property owner could face if the owner "does not in good faith diligently" move to evict the tenant (Real Property Actions and Proceedings Law, Section 715). The neighborhood association won its case: the tenant was evicted, the house was sold, and the legal costs of the association were paid from the proceeds. The "bawdy house" statute is now used in similar situations by the Manhattan District Attorney's Office.

Another early pioneer in civil remedies was Portland, OR's Office of Neighborhood Associations, which helped enact a municipal drug house ordinance in 1987 enabling the city to impose civil penalties on owners of properties used for drug dealing. Within a month of the ordinance's enactment, 12 civil suits were filed against property owners (Davis and Lurigio, 1996). Rather than needing to prove beyond a reasonable doubt that a crime had been committed, the civil suits were simply predicated on evidence that a drug nuisance existed. Ironically, the case is often made that a drug nuisance problem exists by virtue of a history of vice arrests at the property.

One reason behind the rapid development and acceptance of civil remedies for crime prevention and control is the recognition that criminal remedies — arrest, prosecution and incarceration — often fail to resolve the problem, even in the short term and especially in the long-term (Moore and Kleiman, 1989; Sherman, 1990; Uchida, et al., 1990). For example, drug dealers may continue to deal while out on bail and on probation; if they are jailed, others are likely to quickly take their place. A motel that harbors drug use and prostitution with a long history of vice arrests is likely to persist unless there are changes in the management of the motel.

Unlike traditional criminal sanctions, civil remedies attempt to resolve underlying problems: the motel's poor management, the absentee owner's neglect. The use of civil remedies tends to be proactive and oriented toward prevention (Hansen, 1991), while at the same time aims at enhancing the quality of life (Rosenbaum, et al, 1992) and eliminating opportunities for problems to occur or reappear (Feldman and Trapp, 1990; National Crime Prevention Council, 1992). A number of civil remedy approaches move beyond coercing and pressuring owners to evict, renovate, repair and clean up their properties to efforts that provide training and assistance to the owner/landlord to prevent his or her other properties from becoming crime magnets (Green, 1996; Skogan and Hartnett, 1997).

Civil remedies also offer an attractive alternative to criminal remedies since they are relatively inexpensive and easy to implement (Davis and Lurigio, 1996). A single citizen can make a difference by documenting a problem, pressuring police and prosecutors to take appropriate civil action, or spearheading a drive to establish useful local ordinances (Davis, et al., 1991). A group of neighbors can pursue a nuisance abatement action in small claims court without the assistance of police or public prosecutors (Roehl, et al., 1997). Moreover, civil laws require a lower burden of proof than criminal actions and loosen the requirements of due process, making them easier to apply yet open to concerns about fairness and equity (Cheh, 1991).

CIVIL REMEDIES IN A CRIME PREVENTION CONTEXT

Civil remedies are relatively new tools for reducing and preventing crime and incivilities. As shown by the recent application of the century-old bawdy house statute, many rely on civil statutes that have been on the books for years. In form, and in the underlying principles, civil remedies are consistent with the myriad of crime prevention and control strategies implemented in the 1970s and 1980s and their underlying theoretical frameworks (e.g., see Clarke, 1992; Crowe, 1991; Jeffrey, 1977; Newman, 1972; Rosenbaum, 1988). Civil remedies are also primary tools found in many problem-solving efforts (Eck and Spelman, 1987; Goldstein, 1979, 1990).

The emerging emphasis on place (see Eck and Weisburd, 1995) — heavily influenced by rational choice theory (Cornish and Clarke, 1986) and routine activity theory (Cohen and Felson, 1979; Felson, 1986, 1994) — parallels the trend to use civil remedies to control crime and quality-of-life problems at crime-prone places. The goals underlying many civil remedy actions also have some theoretical connection to what Wilson and Kelling (1982) describe as the "broken windows" hypothesis.

Many civil remedy actions seek to reduce signs of physical (broken windows, graffiti, trash, etc.) and social (public drinking, loitering, public urination, etc.) incivilities in the hope that cleaned-up places will break the cycle of neighborhood decline and decrease victimization, fear of crime, and alienation. In fact, reducing the signs of physical disorder and preventing their occurrence (or recurrence) is the primary purpose of many civil remedies, including code enforcement, nuisance abatement, neighborhood clean-up and beautification, and CPTED interventions. Other civil remedies focus on reducing social incivilities and preventing criminal opportunities. Youth curfews, gang injunctions, ordinances controlling public behavior and restraining orders are all civil remedy examples that seek to alter criminal opportunities and prevent crime problems from escalating. These types of civil remedies also have much in common with community policing (Skolnick and Bayley, 1986; Pate et al., 1986; Trojanowicz and Bucqueroux, 1989); cooperative partnerships among law enforcement, the community, public agencies and the private sector; and solutions aimed at resolving problems for the long-term and improving the quality of neighborhood life.

Civil remedies that seek to reduce criminal opportunities represent a pragmatic application of "opportunity reduction theory," which posits that crime can be reduced or prevented by removing opportunities for crime. Civil remedies that aim to reduce criminal opportunities tend to be directed at potential offenders (e.g., gang members congregating on street corners and youths out late at night) yet may also focus on places, an area that will be examined later. Many target-hardening strategies and CPTED approaches that have a civil basis to ensure compliance are examples of place-oriented remedies that focus on reducing criminal opportunities.

Situational crime prevention also "relies, not upon improving society or its institutions, but simply upon reducing opportunities for crime" (Clarke, 1992:3). Many situational initiatives involve changing the environment and the opportunities for crime in order to deter the illicit use of spaces and encourage beneficial territoriality, ownership and licit use. When a situational crime prevention initiative has a civil basis to coerce compliance then we would classify the initiative as a civil remedy. One example of a civil remedy tactic with a situational component is when an owner of a property that is classified as an "environmental hazard" is compelled to seal the building and, in some cases, demolish or refurbish it in order to put the property toward positive community use.

The goals of many civil remedy activities also have theoretical support from routine activities and rational choice theory. Rational choice theory posits that offenders select targets and make rational choices about committing crimes in order to benefit from their criminal behavior, and that the information and decision processes used by offenders vary dramatically depending on the type of offense contemplated (Cornish and Clarke, 1996). Routine activity theory states that crime occurs when three sets of circumstances are present at the same time and place: a motivated offender, a suitable target and the absence of human controllers who are in a position to protect a target or place constraints on the offender (Felson, 1994). These theories explain how offenders, targets, various types of controllers, and physical and social environments combine or interact to hinder or encourage crime. Many civil remedies aim to change the pattern of people's routine activities, reduce the potential for a place to become a problem and lessen the opportunities for people to engage in criminal conduct. For example, gang injunctions that fine gang members if they congregate in specific areas seek to alter the underlying routine activities of gang members with the intention of blocking some of their criminal opportunities. Ordinances that define parental responsibilities for delinquent youths aim to create or improve the role of what Felson (1987) describes as "intimate handlers."

Another theoretical foundation underlying many civil remedies is deterrence theory, which contends that increasing the costs of crime at places deters the recurrence or persistence of future problems (see Clarke, 1992; Paternoster, 1987; 1989). For example, code enforcement actions that increase the costs of criminal activities at places with crime problems seek to encourage property owners to manage their properties better. Principles of deterrence theory inform many attempts to solve problems using the civil remedy approach by increasing the costs of crime, disorder or non-compliance.

DIMENSIONS OF CIVIL REMEDIES

Civil remedies vary on a number of dimensions (see also Finn and Hylton, 1994), including: the purpose of the action (prevention or control); the type of user who initiates or applies civil remedies (private citizens, police departments, city prosecutors, community organizations); the immediate targets or the "burden bearers" of civil remedy action (suspected offenders, potential offenders, third parties); the focal point of the activities (people versus places); the types of problems addressed (e.g., crime, quality-of-life problems); the types of sanctions applied (e.g., fines, eviction, license restrictions); and the statutory basis of the civil remedy (e.g., municipal ordinances, town bylaws, health and safety codes). In this section we explore these dimensions of civil remedies and present a typology to organize common civil remedies.

Civil remedies have two primary purposes that are not mutually exclusive: they may aim to prevent behaviors and situations before they become a problem, or they may aim to reduce or eliminate problems that already exist. Civil remedies used as preventive mechanisms include such tactics as: youth curfews; bans on alcohol advertising; bans on cigarette machines in high-crime areas; restrictions on bars and liquor stores; landlord training in drug-free management; drug-free zones; and CPTED applications. Civil remedies used to mitigate problems already in progress incorporate many of the preventive mechanisms but also encompass drug abatement, nuisance abatement, enforcement of health and safety codes, restraining orders, gang injunctions, and neighborhood clean-ups.

Civil remedies may be initiated by just about anybody: private citizens, grassroots neighborhood groups, community organizations, police officers, code enforcement officers, prosecutors and others. In cities and counties across the U.S., police, code enforcement officers, businesses and community groups are working together to solve neighborhood problems using civil remedies, often under community policing or problem-oriented policing umbrellas. As problems are identified by the police and community, civil sanctions are brought to bear on the problem through violations cited by local health, safety, and building officials and by public prosecutors.

Oftentimes, citizens and community organizations identify problems and problem properties, gather data on them and use this information to persuade other regulatory officials (police officers, building inspectors, city attorneys, etc.) to take action against the property owners and/or the offenders themselves. Citizens and community organizations may also take actions themselves; for example, when they sue a property owner in small claims court for knowingly maintaining a public nuisance. In all forms of civil remedies, however, the ultimate sanctions are applied by the courts, which can order the forfeiture of property or incarceration of offenders.

Many civil remedies are aimed at non-offending third parties — the property owners, business owners and place managers believed to be able to exert some control over an immediate environment and the people who frequent it (see also Buerger and Mazerolle, 1998). Many nuisance and drug abatement processes are applied against third parties, including owners of rental properties, storekeepers, and bar and liquor store owners. A large proportion of civil remedies, however, are directed against potential offenders or those people engaged in activities thought to lead to criminal activity. Civil remedies that target potential offenders typically seek to regulate and control social activity. Many of these social activities (e.g., sleeping in public) become the target of civil remedy action only under "certain circumstances." These "certain circumstances" are, however, defined within a complex understanding of acceptable social norms that vary by beat and neighborhood. Finally, other forms of civil remedies are targeted against offenders themselves. Injunctions against gang members and domestic violence restraining orders, for example, are used to directly control the behaviors of offenders. These forms of civil remedies are typically and ultimately enforced by criminal remedies: if the civil sanctions of fines fail to eliminate behaviors, offenders may be arrested and prosecuted.

Civil remedies are applied to a wide range of problems, from serious crimes (e.g., drug trafficking, gang-related crime) to incivilities and quality-of-life issues (e.g., panhandling, cruising, blight) to legal practices that run counter to positive neighborhood life (e.g., operating hours of bars, billboard advertising). The National Crime Prevention Council (1996) presents a long list of incivilities and serious crimes that may be prevented by the application of civil laws (see also Finn and Hylton, 1994).

The sanctions of civil remedies vary greatly and include required repairs of properties, fines, forfeiture of property or forced sales to meet fines and penalties, eviction, padlocking or temporary closure (typically up to a year) of a rented residential or commercial property, license restrictions and/or suspensions, and ultimately arrest and incarceration. Oftentimes, several civil remedies may be initiated simultaneously to solve one problem. To solve a drug problem, for example, a suspected offender might be evicted and the property owner cited for building code violations and asked to attend a landlord training seminar.

The authority for civil remedies lies in a variety of civil statutory bases including municipal ordinances; local, state, and federal statutes; health and safety codes; and uniform building standards. Most states and local jurisdictions have a wide range of civil statutes currently on the books that are being rediscovered and applied to problems in new and different ways. Where civil statutes are not available, community organizations, legislators, and policymakers are passing new laws or refining old ones.

Civil remedies represent a growing area for crime prevention that has been, until now, largely unexplored in the academic literature. We suggest that future discourse on the use of civil remedies could be guided by conceptualizing civil remedies into a typology. Two dimensions appear to help organize the application of civil laws, ordinances and regulations to crime control and prevention: the focal points of the anti-social (or illegal) activity (persons or places), and the persons who bear the burden of the enforcement action (suspected offenders, potential offenders or non-offending third parties). We provide some examples of civil remedies within this conceptual framework in Figure 1.

The person/place dichotomy is an important distinction given the increased attention in recent years to controlling the anti-social behavior in "hot spots" and high-crime places (see Eck and Weisburd, 1995). In particular, community and problem-oriented policing efforts often have a "place" focus as opposed to a "person" focus. Place-oriented enforcement action still seeks to control the activities of persons at these places, yet the focus of place-control efforts are to alter the environmental landscape in ways that deter persons from frequenting these problem places. Changing the physical and routine activity patterns of a place constitutes the primary focus of civil remedies that we define as being place-oriented. Examples of place-oriented civil remedies include cleaning up graffiti and trash, padlocking crack houses, changing street configurations, removing incoming-call capacities of public pay phones in drug market locations, and enacting "cruising" laws along problem streets. In contrast, person-oriented civil remedies focus on the specific actions of individuals, regardless of where the action takes place. For example, we define youth curfew laws that are citywide as "person-oriented." While the enforcement of youth curfews often informally focuses attention on certain problem places, this type of civil remedy is designed more to concentrate on the people who are perceived as "problem youths" as opposed to what is perceived as a "problem place."

The second dimension that we present in Figure 1 distinguishes between those people who become the "bearers of the burden" of civil remedy action. We identify three groups of people who tend to bear the enforcement burden of civil remedy actions: suspected offenders, potential offenders and non-offending third parties. Suspected offenders are those people who are thought to have engaged in criminal conduct yet are not criminally charged for the transgression. Nonetheless, the activities of these "suspected offenders" are controlled through civil remedy action, either directly (person-focused remedy) or indirectly (place-focused remedy). Domestic violence restraining orders, for example, control the activities of a suspected batterer and thus we classify this remedy as a person-oriented remedy where the burden bearer is the "first person" (the batterer). A gang area ban that prohibits gang members from frequenting specified locations is an example of a civil remedy action that targets suspected offenders and is place-oriented. In San Fernando, CA, for example, the city council passed an "urgency" ordinance that provided a fine for entry of a gang member into Las Palmas Park. The ordinance used a two-step approach in which known gang members were given written notice not to re-enter the park, and were cited for violating the ordinance and fined $250 if they were subsequently found in the park (see National Crime Prevention Council, 1996:43). The burden-bearer in this example is the gang member, yet he or she only bears the burden when frequenting a specific place: Las Palmas Park.

We define "potential offenders" as those people who are not necessarily engaged in criminal activities (such as drug dealing, robberies, burglaries) but behave in a manner that is perceived as being troublesome (e.g., loitering, public urination, sleeping in public). In many ways, it is this type of public disorderly behavior that paved the way for increasing reliance on civil remedy actions. Criminal laws typically could not be enforced to control these types of disorderly behavior (formal social control), and informal social control mechanisms failed to control the actions of people behaving in disorderly ways. Therefore, the murky in-between concept of "civil remedies" emerged to provide a legislative basis to control potentially troublesome behavior. Youth curfews, restrictions on who can purchase spray paint and prohibition against obscene language are examples of person-oriented civil remedies that target these types of "potential offenders." Importantly, the behaviors that are the target of the civil remedy action are illegal only within a defined context. When that "defined context" becomes a place (e.g., a particular street along which cruising occurs, alcohol-free zones, a school enforcing "codes of conduct"), then we classify the civil remedy as being place-oriented (see Figure 1).

The final dimension of our civil remedy typology includes those remedies where the burden-bearer is a non-offending third party; landlords, parents, guardians, leaseholders and property owners figure prominently in this category. We define "person-oriented" civil remedies that target third parties as those that define the specific responsibilities of non-offending individuals believed (or expected) to have control over other people (e.g., parents controlling their children, leaseholders in public housing sites controlling the people living in their household). Conversely, when non-offenders are urged to remedy the general appearance or an undesirable attribute of a place (e.g., blighted properties, drug dealing from an abandoned house, repeat burglaries of a business), then we define the civil remedy as being "place-oriented." Figure 1 presents our civil remedy typology and provides examples of civil remedies identified as place and person-oriented where the burden bearers are non-offending third parties, suspected offenders or potential offenders.

Figure 1: Typology of Civil Remedies

	Suspected Offenders	Potential Offenders	Non-Offending Third Parties
People	Gang injunctions Domestic violence restraining orders Publishing photos of prostitution clients	Youth curfews Evictions License restrictions Loitering laws Panhandling laws Regulations on sleeping in public Prohibition of obscene/threatening language	Parental responsibility for delinquent youths Youth curfews (parent/guardian clauses) Public housing lease restrictions Laws against cigarette sales to youths Laws against spray paint sales to youths Laws against alcohol sales to youths
Places	Gang area bans	Cruising Alcohol-free zones School "codes of conduct"	Restricted hours of alcohol-serving establishments Restricted locations of liquor stores Code enforcement (building, fire, health, safety) Public pay phone restrictions on incoming calls Property forfeiture Property improvement Padlocking Repair of property Cigarette machine placement Nuisance abatement Mandated graffiti removal Insurance requirements on properties in high crime neighborhoods Restrictions on billboard advertising CPTED interventions (e.g., lighting, traffic controls)

THIS VOLUME

Our book brings together researchers and practitioners with an interest in the proliferation of civil remedies both as a crime control and crime prevention tool. We explore some of the social, legal and political issues that surround the use of civil remedies, as well as examine the effectiveness of various civil remedy approaches. As such, we believe that the collection of papers assembled in this volume provide cutting-edge, thoughtful, provocative and well-researched analyses of the theory and practice of civil remedies.

Part I explores some of the social, legal, political and theoretical issues that are raised in using civil remedies for crime control and preventive purposes. In this section, we asked authors to tease out some of the critical issues that underpin the use of civil remedies in controlling crime problems. The first and third papers (by Sharyn L. Roach Anleu and Martha Smith, respectively) examine some of the theoretical dimensions of civil remedies within a crime prevention context. Roach Anleu tracks the theoretical dimensions of the proliferation of civil remedies within a long history of social control mechanisms. She examines a general worldwide trend toward using alternative means to control crime and social behavior, pointing to the use of insurance within the context of an actuarial model of social control. From a pragmatic perspective, Smith offers an interesting analysis of the way that civil remedies can be used to regulate and control crime opportunities. She suggests that civil remedies play a direct role in bringing about "situational controls" and an indirect role in influencing the decisions of those who control crime opportunities. Using a script analytic model, Smith examines the utility of civil remedies to prevent crime.

Mary M. Cheh draws from her earlier research on the "blurring" of the criminal and civil laws to provide a legal analysis of the different types of civil laws that are used for crime control, summarizing their legal foundations and constitutional challenges to date. Beginning with the limitations and inadequacies of criminal procedures and sanctions, Cheh outlines the reasons why civil remedies have become attractive alternatives and complements to the use of criminal law for preventing or punishing criminal behavior. For the two most widely used civil tools — asset forfeiture and injunctive relief — she outlines the civil laws, legal procedures and substantive rules of application, highlighting the relative ease of their use and seriousness of their penalties. Cheh also presents a layperson's analysis of constitutional challenges to these two civil remedies based on U.S. Supreme Court rulings, concluding that the court has confirmed a "relatively permissive approach to new uses of civil remedies to fight crime."

The final two papers in this section examine some of the political issues concerning the use of civil remedies in crime prevention. Michael E. Buerger examines the elements of the political process that led to the recruitment of third parties to engage in crime management. Buerger points out that the police unilaterally created new forms of public duty using civil remedies as their primary tool to coerce third parties to engage in crime management. Buerger then explores the individual and collective forms of resistance to the use of civil remedies in policing through third parties.

The final contribution in this section is from Robert White, who critiques the use of civil remedies in efforts to control the activities of young people. White focuses especially on the use of curfews, special police operations and the variety of legislation enacted to enforce controls over the behavior of youths.

Part II focuses on civil remedy programs that are designed to control drug problems. Lorraine Green Mazerolle and her colleagues report results from a randomized field trial in which the Oakland (CA) Police Department's drug abatement program (Beat Health) and traditional police patrols were randomly assigned to 100 street blocks with drug problems. Using on-site observations before and after the intervention period, Mazerolle et al. found significant declines in disorder and drug dealing in the Beat Health-targeted blocks compared to the patrol-target blocks. Their research points to the effectiveness of the use of civil remedies to control drug problems, particularly when compared to traditional policing efforts that are targeted at drug dealing places.

The San Diego (CA) Police Department's Drug Abatement Response Team, similar in many ways to Oakland's Beat Health program, is the subject of John E. Eck and Julie Wartell's paper. Using a randomized evaluation design, Eck and Wartell found decreases in drug problems when the police and code enforcement officials met with property owners following traditional drug enforcement action. The results reported by Eck and Wartell support Eck's (1995) theory of the geography of retail drug dealing in that poor place management tends to increase the chances of drug dealing.

The community-based narcotics nuisance abatement program operated by the Cook County (Chicago) State's Attorney Office is similar to others in a number of U.S. cities. Arthur J. Lurigio and his associates present the results of a study of the procedures and outcomes of this large and well-established abatement program. The initiative relies on citizens and police to identify properties involving narcotics sales, and uses three primary strategies — voluntary abatement, prosecutorial abatement and community outreach — to ameliorate such problems.

Address correspondence to: Lorraine Green Mazerolle, Director, Center for Criminal Justice Research, and Assistant Professor, Division of Criminal Justice, University of Cincinnati, P.O. Box 210389, Cincinnati, OH 45221.

REFERENCES

Buerger, M. and L.G. Mazerolle (1998). "Third-Party Policing: A Theoretical Analysis of an Emerging Trend." *Justice Quarterly* 15(3):301-327.

Cheh, M.M. (1991). "Constitutional Limits on Using Civil Remedies to Achieve Criminal Law Objectives: Understanding and Transcending the Criminal-Civil Law Distinction." *Hastings Law Journal* 42:1325-1413.

Clarke, R.V. (1992). *Situational Crime Prevention: Successful Case Studies.* Albany, NY: Harrow and Heston.

Cohen, L.E. and M. Felson. (1979). "Social Change And Crime Rate Trends: A Routine Activity Approach." *American Sociological Review* 44:588-608.

Cornish, D. and R.V. Clarke, eds. (1986). *The Reasoning Criminal: Rational Choice Perspectives on Offending.* New York, NY: Springer-Verlag.

Crowe, T.D. (1991). *Crime Prevention Through Environmental Design: Applications of Architectural Design and Space Management Concepts.* Boston, MA: Butterworth-Heinemann.

Davis, R.C. and A.J. Lurigio (1996). *Fighting Back: Neighborhood Antidrug Strategies.* Thousand Oaks, CA: Sage.

Davis, R.C., B A. Smith, , A.J. Lurigio and W.G. Skogan (1991). *Community Responses to Crack: Grassroots Anti-drug Programs.* Report to the U.S. National Institute of Justice. New York, NY: Victim Services Agency.

Eck, J.E. (1995). "A General Model of the Geography of Illicit Retail Marketplaces." In J.E. Eck and D. Weisburd (eds.), *Crime and Place.* Crime Prevention Studies, vol. 4. Monsey, NY: Criminal Justice Press.

—— and W. Spelman (1987). *Solving Problems: Problem-oriented Policing in Newport News.* Washington, DC: Police Executive Research Forum.

—— and D. Weisburd (1995). *Crime and Place.* Crime Prevention Studies, vol. 4. Monsey, NY: Criminal Justice Press.

Feldman, J. and S. Trapp (1990). *Taking Our Neighborhoods Back.* Chicago, IL: National Training and Information Center.

Felson, M. (1986). "Linking Criminal Choices, Routine Activities, Informal Control, and Criminal Outcomes." In: D. Cornish and R.V. Clarke (eds.), *The Reasoning Criminal: Rational Choice Perspectives on Offending.* New York, NY: Springer-Verlag.

—— (1987). "Routine Activities and Crime Prevention in the Developing Metropolis." *Criminology* 25:911-932.

—— (1994). *Crime and Everyday Life: Insight and Implications for Society.* Thousand Oaks, CA: Pine Forge Press.

Finn, P. and M.O. Hylton (1994). *Using Civil Remedies for Criminal Behavior: Rationale, Case Studies, and Constitutional Issues.* Washington, DC: U.S. National Institute of Justice.

Goldstein, H. (1979). "Improving Policing: A Problem-Oriented Approach." *Crime & Delinquency* 25:236-258.

—— (1990). *Problem-Oriented Policing.* New York, NY: McGraw Hill.

Green, L. (1996). *Policing Places with Drug Problems.* Thousand Oaks, CA: Sage.

Hansen, K.J. (1991). "An Exploratory Study of the Extension of Local Empowerment through Community Policing." Unpublished paper.

Jeffrey, C. R. (1977). *Crime Prevention Through Environmental Design.* Beverly Hills, CA: Sage.

Moore, M.H. and M.A. Kleiman (1989). "The Police and Drugs." *Perspectives on Policing,* vol. 11. Washington, DC: U.S. National Institute of Justice.

National Crime Prevention Council (1992). *Creating a Climate of Hope: Ten Neighborhoods Tackle the Drug Crisis.* Washington, DC: author.

—— (1996). *New Ways of Working with Local Laws to Prevent Crime.* Washington, DC: author.

Newman, O. (1972). *Defensible Space: Crime Prevention Through Urban Design.* New York, NY: Macmillan.

Pate, A.M., M.A Wycoff., W.G. Skogan and L.W. Sherman (1986). *Reducing Fear of Crime in Houston and Newark: A Summary Report.* Washington, DC: U.S. National Institute of Justice.

Paternoster, R. (1987). "The Deterrent Effect of the Perceived Certainty and Severity of Punishment: A Review of the Evidence and Issues." *Justice Quarterly* 4:173- 217.

—— (1989). "Decisions to Participate In and Desist From Four Types of Common Delinquency: Deterrence and the Rational Choice Perspective." *Law & Society Review* 23:7-40.

Roehl, J., H. Wong and C. Andrews (1997). *The Use of Civil Remedies by Community Organizations for Neighborhood Crime and Drug Abatement.* Pacific Grove, CA: Institute for Social Analysis.

Rosenbaum, D.P. (1988). "Community Crime Prevention: A Review and Synthesis of the Literature." *Justice Quarterly* 5: 323-95.

—— S.F. Bennett, B.D. Lindsay, D.L. Wilkinson, B.D. Davis, C. Taranowski and P.J. Lavrakas (1992). *Executive Summary: The Community Re-*

sponses to Drug Abuse National Demonstration Program Final Process Evaluation Report. Chicago, IL: Center for Research in Law and Justice, University of Illinois.

Sherman, L.W. (1990). "Police Crackdowns: Initial and Residual Deterrence." In: M. Tonry and N. Morris (eds.), *Crime and Justice: A Review of Research,* vol. *12.* Chicago, IL: University of Chicago Press.

Skogan, W. and S. Hartnett (1997). *Community Policing, Chicago Style.* New York, NY: Oxford University Press.

Skolnick, J.H. and D.H. Bayley (1986). *The New Blue Line: Police Innovation in Six American Cities.* New York, NY: The Free Press.

Trojanowicz, R.C. and B. Bucqueroux (1989). *Community Policing: A Contemporary Perspective.* Cincinnati, OH: Anderson.

Uchida, C.D., B. Forst and S. Annan (1990). *Modern Policing and the Control of Illegal Drugs: Testing New Strategies in Two American Cities.* Washington, DC: Police Foundation.

Wilson, J.Q. and G.L. Kelling (1982). "Broken Windows: The Police and Neighborhood Safety." *Atlantic Monthly:* 29-38.

Part I: Social, Legal and Political Considerations

THE ROLE OF CIVIL SANCTIONS IN SOCIAL CONTROL: A SOCIO-LEGAL EXAMINATION

by

Sharyn L. Roach Anleu
Flinders University

Abstract: *This chapter examines the concept of social control in discussions of crime and deviance. Discussions of informal social control identified the ways in which the management of deviance emerged and was embedded in social relations: it was unplanned, unconscious, automatic, private and often diffuse. This was then contrasted with formal social control, most closely associated with the criminal justice system which was planned, specific, public, and oriented to specific individuals for their punishment or rehabilitation. Many theorists (for example, Durkheim and Black) argue that formal social control will gradually take over more of the responsibility of crime control in contemporary society. Durkheim also points to the shift from repressive to restitutive law. Current interest in crime prevention again focuses on social relations as sources of crime management in addition to punishing offenders. Using civil sanctions (including insurance) to encourage, influence, require and even coerce people to modify what are perceived to be opportunities for crime commission is an example. Crime management is more indirect, more private and more diffuse, thus having similarities with earlier descriptions of informal social control. This chapter examines new developments in crime control, including the establishment of alternative tribunals that are less formal than criminal courts and that provide opportunities for community participation, mediation and negotiation; situational crime prevention initiatives; and the greater role of insurance.*

INTRODUCTION

Social control has been a central concept in sociological discussions of crime and deviance for the past century. However, it has undergone a number of transformations, most recently in the wake of the writings of Foucault (1979, 1981, 1991). This has led to new interest in the topics of discipline and governance, apart from the institutions of social control, particularly the police, courts and prisons. This chapter maps various changes in theories of social control and identifies new directions in social control mechanisms in contemporary society. It does not propose that these new directions are evolutionary, purposive, instrumental or intentional but seeks to identify some general trends that are occurring in the shadow of traditional criminal justice concerns with punishment and crime control. Among recent developments are the increasing use of civil remedies for crime control purposes, greater input by victims and the community into the criminal justice process, and more opportunities for mediation and negotiation in less adversarial tribunals. There appears to be less faith in rehabilitation as a goal of criminal sanctions, and more policies and programs are oriented to crime prevention. Current developments are neither necessarily alternative social control strategies, nor do they inevitably replace or extend state-centered social control. Empirical investigation is essential to gauge the conditions under which new initiatives for social control emerge, and to examine the relationships between different ideologies and practices of social control.

Using civil remedies to control criminal or antisocial behavior has a long history; what is new is the vast expansion of the kinds of responses to deviance and the admixture of civil and criminal sanctions. Civil remedies — for example, compensation, restitution and apology — can be incorporated directly into the criminal justice process by replacing imprisonment and other criminal penalties. Second, many matters previously dealt with by the criminal justice system are now referred or delegated to or dealt with in such alternative tribunals as youth courts and local courts where there is greater scope for mediation and negotiation, the process is less adversarial, and there is more opportunity for participation by victims and less involvement of legal personnel. These new fora are sponsored by the state but involve members of the community in tandem with criminal justice officials. Third, the decriminalization of some offenses — for example, possession of small amounts of cannabis — has led to the greater use of expiation notices and on-the-spot fines without criminal proceeding. Fourth, there has been an expansion of administrative law, including local government regulations and ordinances, licensing procedures, orders to cease and desist from certain behaviors, and the statutory establishment of specialized crime investigation and prosecution agencies, all of which aim to curb antisocial, harmful and criminal activities but emerge outside or in the shadow of the criminal justice system. Administrative law and civil remedies are also being used to control corporate crime where establishing individual culpability may be difficult or impossible. It is more relevant to talk about the regulation of behavior to achieve conformity than about the social control of deviant activities. The expansion of regulatory action encompasses those deviating from some social norms, including criminal laws, as well as those who conform and have no intention of engaging in illegal activities.

Trends signaling a general movement away from the criminal justice system's monopoly on formal social control for some offenses have variously been termed decarceration, informalism and privatization. Social contract theory underpins the themes of community, apology, restitution and conciliation: crime and anti-social behavior breach individuals' responsibilities and obligations to the community, especially the victim(s)', and social control is needed to restore the status quo. At the same time, there is a return to classical conceptions of crime and punishment: crime is viewed as an outcome of rational action in the context of criminogenic opportunities, and sanctions are equated with the seriousness of the criminal offense. A further important component in contemporary approaches to crime management is insurance and the increasing expectation that potential victims of crime will insure themselves against the risk of victimization.

The following discussion examines sociological approaches to social control and locates new criminal justice programs within this context. The central point is that social relations remain key aspects of crime control and management, but these relations are not necessarily intimate or personal. Crime management is more indirect, private, diffuse and oriented to communities as the location of social control, thus having some similarities with earlier descriptions of informal social control. A significant difference is that contemporary crime prevention programs and attempts to incorporate the community into the criminal justice process are explicit, consciously planned strategies for establishing order rather than emergent qualities of the social setting.

SOCIAL CONTROL

Traditional approaches view social control as an essential integrative mechanism that is necessary for social order. For Parsons

(1951), the theory of social control "is the analysis of those processes in the social system which tend to counteract the deviant tendencies, and of the conditions under which such processes will operate" (p. 297). Social control is contingent upon norm-breaking behavior. It reacts to and seeks to eradicate or contain deviance, and is something positive and ameliorative that facilitates social life. In the 1960s labeling theorists pointed out the lack of consensus on criminal laws and the relativity of deviance, and in the 1970s more critical theorists focused on the oppressive elements of social control. While sanctions might be functional to the continuation of social life at a macro level, or to reestablish social order, the individuals subject to social control experience sanctions as oppressive and often discriminatory. Rather than reflecting a general consensus, social control — especially the criminal justice system — actually reinforces the interests of dominant segments of society, and is used to control those whose interests and activities are defined as contrary to the former. Countless examples of sociolegal research point to the abuse of police powers, the lack of due process, the alienating experience of the trial process and the inhumanity of prisons. Since the 1970s there has also been renewed attention to informal social control within the private sphere of family relationships. Investigations of the plight of women and children subject to both economic and physical discipline and control meted out by fathers and husbands has led to social movements aimed at reforming the justice system's responses to domestic violence, child abuse and rape.

A primary concern among researchers has been to distinguish formal from informal social control, and to identify different kinds of sanctions and the social conditions in which different forms of social control prevail. Formal social control refers to broad institutional expressions of collective or accepted definitions of appropriate behavior, while informal control refers to interpersonal influence or evaluations of conduct related to group membership (Radcliffe-Browne, 1952; Roach Anleu, 1995a). Informal social control predominates where little individualism or privacy exists, strong primary relationships prevail and the community or extended family retains primary authority. It is embedded in social relations; emerges in social situations; and is unplanned, unconscious, automatic and personal (Nader and Metzger, 1963; Schwartz, 1954). Formal social control, analytically constructed as the antithesis of informal control, usually engages specialized officials with the authority to apply sanctions following a trial process. The central concern is with the rule of law, which entails enforcing the rules and punishing the offender who is protected in varying degrees by due process. Different types of social control can operate in the same social setting. For example, in the criminal justice arena much of the processing of cases occurs outside the court and involves informal relationships and expectations among criminal justice officials (Blumberg, 1967; Mack and Roach Anleu, 1995).

Social Control and Social Structure

Changing forms of social control and approaches to punishment are linked with other dimensions of social structure, in particular, market relations and state formations. A stark and controversial statement of the relationship between types of social control is Black's (1976, 1993) behaviorist theory. For Black law is governmental social control that prescribes the normative life of a community, and includes legislation, litigation and adjudication. Law varies inversely with non-legal social control, and includes etiquette, custom, ethics, bureaucracy and medicine. Governmental social control increases as societies become more complex and the style of law moves from penal to compensatory, therapeutic and conciliatory (Black, 1976; 1993). The penal style of conflict management, most closely aligned with the criminal justice system, refers to prohibitions, violations, guilt and punishment of an offender. In contrast, the compensatory style, associated with civil laws, emphasizes the consequences of the conduct rather than the conduct itself, and focusing on obligations, damages, debts and restitution. The therapeutic style deals with individuals deemed to be experiencing abnormalities, while the conciliatory approach seeks to restore social relationships. Increasingly, compensation is becoming the common mode of conflict management in modern societies, including within the criminal justice sphere (Black, 1987).

Durkheim (1938, 1973) is interested in the ways in which types of law reflect and indicate the prevailing social solidarity. He describes differences between repressive and restitutive law, with the former more prevalent in small-scale, structurally simple societies with a strong collective consciousness and the latter predominant in societies that are larger and more heterogeneous, with a more abstract collective consciousness that allows for greater individual variation. Criminal acts offend the collective consciousness and are dealt with by repressive sanctions that aim to punish an offender with some proportionality between the crime and the punishment. Durkheim states that "penal law prescribes only sanctions and says nothing about the obligations to which they relate" (Lukes and Scull, 1983:43). In contrast, restitutory law is concerned with obligations, rights and duties between individuals; the sanctions — in the form of damages, orders to perform specific tasks or requirements to cease or desist from some activities — are not expiatory but aim to restore the status quo. Contract law, torts and administrative law are all concerned with the regulation of personal status and the associated obligations between particular sectors of society rather than between the individual and society. By definition transgressions of restitutory law do not deeply offend the common consciousness (Lukes and Scull, 1983).

In his essay entitled "Two Laws of Penal Evolution," Durkheim (1973) attends to the role of state/governmental power and proposes the law of quantitative change as follows: "The intensity of punishment is greater the more closely societies approximate to a less developed type — and the more the central power assumes an absolute character" (p. 285). He says that the apogée of absolute monarchy coincides with the period of the greatest repression, that is, punishments become less severe as one moves from the most primitive to the most advanced societies. The law of qualitative changes posits that: "Deprivations of liberty, and of liberty alone, varying in time according to the seriousness of the crime, tend to become more and more the normal means of social control" (Durkheim, 1973:294). There is not in reality a general weakening of the whole apparatus of repression; rather, one particular system weakens but is replaced by another, which despite being less violent and less harsh does not cease to have its own severities. For Durkheim, punishment is an expressive institution; its essence is emotion that arises when the collective conscience has been offended (Garland, 1990). Punishments often become a site of collective outrage and political contestation, providing opportunities for citizens to make claims about their perceptions of crime and the kind of society or community they seek.

Reintegrative Shaming

Braithwaite's (1989) theory of reintegrative shaming represents a recent elaboration of a perspective on crime control that proposes the move to restitutive law as an important resource in crime management. It is an example of incorporating civil remedies — especially restitution and apology — into the punishment process. Communitarian philosophy underpins the theory in which crime represents a violation of social relationships, mutual obligations and collective responsibilities (Braithwaite, 1989). This is a valuable antidote to conceptions of crime as rational, pragmatic and hedonistic action. Rather than viewing punishment as ostracizing and only dealing with the offense, that is past actions, sanctions and responses will help restore an individual's obligations to and ties with the community. "Reintegrative shaming means that expressions of community disapproval, which may range from mild rebuke to degradation ceremonies, are followed by gestures of reacceptance into the community of law-abiding citizens" (Braithwaite, 1989:55).

The community can be represented by the state/criminal justice system or it might be more local, consisting of families or neighborhoods, including victims. This provides scope for restitution, reparation, apology and compensation contrasting with the classical approach in which official responses to criminal behavior only involve punishment for the offense, which is usually stigmatizing and where victims have little or no input into the sanctioning or rehabilitative processes. Shaming by the state is less potent than shaming by proximate communities, although effective state shaming is one of the factors that assist societies to maintain low crime rates. Their effects are complementary: reintegrative shaming often is achieved via state punishment, which delivers most of the shame combined with reintegration facilitated by intimates (Braithwaite, 1989). For Braithwaite, social control is effective to the degree that it is expressive and has a moral, denunciatory component (Scheff, 1990).

Some criminal justice policies do incorporate community input into state crime control and punishment structures. Examples include neighborhood watch schemes and community initiatives to rid neighborhoods of specific crimes, including illicit drug trading and property damage. Perhaps the most explicit incorporation of reintegrative shaming has been in juvenile justice systems with the establishment of family group conferences. In New Zealand, the Children, Young Persons and Their Families Act 1989 provides for the integration of Western and Maori approaches to juvenile offending, the involvement of family members in decision making, victim/offender mediation and victims' participation in negotiations over possible penalties in family conference settings (Morris and Maxwell, 1993). Similarly, in South Australia the Young Offenders Act 1993 establishes family conferences that aim to bring together the people most affected by the young person's behavior, especially the victim(s) of the offense and family members, in a relatively informal, non-adversarial setting that emphasizes negotiation and mediation rather than adjudication. Here victims, family members and the police are the proxies for community. Family conferences formalize the opportunity to make amends: to apologize, provide compensation and remedy the harm done. They are also supposed to offer an educative experience and to instill a sense of responsibility. Family conferences have the authority to punish young people who admit offenses, but there is no guilt-producing process or testing of evidence. The Young Offenders Act says nothing about the interests, needs or welfare of the young person being paramount but is concerned instead with responsibility, the involvement of victims, and the perceived interests and concerns of the community, especially regarding protection and security (Roach Anleu, 1995b). The Act minimizes the input of social workers and the department of Family and Community Services, thus reflecting disfavor with welfarist approaches. The other side of these developments is that families and communities must take greater responsibility for the criminal activities of their members. The extent and nature of these responsibilities is a subject of great contention.

Discipline, Power and Control

Much contemporary interest in social control arises from Foucault's (1979, 1981, 1991) key concerns with discipline, power, knowledge, punishment, regulation and governmentality. Current broad understandings of control are not restricted to examining criminal deviance or punishment as the exclusive domain of the state and its legal institutions. In *Discipline and Punish* (1979), Foucault establishes his perspective on punishment as a set of power/knowledge techniques located in a field of political forces, as well as mechanisms for administering the bodies of individuals and through them the body politic. Foucault (1979) views punishment as a set of disciplinary mechanisms, with discipline being a type of power that may be taken over by such specialized institutions as penitentiaries or other authorities that use it to reinforce or reorganize their internal mechanisms of power. He describes a movement from the discipline blockade, characterized by the enclosed institution to, at the other extreme, the discipline mechanism, which entails generalized surveillance. Disciplinary mechanisms tend to become deinstitutionalized and broken down into flexible methods of control, which are exercised by the human sciences adopting a therapeutic model.

Notably educationalists, followed by the medical, psychiatric, psychological, social work and counseling professions, have made the family the privileged locus of emergence for the disciplinary question of the normal and the abnormal (Foucault, 1979). The disciplines function as diffuse, multiple and polyvalent throughout the whole social body; their distinctiveness as techniques for assuring the ordering or administering of human multiplicities derives from their being economical, relatively invisible and provoking little resistance. Historically, juridical frameworks — formally, at least — are more egalitarian as they acknowledge legal rights and due process, and provide various protections for the person defending criminal charges. However, the disciplines are non-egalitarian and asymmetrical. Foucault (1979) nonetheless underestimates the power of law that in many jurisdictions seeks, with success, to curtail the role and authority of some professional occupations. Informed consent requirements, legislation regulating some medical practices and judicial decisions on negligence have evoked open conflict between law and medicine.

The rise of the disciplines in criminal justice policy has been primarily concerned with rehabilitation of the offender, rather than punishment for a crime, which remained a dominant ideal until the late 1960s. Human services personnel — psychiatrists, psychologists, social workers, educationalists and probation and parole officers — provided presentence reports to the court evaluating the needs of the offender, and made recommendations for her or his treatment or punishment. Classification of offenders in terms of their perceived needs was an essential aspect of correctional policy. Wide discretion enabled sentencing judges to impose a penalty most appropriate to offenders and their individual situation as assessed by non-judicial personnel. Community-based corrections — especially parole, probation and work orders — were viewed as less stigmatizing than imprisonment and more suitable for most offenders as they enabled the offender to remain in the community and to repair broken social relationships. These strategies also required the establishment of a casework (therapeutic) relationship with probation and parole officers, who are often trained in psychology or social work. Counseling was a linchpin in the quest for an individual to modify his or her criminal behavior and become a conforming citizen. The rehabilitative ideal marked a shift from an ideology emphasizing punishment for a crime to one oriented to treatment and regulation of the criminal offender; social control is now concerned not just with the criminal offense but with offenders and their criminality. The identity of those engaged in social control has in the process become less clear and the tools of control and punishment less visible (Simon, 1993).

Debate continues about the extent to which, or even whether, non-penal punishments are alternatives to or an extension of state control, albeit in a diluted form (Cohen, 1985). Punishment, once centralized in the prison, is diffused, and the power to punish has become fragmented and less visible. The punitive and juridical functions of the probation officer, the psychologist, the psychiatrist, the social worker and the medical practitioner are less visible and less identifiable than those of criminal justice personnel. Cohen (1979) argues that expansions of community-based forms of punishment blur the boundaries between inside/outside, guilty/innocent, freedom/captivity, punishment/treatment and imprisoned/released (Cohen, 1979). Diversion of most people from the formal justice system expands the amount of official intervention and increases the total number of people coming into contact with the criminal justice system, including those who have not been convicted of criminal offenses, for example, the offender's family and friends. Rather than limiting social control and preserving individual liberty and autonomy, the growth of community corrections widens the net, disperses social control, extends and diffuses juridical functions, and blurs the boundaries between the community and imprisonment (Foucault, 1979).

Foucault (1981) suggests it is not that the institutions of justice tend to disappear or that the disciplines supplant judicial authority, but that increasingly, the judicial institution is being incorporated into a continuum of apparatuses (medical, administrative, and so on) whose functions are for the most part regulatory. Thus, rather than thinking about formal social control mechanisms as synonymous with a criminal justice system concerned only with punishment (or rehabilitating individuals convicted of criminal offenses), it is more relevant to consider how populations, or sub-populations, are subject to governmental and other regulatory forces (Hunt, 1993).

Governments attempt to unify and centralize various forms of regulation in their quest to manage populations. In this process, legal techniques increasingly are directed toward setting up the procedural mechanisms of a wide variety of systems of surveillance (Hunt and Wickham, 1994). This entails incorporating nongovernmental (including market and voluntary sectors), as well as governmental resources and institutions in the quest for crime control. Governments may command that third parties assist with law enforcement; for example, requiring financial institutions to report large transactions is an attempt to identify and deter money laundering and embezzlement. Governments also place an onus on a range of professional occupations — from tax advisers and auditors to general medical practitioners — to report suspected law infractions and the relevant legislation attaches penalties for a failure to do so (Grabosky 1996).

The concept of governmentality describes the dramatic expansion in the scope of government facilitated by the emergence of the human sciences, which provide new mechanisms of calculation, especially statistics, that enable particular kinds of knowledge about populations (Foucault, 1991; Hunt and Wickham, 1994). Statistics on crime rates, numbers of convictions, guilty pleas and the size of prison populations, for example, are correlated with geographic and demographic data to become critical components in contemporary criminal justice (or law and order) programs and policies that constitute a major aspect of governments' mandate. Criminological researchers advise which areas of a city or neighborhoods experience high crime rates, and identify which categories of people — in terms of age, sex, employment, marital status, geographical mobility and socioeconomic status — are at risk of criminal offending or victimization. Based on such knowledge, governments can attempt to regulate populations via legal and quasi-legal forms of intervention in order to achieve such specific ends as crime control or crime prevention (Hunt, 1993).

SITUATIONAL CRIME PREVENTION

Situational crime prevention is an important perspective in contemporary discussions of crime control, and policy makers have adopted crime prevention programs with alacrity. New programs emerge alongside, not necessarily replacing or providing alternatives to, traditional crime control pursuits. The underlying theory is that criminal events occur within opportunity structures. Proponents concentrate on the circumstances or situations in which criminal activities are conducted and not on the sociopsychological characteristics of offenders. Cohen and Felson's (1979) routine activity approach assumes criminal inclination, and examines the ways in which the spatio-temporal organization of social life affects opportunities for criminal activity and facilitates individuals' realization of their criminal tendencies. They propose that the convergence in time and space of potential offenders, suitable targets and an absence of capable guardians is conducive to predatory crimes. Mobility afforded by cars; the increase in empty residences because household members are away at work, school or on vacation; and light, portable electronic durables all increase the opportunities for predatory crimes and the risk of victimization (Cohen and Felson, 1979).

Opportunity theory has always been a central perspective in criminology that has been important in giving a sense of the social structure of criminal activity rather relying on the personal, individualistic characteristics of offenders (Birkbeck and LaFree, 1993). What is new is that rather than looking at the opportunities from a macro perspective, there is more specific identification of situational opportunities and recommendations on how to modify them. Situational crime prevention approaches are policy-oriented and provide explicit and practical suggestions on reducing the risk of victimization. Advocates of this approach conceptualize criminal activity as the outcome of rational decision making in the context of perceived available opportunities and the lack of adequate social control (Clarke, 1980, 1992; Gottfredson and Hirschi, 1990). Accordingly, a strategy to prevent or manage crime must modify the spatial, temporal, social and physical opportunities, thereby indirectly affecting criminal behavior. Clarke offers 12 techniques of situational crime prevention that involve increasing potential offenders' effort, increasing their risks and reducing their rewards (Clarke, 1992).

Crime prevention also entails attention to geographic and spatial locations — 'hot spots' — where crimes frequently and are likely to occur, for example, some neighborhoods, specific kinds of buildings or sites, and such public spaces as parks or beach foreshores, shopping malls, public transport systems and central business districts. Behaviors deemed to be ancillary to or even causing criminal deviance, for example, alcohol consumption, are also targeted. Situational crime prevention programs rely on the collection of data about crime problems, input by criminologists and evaluation research (Clarke, 1992). Statistical information correlates crime rates with a range of such independent variables as neighborhood, location and building type in order to formulate crime profiles that then lead to discussions about probabilities and the distribution of crime risks. The categories — that is the specific situations calculated as presenting criminogenic opportunities — then become subject to regulation/governance/surveillance. Those same locations or situations are also the sites of conformity: the same opportunities may be taken for legitimate or illegitimate pursuits. Regulating or modifying these situations also affects conforming behavior and individuals who do not intend to engage in criminal or antisocial activity. A stark example of this is the way in which Disney World, the quintessential American leisure and fun park, melds childhood fantasies and uninhibited enjoyment with surveillance, crowd management and private corporate policing to achieve conformity and control. Physical barriers and constant direction from well-known Disney characters reduce opportunities for individuals' free movement and disorder. Social control is embedded in the very structure of Disney World and thus goes unnoticed by most visitors (Shearing and Stenning 1992).

At a practical/policy level, this method of social control parallels a shift away from punishing or rehabilitating individuals for breaking the law to regulating the behavior and activities of various people in specific locations with the aim of crime prevention. This involves identifying and reducing criminogenic places constituted by situations, opportunities and conditions. Current crime prevention programs that seek to modify opportunities are less concerned with wider economic and social causes of crime, the motivational factors preceding criminal activity or the politics of crime control. There is little attention to the definitions behind criminalizing some activities but not others, or to the kinds of activities deemed to be antisocial and subject to crime prevention strategies.

Altering opportunities for criminal activity can also involve regulating the activities of individuals (third parties) who are not engaged in criminal activity, but who because of their relations with potential offenders can actually but unintentionally enhance criminal opportunities. Their facilitation of crime can be inadvertent and unconscious. This approach also involves using administrative laws and regulatory codes initially established to achieve other non-crime related goals, for example, protecting the rights of tenants vis-à-vis property owners, public health and safety, and protecting employees from dangerous or unhealthy workplaces. Examples of regulating the activities of third parties in the quest to modify crime locations or situations include:

- *Property owners*: Various planning, health and housing regulations can be used to require property owners to maintain their premises, especially if they are rental properties, in order to reduce the likelihood that they will become crime sites. Green (1996) evaluates the Specialized Multi-Agency Response Team program, a central tactic of which is administering civil codes to ensure that property owners take responsibility for properties showing evidence of drug and disorder problems. Representatives from city agencies inspect drug nuisance locations and enforce local housing, fire and safety codes where necessary. This allows the police to improve the physical appearance of problem places and create an environment where people are less able or willing to engage in illegal activity. Thus, the program extends the responsibility for crime control into the realm of non-offending third parties (Buerger and Mazerolle, 1998).

- *Business owners*: Local government regulations can specify who may purchase certain goods or services as a way of rendering criminal activity more difficult. For example, some industry codes of practice limit access to and possession of spray paint that can be used to deface property. Some local councils in Adelaide, Australia have appointed crime prevention officers whose tasks include establishing a graffiti register to document tags and suspected culprits, and conducting random checks on shops selling graffiti tools to obtain compliance to an industry code of practice (Cowham, 1996). Administrative laws, including health and safety legislation and the granting or withdrawal of licences, also regulate behavior to reduce the incidence of criminal or illegal activity. In some jurisdictions it is an offense for alcohol to be sold to an intoxicated person. The South Australian

Liquor Licensing Act 1997 specifies that: "If liquor is sold or supplied on licensed premises to a person who is intoxicated the licensee, the manager of the licensed premises and the person by whom the liquor is sold or supplied are each guilty of an offense" (sec. #108 [1]), with a maximum penalty of AUS$20,000. The legislation also provides for defenses to potential allegations regarding its breach. Other crime prevention activities include reducing cash holdings, installing security personnel and video surveillance cameras, making entry (and exit) more complicated, and attaching security tags to goods.

- *Potential victims*: Increasingly, the onus falls on individuals to minimize their chances of becoming a crime victim. Police and insurance companies expect home and business owners to have appropriate and adequate security and not to act negligently, for example, by leaving a door or window open. Much of the responsibility for the management of such property crimes as house break-ins and household burglary has shifted from the police to insurance companies. As victims of burglaries will get little satisfaction from the criminal justice system due to the very low clearance rate for these crimes, insurance policies are necessary to provide some compensation and security.[1] This means, of course, that those who cannot afford adequate or any insurance are unlikely to recover their stolen goods or be compensated for any loss due to theft. Interestingly, to some extent criminal justice officials (and others) have always considered female victims of sexual assault and rape as responsible for failing to minimize the opportunities for the offense.

- *Guardians:* The establishment of family group conferences in some juvenile justice systems aims to reinstate parental discipline and encourage young people's law-abiding activities. Parental responsibility laws, where they exist, seek to ensure that parents take disciplinary or corrective action by making them liable for the damage caused by their children (National Crime Prevention Council, 1996). For example, in New South Wales, Australia, the Children (Parental Responsibility) Act 1994 provides that in some cases where a court finds a child guilty of an offense instead of imposing criminal penalties it may require the child to submit to parental (or other guardian) supervision and require that the parent(s) undertake to guarantee the child's compliance with requirements specified by the court. The legislation also criminalizes parental behavior in stating that: "A parent who, by wilful default, or by neglecting to exercise proper care and guardianship of the child, has contributed to the commission of an offence of which the child has been found guilty, is guilty of an offence" (sec. # 9[1]).

Crime as Risk

The growing reliance on probability, opportunity reduction and loss prevention signals a trend toward an insurance or actuarial model of social control. This model tends to treat crime as a fortuitous event the effects of which can be spread across communities of risk takers (Reichman, 1986). Risk becomes something calculable when it is spread across a population and insurers identify populations (or risk categories) by correlating relevant characteristics, so that individuals are categorized according to the same characteristics they share with others in the classification (Ewald, 1991). Property insurance operates to manage the consequences of criminal activities by spreading the risks across categories of non-offenders, that is, potential victims. The categories that insurers create are not moral communities engendering a sense of collective solidarity among members, but artificial actuarial groupings compared and ranked according to knowledge and predictions about risk (Ewald, 1991; Simon, 1987; 1988).

Managing crime risks shifts the focus of control from the offenders to potential victims. From an insurance viewpoint the spreading of the risk requires individual policy holders to conform with certain criteria, some of which will relate to being individually responsible for reducing crime risks. There is also pressure (financial incentives in the form of lower premiums or more advantageous policies) for potential victims to modify their own behavior, often taking the form of regulation and social control, in order to reduce the risk of victimization. Before property insurance is granted, homeowners must ensure that their home has a certain level of security indicated by locks, the marking of electrical goods and a monitored alarm system. Alternatively, insurance companies can create incentives by offering rebated premiums to householders who install a burglar alarm or adopt other (legal or approved) self-protection mechanisms.[2] For example, the NRMA insurance company in Australia offers a 6% discount on home contents policies for homes in urban areas —defined as high risks for burglary — where an alarm has been installed. The discount is not available in areas not defined as high risk (NRMA 1996).

Some property owners in high-crime areas may be considered a bad risk and denied insurance altogether, and are faced with the "choice" of coping with victimization themselves, relying on the criminal justice process or relocating. Insurance companies are able to require that individuals modify their behaviors to reduce risks. Companies thereby constitute agencies of regulation and social control.

While insurance spreads risk across a collectivity, it is the responsibility of individuals to obtain insurance. Given that the clearance rate for housebreaking is so low, this type of crime is more likely to be managed via insurance than the criminal justice system. This trend is an example of the deregulation or privatization of crime management. Only those who do not have access to insurance — either because the insurance company deemed the person (or more accurately, deemed characteristics of the person) an unacceptable risk, or because the person could not afford insurance payments — will have to depend on the criminal justice system for compensation, justice and recovery of their stolen goods. This reliance on insurance also creates new opportunities for fraud, which companies manage by hiring insurance adjusters to validate the bona fides of a claim. Victims of a crime can also be suspects.

The language of probability, statistics, and actuarial categories appears neutral and not discriminatory or exclusionary (Simon, 1987). Yet categories and forms of classification are the outcome of political and value-laden decisions. As many crime prevention programs target inanimate objects — buildings, consumer goods, public transport systems and geographic locations — arguably they do not discriminate against particular individuals or selectively police some segments of society. However, some types of people are more likely than others to be present, perhaps for non-deviant activities, in the locations targeted. The impact of many crime prevention programs that focus on the prevention of street crime and what is perceived as antisocial behavior in public places falls most heavily on the more marginalized: poor, unemployed, young and indigenous people. These programs often emphasize safeguarding property and maintaining public order, especially in visible locations including parks, shopping precincts and beaches (White and Sutton, 1995). As different social groups use public space differently, programs to alter opportunities for criminal activity also alter the availability of resources for the users of the public space. Crime prevention initiatives can reduce (perhaps intentionally) the presence and visibility of these people in public and semi-public spaces. Their effect is then exclusionary (White and Sutton, 1995).

Unresolved Issues

Situational crime prevention programs do not provide a panacea for the existence of crime in society, and they raise some general issues about social control and crime management. Critics question programs' implications for citizens' rights, their linkages with conservative political philosophies and the increasing privatization or deregulation of governmental/collectivist/welfare activity, and point out potential enforcement problems. Crime prevention initiatives potentially compromise individual rights, as the behavior and activities of a wider range and greater number of people — not just those engaging in criminal deviance — are subject to regulation and surveillance. The confidential relationship between professionals and their clients is being transformed as a result of increasing legal obligations to identify and report suspected law infringements or evasions and even to detect fraud on the part of the clients to avoid possible civil action (Grabosky 1990; Partlett and Szweda 1991). This increases the need for professional indemnity insurance to manage the risks of such legal action.

Individuals may be subject to surveillance — even stigmatized as perpetrators — without having been convicted by a court and without the opportunity to either defend their actions or deny any accusation against them. They may have little opportunity to effectively demonstrate their innocence. This is especially true where non-offending third parties are convinced or coerced into taking actions designed to minimize disorder caused by other persons, or to or reduce the probability that crime may occur (Buerger and Mazerolle, 1998). The establishment of administrative agencies and personnel to administer various statutory codes and regulations also will have fewer protections than those provided by the criminal law. The power of decision makers can be challenged by claims that natural justice was denied or that the enforcers acted beyond their sphere of legitimate competence and designated authority. However, challenging the decisions of administrative agencies is very costly and can involve protracted cases in the civil courts.

A second concern is the affinity between criminological theories and criminal justice policies based on a model of crime as rational action and conservative political agendas and ideologies. O'Malley (1994) proposes that the ascendancy of post-Keynesian, neo-liberal political rationalities provides a much better explanation for the popularity of situational crime prevention than do arguments about its efficiency or its necessity to counter rising crime rates. He argues that approaches to crime control as risk management that underpins situational crime prevention "deals hardly at all with individual offenders, is uninterested in the causes of crime, and generally is hostile or at best agnostic toward correctionalism" (O'Malley, 1992:262). The focus on individuals as rational decision makers in criminogenic situations shifts concern away from more macro conditions that have traditionally been central sociological concerns for understanding so-called everyday or ordinary crimes, namely, the class structure, inequality, education, unemployment, poverty, value systems and cultures or sub-cultures. More recent sociological attention to questions of gender and masculinity and the ways in which they are institutionally structured are not amenable to analyses of individuals making choices in given situations. Attention to the social, economic and political causes of crime and criminalization and social amelioration via long-term collective welfare programs has been displaced by enthusiasm for the situational manifestation of crime and the appeal of short-term programs to rid areas of criminal deviance. There is also a debate about the extent to which crime prevention programs merely displace or diffuse criminal activity (Green, 1996).

Third, the enactment of new codes and regulations to reduce criminogenic situations raises the specter of enforcement. Crime prevention programs may be politically inspired, which means that funding for enforcement may be tenuous and dependent on demonstrable and quick effects. A study of housing code inspection in three industrial cities in the northeastern U.S. finds that much of the failure of these codes derives from inadequate resources. Negotiation is central in regulatory enforcement, which is seen as exchanging information and forbearance for compliance (Grabosky and Braithwaite, 1986). The application of the formal law by inspectors who, like police, are field operators involves considerable discretion and renders the law in action simplified, liberalized and often arbitrary. Most inspections occur in response to complaints rather than as part of the systematic enforcement of relevant codes. A major problem is that not all urban properties are owned by wealthy people and maintenance of property to the code can be very expensive (Ross, 1995). Ross (1995) concludes that housing code enforcement provides an ineffective counter to problems of urban decline because it cannot address the fundamental causes of blight: poverty, racism, crime, drugs and inadequate school and social control institutions. In other words, deteriorated housing and the appearance of neglect do not cause crime suggesting that using such codes as a way of preventing crime in specific situations cannot deal with the causes, only the manifestation or location, of crime. Nevertheless, attempts to improve the appearance and condition of a neighborhood by effectively enforcing housing and other codes can be carried out successfully by citizens and residents even in poor and disadvantaged areas. Reductions in burglary rates, property damage and drug dealing have resulted directly from improvements in local environments (Wilson and Kelling 1982; 1989).

It is salutary to contemplate Durkheim's (1938) discussion of a society of saints, where he cautions that "faults which appear venial to the layman [sic] will create there the same scandal that the ordinary offence does in ordinary consciousness" (p. 68-69). Because crime exists in all societies (although its form or expression changes), it contributes to social cohesion by offending collective sentiments; it unites people in shared indignation and outrage. Concerns over the amount of graffiti, drug-related crime in neighborhoods, and antisocial behavior have all become pivots on which to assert the value of community as an antidote to individualism and hedonism. Often the ideology underpinning crime prevention programs and concerns about community security and safety without question assume that the community is a collective good that will have a therapeutic and healing effect (Lacey and Zedner, 1995).

CONCLUSION

Current interest in crime prevention again focuses on social relations as sources of crime management, in addition to punishing offenders. But the social relations are not necessarily intimate, personal or familiar. Crime management is more indirect, private and diffuse, thus having some similarities with earlier descriptions of informal social control. Crime prevention programs and attempts to incorporate the community (or at least some members of it) into the criminal justice process are explicit, consciously planned strategies for establishing order rather than emergent qualities of the social setting. The criminal justice system and criminal sanctions are incorporating more elements from civil law, thus blurring the distinction between criminal and civil law (Cheh, 1991). This reconfirms Durkheim's (1973) predictions that more and more areas of life will be subject to restitutive law, and that the punitive role of the state will decline as crimes come to be seen as conflicts between private individuals — perpetrators and victims — instead of offenses against the entire conscience collective. Additionally, increasing reliance on insurance to prevent crime risks and to curtail the consequences of crime indicates further privatization of crime control.

The role of the state is not declining in an absolute sense. Many of the crime prevention programs are initiated by state officials, require public funding and involve changing relations between criminal justice personnel and other agencies responsible for obtaining compliance to building or health and safety codes, for example. This indicates some privatization or deregulation of crime management, as well as a greater reliance on the community (however constructed in criminological and governmental discourse) in tandem with the activities of the state. In this context, privatization has two meanings: greater input by communities, neighborhoods and families as well as more reliance on the market, especially insurance, in order for individuals to manage the risk of victimization themselves.

Address correspondence to: Sharyn L. Roach Anleu, Sociology Department, Flinders University, G.P.O. Box 2100, Adelaide, South Australia 5001. E-mail: <sharyn.roachanleu@flinders.edu.au>.

Acknowledgments: The author expresses appreciation to Megan Morgan and John Schwartz for their research assistance on this chapter, and to the external reviewer for very useful comments.

REFERENCES

Birkbeck, C. and G. LaFree (1993). "The Situational Analysis of Crime and Deviance." *Annual Review of Sociology* 19:113-137.

Black, D. (1976). *The Behavior of Law*. New York, NY: Academic Press.

—— (1987). "Compensation and the Social Structure of Misfortune." *Law & Society Review* 21:563-584.

—— (1993). *The Social Structure of Right and Wrong*. San Diego, CA: Academic Press.

Blumberg, A.S. (1967). "The Practice of Law as a Confidence Game: Organizational Cooptation of a Profession." *Law & Society Review* 1:15-39.

Braithwaite, J. (1989). *Crime, Shame and Reintegration*. Cambridge, UK: Cambridge University Press.

Buerger, M. and L.G. Mazerolle. (1998). "Third-Party Policing: A Theoretical Analysis of an Emerging Trend." *Justice Quarterly* 15(2):301-327.

Cheh, M. (1991). "Constitutional Limits on Using Civil Remedies to Achieve Criminal Law Objectives: Understanding and Transcending the Criminal-Civil Law Distinction." *Hastings Law Journal* 42:1325-1413.

Clarke, R.V. (1980). "Situational Crime Prevention: Theory and Practice." *British Journal of Criminology* 20:136-47.

—— (ed.) (1992). *Situational Crime Prevention: Successful Case Studies.* New York, NY: Harrow and Heston.

Cohen, L. and M. Felson (1979). "Social Change and Crime Rate Trends: A Routine Activity Approach." *American Sociological Review* 44:588-608.

Cohen, S. (1979). "The Punitive City: Notes on the Dispersal of Social Control." *Contemporary Crises* 3:339-363.

—— (1985). *Visions of Social Control: Crime, Punishment and Classification.* Cambridge, UK: Polity.

Cowham, S. (1996). "Marion Takes on Vandals in New $70,000 Strategy." *Guardian Messenger,* Wednesday August 21:1.

Durkheim, E. (1938). *The Rules of Sociological Method.* New York, NY: Free Press.

—— (1973). "Two Laws of Penal Evolution." Translated by T.A. Jones and A. T. Scull. *Economy and Society* 2:285-308.

Ewald, F. (1991). "Insurance and Risk." In: G.Burchell, C. Gordon and P. Miller (eds.), *The Foucault Effect: Studies in Governmentality.* London, UK: Harvester Wheatsheaf.

Foucault, M. (1979). *Discipline and Punish: The Birth of the Prison.* translated by A. Sheridan. New York, NY: Vintage.

—— (1981). *The History of Sexuality: An Introduction.* translated by R. Hurley. Harmondsworth, UK: Penguin.

—— (1991). "Governmentality." In: G. Burchell, C. Gordon and P. Miller (eds.), *The Foucault Effect: Studies in Governmentality.* London, UK: Harvester Wheatsheaf.

Garland, D. (1990). "Frameworks of Inquiry in the Sociology of Punishment." *British Journal of Sociology* 41:1-15.

Gottfredson, M. R. and T. Hirschi (1990). *A General Theory of Crime.* Stanford, CA: Stanford University Press.

Grabosky, P. (1990). "Professional Advisers and White Collar Illegality: Towards Explaining and Excusing Professional Failure." *University of New South Wales Law Review* 13:73-96.

—— (1996). "The Future of Crime Control." *Trends and Issues in Criminal Justice,* no. 63. Canberra, AUS: Australian Institute of Criminology.

—— and J. Braithwaite (1986). *Of Manners Gentle: Enforcement Strategies of Australian Business Regulatory Agencies.* Melbourne, AUS: Oxford University Press.

Green, L. (1996). *Policing Places with Drug Problems.* Thousand Oaks, CA: Sage.

Hunt, A. (1993). *Explorations in Law and Society: Toward a Constitutive Theory of Law.* New York, NY: Routledge.

—— and G. Wickham (1994). *Foucault and Law: Toward a Sociology of Law as Governance.* London, UK: Pluto Press.

Lacey, N. and L. Zedner (1995). "Discourses of Community in Criminal Justice." *Journal of Law & Society* 22:301-25.

Lukes, S and A. Scull (1983). *Durkheim and the Law.* Oxford, UK: Basil Blackwell.

Mack, K. and S. Roach Anleu (1995). *Pleading Guilty: Issues and Practices.* Melbourne, AUS: Australian Institute of Judicial Administration.

Morris, A. and G. Maxwell (1993). "Juvenile Justice in New Zealand: A New Paradigm." *Australian & New Zealand Journal of Criminology* 26:72-90.

Nader, L. and D. Metzger (1963). "Conflict Resolution in Two Mexican Communities." *American Anthropologist* 65:584-592.

National Crime Prevention Council (1996). *Working with Local Laws to Reduce Crime.* Washington, DC: author.

NRMA (1996). *Household Burglary in Eastern Australia, 1995-96.* Sydney, AUS: NRMA Insurance Ltd.

O'Malley, P. (1992). "Risk, Power and Crime Prevention." *Economy and Society* 21:252-275.

—— (1994). "Neo-Liberal Crime Control Political Agendas and the Future of Crime Prevention in Australia." In: D. Chappell and P. Wilson (eds.), *The Australian Criminal Justice System: The Mid 1990s.* Sydney, AUS: Butterworths.

Partlett, D. and E.A. Szweda (1991). "An Embattled Profession: The Role of Lawyers in the Regulatory State." *University of New South Wales Law Review* 14:8-45.

Parsons, T. (1951). *The Social System.* New York, NY: Free Press.

Petersen, A.R. (1996). "Risk and the Regulated Self: The Discourse of Health Promotion as Politics of Uncertainty." *Australian and New Zealand Journal of Sociology* 32:44-57.

Radcliffe-Browne, A.R. (1952). *Structure and Function in Primitive Society.* London, UK: Cohen & West.

Reichman, N. (1986). "Managing Crime Risks: Toward an Insurance Based Model of Social Control." *Research in Law, Deviance and Social Control* 8:151-172.

Roach Anleu, S.L. (1995a). *Deviance, Conformity and Control. (2nd ed.)* Melbourne, AUS: Longman.

—— (1995b). "Lifting the Lid: Perspectives on Social Control, Youth Crime and Juvenile Justice." In: C. Simpson and R. Hil (eds.), *Ways of Resistance: Social Control and Young People in Australia.* Sydney, AUS: Hale and Iremonger.

Ross, H.L. (1995). "Housing Code Enforcement as Law in Action." *Law & Policy* 17:133-160.

Scheff, T.J. (1990). "Review Essay: A New Durkheim." *American Journal of Sociology* 96:741-746.

Schwartz, R.D. (1954). "Social Factors in the Development of Legal Control: A Case Study of Two Israeli Settlements." *Yale Law Review* 63:471-491.

Shearing, C.D. and P.C. Stenning (1992). "From Panopticon to Disney World: The Development of Discipline." In: R.V. Clarke (ed.), *Situational Crime Prevention: Successful Case Studies.* Albany, NY: Harrow and Heston.

Simon, J. (1987). "The Emergence of a Risk Society: Insurance, Law, and the State." *Socialist Review* 95:61-89.

—— (1988). "The Ideological Effects of Actuarial Practices." *Law & Society Review* 22:771-800.

—— (1993). *Poor Discipline: Parole and the Social Control of the Underclass, 1890-1990.* Chicago, IL: Chicago University Press.

Wilson, J.Q. and G.L. Kelling (1982). "Broken Windows." *Atlantic Monthly* 249:29-38.

—— and G.L. Kelling (1989). "Making Neighborhoods Safe." *Atlantic Monthly* 263:46-52.

White, R. and A. Sutton (1995). "Crime Prevention, Urban Space and Social Exclusion." *Australian and New Zealand Journal of Sociology* 31:82-99.

NOTES

1. For example, in Australia in the period 1991-92, the clearance rate for break, enter and steal offenses reported to the police was 11% (Roach Anleu 1995a).

2. Similarly, in the medical sphere individuals are increasingly expected or required to take responsibility for their own health and illness. Insurance companies adjust policy premiums, or even deny them, based on such lifestyle factors as tobacco use, alcohol consumption and sexual practices (Petersen, 1996).

CIVIL REMEDIES TO CONTROL CRIME: LEGAL ISSUES AND CONSTITUTIONAL CHALLENGES

by

Mary M. Cheh

George Washington University

Abstract: *The use of civil remedies by criminal justice officials to prevent or punish criminal behavior has grown rapidly in the U.S. in recent years, in part because criminal remedies are often cumbersome, inefficient, and ineffective. Along with the increased use of civil remedies have come legal challenges. In this chapter, the workings of two of the most widely used civil tools — civil asset forfeiture and injunctive relief — are reviewed, followed by an analysis of the constitutional challenges each has faced. The principal legal assaults have involved procedural and substantive constitutional claims. The chief constitutional issues raised by anti-gang injunctions and other forms of injunctive relief are the proper scope of the orders entered and the procedures used to protect the enjoined party's rights. The U.S. Supreme Court's rulings have resulted in some constitutional boundaries limiting the application of the two civil remedies, but with few exceptions the court has confirmed a relatively permissive approach to new uses of civil remedies to control crime. Officials have been left with enormous discretion to employ civil remedies creatively and expansively. As civil remedies proliferate, however, the challenge to maintain principles of fairness and sensitivity continues.*

THE APPEAL OF CIVIL REMEDIES IN FIGHTING CRIME

Society relies on a variety of means to force or encourage people to follow its rules. The most familiar and most potent tool of societal control is the criminal law. A person convicted of a crime suffers the stigma and condemnation of being adjudged a criminal and faces the punishment of fines, incarceration and even death. The criminal law deters misconduct, reaffirms the moral boundary line of acceptable behavior, incapacitates wrongdoers and exacts retribution. But, as powerful and as special a tool of social control as the criminal law may be, it is also inadequate.

In the U.S., the use of criminal procedures and the imposition of criminal sanctions are strictly limited by constitutional guarantees. Criminal defendants are entitled to a trial by jury and appointed counsel; they are innocent until proven guilty beyond a reasonable doubt; they may stand mute in the face of accusation, and no inference may be drawn from their silence. Because of constraints such as these, the use of criminal remedies is often cumbersome, inefficient and ineffective. By its nature, the criminal law focuses on specific wrongdoers, relies on government initiative and prosecution, generally responds to crime only after its commission, and, by itself, does little to upset the conditions or remove the resources that permit crime to flourish.

Because of these inadequacies, criminal justice officials are now vigorously pursuing a range of alternative and supplementary methods to prevent or to punish criminal behavior. They have found a treasure trove of possibilities in the civil law, and have turned to restitution, injunctions, equitable relief such as constructive trusts, nuisance abatement, asset forfeitures and civil commitment. In addition, officials have drawn upon devices characteristic of the modern regulatory state such as statutory fines and loss of government benefits (Cheh, 1991).

Civil remedies offer a range of advantages that the criminal law cannot match in either scope or flexibility. First, through a variety of devices such as reporting requirements or threats of confiscation of property, the civil law can enlist or dragoon third parties to monitor or control would-be criminals. Under the Bank Secrecy Act (31 U.S.C. sec. 5311-5322), for example, banks and other financial institutions are required to report currency transactions of more than $10,000. This reporting alerts the government to possible money laundering and is the principal means by which the government can measure, detect and punish the concealment of illegally obtained income (President's Commission on Organized Crime, 1984). Landlords, parents and spouses at risk of forfeiting houses, apartments, or cars must insure that their business or the family property is not used to carry on criminal activities (21 U.S.C. sec. #881 authorizing civil forfeiture of property connected to narcotics activity). These obligations go well beyond criminal prohibitions on aiding and abetting. In general, the criminal law prohibits culpable behavior; it does not require reporting on or intervention in the bad behavior of others. Under civil forfeiture laws, property may be at risk even where the owner did not condone or did not even know of the illegal use of his or her property.

Second, civil remedies may be employed to strike at the direct supports of crime. Rather than simply prosecuting wrongdoers, civil remedies can target for destruction or confiscation the resources devoted to crime such as entire criminal business enterprises or the warehouses, supplies or other tools of a criminal trade. Drug traffickers, for example, may face not only jail but loss, through civil forfeiture, of boats, planes, safehouses and other assets that would allow others simply to step into their shoes. Law enforcement personnel have long recognized that arrest and prosecution of individuals, even on a massive scale, is often ineffective in ending political corruption, organized crime or the operation of illicit businesses (President's Commission on Organized Crime, 1986).

Third, civil remedies can also target the indirect supports of crime or affect the "habitat," environment, or circumstances within which crime flourishes. Laws such as teen curfews or even simple regulatory measures such as requiring all-night stores to be specially lit may deter crime (Hunter and Jeffrey, 1992). More specifically, the civil law may provide the mechanism for removing guns from felons or the mentally ill, or, through the old-fashioned remedy of nuisance abatement, may close down houses of prostitution or gambling sites. Injunctions may be sought to disband gangs or protect individuals from abusive domestic partners.

Finally, civil remedies expand the punishments that can be meted out to wrongdoers, and they permit punishment without the same cumbersome and time-consuming constraints associated with the criminal law. Civil asset forfeiture is an excellent example. Property owners stand to lose any assets that are used or intended for use in the commission of a crime. Thus, even if the government is unable to prove beyond a reasonable doubt that a property owner has committed a crime, the more lenient burdens of proof of asset forfeiture may permit a sufficient penalty to punish or deter wrongdoing.

Although it is hard to gauge the precise crime-fighting benefits of civil remedies, such remedies — particularly asset forfeitures — have stripped many criminals of the tools of their trade and the proceeds of their crimes, and have successfully broken up criminal enterprises and deterred or prevented criminal activity. Perhaps more importantly, by blending criminal and civil remedies as part of a single law enforcement strategy, officials have taken a more systematic look at the immediate causes and effects of criminal activity. And, on the local level, communities have been enlisted to think strategically about how to rout crime from their neighborhoods (Finn and Hylton, 1994). Nevertheless, civil remedies, freed of many of the individual liberty protections that apply to criminal proceedings, have sometimes produced unfair, disproportionate or harsh results. Individuals have suffered multiple punishments for a single offense, been denied due process of law through procedures calculated to limit notice and one's opportunity to defend, and have lost property, such as their homes or cars, even though they were uninvolved in or unaware of criminal activity.

As the use of civil remedies has increased so, too, have the legal challenges. In a series of cases, lower courts and the U.S. Supreme Court have now met and answered many of the constitutional objections raised against these devices of social control. Many of the courts' rulings have come in cases involving two of the most widely used civil tools, namely, civil asset forfeiture and injunctive relief. To understand the very generous boundary lines the courts have drawn, it is necessary to understand how civil forfeiture and injunctive relief actually work.

CIVIL FORFEITURE

Civil forfeiture is an in rem action, that is, a proceeding directed against property and not against any person having an interest in the property. It is based on the legal fiction that property used in or derived from violations of law is "guilty" and may be confiscated. Although the most popular and well-known use of forfeiture is against assets connected with drug trafficking or narcotics use, property is subject to forfeiture under a wide array of federal and state laws. Forfeiture is authorized in over 140 federal laws, and all states have one or more statutes permitting seizure of assets (Kessler, 1994). The federal and state governments may, for example, seize property smuggled into the country in violation of custom laws, property used to violate gambling or liquor laws, property obtained in violation of antitrust statutes and misbranded food or medicine. Many states have general forfeiture statutes permitting confiscation of "any property" used as an instrument of crime. Under these various statutes, state and federal officials have seized property ranging from cars and planes to currency, jewelry, businesses and farm equipment.

Civil asset forfeiture is easy to use and offers distinct procedural advantages to seizing authorities. In federal and most state forfeiture proceedings, the government may seize property when it has probable cause to believe that the property was used or intended to be used to commit a crime. Probable cause is the weakest of all evidentiary burdens requiring only a "fair probability" that property was used contrary to law (United States v. United States Currency, 1982). It involves more than mere suspicion but constitutes less than a prima facie case. Typically the government seizes property without notice to the owner and without giving the owner any prior opportunity to object. The property owner need not have been charged or convicted of a crime, either at the time of seizure or ever. Indeed, most people who lose property through civil forfeiture are never charged with a crime and, because of the fiction that it is the property that is guilty, they need not be. Alternatively, asset seizures may come long after conviction, even years after a criminal defendant has served his or her sentence (United States v. James Daniel Good Real Property, 1993).

Once the property owner is notified that a seizure has occurred, he or she has a stunningly brief period of time (usually 10 to 20 days) within which to file a notice indicating a wish to contest the seizure. At a court hearing on the matter, the law effectively assumes that the property is subject to forfeiture, and the property owner — not the government — must now prove, by a preponderance of evidence (meaning that it is more likely than not), that the property is "innocent." This shift in the burden of proof is at odds with ordinary civil practice where the party taking adverse action — in this case, the government — must prove it was entitled to do so. In addition, the property owner must pay all of the costs and expenses associated with this legal proceeding and must do without his or her property in the meantime. Expenses include lawyers' fees because indigent civil defendants have no right to an appointed counsel. Lawyers will not take forfeiture cases on a contingent-fee basis because, of course, there is no recovery for the defendant and only a return of the property. And, again, because civil forfeiture proceeds against "guilty" property, property is subject to forfeiture even if the property owner was uninvolved in crime and did not know the property was used for or derived from criminal activity (Kessler, 1994). This harsh 'result is somewhat softened by statutes that may, but need not, recognize an "innocent owner" defense. Federal statutes and some state statutes provide such a defense, but it applies only if property owners prove that they had no knowledge of any wrongdoing or that they did all that they reasonably could to prevent the wrongdoing. For example, the Comprehensive Drug Abuse Prevention and Control Act provides, in part, that "no conveyance shall be forfeited under this paragraph to the extent of an interest of an owner, by reason of any act or mission established by that owner to have been committed or omitted *without the knowledge, consent, or willful blindness of the owner*" (21 U.S.C. sec. 881(a)(4)(c) (1994, emphasis added).

These extraordinarily congenial features of civil asset forfeiture make the tool quite attractive to law enforcement authorities and sharply distinguish it from criminal forfeiture. Criminal forfeiture is an in personam proceeding, that is, an action taken against an individual as part of the criminal case against him or her, for example, 21 U.S.C. sec. 853 (1994), criminal forfeiture in federal drug cases. Criminal forfeiture affects only the defendant's interest in the property, not the property itself. Because criminal forfeiture is part of the criminal process, the defendant enjoys all rights recognized in criminal cases, such as a right to counsel, government proof of guilt beyond a reasonable doubt, and the privilege not to testify. And, ordinarily, property may not be adjudged forfeit until the defendant is convicted of the underlying crime.

In addition to civil asset forfeiture, many states also permit forfeiture of property under public nuisance laws. Such laws declare that certain property or activity is harmful to the public, and they permit the government to bring an action to "abate," or end, the nuisance. Abatement remedies include injunctions that order an end to the activity and forfeitures or orders to seize or destroy the property that constitutes or facilitates the nuisance. State and local officials have used public nuisance laws to close illicit sex shops, seize apartments used as havens for drug use and confiscate cars in which the owners committed lewd acts. Although nuisance forfeiture typically does not proceed on the minimal probable cause standard used in many civil asset forfeiture statutes, this form of forfeiture is still quite congenial to the government. An action to abate a nuisance is a civil proceeding usually held before a judge without a jury; the protections afforded to persons accused of crime are not applicable; and, once the government proves the existence of a nuisance by a preponderance of evidence (meaning more likely than not), an order of forfeiture against the offending or facilitating property follows as a matter of course. Public nuisance statutes vary, but the following Michigan law (Michigan Statutes Annotated 27A:3801) is illustrative:

> Any building, vehicle, boat, aircraft, or place used for the purpose of lewdness, assignation, or prostitution or gambling . . . or used for the unlawful manufacturing, transporting, sale, keeping for sale, bartering, or furnishing of any controlled substance . . . . is declared a nuisance, and the furniture, fixtures, and contents of the building, vehicle, boat, aircraft, or place and all intoxicating liquors therein are also declared a nuisance, and all controlled substances and nuisances shall be enjoined and abated. . . .

Civil forfeiture is justified as a means of depriving criminals of their profits, confiscating the tools of the criminal trade and destroying criminal enterprises. But asset forfeiture has also become big business for the law enforcement community. On the federal level, for example, the Department of Justice's Asset Forfeiture Program reports that, over the last decade, deposits to the Asset Forfeiture Fund have exceeded $3 billion (U.S. Department of Justice, 1985-1995). State and local law enforcement officers have seized millions more over the same period. As one illustration, between 1989 and 1992, the sheriff's office in Volusia County, FL seized an astonishing $8 million in cash in roadside stops of motorists. Although about half the money was returned to property owners in settlements, the sheriff's office netted nearly $4 million over the three-year period (Brazil and Berry, 1992).

Law enforcement benefits directly from seizing assets through forfeiture. The confiscated money and property have been used for a variety of needs such as prisons, prosecutors' salaries, police equipment, payments to informants, and other subsidies to state and local law enforcement programs. Sensing the potential, some local police agencies have been particularly aggressive in setting up criminal opportunities in order to seize property. For example, in certain drug stings, police agents instructed their informant/buyers to arrange purchases in homes or condominiums knowing this would permit seizure of the seller's real estate (United States v. 41430 De Portola Rd., 1992).

Although the government finds civil forfeiture easy to use and highly profitable, courts and commentators frequently describe it as harsh, oppressive and disfavored (United States v. $31,990, 1993). This is because forfeiture, although formally a proceeding against offending property, carries the implication that the property owner either participated in, obtained profits from, or somehow aided others in the commission of a crime. Moreover, whether the property owner did or did not participate in criminal activity, the effect of a forfeiture may be altogether disproportionate to the underlying transgression. It is the hallmark of civil forfeiture that the nature or value of seized property may bear no equivalence to the harms caused by use of the property or the culpability of the property owner. Drug cases are instructive. Inattentive parents may lose the family car because their teenager smoked marijuana in the vehicle (United States v. 1978 Chrysler LeBaron Station Wagon, 1986). A parent's home may be seized because a son is selling cocaine from the premises (United States v. 141st St. Corp., 1990). A boat rental business may forfeit a yacht because, unknown to the owner, the rental party used marijuana on board (Calero-Toledo v. Pearson Yacht Leasing Co., 1974).

Of course, not all forfeitures are disproportionate. It is perfectly appropriate to seize contraband, such as cocaine or stolen property, because, by definition, such property is illegal and may not be possessed. It is also perfectly appropriate to confiscate the proceeds derived from crime because criminals should not be able to profit from their wrongdoing. The real unfairness arises when the government seizes property as "instruments" of crime, that is, any property used or intended to be used to commit a crime. Instrumentality forfeiture is broadly applied and may reach the assets of an organized-crime-infiltrated business, the entire property where a group planning a crime may have met, the apartment of a family where one member is storing drugs or the car used to drive to the crime scene. Moreover, the entire property may be seized even if illegality only took place on part of it (United States v. Santoro, 1986).

CONSTITUTIONAL BOUNDARIES

Since federal and state statutes permit civil forfeiture under very generous procedural and substantive rules, few forfeitures are questioned as unauthorized by law. Rather the principal legal assaults have involved procedural and substantive constitutional claims. The constitutionally based procedural challenges begin with the observation that even ordinary civil actions must comport with procedural due process protected by the Fifth and Fourteenth Amendments. Parties are entitled to fair notice, an opportunity to be heard and such other procedures as will insure an accurate and rational decision. Critics of civil forfeiture have argued that the entire civil forfeiture regime, crafted as it is to be a "prosecutor's tool and a defendant's nightmare" (Kessler, 1994: sec. 3.01[1], 3-4), violate these minimal procedural requirements. They have taken particular aim at summary, no-notice seizures of property and the shifting of the burden of proof to the property owner.

The federal courts have, with one exception, been entirely unsympathetic. Facial challenges to federal forfeiture laws have been uniformly rejected, with courts concluding that minimal fairness and an opportunity to be heard are adequately provided for. In particular, challenges to burden shifting have been shrugged off with the observation that forfeiture statutes specifically allow for the practice, and there has been long historical acceptance of such an approach (J.W. Goldsmith, Jr.-Grant Co. v. United States, 1921; United States v. Premises and Real Property at 4492 S. Livonia Rd., 1989).

However, in United States v. James Daniel Good Real Property (1993), the Supreme Court tugged slightly on the government's broad powers to seize property with no advance notice or an opportunity to be heard. At least with respect to real property, such as land, houses, and farms, the Court held that, absent exigent circumstances, procedural due process requires the government to afford notice and a meaningful opportunity to be heard before seizure. While this was a welcome development for property owners, including those living in private and government owned apartments, its significance must not be overstated. The rule applies only to real property; cars, boats, planes, currency and other "movables" remain automatically covered by the "exigent" need to seize-first-ask-questions later (United States v. James Daniel Good Real Property, 1993).

With no substantial federal constitutional basis to challenge the procedural rules of forfeiture, some state courts, such as the Florida Supreme Court, have looked to state law to rein in the harshness of their state forfeiture regimes (Department of Law Enforcement v. Real Property, 1991). But in most states and at the federal level, it is starkly apparent that any greater procedural protections for property owners must come, if they are to come at all, from statutory reform.

Substantively, parties and legal scholars have argued that, as applied in particular circumstances, civil forfeiture violates the excessive fines clause of the Eighth Amendment, constitutes double jeopardy under the Fifth and Fourteenth Amendments, and is fundamentally unfair to innocent owners under basic principles of due process of law. There are two main ways to press these constitutional claims. The first is to say that civil forfeiture, although called "civil" and enacted as "civil" law, is actually a criminal proceeding. If civil forfeiture were deemed to be a criminal proceeding, then all of the constitutional provisions ordinarily associated with criminal proceedings, such as proof beyond a reasonable doubt, would apply. Since no current civil forfeiture statute satisfies these requirements, all would be declared unconstitutional. Not surprisingly, the Supreme Court has rejected this maneuver, and in United States v. Ursery (1996) it specifically held that in rem forfeitures are civil, not criminal, proceedings.

In Ursery, the Supreme acknowledged, as it had in previous cases, that a civil proceeding could exhibit certain features and invoke punishment that was so punitive that, although called civil, it was really a criminal proceeding. Yet the test the Court used to reach this result is, in practice, so difficult to satisfy that it is exceedingly unlikely that any of the civil remedies currently used to combat crime will be deemed criminal proceedings for constitutional purposes. The Court asked, first, did Congress (or a state legislature) intend a proceeding to be civil. If it did, that is conclusive unless a party establishes, "on the clearest proof," that the proceedings are so far punitive that they may not legitimately be viewed as civil in nature, despite Congress's intent (Kennedy v. Mendoza-Martinez, 1963; United States v. One Assortment of 89 Firearms, 1984). Among the factors that would be relevant are whether: (1) the sanction involves an affirmative disability or restraint; (2) it has historically been regarded as a punishment; (3) it comes into play only on a finding of scienter (that is, intent); (4) its operation will promote the traditional aims of punishment — retribution and deterrence; (5) the behavior to which it applies is already a crime; (6) an alternative purpose to which it may rationally be connected is assignable for it; and (7) it appears excessive in relation to the alternative purpose assigned (Kennedy, 1963: 168-169).

But it is obvious that the Court did not take its test very seriously. Except for a single case where it found that loss of citizenship, though a civil proceeding, was a criminal punishment (Kennedy, 1963), no civil punishments have been found to be criminal for constitutional purposes. In addition, lower courts have routinely and consistently found that the federal drug forfeiture laws are civil and not criminal in nature (United States v. 6109 Grubb Rd., Millcreek Township, Erie County, 1989 [collecting many cases]). They then readily concluded that "claimants....are not entitled to the wide range of constitutional protections afforded to a criminal defendant....[including]....the presumption of innocence....or proof beyond a reasonable doubt" (p. 701).

However, even if proceedings are regarded as civil for constitutional purposes — and most, if not all, will be — they may still run afoul of constitutional guarantees that apply to both civil and criminal proceedings. For example, the Supreme Court has long held that the Fourth Amendment protection against unreasonable searches and seizures applies in the civil and criminal context. Indeed, the Court has specifically ruled that the Fourth Amendment and the protections of the exclusionary rule extend to forfeitures (One 1958 Plymouth Sedan v. Commonwealth of Pennsylvania, 1965). This, then, is the second way to apply constitutional limits to civil remedies.

Recently the Court grappled with the question of whether Eighth Amendment protection against excessive fines ("Excessive bail shall not be required, nor excessive fines imposed..."), or the Fifth and Fourteenth Amendment protections against double jeopardy ("nor shall any person be subject for the same offense to be twice put in jeopardy of life or limb..."), apply to civil proceedings, particularly forfeiture proceedings. The verdict has been mixed.

In Austin v. United States (1993), the Supreme Court decided that some civil forfeitures can impose punishments so severe and disproportionate to the underlying wrong that they will violate the prohibition against excessive fines. Richard Austin was convicted of cocaine possession, and, thereafter, the government seized his mobile home and auto body shop. The government considered these properties "instruments" of crime because Austin stored the cocaine in his home and sold it in his body shop. The heart of the Court's opinion was its realistic appraisal of the nature of forfeiture. The Court pierced the fiction of forfeiture as simply a proceeding against property: it acknowledged that many forfeitures are forms of punishment, and that, as punishment akin to fines, they can be constitutionally excessive.

Not all forfeitures, particularly confiscation of contraband and proceeds, are punishment. Yet, instrumentality forfeiture, particularly loss of one's entire house and business solely because they served as the location to store drugs, plainly could be. The Austin Court gave little guidance on how to calculate excessiveness, but lower courts have judged the nature and value of the forfeited property against factors such as the degree of culpability of the defendant, the relationship of the property to the offense, the duration of the wrongdoing and the harm that resulted. Austin has thus put into place at least some outer limits on grossly disproportionate forfeitures. These limits may be invoked whenever any property is seized as an instrumentality of crime, and they may be claimed by any property owner whether or not guilty or innocent of the underlying offense.

Many commentators believed that three court decisions signaled that forfeitures would also be limited by the double jeopardy clause. These were: Austin; United States v. Halper (1989), which held that double jeopardy barred noncompensatory statutory fines imposed on a defendant for the same conduct that led to a criminal conviction for fraud; and Montana Department of Revenue of Montana v. Kurth Ranch (1994), which held that a state tax imposed on marijuana was invalid under the double jeopardy clause where the taxpayer had already been convicted of owning the marijuana

That idea was dispelled in United States v. Ursery (1996), in which defendants who had been convicted of drug offenses or who had suffered forfeitures because of such activity claimed that criminal punishment and forfeiture for the same offense amounted to double jeopardy. The Court ruled otherwise. The majority began by noting that double jeopardy protects against double prosecutions or double punishments for the same offense. Double jeopardy was not applicable, the Court said, because forfeiture did not count as a punishment for the purposes of the double jeopardy clause. Civil forfeitures, it said, are primarily civil regulatory measures. They were so identified by Congress and, viewed in their overall operation, were not so punitive in form and effect as to render them a form of double jeopardy punishment despite Congress's intent to the contrary. Forfeitures, the Court explained, encourage people to ensure that their property is not used for illegal purposes, prevent further illicit use of property, abate nuisances, confiscate contraband and deprive criminals of their profits. The Court declined to look at the application of particular forfeitures to determine whether they were sufficiently punitive to invoke the double jeopardy clause. It was enough to conclude that, historically, in rem forfeitures had not been regarded as punishment and that although forfeitures may have some punitive aspects, they have not been so regarded under prior precedent. Thus, for double jeopardy purposes, criminal punishment and loss of property through asset forfeiture did not constitute double punishment for the same offense.

The conclusion that forfeiture of a defendant's house because police found marijuana seeds, stems, stalks and a grow light inside was anything but punitive was too much for Justices Kennedy and Stevens. Justice Kennedy agreed that civil forfeiture and criminal punishment did not violate double jeopardy, but he offered a different rationale. Justice Kennedy recognized that "[f]orfeiture [in fact] punishes an owner by taking property involved in a crime," (Ursery, 1996:2150) but he found that a forfeiture punishes for misuse of property and not for the same offense as the underlying transaction. Thus, for him, there could be no double jeopardy because the person was not being twice punished for the same wrong.

Justice Stevens, in a lone dissent, also found one of the challenged forfeitures to be a form of punishment, but he believed this did amount to a violation of double jeopardy. Justice Stevens began with the proposition that forfeitures apply to different categories of property — proceeds, contraband, and instrumentalities — and that instrumentality forfeiture may sometimes constitute punishment. He said, "[t]here is simply no rational basis for characterizing the seizure of respondent's home as anything other than punishment for his crime. The house was neither proceeds nor contraband and its value had no relation to the Government's authority to seize it" (Ursery, 1996:2161). Despite Justice Steven's view, Ursery finally settled — in favor of the government — the double jeopardy issue that had bedeviled the lower courts in numerous cases. Indeed the Supreme Court has now altogether retreated from its earlier ruling in United States v. Halper (1989): double jeopardy no longer applies to any proceeding found to be civil in nature (Hudson v. United States, 1997).

The final substantive challenge to forfeiture involved the protection of "innocent owners," a matter addressed most recently in Bennis v. Michigan (1996). In an earlier case, Calero-Toledo v. Pearson

Yacht Leasing Co. (1974), the Supreme Court held that forfeiture laws do not violate due process simply because they apply to the property of innocent owners. This makes sense if the property is contraband because, by definition, contraband may not be owned or possessed. Applying forfeiture to the property of innocent owners also makes sense if the property constitutes the traceable proceeds of crime, because the criminal should not gain from wrongdoing. This is true even if such proceeds rest in the hands of an unknowing third party. The idea is that, as between harm to the innocent party and closing off avenues for criminals to launder their profits, a legislature may choose to frustrate the criminal. Moreover, a third party, like a lawyer, may be in a position to consider whether property was obtained from a known or suspected criminal.

Commentators have argued, however, that forfeitures applied to innocent persons whose property is simply used by another to commit a crime may be irrational and, therefore, unconstitutional under due process of law (Cheh, 1991). The Supreme Court appeared to acknowledge this possibility in the Calero-Toledo case. There the Court upheld the forfeiture of a yacht because a single marijuana cigarette was recovered on board. The leasor boat company had no knowledge of the drug use but, at the same time, offered no evidence of its degree of care in superintending how the yacht was used. The Court upheld the forfeiture, saying, "confiscation may have the desirable effect of inducing [the lessors] to exercise greater care in transferring possession of their property" (Calero-Toledo, 1974:688). But the Court also said:

> .... it would be difficult to reject the constitutional claim of an owner....who proved not only that he was uninvolved in and unaware of the wrongful activity, but also that he had done all that reasonably could be expected to prevent the proscribed use of his property; for, in that circumstance, it would be difficult to conclude that forfeiture served legitimate purposes and was not unduly oppressive [pp. 689-699].

In Bennis v. Michigan (1996), however, a bare majority of the Supreme Court permitted the forfeiture of an innocent wife's interest in a car seized from her husband. He had been convicted of an indecent act with a prostitute while the two were in the vehicle. The wife's interest was sacrificed even though she had no awareness whatsoever that her husband had behaved or would behave as he did. Nevertheless, the plurality opinion reasoned that there was long-standing precedent permitting forfeiture against innocent owners, that there was no reason to make different rules for forfeiture of instrumentalities and that such forfeitures serve purposes distinct from punishment such as preventing further illicit use of property. The plurality said that, just as Michigan makes a motor vehicle owner liable for the negligent operation of the vehicle by a driver who had the owner's consent, so too it could make Mrs. Bennis liable for her husband's use of the car contrary to decency laws.

Even if the Bennis Court had gone the other way and had mandated a constitutionally based innocent-owner defense, it is unclear whether property owners would have much to cheer about. Many federal and state laws already recognize an innocent-owner defense in their forfeiture statutes, but proving innocence is very difficult. To be innocent, one must have no knowledge of any wrongdoing or prove that he or she did all that reasonably could have been done to prevent the wrongdoing. To illustrate, a court found lack of reasonable care where a parent loaned the family car to a son who had a minor record. When the son later used the car to transport drugs, the car was forfeited (United States v. 1978 Chrysler LeBaron Station Wagon, 1986). Courts have, for example, permitted forfeiture of homes from law-abiding parents because they failed to report their children's drug use to police or failed to throw them out of the house (Guerra, 1996).

INJUNCTIVE RELIEF

Many of the civil tactics now used to prevent crime employ the ancient and widely used injunction remedy. An injunction is a court order directing particular persons to do or refrain from doing specific acts. The order is typically enforced through a criminal contempt proceeding. Injunctive relief is the basis of many statutory programs aimed at unsocial or criminal behavior, including laws prohibiting domestic violence, interference with another's civil rights, participation in gang activity and maintenance of a public nuisance. Injunctions have been obtained against labor picketing, anti-abortion protests, gang activity, and the operation of drug and gambling rings.

Using the injunctive remedy to curb antisocial or criminal activity ordinarily involves a two-step process. First, relying on equitable rules or statutes that permit the granting of injunctive relief, a private individual or government officials apply to a court for an injunction. Because this part of the process is civil in nature, only civil procedural protections apply. This ordinarily means that private litigants or the government have a better chance of success because rules such as proof by a preponderance of evidence and no appointed counsel for indigent defendants apply. Moreover, if the proving party (usually government officials) presents a particularly urgent case, a court will award immediate and ex parte (one side only) relief on a temporary basis. Based on the government's proofs, courts have enjoined defendants from engaging in a wide variety of conduct including appearing in certain public places; having contact with specific persons; annoying, harassing or threatening other persons; or committing other antisocial or criminal acts. In nuisance abatement actions, courts have also entered affirmative injunctions: that is, orders telling the defendant to perform certain acts as opposed to orders stopping him or her from performing them. Property owners have been ordered to repair their buildings, comply with fire and safety codes and evict drug-abusing tenants. Injunctive orders can be modified but may remain in effect for months, a year or even longer with renewals. Some injunctions might be "permanent," that is, remain in place indefinitely until modified or lifted by the courts that entered them.

The second step in using an injunctive remedy is enforcement. Once an injunction is obtained and served on a party, violation of the order is a crime, enforced either by contempt proceedings or the ordinary criminal process. Although some courts have erroneously concluded that minor punishments for violation of court orders are a form of civil contempt, it is clear that any determinate contempt sentence is criminal in nature. It follows that, in these instances, all of the procedural protections applicable to criminal cases must be honored. However, the government retains one distinct advantage even in the criminal contempt phase. Under a doctrine known as the "collateral bar rule," defendants may not, in the enforcement stage, challenge the constitutionality of the scope or nature of the underlying injunction. The only relevant issues in the criminal contempt proceeding are whether the court has jurisdiction to enforce the injunction, and whether the defendant knowingly violated it (Yoo, 1994).

Since punishing the violation of an injunction through criminal contempt is itself a criminal proceeding, complete with all constitutional criminal procedural protection for the accused, one might question why, apart from the collateral bar rule, the injunctive remedy is used at all. Why don't the authorities simply rely on criminal prosecution to deal with the defendant's underlying behavior?

Injunctive relief is attractive for a number of reasons. First, as indicated, injunctions may prohibit behavior that is not criminal, such as ordering named gang members not to associate with other named gang members in a certain area. In addition, unlike criminal prosecution, injunctions are a form of relief that can be molded to particular circumstances, such as specifying the precise conditions under which a batterer may have contact with an abused spouse or how a landlord must end drug use in an apartment complex. Second, injunctions may be sought even though the conduct enjoined would, if continued, amount to a criminal act. Thus, they can serve as an alternative to prosecution in circumstances where it is easier to obtain or to prove violation of the injunction than it is to prove the underlying offense, or in any other circumstances where obtaining or enforcing the injunction is speedier or more practicable. Noting this use of the injunction, one commentator observed that enjoining crime is easier than prosecution because it will, at the injunction stage, result in a non-jury trial and may, at the criminal contempt phase, result in penalties more severe than those prescribed for committing any underlying crime (Dobbs, 1973). Third, some injunctions may be sought by "victims," and thus provide a "self-help" remedy where a prosecutor is unwilling to bring an action. Finally, and perhaps most importantly, the very process of obtaining an injunction serves notice on an offender that his or her conduct is in question, that the courts are involved and that serious consequences may follow if the behavior persists. This by itself may deter future misconduct. There is growing evidence that the California anti-gang injunctions have had this effect (Boga, 1994).

CONSTITUTIONAL BOUNDARIES

The chief constitutional issues raised by anti-gang injunctions and other forms of injunctive relief are the proper scope of the orders entered, and the procedures used to protect the enjoined party's rights. Civil injunctions frequently restrain an individual from committing acts that are not, in themselves, criminal. Since the individual will face criminal contempt for violation of the injunction, the injunction operates as a personal criminal code that the individual alone must obey. Principles of due process require that the individual have fair notice of the conduct that will entitle the government to obtain an injunction, and that he or she have an adequate opportunity to defend and limit any order that may be entered. Moreover, if the enjoined behaviors are too broadly stated, the order may violate constitutionally protected freedom of speech, association and movement.

The place to start is the underlying statute or law that permits an injunction to be entered. If a statute specifically identifies behavior that may be enjoined, due process is satisfied. If officials rely on broad and open-ended laws that permit, for example, "abatement of any public nuisance," then court specification of some standards is necessary. The California courts, for example, have tried to tailor that state's general nuisance law, as applied to anti-gang activity, by requiring that the enjoined conduct pose an actual or threatened, substantial and unreasonable interference with health, property or rights common to the public (Gallo v. Acuna, 1997). The behavior may be — but need not be — criminal, and, in most instances, will be based on allegations of extreme and continuing interference with others' personal and property rights. So refined and narrowed, these nuisance laws can meet the fair notice requirements of due process.

The scope of an injunctive order must also be scrutinized, both as to persons to whom it is addressed and the activities prohibited. To avoid infringing on constitutional rights such as freedom of expression and free association, injunctions may be entered only against persons who have actively participated in a gang's unlawful activities. One's simple association with other gang members or even one's self-identification as a gang member is an inadequate proxy for proving that a specific individual has created a public nuisance.

Courts and individual judges have disagreed over the precise behavior that will justify an order binding a particular individual. The debate centers on whether an injunction may bind only those defendants who are proved to have "a specific intent to further an unlawful aim embraced by [the gang]," as suggested by at least one Supreme Court opinion, NAACP v. Claiborne Hardware Co. (1982); or, whether it is permissible, with notice, to allow an injunction to run to classes of persons (such as all gang members, all union members, all members of an abortion protest group) who are agents, employees or others acting in concert with other enjoined persons. The key, it appears, is whether the broader scope of the injunction rests on specifically describing the coercive and prohibited conduct, and, in effect, enjoining agents from aiding others continuing in that specific conduct (Milk Wagon Drivers v. Meadowmoon Dairy, 1940). Of course, no one may be bound by an injunction without notice. The issue of precisely who may be enjoined under anti-gang decrees will continue to arise as courts struggle to refine the appropriate reach of orders in particular cases.

The scope of a court's order against gang activity must also be carefully considered and tailored. If an order curtails expression, association or free assembly, it must burden no more activity than is necessary to serve the government's legitimate interests (Madsen v. Women's Health Center, 1994; Schenck v. Pro-Choice Network of Western New York, 1997). In California, officials have obtained injunctions that prohibit gang members from associating with one another in various ways (e.g., "standing, sitting, walking, driving, gathering or appearing anywhere in public view"), from wearing distinctive gang clothing or insignia or using certain hand signs or signals to communicate with one another, from fleeing from police or being in a public place after a certain hour at night, and from engaging in a variety of behaviors that "annoy, harass, intimidate, threaten, [or] challenge...any person." Prohibitions that are too broad or too indefinite may also run afoul of the due process requirement that people have fair notice of what conduct is proscribed, and that officials not be permitted to apply the law with completely unfettered discretion.

State courts have grappled with the degree of precision they will require, and, to date, there is considerable variability in the decisions. To illustrate, the California Supreme Court upheld an injunction against certain gang members, applicable in a four-block neighborhood of San Jose known as Rocksprings that, among other restraints, enjoined named defendants from being in the company of any other gang member while "standing, sitting, walking, driving, gathering or appearing anywhere in public view" (Gallo v. Acuna, 1997). The majority acknowledged the breadth of the order but concluded that the order was valid in light of: the extensive misbehavior that led to the granting of the injunction (threats, destruction of property, drug use, violence, etc.); the limited four-block area within which the order operated; the minimal affect on actual rights of free speech or intimate association; the alternate opportunities for gang members to congregate with one another; and the need to show some deference to the trial court's superior knowledge of the conditions calling for the specific order. In dissent, Justice Kennard disagreed, saying: "The evidence presented in this case falls far short of establishing that so drastic a restriction on the rights of defendants and [other gang members] to peacefully assemble is necessary to abate the public nuisance....[W]hen a constitutionally protected interest is at stake....the injunctive relief must be narrowly tailored so as to minimally infringe upon the protected interest" (pp. 619-620).

Finally, because of the special dangers to individual liberties posed by the injunctive remedy, and given the growing attraction of this device to law enforcement officials, commentators and some judges have expressed concern that the procedures used to obtain an injunction do not give a target a complete and fair opportunity to contest the action (Yoo, 1994). The most troubling procedural feature of the injunction regime is the award of a temporary restraining order obtained without notice and without any opportunity to be heard. In many cases, government officials may apply to a court ex parte (one side only), allege a public nuisance and ask for immediate relief. An order is then entered and the affected parties are served with a notice (called an order to show cause) requiring them to explain why a preliminary and then a permanent injunction should not be issued.

If the party does not show up, the injunction is entered by default. But even if the party does appear, the burden of proof may be shifted, thus requiring the individual to show that the order was not improperly entered. Moreover, indigent defendants have no right to appointed counsel to assist them in challenging the basis for or the scope of any injunction, and there is no trial by jury. The standards for granting the injunction, especially under general "public nuisance" statutes, are left largely to the trial judge's discretion. Under the circumstances, it is quite clear that "the injunction...[is] an instrument of some danger in a free society, as well as an instrument of considerable power" (Dobbs, 1973:105). To date, however, courts have rejected facial constitutional challenges to these procedures. As with the procedures used to obtain forfeitures, it appears that any systematic reform or enhanced procedural protections for persons made subject to injunction orders, such as appointed counsel or bans on ex parte relief, must come from an unlikely quarter — the legislature.

CONCLUSION

In Bennis v. Michigan (1996), Justice Thomas joined with a majority of the Court to hold that it was constitutional to forfeit a wife's interest in the family car even though she was completely innocent of her husband's illegal use of the car. Justice Thomas said that history and precedent supported that outcome, but that, not knowing the courts' treatment of forfeiture laws in the past, one "might well assume that such a scheme is lawless — a violation of due process" (p: 1001). The Bennis case, he said, "is ultimately a reminder that the Federal Constitution does not prohibit everything that is intensely undesirable" (pp. 1001-1002). With few exceptions, that sober observation sums up the Supreme Court's relatively permissive approach to new uses of civil remedies to fight crime.

Some constitutional boundaries have been marked. With civil forfeitures, seizure of valuable property only incidentally or haphazardly associated with criminal activity may, for example, constitute the equivalent of an excessive fine. Furthermore, confiscating real property like a home, requires prior notice and a pre-seizure chance to be heard. With injunctive relief, there must be fair notice of what constitutes proscribed conduct and appropriate tailoring of injunctive decrees. Yet, in the main, officials are left with enormous discretion to employ civil remedies creatively and expansively. With modest care, they can avoid most constitutional difficulties.

At the same time, the allure of civil remedies presents a challenge. As the use of this tool proliferates, particularly forfeiture and injunctive decrees, legislators and enforcement officials must maintain principles of fairness and sensitivity. Practices that are constitutional are not necessarily wise. Indeed they may be "intensely undesirable."

Address correspondence to: Mary M. Cheh, School of Law, George Washington University, 720 20th Street, N.W., Washington, DC 20052; 202/994-6748; 202/994-9446 (fax).

REFERENCES

Austin v. United States (1993). 509 U.S. 602.

Bennis v. Michigan (1996). 116 S. Ct. 994.

Boga, T.R. (1994). "Turf Wars: Street Gangs, Local Governments, and the Battle For Public Space." *Harvard Civil Rights-Civil Liberties Law Review* 29:477-503.

Brazil, J. and S. Berry, (1992). "Tainted Cash or Easy Money?" *Orlando Sentinel*, June 14, pp.A1, A16-17.

Calero-Toledo v. Pearson Yacht Leasing Co. (1974). 416 U.S. 663.

Cheh, M.M. (1991). "Constitutional Limits on Using Civil Remedies to Achieve Criminal Law Objectives: Understanding and Transcending the Criminal-Civil Law Distinction." *Hastings Law Journal* 42:1325-1413.

Department of Law Enforcement v. Real Property 1991, 588 So. 2d 957 (FL).

Dobbs, D.B. (1973). *Remedies: Handbook on the Law of Remedies.* St. Paul, MN: West Publishing.

Finn, P. and M.O. Hylton (1994). *Using Civil Remedies for Criminal Behavior: Rationale, Case Studies, and Constitutional Issues.* Washington, DC: U.S. Department of Justice.

Gallo v. Acuna (1997). 929 P.2d 596 (CA).

Guerra, S. (1996). "Family Values?: The Family As An Innocent Victim of Civil Drug Asset Forfeiture." *Cornell Law Review* 81:343-392.

Hudson v. United States (1997). U.S. 118 S.CT. 488.

Hunter, R.D. and C.R. Jeffrey (1992). In R.V. Clarke (ed.), *Situational Crime Prevention: Successful Case Studies.* Albany, NY: Harrow and Heston.

J.W. Goldsmith, Jr.-Grant Co. v. United States (1921). 254 U.S. 505.

Kennedy v. Mendoza-Martinez (1963). 372 U.S. 144.

Kessler, S.L. (1994). *Civil and Criminal Forfeiture: Federal and State Practice.* Deerfield, IL: Clark Boardman Callaghan.

Madsen v. Women's Health Center Inc. (1994). 512 U.S. 753.

Milk Wagon Drivers v. Meadowmoon Dairy (1940). 212 U.S. 287.

Montana Department of Revenue v. Kurth Ranch (1994). 511 U.S. 767.

NAACP v. Clairborne Hardware (1982). 458 U.S. 886.

One 1958 Plymouth Sedan v. Commonwealth of Pennsylvania (1965). 380 U.S. 693.

President's Commission on Organized Crime, Report to the President and the Attorney General (1984). *The Cash Connection: Organized Crime, Financial Institutions, and Money Laundering.* Washington, DC: U.S. Government Printing Office.

—— (1986). *The Edge: Organized Crime, Business, and Labor Unions.* Washington, DC: U.S. Government Printing Office.

Schenck v. Pro-Choice Network of Western New York (1997). 117 S.Ct. 855.

United States v. 1978 Chrysler LeBaron Station Wagon (1986). 648 F. Supp. 1048 (E.D. N.Y.).

U.S. Department of Justice, Executive Office for Asset Forfeiture. *Annual Reports of the Department of Justice Asset Forfeiture Program: Fiscal Years 1985-1995.* Washington, DC: U.S. Government Printing Office.

United States v. 41430 De Portola Road (1992). 959 F.2d 243 (9th Cir.).

United States v. James Daniel Good Real Property (1993). 510 U.S. 43.

United States v. 6109 Grubb Road, Millcreek Township, Erie County (1989). 708 F. Supp. 698.

United States v. Halper (1989). 490 U.S. 455.

United States v. One Assortment of 89 Firearms (1984). 465 U.S. 354.

United States v. Premises and Real Property at 4492 South Livonia Road, Livonia (1989). 889 F.2d 1258; rehearing denied, 897 F.2d 659 (1990).

United States v. Santoro (1986). 647 F. Supp. 153 (E.D. N.Y.).

United States v. 141st Street Corp. (1990). 911 F.2d 870 (2nd Cir.).

United States v. Ursery (1996). 116 S. Ct. 2135.

United States v. United States Currency (1982). 546 F. Supp. 1120 (S.D. Ga.).

United States v. $31,990 (1993). 982 F.2d 851 (2nd Cir.).

Yoo, C.S. (1994). "The Constitutionality of Enjoining Criminal Street Gangs As Public Nuisances." *Northwestern University Law Review* 89:212-267.

REGULATING OPPORTUNITIES: MULTIPLE ROLES FOR CIVIL REMEDIES IN SITUATIONAL CRIME PREVENTION

by

Martha J. Smith

Abstract: *This chapter attempts to provide a first step toward systematically examining the part that civil remedies can play in situational crime prevention. First, it reviews the main features of the concept and uses the script-analytic model to describe the mechanisms by which this approach seeks to prevent crime. The model is expanded to incorporate concepts useful for examining how situational controls are implemented. Second, two main roles for civil remedies in situational crime prevention are discussed: (1) a direct role in the implementation of situational controls as formal inducements for those who influence or control crime opportunities; and (2) an indirect role, either influencing the decisions of those who control crime opportunities or increasing the likelihood that potential offenders will perceive that situational controls have been implemented.*

INTRODUCTION

As advocates of situational crime prevention have long noted, the criminal law is not the only mechanism available for dealing with criminal behavior (Clarke, 1997). Recently, lawyers, researchers and crime prevention advocates have discussed the use of civil remedies as non-penal interventions directed against criminal behavior (e.g., Buerger and Mazerolle, 1998; Cheh, 1991; Davis et al., 1991; Finn and Hylton, 1994; Fried, 1988; Green, 1996; Jensen and Gerber, 1996; Mann, 1992; National Crime Prevention Council, 1996). A remedy is "an action taken by an authoritative body — a legislature, a court, or an administrative agency – to enforce compliance with prescribed conduct or to impose a cost for failure to comply" (Mann, 1992:1809). Traditionally, this term has been applied to actions that are civil in nature. Much of the recent focus on civil remedies in crime prevention has been on their role as regulators of offenders, noting their flexibility (see, e.g., the use of restraining orders in domestic violence cases in Cheh, 1991; Finn and Hylton, 1994) or discussing the potential pitfalls of their use from a legal or constitutional perspective (e.g., Cheh, 1991; Mann, 1992). When used as offender regulators, civil remedies are directed toward an identified person as offender or potential offender.

There has also been recognition that civil remedies can be used in situational crime prevention — to control the crime opportunities of the unidentified offender or potential offender rather than the offender him or herself. For example, in a discussion of the particular types of interventions applied in the SMART program in Oakland, CA, Green (1996) drew upon situational crime prevention concepts (Clarke, 1992) in her description of how the police used existing regulatory statutes, and other forms of inducements, to try to get landowners and tenants (acting as place managers) to clean up properties where drug dealing had occurred so that these places would be less attractive sites for future drug offenses. "Place manager" is the concept developed by Eck (1995) from previous work by Felson (1986) and Cohen and Felson (1979) to describe the non-offending third party who controls a potential crime place. Buerger and Mazerolle (1998) have used the term "third-party policing" to describe the police use of civil controls against place managers. This emphasis on directing crime prevention measures toward the place manager demonstrates the importance of place in crime commission and prevention (see, e.g., Brantingham and Brantingham, 1981; Cohen and Felson, 1979; Eck and Weisburd, 1995; Jeffery, 1971; Newman, 1972; Sherman et al., 1989), as well as the suitability of directing prevention measures at crime opportunities rather than at identified criminal actors (see, e.g., Clarke, 1995).

Recognition of the importance of place in crime prevention should not obscure the potential of directing crime prevention efforts toward others who control or influence crime opportunities, that is, toward: (1) the target guardian (Felson, 1995), who oversees the victim or crime target (Cohen and Felson, 1979); (2) the offender handler (Felson, 1986; 1995) who influences the offender; and (3) the "props controller," a concept developed here to describe the person who controls the instrumentalities of the crime, the so-called "props" used by the offender as part of crime-commission scripts (Cornish, 1994a; 1994b). Civil remedies can assist crime prevention efforts involving each of these actors whose roles deserve wider recognition within both civil remedy and situational crime prevention contexts. Given the four types of persons who can exert control over crime opportunities — the place manager, target guardian, offender handler, and props controller — and the possibility that civil remedies can be used to influence each of these actors, there promise to be a large number of ways to use civil remedies to control crime opportunities.

This chapter draws upon situational crime prevention theory and related models and concepts to emphasize the broad reach that civil remedies can have in the regulation of crime opportunities. The discussion is divided into three parts. The first section is designed to provide the reader with a brief, general description of civil remedies and some of their potential advantages and disadvantages. Section two provides a background discussion of theoretical concepts developed to explain the operation of situational crime prevention, as a framework for describing how civil remedies can be used to help regulate crime opportunities. The third section discusses the direct role that civil remedies can play in situational crime prevention, focusing on the implementation of situational initiatives, as well as the indirect role they can have in regulating opportunities.

CIVIL REMEDIES

What are Civil Remedies?

As noted earlier, Mann (1992) defined a remedy as "an action taken by an authoritative body — a legislature, a court, or an administrative agency — to enforce compliance with prescribed conduct or to impose a cost for failure to comply" (p.1908) The prescription can be based on a legal duty (which is, in turn, based on statute or the common law) or a contractual agreement. Thus, under this definition, civil remedies would include fines imposed for the violation of a civil statute. Cheh (1991) listed the following as civil remedies: "compensatory damages, punitive damages, restitution, special performance, injunctive relief, constructive trusts [on property fraudulently transferred], abatement of nuisances, and forfeitures" (p.1333). With the exception of compensatory and punitive damages, all of these measures involve an attempt to force a party to do something (or to stop doing something), with the variety of names attesting to the many different legal duties that one can fail to meet. These remedies seek primarily to change the situation in which the harm is occurring rather than to punish the person. "Remedy" implies that an aggrieved party can seek relief from the non-compliance of another.

Historically, such remedies were primarily used in disputes between private parties: the harm was to the individual and the individual sought redress.

Potential Advantages and Disadvantages of Civil Remedies

Whether civil remedies regulate criminal offenders or crime opportunities, they are useful when they can force someone to do or not to do something in a way that is not otherwise possible using the usual measures in these two areas — criminal penalties (for regulating offenders), or forms of non-coercive encouragement (for most forms of situational crime prevention). For example, an offender convicted of assault following a domestic violence case may serve a jail sentence (a criminal penalty) and have no further restrictions made on his or her movement, while another person involved in the same type of assault might be the subject of a restraining order (a civil remedy) restricting access to the home of the victim. With situational prevention, the police could seek to get property owners to clean-up their property voluntarily (a form of non-coercive encouragement), or they could use an existing vermin ordinance (a civil remedy) to force property owners to clean up their property (see Green, 1996).

Regulating Offenders

Civil remedies used to regulate offenders also have advantages over criminal penalties purely because they involve the civil rather than the criminal law. They do not require the same level of proof that is required with a criminal prosecution, nor do they call into operation the same constitutional protections that criminal cases do, such as the right to counsel and the right to cross-examine witnesses (see Cheh, 1991). This can make civil remedies speedier to apply (see Finn and Hylton, 1994), as well as increasing the likelihood that they will be applied. Also, the underlying prohibitions or duties do not have to be serious enough to warrant criminal penalties, so they can be imposed prior to the occurrence of serious harm (see Finn and Hylton, 1994). Interestingly, civil remedies can themselves sometimes hold out the threat of criminal penalties. For example, non-compliance with some civil remedies, such as restraining orders, can result in the imposition of criminal penalties on the ground that the judges' orders were violated (Cheh, 1991).

The legal and constitutional problems with the use of civil remedies to regulate offenders or potential offenders are well-documented (e.g., Cheh, 1991; Finn and Hylton, 1994; Mann, 1992; von Hirsch et al., 1995), as are the adjustments made to address these issues (Cheh, 1991; Finn and Hylton, 1994), so they will not be reviewed here. The primary focus of this chapter is on the use of civil remedies to regulate crime opportunities.

Regulating Opportunities

Civil remedies are particularly useful in regulating opportunities because they can not only force the subjects of the legal prescription to act (or refrain from acting), but they also can determine who enforces the remedy. As Engstad and Evans (1980) noted nearly 20 years ago, when civil remedies are used to regulate crime opportunities, then the lines of responsibility for enforcement of the situational control are clearly set out. In addition, the areas of responsibility are wider than just police departments since they include regulatory departments as well. Wider responsibility for enforcement spread throughout other parts of the community demands cooperation among agencies, since the mere existence of regulatory schemes does not guarantee that enforcement will occur. As Ross (1996) has documented in the area of housing code enforcement, those who enforce regulations use a great deal of discretion in deciding which ones to enforce in particular situations. The use of civil remedies, especially that involving the passage of new legislation, brings the possibility of over-regulation, which could result in backlashes from those regulated as well as the regulators. As a first step toward examining systematically the actual advantages and disadvantages of using civil remedies to regulate crime opportunities, the language of situational crime prevention and its related models and concepts will be used and expanded in the next section.

SITUATIONAL CRIME PREVENTION

What is Situational Crime Prevention?

Clarke (1983) has defined situational crime prevention as "comprising measures (1) directed at highly specific forms of crime (2) that involve the management, design, or manipulation of the immediate environment in as systematic and permanent a way as possible (3) so as to reduce the opportunities for crime and increase its risks as perceived by a wide range of offenders" (p.225). This may, at first, sound very similar to Crime Prevention Through Environmental Design (Jeffery, 1971) and defensible space (Newman, 1972), with their emphases on the physical environment and crime. Yet, though situational crime prevention was developed at roughly the same time as these perspectives, it has a different etiology and different theoretical underpinnings (see Clarke, 1995, for a discussion of the history of situational crime prevention).

The rational choice perspective (Clarke and Cornish, 1985; Cornish and Clarke, 1986) was developed to provide a theoretical framework for thinking about situational crime prevention (Clarke, 1995; Cornish, 1993). By assuming that human actors make broadly rational choices, it looks at offenders' perceptions of the risks, rewards and efforts in situations to guide its analysis of crime prevention possibilities. It does this by focusing on the instrumentality of person-situation interactions. This perspective has a number of ramifications for situational crime prevention. For example, Clarke and Homel (1997) have noted the need for situational measures to be very crime-specific and delivered at the point where the criminal decisions are made. This means that they are not designed primarily to produce long-term changes in dispositions to offend. One of the advantages of this situational approach to crime prevention is that "offenders do not have to be identified before they can be dealt with" (Cornish, 1994b:153).

Classifying Situational Techniques

Beginning with Clarke and Mayhew's (1980) eight techniques of preventing crime, classification schemes have been used to highlight similar features among various situational measures (Clarke, 1992; Clarke and Homel, 1997). These classification schemes categorize measures, first, according to the technique used, that is, according to the way that the measure affects the environment (e.g., by removing the target or through the use of some form of surveillance). These techniques are then classified into broad categories according to the purpose served. The most-recent scheme (Clarke and Homel, 1997) sets out 16 different techniques and four broad purposes: (1) increasing perceived effort; (2) increasing perceived risk; (3) reducing anticipated reward (identified in Clarke, 1992); and (4) inducing guilt or shame.

Fitting the Technique to the Crime

There are several models that could be used to match crime prevention controls and crimes. For example, Ekblom (1994a; 1994b; Ekblom and Pease, 1995) has designed a model of the crime prevention intervention process for use in the evaluation of the wide variety of situational and non-situational interventions used in the Safer Cities Programme in Great Britain. The SARA model (Eck and Spelman, 1987), used in problem-oriented policing (an approach complementary to situational crime prevention), emphasizes the need to gather information about the problem presented, analyze its operation and respond to it. Although routine activity theory (Cohen and Felson, 1979) was not developed with situational crime prevention in mind, some of its concepts, as shown in the introduction to this chapter, have direct application to situational prevention and are very useful for explaining the reach of civil remedies. Here, however, the script-analytic approach (Cornish, 1994a; 1994b) will be used as the underlying model for describing the operation of situational crime prevention, because it was designed to deal with situational crime prevention and is very flexible.

Crime Scripts

Cornish's (1994a, 1994b) script-analytic approach provides a way of conceptualizing how crime prevention measures can be focused in a crime- and situation-specific manner, that is, at the successive points in the crime where various criminal decisions are made. Cornish (1994b) used the concept of a script as "a way of generating, organizing and systematizing knowledge about the procedural aspects and procedural requirements of crime commission.... helping to enhance situational crime prevention policies by drawing attention to a fuller range of possible intervention points" (p.151).

An example from Cornish's analysis of how intervention points can be combined with particular situational measures is reproduced here as Figure 1, which describes the graffiti offense known as tag writing. Although crimes can be described at various levels of abstraction — e.g., the protoscript (vandalism), the script (graffiti writing) and the track (tag writing) — only the levels of script and track are usually crime-specific enough to generate information effective for situational crime prevention purposes. Figure 1 shows: (1) various general scenes (or functions) — such as preparation, entry and doing — that together make up the criminal act; (2) identified script actions occurring within each scene that are specific to the particular crime; and (3) the situational controls that are linked to script actions and scenes. If a measure is effective, then it will disrupt the crime script. If the offender does not overcome the disruption through innovation, then the crime will be prevented.

Figure 1: Cornish's (1994b) Script Disruption Figure for Graffiti Tag Writing

PROTOSCRIPT:	VANDALISM	
SCRIPT:	GRAFFITI WRITING	
TRACK	"TAG WRITING"	

SCENE/FUNCTION	SCRIPT ACTION	SITUATIONAL CONTROL
PREPARATION	Buy spray-can Find good setting	Sales regulation City paint-out program
ENTRY	Enter setting	Access control Entry/exit screening
PRE-CONDITION	Loiter	Surveillance
INSTRUMENTAL PRE-CONDITION	Select target	Remove target
INSTRUMENTAL INITIATION	Approach target	Surveillance
INSTRUMENTAL ACTUALIZATION	Reach target	Protective screens Legal target provided
DOING	Spray graffiti	Graffiti-resistant paint
POST-CONDITION	Get away quietly	Moisture-activated alarm
EXIT	Leave setting	Entry/exit screening
DOING (later)	"Getting up"	Rapid cleaning

From "A Procedural Analysis of Offending" by Derek Cornish. In: R.V. Clarke (ed.), *Crime Prevention Studies,* vol. 3, p.165.

Key to the script-analytic approach is the identification of the crime problem as the first step in a method that goes on to analyze criminal and intervention processes. There should be tight theoretical links between the crime to be disrupted, the actions and the conditions (props, accomplices and settings) under which these scripts are carried out. Crime-script specificity can force a crime preventor to consider a range of alternative measures or some combination of measures to disrupt a crime script. It may also be used to limit the reach of a proposed measure so that it only targets areas where the scripts are operating. This focus on crime-script specificity does not mean that a measure can only address one crime script at a time, only that each script should be identified and analyzed separately.

This should help ensure that the measure will be targeted against the undesirable behavior in a way that increases its likely success without wasting valuable crime prevention resources. For example, curfews might be successful in keeping a designated group off the street at particular times, but will only affect crimes that had this factor as part of their crime scripts. This is why it is important to discuss situational controls in terms of the crime scripts to which they are linked: they may be successful against one crime but not another. The script-analytic model for situational crime prevention is still relatively new, so it has yet to be used to explore questions related to the comparative ease of disrupting various crime scripts or the part that script complexity may play in disruption or in offender innovation.

Describing the Mechanism

Implicit in the script approach are its connections with the purposes and techniques of situational crime prevention discussed earlier (Clarke, 1992; Clarke and Homel, 1997). Columns could be added to Figure 1 to illustrate the purpose of and technique for each situational control. For example, the city paint-out program against tag writing shown in Figure 1 may act to reduce temptation (the technique), thereby reducing the anticipated rewards for the potential offender (the purpose). When planning prevention initiatives, the mechanism by which the control is to operate should be clearly identified (see Ekblom, 1994a).

Implementation

Despite the importance of correctly analyzing the processes of crime commission and script disruption, crimes will not be prevented if the situational controls are not implemented effectively. Cornish's (1994a, 1994b) discussion of the script disruption process did not include a section on implementation, but, because civil remedies can be used most directly in situational prevention at this stage of the disruption process, it is important to set out some of the key factors related to implementation. These factors can be easily added to the script-analytic model, and displayed in figure form. For example, as Figure 1 stands now, situational control is the last column listed. Additional columns could be added for each new implementation factor to be considered, with the characteristics of the new factors that apply for a particular situational control added along each row under each new factor heading.

Five important factors to be considered in this context are identified here (although others could be considered as well):

(1) the intervenor (i.e., individuals, governmental agencies, businesses, community groups and multi-agency partners);
(2) the focus of the situational control (i.e., offenders, crime targets, accomplices, props, scenes);
(3) the medium of control (i.e., offender handlers, crime target guardians, place managers and props controllers);
(4) the inducement type (i.e., non-coercive encouragement, civil remedies and criminal penalties); and
(5) the inducement enforcer; (i.e., the same groups as in [1]).

These factors will now be discussed.

Intervenors

Intervenors are those who decide to carry out a crime prevention initiative and get it going. They are the people who decide which situational controls to use. They are the organizers. Intervenors include individuals and governmental agencies as well as businesses (see Felson and Clarke, 1997), community groups (see National Crime Prevention Council, 1996) and multi-agency partners (see, e.g., Walters, 1996).

Foci of Control and Media of Control

The foci of situational controls can include any material conditions necessary for the script action to occur — that is, offenders, crime targets (victims), accomplices, props (instrumentalities) and scenes (Cornish, 1994b). These foci of situational controls should directly involve crime opportunities. The media of control are those who control or influence the material conditions (or crime opportunities) of the script action that are to be regulated. They can best be understood by incorporating terminology emanating from routine activity theory (Cohen and Felson, 1979) — offender handler, crime target guardian (Felson, 1995) and place manager (Eck, 1995) — with another category — "props controller" — describing those who exert some control over the instrumentalities of crime.[1] Because accomplices are essentially additional offenders, those who control them are offender handlers. As this scheme is designed to explain the operation of situational crime prevention, offender handlers within it exert situational controls, rather than social control (cf. Felson, 1986). For example, when a parent (as an offender handler) sets limitations over when a teenager leaves the home, this could be considered as access control (a situational control) that increases the perceived effort (the purpose of the control) of carrying out a particular offense.

The foci of the situational controls will differ according to the crime script and the criminal actions or scenes. For example, with graffiti tag writing, certain types of crime targets are likely to be more suitable than others — for example, those with graffiti already present (Ferrell, 1993; Smith, 1996) and those located in places with little opportunity for surveillance (Ley and Cybriwsky, 1974; Mawby, 1977; Mayhew et al., 1979; Poyner, 1992; Sturman, 1980; Webb, 1984). These choice-structuring properties (Cornish and Clarke, 1987) of tag writing mean that situational controls can be focused toward the crime target or the scene, with inducements directed toward those who exert some control or influence over these elements of the crime script. In this example, the media of control would be the crime target guardian and the place manager, respectively. Not all of the script actions in tag writing involve crime targets or scenes (see Figure 1): one of the props used — the spray paint can — could also be a focus of control.

As yet, it is not clear whether one type of focus of control is easier to control than another, or whether one type of medium of control is easier to induce to act than another. The importance of scene and place manager in situational crime prevention (e.g., Eck, 1995; Green, 1996) may be related to the types of crime problems addressed or the ubiquitous nature of scene in crime commission. It may also be that some places — so-called "hot spots" (Sherman et al., 1989) – are the sites of multiple crime scripts, and that it is possible to control crime scenes even if little else is known about the scripts going on there (see discussion of offender lifestyles in Cornish, 1994b).

Inducement Type

A large number of situational controls do not involve any kind of formal inducement by a governmental agency, no actual or threatened sanction by an administrative body or court. For example, the mundane precautions that many of us take for granted, such as locking one's car or front door, as well as such diverse measures as off-street parking, burglar alarms, phonecards and trash bins (Clarke and Homel, 1997), usually involve voluntary cooperation by those in control of the opportunity. Where voluntary cooperation is unlikely or not forthcoming, it may be possible to use a civil remedy (or occasionally even a criminal penalty) as an additional coercive inducement. Existing statutes, ordinances, regulations, and non-statutory legal duties may be used or special legislation may be passed (see National Crime Prevention Council, 1996) to require those in control of crime opportunities (the media of control) to carry out some action that is thought to have a crime-preventive effect. Inducement type is important to the extent that it affects the likelihood that the medium of control will exercise the needed control over the opportunity (the focus of the situational control).[2] While implementation effectiveness is the primary consideration for choosing one type of inducement over another, the decision to try to use a criminal penalty requires additionally that the behavior to be encouraged or discouraged be harmful enough to warrant the use of the censuring power of the criminal law.

Inducement Enforcers

Inducement enforcers include the same group of potential actors as the intervenor, but they play a different role in the process. The enforcer oversees the medium of control to ensure that the situational control the intervenor seeks to use in a particular crime prevention initiative is actually used. For example, with an initiative involving informal encouragement, the intervenor may be a community group that decides that a paint-out program would be a good way to try to eliminate the rewards for graffiti writers, with the same group cajoling individual property owners to paint out graffiti on their property.

The use of other, more formal types of inducement increases the possibility that the intervenor and the enforcer will not, in fact, be the same group of actors. For example, the intervenor may be a community group and the enforcer may be a government agency. The government agency may have formal responsibility for enforcement of a particular civil code, but may not share the crime prevention goals of the local community group. For example, where resources are limited, the relationship between the civil enforcement and the crimes to be prevented may not be widely recognized, or the agency may not view its mission as one involving crime prevention. When the intervenor and enforcer are not the same group of actors, the intervenor does not necessarily have authority over the enforcer, such as in the community group-government agency example. Thus, in effect, when a civil remedy is used, the intervenor's need for voluntary cooperation is no longer focused on the media of control but instead shifts to the enforcer.

REGULATING OPPORTUNITIES WITH CIVIL REMEDIES

To understand how civil remedies operate to regulate opportunities in the dynamic atmosphere of crime commission, it is helpful to look at how they are used within the script-analytic framework of situational crime prevention described in the previous section. The most direct role for civil remedies in situational crime prevention is in the implementation process, providing an inducement for the medium of control (that is, the offender handler, crime target guardian, place manager, or props controller) to exert his or her influence over a crime opportunity, defined above as the focus of control (that is, offender, crime target, scene and props). The direct operation of civil remedies in the implementation of situational crime prevention initiatives will now be illustrated. Attention is also focused on premises liability suits and civil recovery, in which civil remedies can play an indirect role in situational crime prevention.

Civil Remedies and Implementation

While the choice of whether to use a particular civil remedy rather than rely on voluntary cooperation in a situational crime prevention scheme may be one of the last decisions an intervenor makes, its inclusion may have important, possibly determinative, effects on the success of the initiative. The decision requires a balancing of three primary considerations: (1) how successful the situational control will be without the added enforcement power; (2) whether the resources for using the remedy are available; and (3) whether the use of the remedy will have negative effects. These factors are discussed below in the context of using civil remedies to help prevent graffiti tag writing.

Mechanism of Control

Cornish's tag-writing script (Figure 1) will be used again to help describe how civil remedies can be employed to assist in the disruption of a crime script. One of the script actions in tag writing is to enter the setting. Fenced yards could be used to control access (the situational technique) to that crime setting (the focus of control) by increasing the perceived effort (the purpose of the control) of the tag writer. However, if a municipal code were passed requiring property owners (as place managers) to erect fences to control access to particular places, then it would not be the imposition (or threat of imposition) of the civil remedy itself that would be intended to have the crime prevention effect. It would still be the fence that is intended to control access and increase perceived effort. The civil remedy would just be another way of getting owners to erect or keep up fences — that is, a different type of inducement. While the use of the civil remedy could aid in the disruption of the crime script, it would do so through an increase in the complexity of the implementation process — not by changing the mechanism of control.

Choosing the Type of Inducement

One of the tools or props frequently used by graffiti writers is the spray paint can. As noted earlier, this can be one of the foci of control in a tag-writing script-disruption plan (see Figure 1). One medium of control for the spray paint can could be the spray paint retailer, acting as a props controller (for others, see National Crime Prevention Council, 1996). It is possible that a props controller might voluntarily cooperate in whatever situational control is proposed; for example, retailers could limit the sale or display of spray paint cans voluntarily. However, intervenors may judge that (a) such cooperation is unlikely or unworkable without the aid of a threatened civil (or possibly criminal) sanction; (b) the imposition of an actual sanction is needed to force some of them to cooperate (see, e.g., Green, 1996); or (c) enforcement responsibility should fall to another group (Engstad and Evans, 1980).

Despite the added benefit that a prohibition against the sale of spray paint to minors may provide, however, it may still turn out that it is not the right control for the situation. For example, although city ordinances limiting spray paint sales to minors might be a good way to "control facilitators" (Clarke and Homel, 1997) through the props controller and to disrupt the tag-writing crime script, such an ordinance may be impossible to implement effectively in an area if it includes many small jurisdictions or if the enforcement resources are limited. These particular problems with using a civil remedy would not necessarily be solved by trying to secure voluntary cooperation, since non-coercive inducements may also be difficult to coordinate across jurisdictions and can require resources as well (see, e.g., Gladstone, 1980; Hope, 1985). An intervenor may decide not to use a potentially powerful control if it cannot be implemented properly, despite the existence of several different types of possible inducement.

An additional problem that could be encountered with the use of civil remedies is illustrated by another situational control used against tag writing — painting out. Graffiti writers have reported finding places with graffiti already present attractive sites for their handiwork (Ferrell, 1993). As noted previously, painting out existing graffiti may reduce tag writing. Ferrell (1993) reported that the city of Denver, CO, as part of a wider anti-graffiti campaign, used a zoning ordinance to force property owners (as target guardians) to remove graffiti from their premises. The use of this civil remedy, however, may have contributed to the campaigns' limited success for, as the National Crime Prevention Council (1996) has observed, "Legislation that requires removal of graffiti by property owners may meet with resistance from [those] who feel the burden is misplaced and unjust" (p.11). Intervenors may find that attempts to win property owners over and secure voluntary cooperation with clean-up campaigns is a better way to achieve their goal of decreasing perceived rewards for potential tag writers. Furthermore, resources that might go toward enforcing mandatory clean-up by the property owners could be used to finance painting-out by the local government. Such a campaign was carried out in the London Borough of Bromley ("Council Hopes to Rub out Graffiti," 1993). With a government-run paint-out initiative, the property owners might feel as if the government were doing them a favor rather than making them bear the burden for someone else's crime, and they might cooperate more readily in the control.

The decision about the type of inducement to use in a particular situation is likely to involve difficult comparisons for intervenors and deserves wider attention in the crime prevention literature. The review by the National Crime Prevention Council (1996) describes a variety of civil remedies and criminal penalties that have been used across the U.S. to address particular crime problems. More research in this area is needed, particularly controlled comparisons of the use of the three different types of inducements, as well as comparisons of particular inducements used across different situational controls and crime scripts.

An Indirect Role in Situational Crime Prevention

Civil remedies may play an indirect role in the operation of situational crime prevention as well. Two civil remedies that may affect crime opportunities are premises liability suits and civil recovery statutes. These two remedies, unlike those already discussed, are not directly used by crime prevention intervenors to try to get those who control crime opportunities to modify these opportunities. Their potential roles in situational crime prevention follow different paths, as described below.

Premises Liability Suits

Premises liability suits have been cited as another means by which a civil action can be used for crime-preventive purposes (Gordon and Brill, 1996). The theory is that a civil suit by a crime victim against the person responsible for the place where the crime occurred (the place manager) leads other landlords to use measures that will reduce the likelihood of future similar crimes occurring on property under their control. Eck (1997) examined three possible models of attorney and business decision making in this area, looking at factors such as individual risk, place risk, area crime rates, costs of being sued and risk of suit. He predicted differing levels of investment in crime prevention by businesses depending on which model was applied. Although all of the models predicted an increase in investment, only one anticipated that the threat of premises liability suits improved public safety. Some of the models predicted investment that would reflect the risk of suits more than the risks of crime at a particular place, while another foresaw a lack of correspondence between risk of victimization and investment.

Eck's (1997) analysis lends support to the view that civil remedies may sometimes have indirect situational crime prevention effects. Individual plaintiffs bring premises liability suits primarily to receive compensation. Unlike the potential uses of civil remedies against graffiti tag writing described earlier, such suits are not designed to make the medium of control change the situation in which scripts are played out or to directly control crime opportunities. Changes made by similarly placed persons who seek to avoid having premises liability suits brought against them do not ensure that they will actually avoid these suits by making the changes. The fit between the situational controls (e.g., locks, lighting, surveillance) and the civil remedy (compensation following a criminal harm) is neither tight nor direct. In addition, there is no single intervenor to oversee the remedy's crime prevention effects, overcome this lack of fit, or initiate other control measures, nor is there a single enforcer. Given these features, it is not surprising that premises liability suits may not have a situational crime-preventive effect (Eck, 1997). What is perhaps more unexpected is that, despite their indirect relationship to those who control crime opportunities, these suits may in fact have such an effect.

Civil Recovery

Civil recovery is also indirectly linked to potential situational controls. About half of the U.S. states have expanded the normal civil tort action available to store owners into a civil recovery action that allows them to choose whether to prosecute offenders, or to bring a civil recovery action involving restitution and, depending on the statute, some type of punitive damages (Davis et al., 1991). The primary thrust of the statutes appears to be compensatory rather than crime preventive. However, if store owners find that the advantages of seeking civil recovery outweigh the burdens of criminal prosecution and use it, then this civil restitution option could have an increased crime prevention effect through situational means. This could happen, for example, if the increased financial incentive to pick up shoplifters leads to increased surveillance or exit screening, and the increase in risk of capture from the use of these controls leads to less shoplifting. Crime would also be prevented if the existence or use of the civil recovery option alone resulted in a perception of greater risk among offenders, and this led to less shoplifting.

On the other hand, at least three conditions could operate to lessen any crime prevention effect from civil recovery. First, where arrests for shoplifting are the normal response in all cases (as in the store described by Davis et al., 1991), a switch to civil recovery actions may result in owners pursuing a policy that does not decrease the amount of shoplifting but merely provides enough compensation to cover the costs of the thefts. Second, if potential offenders were to learn that they might not face prosecution if apprehended and this was seen as a less risky result, then they might increase the level of their stealing to cover the risks of paying compensation if discovered. Finally, Hollinger (1997) warned that although there may be financial incentives for retailers to eschew criminal prosecution and pursue monetary restitution, if they have trouble getting money from apprehended shoplifters who have little incentive to pay, then the retailers may find themselves without an effective option — and in the same position regarding crime prevention that they were in before.

Again, unlike the use of civil remedies against tag writing discussed earlier, the sanction available with civil recovery statutes is not directed against those who control crime opportunities. Instead, it is targeted at identified offenders, with the retailers (acting as both place managers and target guardians) carrying out the enforcement role. And, like premises liability suits, even though the remedy is not directed against those who control the crime opportunities for shoplifting, there may be a situational crime-preventive effect — though, again, it is an empirical question as to whether there is such an effect. Here, the situational effect will occur if the remedy increases the perception of risk among unidentified potential offenders or makes the reduction of crime opportunities by the retailers profitable enough for them to increase their situational controls.

It remains to be seen whether the indirect roles of particular civil remedies in situational crime prevention will be shown to have a crime-preventive effect, and, if they do, whether they will prove as successful as some of the direct applications of remedies at the implementation stage (see, e.g., Green, 1996). Indirect roles for civil remedies may be fairly rare occurrences, certainly less common than the potential uses of civil remedies to influence the four groups — offender handlers, crime target guardians, place managers and props controllers — that control or influence crime opportunities.

CONCLUSION

Civil remedies can be used in several different ways to prevent crime. In addition to regulating identified offenders or potential offenders, they can also regulate crime opportunities. Most notably, civil remedies can be used directly as formal inducements to increase the likelihood that those with influence or control over crime opportunities carry out activities designed to affect a situational control over these opportunities. Other possible inducements, including noncoercive encouragement and criminal penalties, may be used as well. The decision to choose one inducement over another to affect a particular situational control requires that the intervenor evaluate the following for each inducement: (1) how well it will work; (2) necessary and available resources; and (3) potential negative effects.

It is also possible that civil remedies can be used indirectly to produce a situational crime prevention effect, that is, to regulate crime opportunities. Such an effect may occur where the existence or use of a remedy (usually invoked to serve some other purpose) increases the likelihood that those in control of opportunities will perceive that it is in their interest to increase effective situational controls, or where the remedy increases the likelihood that potential offenders will perceive that increased situational controls have been implemented, whether or not they have been.

Address correspondence to: Martha J. Smith, 7 Farnborough Court, High Street, Farnborough, Kent, BR6 7AY, U.K.

Acknowledgments: I am grateful to Derek Cornish, Ron Clarke and to two anonymous reviewers for their comments on earlier versions of this paper.

REFERENCES

Brantingham, P.J. and P.L. Brantingham (eds.) (1981). *Environmental Criminology.* Beverly Hills, CA: Sage.

Buerger, M.E. and L.G. Mazerolle (1998). "Third-Party Policing: A Theoretical Analysis of an Emerging Trend." *Justice Quarterly* 15(2):301-327.

Cheh, M. (1991). "Constitutional Limits on Using Civil Remedies to Achieve Criminal Law Objectives: Understanding and Transcending the Criminal-Civil Law Distinction." *Hastings Law Journal* 42:1325-1413.

Clarke, R.V. (1983). "Situational Crime Prevention: Its Theoretical Basis and Practical Scope." In: M. Tonry and N. Morris (eds.), *Crime and Justice: An Annual Review of Research*, vol. 4. Chicago, IL: University of Chicago Press.

—— (ed.) (1992). *Situational Crime Prevention: Successful Case Studies.* Albany, NY: Harrow and Heston.

—— (1995). "Situational Crime Prevention." In: M. Tonry and D.P. Farrington (eds.), *Building a Safer Society: Strategic Approaches to Crime Prevention.* Crime and Justice: A Review of Research, vol. 19. Chicago, IL: University of Chicago Press.

—— (ed.) (1997). *Situational Crime Prevention: Successful Case Studies* (2nd ed.) Guilderland, NY: Harrow and Heston.

—— and D.B. Cornish (1985). "Modeling Offenders' Decisions: A Framework for Research and Policy." In: M. Tonry and N. Morris (eds.), *Crime and Justice: An Annual Review of Research*, vol. 6. Chicago, IL: University of Chicago Press.

—— and R. Homel (1997). "A Revised Classification of Situational Crime Prevention Techniques." In: S.P. Lab (ed.), *Crime Prevention at a Crossroads.* Cincinnati, OH: Anderson.

—— and Pat Mayhew (eds.) (1980). *Designing Out Crime.* London: Her Majesty's Stationery Office.

Cohen, L.E. and M. Felson (1979). "Social Change and Crime Rate Trends: A Routine Activity Approach." *American Sociological Review* 44:588-608.

Cornish, D.B. (1993). "Theories of Action in Criminology: Learning Theory and Rational Choice Approaches." In: R.V. Clarke and M. Felson (eds.), *Routine Activity and Rational Choice. Advances in Criminological Theory*, vol. 5. New Brunswick, NJ: Transaction Press.

—— (1994a). "Crimes as Scripts." In: D. Zahm and P. Cromwell (eds.), *Proceedings of the International Seminar on Environmental Criminology and Crime Analysis.* Coral Gables, FL: Florida Statistical Analysis Center and Florida Criminal Justice Executive Institute.

—— (1994b). "The Procedural Analysis of Offending and Its Relevance for Situational Prevention." In: R.V. Clarke (ed.), *Crime Prevention Studies*, vol. 3.. Monsey, NY: Criminal Justice Press.

—— and R.V. Clarke (1986). "Introduction." In: D.B. Cornish and R.V. Clarke (eds.), *The Reasoning Criminal: Rational Choice Perspectives on Offending.* New York, NY: Springer-Verlag.

—— and R.V. Clarke (1987). "Understanding Crime Displacement: An Application of Rational Choice Theory." *Criminology* 25:933-947.

"Council Hopes to Rub Out Graffiti." (1993). *Orpington and Chiselhurst News Shopper*, February 10, p. 16.

Davis, M.G., R. Lundman and R. Martinez (1991). "Private Corporate Justice: Store Police, Shoplifters, and Civil Recovery." *Social Problems* 38(3):395-411.

Eck, J.E. (1995). "A General Model of the Geography of Illicit Retail Marketplaces." In: J.E. Eck and D. Weisburd (eds.), *Crime and Place*. Crime Prevention Studies, vol. 4. Monsey, NY and Washington, DC: Criminal Justice Press and Police Executive Research Forum.

—— (1997). "Do Premises Liability Suits Promote Business Crime Prevention?" In: M. Felson and R.V. Clarke (eds.), *Business and Crime Prevention*. Monsey, NY: Criminal Justice Press.

—— and W. Spelman (1987). *Problem-Solving: Problem-Oriented Policing in Newport News*. Police Executive Research Forum. Washington, DC: National Institute of Justice.

—— and D. Weisburd (eds.). (1995). *Crime and Place*. Crime Prevention Studies, vol. 4. Monsey, NY and Washington, DC: Criminal Justice Press and Police Executive Research Forum.

Ekblom, P. (1994a). "Proximal Circumstances: A Mechanism-based Classification of Crime Prevention." In: R.V. Clarke (ed.), *Crime Prevention Studies*, vol. 2. Monsey, NY: Criminal Justice Press.

—— (1994b). "Scoping and Scoring: Linking Measures of Action to Measures of Outcome." In: D. Zahm and P. Cromwell (eds.), *Proceedings of the International Seminar on Environmental Criminology and Crime Analysis*. Coral Gables, FL: Florida Statistical Analysis Center and Florida Criminal Justice Executive Institute.

—— and K. Pease (1995). "Evaluating Crime Prevention." In: M. Tonry and D.P. Farrington (eds.), *Building a Safer Society: Strategic Approaches to Crime Prevention*. Crime and Justice: A Review of Research, vol. 19. Chicago, IL: University of Chicago Press.

Engstad, P. and J.L. Evans (1980). "Responsibility, Competence and Police Effectiveness." In: R.V.G. Clarke and J.M. Hough (eds.), *The Effectiveness of Policing*. Farnborough, Hants, UK: Gower.

Felson, M. (1986). "Routine Activities, Social Controls, Rational Decisions, and Criminal Outcomes." In: D.B. Cornish and R.V. Clarke (eds.), *The Reasoning Criminal: Rational Choice Perspectives on Offending*. New York, NY: Springer-Verlag.

—— (1995). "Those Who Discourage Crime." In: J.E. Eck and D. Weisburd (eds.), *Crime and Place*. Crime Prevention Studies, vol. 4. Monsey, NY and Washington, DC: Criminal Justice Press and Police Executive Research Forum.

—— and R.V. Clarke (eds.) (1997). *Business and Crime Prevention.* Monsey, NY: Criminal Justice Press.

Ferrell, J. (1993). *Crimes of Style: Urban Graffiti and the Politics of Criminality.* New York, NY: Garland.

Finn, P. and M.O. Hylton (1994). *Using Civil Remedies for Criminal Behavior: Rationale, Case Studies, and Constitutional Issues.* Washington, DC: U.S. National Institute of Justice.

Fried, D.J. (1988). "Rationalizing Criminal Forfeiture." *Journal of Criminal Law and Criminology* 79(2): 328-436.

Gladstone, F.J. (1980). *Co-ordinating Crime Prevention Efforts.* Home Office Research Study No. 62. London, UK: Her Majesty's Stationery Office.

Gordon, C.L. and W. Brill (1996). *The Expanding Role of Crime Prevention Through Environmental Design in Premises Liability.* Research in Brief Series. Washington, DC: U.S. National Institute of Justice.

Green, L. (1996). *Policing Places with Drug Problems.* Drugs, Health, and Social Policy Series, vol. 2. Thousand Oaks, CA: Sage.

Hollinger, R.C. (1997). "Measuring Crime and Its Impact in the Business Environment." In: M. Felson and R.V. Clarke (eds.), *Business and Crime Prevention.* Monsey, NY: Criminal Justice Press.

Hope, T. (1985) *Implementing Crime Prevention Measures.* Home Office Research Study, No. 86. London, UK: Her Majesty's Stationery Office.

Jeffery, C.R. (1971). *Crime Prevention through Environmental Design.* Beverly Hills, CA: Sage.

Jensen, E.L. and J. Gerber (1996). "The Civil Forfeiture of Assets and the War on Drugs: Expanding Criminal Sanctions While Reducing Due Process Protections." *Crime & Delinquency* 42(3):421-434.

Ley, D. and R. Cybriwsky (1974). "The Spatial Ecology of Stripped Cars." *Environment and Behavior* 6:54-68.

Mann, K. (1992). "Punitive Civil Sanctions: The Middleground between Criminal and Civil Law." *Yale Law Journal* 101:1795-1873.

Mawby, R.I. (1977). "Kiosk Vandalism: A Sheffield Study." *British Journal of Criminology* 17:30-46.

Mayhew, P., R.V.G. Clarke, J.N. Burrows, J.M. Hough and S.W.C. Winchester (1979) "Natural Surveillance and Vandalism to Telephone Kiosks." In: *Crime in Public View,* Home Office Research Study, No. 49. London, UK: Her Majesty's Stationery Office.

National Crime Prevention Council. (1996). *Working with Local Laws to Reduce Crime.* Washington, DC: author.

Newman, O. (1972). *Defensible Space: Crime Prevention through Urban Design.* New York, NY: Macmillan.

Poyner, B. (1992) "Video Cameras and Bus Vandalism." In: R.V. Clarke (ed.), *Situational Crime Prevention: Successful Case Studies.* Albany, NY: Harrow and Heston.

Ross, H.L. (1996). "Housing Code Enforcement and Urban Decline." *Journal of Affordable Housing and Community Development Law* 6(1):29-46.

Sherman, L., P. Gartin and M.E. Buerger (1989). "Hot Spots of Predatory Crime: Routine Activities and the Criminology of Place." *Criminology* 27:27-55.

Smith, M.J. (1996). "Assessing Vandalism Cues in an Experimental Setting: A Factorial Design Involving State of Repair, Presence of Graffiti, Target Vulnerability, and Target Suitability." Doctoral dissertation, Rutgers–The State University of New Jersey.

Sturman, A. (1980). "Damage on Buses: The Effects of Supervision." In: R.V.G. Clarke and P. Mayhew (eds.), *Designing Out Crime.* London, UK: Her Majesty's Stationery Office.

von Hirsch, A., A. Ashworth, M. Wasik, A.T.H. Smith, R. Morgan and J. Gardiner (1995). "Overtaking on the Right." *New Law Journal* (Oct.): pp. 1501-1502, 1516.

Walters, R. (1996). "The 'Dream' of Multi-agency Crime Prevention: Pitfalls in Policy and Practice." In: R. Homel (ed.), *The Politics and Practice of Situational Crime Prevention.* Crime Prevention Studies, vol. 5. Monsey, NY: Criminal Justice Press.

Webb, B. (1984). "Is There a Place for Vandalism?" In: C. Levy-Leboyer (ed.), *Vandalism: Behaviour and Motivations.* Amsterdam, NETH: North-Holland.

NOTES

1. Controlling the instrumentalities of the crime — "the props" in Cornish's (1994b) script approach — is analogous to "controlling facilitators," a situational crime prevention technique described in Clarke (1992) and in Clarke and Homel (1997).

2. According to Clarke and Homel (1997), criminal penalties can be used situationally in a way that does not involve inducements to the media of control in the manner described. Harassment codes (for rule setting) and drinking age laws (controlling disinhibitors) are situational because, by inducing guilt or shame, they can be used to change the situation in which offending decisions are made. Their purpose is not to identify and prosecute an individual offender, or to produce long-term changes in dispositions to offend, but to act upon the general public in particular situations.

THE POLITICS OF THIRD-PARTY POLICING

by

Michael E. Buerger

Northeastern University

Abstract: *The recent emphasis upon the use of civil remedies as a problem-solving tool for the police has created a new quasi-doctrine called "third-party policing." The concept refers to police insistence upon the involvement of non-offending third parties (usually place managers) in the control of criminal and disorderly behavior, creating a de facto new element of public duty. Police efforts may be opposed in a variety of different ways, many of which transpire in the political arena. With references to a formal, multi-agency city program (SMART in Oakland, CA), and using examples from a small start-up police initiative (RECAP in Minneapolis, MN), this chapter examines both individual and collective resistance to third-party policing. Documented and potential forms of resistance are discussed, as are the political backdrops and mechanisms that lend themselves to each and the possible avenues by which police and city officials can overcome or thwart political interference.*

Politics is one of the means by which we resolve our differences over the forms and degrees of our public participation. It is also the means by which the larger polity imposes duties, limits and benefits upon private individuals (from taxes and selective military service to welfare eligibility and Social Security entitlements). Each new law, ordinance and government regulation is the culmination of a political process, altering slightly the dividing line between public and private life. This chapter examines salient elements of the political processes that created, and are being created by, a new change in that public/private boundary: the forced recruitment of agents, primarily place managers (Eck, 1994), to act on behalf and direction of the police to control human behavior.

Buerger and Mazerolle (1998) first described the nascent doctrine of third-party policing as:

> police efforts to convince or coerce non-offending persons to take actions which are outside the scope of their routine activities, and that are designed to indirectly minimize disorder caused by other persons, or reduce the possibility that crime may occur. Though the ultimate target of police action remains a population of actual and potential offenders, the proximate target of third-party policing is an intermediate class of non-offending persons who are thought to have some power over the offenders' primary environment. The police use coercion to create place-guardianship that was previously absent, in order to decrease crime and disorder opportunities. Third-party policing is both defined and distinguished from problem- and community-oriented policing by the sources and the targets of that coercive power [p. 301].

They identified increased enforcement of civil regulatory provisions (or the threat of such enforcement) as the lever to force property owners and place-managers to take actions that are not formally required by any regulatory code. The tentative nature of the authority of third-party policing suggests that there will be challenges to the new practices by persons seeking to avoid either the responsibility or the penalties. After first outlining the origins and mechanics of third-party policing, the following pages explore the individual and collective forms such resistance might take, and discuss the ramifications for problem-solving and third-party policing.

ORIGINS

Third-party policing is an outgrowth of the community policing movement of the 1980s and 1990s, the product of a convergence of three concurrent trends: computerized crime analysis, the application of civil remedies to crime problems, and an emphasis upon "quality-of-life issues" as a legitimate police strategy.

The introduction of computerized crime analysis created a new place-based focus for American police tactics.[1] Although police have long constructed "pin maps" showing the locations of certain crimes, the computer age has greatly expanded the ability to examine the full range of police activity, not just felony crimes. Through links to telephone companies' enhanced 911 databases[2] and cities' property management databases, crime analysts can quickly display patterns of call activity, property ownership and other factors not reflected in official crime statistics. Among the new abilities are summarizing disorderly conditions from call data, and linking calls for police service that normally do not generate official reports to those that do (the relationship of "prowler" or "suspicious person" calls to burglaries or auto break-ins, for example). This new capacity has become a powerful force in shaping police strategy, beginning with the identification of problem properties as crime facilitators.

The use of civil ordinances as a remedial tool surfaced as part of problem-oriented policing (Goldstein, 1979; 1990) as early as 1985 in Newport News, VA (Eck and Spelman, 1986), and has been expanding ever since. It has been applied formally, as in the case of Oakland, CA's SMART Teams (Green, 1996) and the Tampa anti-drug initiatives (Kennedy, 1993), as well as informally, illustrated by the Minneapolis, MN, RECAP Unit (Buerger, 1992; 1994). The use of civil remedies discussed throughout this volume targets the conditions of ownership and guardianship that, when absent or insufficiently discharged, facilitate disorderly conditions and criminal activity.

The phrase quality-of-life issues has become central to the working vocabulary of a police establishment as it operationalizes the philosophical tenets of community and problem-oriented policing. Intellectually justified by the "Broken Windows" hypothesis (Wilson and Kelling, 1982), the new focus on quality-of-life issues stems from community concerns about things that police have traditionally dismissed as unimportant. Some of these issues deal with low-level disorderly behaviors that always have been within the police mandate but were only sporadically enforced: noise complaints, barking dogs, illegal auto repair operations in streets and alleys, public drinking, disorderly groups, public urination, low-level drug sales,[3] illegal parking. Computerized mapping provides quick, easily recognized patterns of such problems from call data. Other community concerns, often articulated through community meetings rather than in calls for direct police service, have presented the police with a new set of duties; abandoned autos, and vacant buildings and unkempt lots, among others, now become police concerns as a matter of routine.

The Need for Third Parties

Some of the new duties can be discharged with the time-honored police response to community agitation: a crackdown. Sherman (1990) documented the predictable pattern of crackdowns, in which (generally) a large amount of police resources[4] is suddenly directed at areas or problems that had received little or no attention before. The initial results are usually dramatic: a steep decline in the targeted activities, with or without a correspondingly large "numbers production" of arrests or tickets. As the targeted activity declines, however, there is less and less for officers to do, and eventually the "back-off" phase begins. Officially or unofficially, the police do less, wander off to find more interesting territory and eventually move on to other problems. At the same time, the target population (whether it be drug peddlers, drinking drivers or parking scofflaws) either figures out the new rules, or comes to recognize that the crackdown is over. Activity resumes, and the measured rates of prohibited activity slowly rise back to (and sometimes beyond) their former levels.

As the police responsibility grows to include quality-of-life conditions as well as criminal incidents and disorderly conduct, the groups with whom the police interact have also grown to include property owners and place managers (Eck, 1994). Over the past decade, the problem of maintaining crackdown effects has led to a strategic shift away from sole reliance upon special units and task force-styles of crackdown. Though special units and large-scale operations continue to be integral to the original suppression of the undesirable activity, they are often unsuited to the separate task of maintaining the effects. Large-scale operations cannot be sustained because of the costs involved, and special units frequently must turn their attentions to similar problems in other parts of the city in order to justify their continued existence.

Largely as a part of the community policing movement, but also out of necessity, police administrators have been delegating greater responsibility to line officers, particularly the beat officers patrolling specific neighborhoods. Beat integrity supports beat knowledge, and beat knowledge is supplemented by crime analysis to produce something called "problem solving." This problem analysis and problem solving, done by officers who are on the streets constantly and have at least a theoretical investment in their areas, constitutes the primary maintenance strategy of American policing. The special nature of the problem-solving approach, and the greater interaction with place managers that it produces, provides considerable impetus for third-party policing.

"Third-party policing" is a double-edged phrase, referring to the policing of both disorderly characters by third parties and of the third parties by the police. Unlike traditional police enforcement, which centers on incidents of individual misconduct, third-party policing focuses on those who own or manage places identified as the locus of a series of such incidents, often over extended periods of time. The places may be identified through a variety of mechanisms: community complaints about the specific property; beat officers' recognition of the regularity with which they are called to the address; routine analysis of crime and calls-for-service data; and occasionally a single heinous crime or event that brings to light unreported dissatisfaction. Police attention to the individual incidents continues, but is supplemented by efforts to enlist the place managers as partners to control undesirable behavior at their properties.

Because third-party policing impinges upon relationships previously considered private, the police need some external legitimizing authority for their intervention. Reiss (1971) noted that police authority is weakest when officers act on their own initiative, and strongest when they act on behalf of a citizen requesting assistance. As the individual call legitimates police intrusion into a private residence, police demands upon managerial practices are justified by the collective weight of calls for assistance, articulated through either crime analysis of call records or communal voices in open meetings or neighborhood surveys.

The police intervention is not justified simply by the failure of the place managers to fulfill their part of the contract with tenants or place-users; those remain civil matters, enforced according to the priorities and schedules of the appropriate agency. Third-party policing is invoked only when managerial neglect creates additional problems for the public peace and other third parties — those not party to the primary landlord-tenant or owner-customer relationship.

TACTICS OF THIRD-PARTY POLICING

When a place-based problem is identified, the first approach to the place managers by the police is usually friendly, or at least non-adversarial. Officers present the problem in terms of mutual concern, provide relevant and simultaneously legitimizing information,[5] and ask for the cooperation of the owner and/or place manager. Depending on the jurisdiction and the history of the property, the request may be only that, with no further communication, or it may be backed with a full panoply of options for complying with the request — and the potential consequences for non-compliance.

Agencies with experience in the problem-solving approach equip their officers with a full range of information, including: public and private sources of funds for making capital improvements; property surveys and suggestions for improvements in Crime Prevention Through Environmental Design (CPTED);[6] improvements, model leases for curbing the excesses of less-than-model tenants; and the like. That way, officers can present not only the problem but the resources available and possible approaches to a solution.

The cooperative approach is important for several reasons. Many owners and managers fully intend to be cooperative citizens and good neighbors. Some are unaware of the problems at or created by their properties; others know that there is a problem, but feel overwhelmed by conditions they do not believe they can control. The offer of police assistance is welcome, and helps to bolster the owners' confidence that the problem can be abated. In these more benign cases, policing through third parties is entirely a cooperative endeavor undertaken to bring a troubled property back to a condition desired by both the community and the owner. The softer, cooperative gambit is necessary in more resistant cases. When dealing with slumlords and persons known to be antagonistic or resistance to police requests, the "soft" approach is nevertheless an important first step, demonstrating that the police tried to gain cooperation before moving to more coercive measures. In courts, before regulative bodies, and in the court of public opinion, police requests for punitive action are almost always more favorably regarded if they represent the final step of a process rather than the first resort.

When the Cooperative Approach Fails

When the cooperative approach fails to achieve its goals, the police focus shifts somewhat from the ultimate targets to the proximate targets. The goals the police seek to achieve are the same; only the tactics differ in the more coercive stages of third-party policing. There is an operational assumption that the conduct of the intermediaries — the place managers, property owners, etc.[7] — acts as a facilitator of the undesirable conduct of others. The strongest cases are those where the place managers are in active collusion with the troublemakers, but third-party policing may also be applied to those who passively enable criminal conduct through inaction and neglect. Because the proximate targets (the place managers) are not directly responsible for the behaviors ultimately targeted (the actions of their tenants, patrons or others), the arrest-based coercive powers of the criminal law are ineffective and the police must look for new tools and weapons.

The civil law codes are the new weapons of criminal law enforcement. Designed to mediate the nominally private transaction between willing seller and willing buyer (of residential space, recreational services or other commodity), civil codes impose minimum standards for things: structural integrity, cleanliness and safety issues such as fire detection and egress. Enforcement of the codes has traditionally followed a compliance model (Reiss, 1984), focusing on the correction of conditions and utilizing negotiated timetables and plans where necessary.

By contrast, the actions demanded of place managers by the police concern the regulation of human conduct: tenant screening, place rules and their enforcement (including evictions) and the like. When place managers resist these suggestions, the police bring in regulators to enforce the civil code violations — deficiencies in things — found on the property. Although the properties are normally subject to such inspections as a condition of doing business, regular inspections are usually distributed over fairly long periods. When corrections are needed, property managers can make them in piecemeal fashion.

When police target a property for action because of behavioral problems associated with it, the normal rules do not apply. Regulators arrive en masse. All of the violations and demands to correct are delivered at once. The customary negotiations ("Well, this has to be fixed right away, but those two things I can cut you some slack on, just as long as you take care of them sometime soon") are no longer possible. Everyone understands that the inspection is no longer just about physical conditions, but also about the owner's/manager's intransigence in responding to the police requests.

The police use the accumulated weight of the code inspections (and repair orders, fines, summonses, etc.) as a weapon to gain compliance on other fronts. The task force visits also carry a symbolic message: there will be no reprieve from scrutiny until everything is corrected, and "everything" includes the behavioral issues that the police first sought action on. To avoid the repeated mass inspections and the close follow up on all repair orders, the place manager must take the other actions (not found in any applicable code) requested by the police.

In this way, the police unilaterally create a new form of public duty that has not been approved though the normal political channels. Police access to private places to deal with specific, time-bound problems of behavior ("the call" for police service) is different from access to nominally private business relationships to deal with less well-defined "conditions" that exist over time but have only a presumed link to specific behaviors. The expectations are different, often more costly, and the authority more open to challenge. As police already know, in both scenarios authority conveyed by third parties[8] is fundamentally weaker than that provided by a direct participant in the situation, and the authority for place-specific problem-solving measures almost always comes from other third parties. In addition, the code enforcers are similarly detached from direct police control, often working well outside the normal guidelines for their offices. The overall dynamic is sufficient to provide fertile ground for resistance.

RESISTANCE AND POLITICAL INFLUENCES

The police have traditionally refused to involve themselves in civil matters where the state is not a party and the disputes are between individuals. When the civil dispute resulted in a call for police services (such as landlord-tenant disputes and neighbor-trouble complaints), the police limited their role to controlling the collateral effects of the dispute (those that created or threatened a public disturbance of the peace). The core dispute was always referred to the civil authorities.

Third-party policing has fundamentally changed that approach, placing the police in a role as primary mediators at one end of the spectrum. At the other end, the police may go so far as to direct a landlord how to conduct his or her rental property business, or force the manager of a local bar considered a "den of iniquity" to take specific management actions dictated by the police. The motive for the actions is the improvement of conditions not associated with the business's "bottom line"; the authority for the intervention comes not from a single incident, but from the cumulative impact of a series of incidents and conditions over time.

Anchored in precedent, politics is nevertheless the mechanism by which laws are changed. Each new law — and new administrative regulations created by law — disturbs the previous balance, creating new demands, questions and conflicts. Under the American system of jurisprudence, our political system provides a forum in which both the substance and the application of laws may be challenged. Third-party policing is an emerging doctrine, not yet law and only haphazardly enshrined in administrative regulations. As such, it is vulnerable to political and legal challenges to its legitimacy.

Given the immense diversity of political forms throughout the country, there are many ways in which challenges to the new controls may be mounted. Individual resistance may take the forms of avoidance, exemption, subversion (corruption), cooptation or abandonment. Collective resistance hinges on the larger political mechanisms of repeal (a legislative or administrative function) or overturning of the legal basis for the controls (a judicial function), but may also extend to collective actions of collusion.

Individual Resistance

Avoidance

Avoidance is the near-universal form of resistance to police requests for third-party policing actions. It is usually accompanied by denial of the problem, or an offer of scapegoat alternatives (claims that the problem is actually the result of some other cause [Buerger, 1994]). If the police have adequate documentation of the problem, denial is fairly easy to overcome.

Even after the police have demonstrated the problem, avoidance can continue. Once the police have made their requests for actions, the place manager may agree fully, giving the impression that he or she is compliant, but do nothing once the police contact ends. In one memorable case in Minneapolis, during a meeting with the RECAP officer, a landlord turned to his resident manager and gave her explicit directions to carry out all the officer's recommendations. Once the meeting was over and the officer left the premises, the landlord countermanded all the instructions and told the manager to continue to do business as usual. The duplicity was not discovered until after the manager was later fired for unrelated reasons. At first there was concern that her revelations were just vindictive falsehoods; it took several months before sufficiently strong corroborative evidence was uncovered to establish that the landlord had just been paying lip service to the officer's requests (Buerger, 1992).

Resistance of this kind may be second nature to experienced place managers, based upon the legacy of prior police initiatives. Some who have been in business for a long time have no doubt seen several generations of earnest police officers at their doors, explaining problems at their properties, outlining plans of action and declaiming in serious tones about the consequences of non-compliance with police directives. Each time an officer left the scene and was never seen or heard from again, the place manager learned a lesson about dealing with the police: promise them anything, and they'll go away.

Effective third-party policing changes the nature of this interaction, but it takes time to effect a common recognition of the new rules of engagement. Avoidance can still be an effective foil to third-party policing in venues with limited capacity to enforce civil codes or to follow up requests for action. Officers who are transferred, work rotating shifts or are infrequently assigned to a particularly area are somewhat limited in their ability to overcome avoidance.

Avoidance has several levels: a place manager or owner may ignore the regulatory summonses and repair orders as well as the police requests. Unless a jurisdiction has a well-constructed political mechanism for boarding delinquent properties, like New York City's "Operation Padlock," avoidance can be an effective, low-cost form of resistance that takes advantage of the weakness of the political environment. Similarly, the "teeth" behind police civil actions against nuisance properties with drug or prostitution problems is the ability to apply civil forfeiture laws and seize the property from the owner. Such a legal process will place demands on the city attorney or corporation counsel's staff, typically already understaffed and overburdened with a wide variety of other duties. Introducing a drug forfeiture case that requires seizing (and running) an entire building can be a daunting task: city attorneys will not necessarily step to the task with the same enthusiasm that police officers propose it.

Making this type of enforcement action a top priority requires a broad consensus among the principals of municipal government. The different perspectives (and different sympathies) of the political players may not be automatically sympathetic to the police proposal. Creating a climate to encourage agreement that the action is important to the city — usually as a demonstration that "it can be done, and we will do it," to nudge reluctant place managers into compliance by symbolically raising the stakes for resistance — is a political exercise that requires slow, deliberate consensus building.

Exemption

When police persistence makes avoidance an impractical response, place managers may take the first step into politics by requesting an exemption: a statement that this request/regulation should not apply to them. The request is usually made of the police officer first, almost certainly without success. The next step is to "go over the cop's head," either to a higher ranking officer in the department or a political figure outside the agency.

Exemption often involve elements of denial and scapegoating. The authority figure is a new audience, and the place manager has the opportunity to present the problem in his or her terms, not those of the police officer. Minimization of the problem, scapegoating, "crying poverty" (Buerger, 1994) and a detailed explanation of every factor that should excuse the place manager from complying with the order are all part of the rationalization for exemption.

When enforcement of the civil codes is an element of the police coercion, place managers may ignore the police chain of command and appeal directly to the hierarchy of the enforcing agency. Knowing that the police do not have the authority or the expertise to enforce the civil codes, the place managers would seek to "pull the fangs" out of the police request by neutralizing the enforcement partner's role.[9]

Depending upon the situation, the chances of success may be even greater by approaching the housing, code or health inspector's office for exemption. Experienced landlords and place managers will have dealt with those offices for years, and have a ready knowledge of how the system works. Minneapolis landlords, for instance, knew exactly how much work had to be done to obtain a stay of enforcement of building inspectors' orders, and one building was so well-maintained physically that the building codes were an ineffective tool for reaching the behavioral problems associated with the premises (Buerger, 1992). In some cases, place managers may already have a comfortable working relationship with senior members of the inspecting staff that gives them more credibility with (and sympathy of) the nominal regulators than that enjoyed by the police.

One of the negative aspects of third-party policing is the new demands it places on the routines of other city or county agencies. Agencies are almost always limited in budgets and staff, and each regulatory agency has its own priorities that were established long before the police initiatives were devised. Place managers in some jurisdictions may find a ready partner for collusion in bureaucrats wishing to avoid the extra demands the police make on their routines. Obtaining an exemption from the administrators of the agency charged with the code enforcement effectively forestalls the police initiative. It can also be a powerful defense against further intervention by other city officials, though it has limits in that respect: the success or failure of this gambit often rests on the amount of grass-roots politics that has preceded the police action.

If the local council person is an ally of the police — or has a personal interest in the success of the initiative because of the volume of constituent complaints — granting an exemption to a problem landlord or place manager may well backfire on the agency bureaucrat. But if the groundwork has not been laid by the police (full documentation of the problem from all sources, prior notification to the municipal council and mayor or manager, etc.), the police request may well appear unreasonable against the self-serving background description that has been provided by the place manager.

It may sound odd to speak of such things as "politics," since the police culture has long held the shibboleth that it should be independent of politics (a legacy of the professionalism movement at the turn of the last century). Politicians sit high on the rank and file's list of stock villains, and most police officers expect their superiors to act as a buffer between them and "the politicians." Nevertheless, the need to build consensus and alliances to advance and defend a new program places the police in the arena of local politics.

The simple act of advance notification, and a summary description of both the problem and the project goals, is often sufficient to win the support of both police administrators and local political figures. Except in locally pathological situations, the police commanders and ward representatives have no particular need to be directly involved in a problem-solving venture. Their interests are usually two-fold: first, not to be surprised by questions about something they know nothing about; and second, to be able to associate themselves with good results.[10]

To some degree, this can be interpreted as a game of "who gets the pol's ear first" as a way of defining the battlefield, but that is too simplistic. Poorly conceived projects will not win support even with early notice, and occasionally there are legitimate differences in priorities. An officer's ardent desire to level a pernicious den of iniquity may run up against a concern about the number of affordable housing units in the community: even though the politicians may agree with the officer's definition of the problem, they may have reason to seek a different resolution to the situation, if possible. For that reason, early consensus building on the nature of the problem, the preferred outcome and the most desirable course of action toward that end are all essential — and inherently political — elements of problem solving.

Subversion/Corruption

The exemption dodge is based on an assumption of good-faith intervention on the place manager's behalf. Exemption has an evil twin in some jurisdictions, however: corruption. Bribing inspectors, judges or politicians is also a viable option in some jurisdictions. It is the seamy underside of politics, but represents an effective countermeasure to police action. Regulatory and enforcement processes are subverted by securing a powerful ally, capable of blocking or vetoing enforcement actions for reasons unrelated to the facts and issues of the case.

The softer side of the corruption issue is that of "influence." Bribery constitutes a direct quid-pro-quo: paying a certain sum of money in return for having a repair order lost or incorrectly written (to obtain procedural dismissal in court or administrative hearings); money changing hands to have a summons quashed or placed in some administrative limbo, etc. Influence rides on campaign contributions, favors, childhood associations, family relationships, club memberships and any number of other personal allegiances that would lead a bureaucrat or politician to intervene on a place manager's behalf. Influence merely means that the place manager's description of the situation will be received more sympathetically than will that of the police.

Influence creates calls to the agency head (the police chief, the head of the regulatory agency or both), or conversations with the municipal attorney or the judge. Influence asks for postponements, set-asides, extra time and other tactics that either delay the orders beyond effectiveness or send fairly direct messages that the resources of the agencies shouldn't be wasted on this particular target. In extreme cases, influence gets the police officer transferred to other duties (as a "promotion" that "utilizes the officer's skills in another needed area" in benign circumstances; as outright punishment transfers in more dire ones), and can even lead to the evisceration of the entire police initiative.

Rarely does influence work for long periods of time, or for a second time, if there is an organized police effort. As they do when an arrest is thrown out of court for procedural violations, the police learn to try again. Because influence works in private space, the best counter tactic is to take the issue into public space. Using the political arena to their own advantage, the police build allegiances to create a groundswell of public criticism of the problem establishment, which in turn generates support for police attempts to change it or shut it down.[11] Embarrassment is the primary weapon, and it can be an effective one in the public realm. The patrons of influence usually do not enjoy unfavorable publicity, particularly if it portrays them in a light contrary to their cultivated public image. No one wants to open the morning paper to the headline, "Local Judge Lets Slumlord Off the Hook," or "Council Member Says Neighbors Must Put Up with Drug Bar."

In most cases, embarrassment is not the first weapon deployed: used prematurely, it creates enemies and can have devastating future repercussions. Like all such weapons, it is most effective when kept in reserve, as a threat. The goal of negative publicity about an establishment is primarily to neutralize the influence in the realm of private space, and it must be supported by equally vigorous lobbying in the private realm. "Politicking" links the vigorous public protest in the public arena to the police description of the situation, quietly conveyed to the Person Of Influence. Public protests create the opening for further behind-the-scenes negotiation, and the opportunity for the competing view of the situation to be heard on an equal footing with the place manager's original description.

Ideally, the police want to create a "turnabout" situation. In a role reversal of sorts, the individual to whom the place manager has appealed for intervention uses his or her influence instead on the supplicant. The political patron becomes the final voice that conveys to the place manager the regulators' orders, and the knowledge that she or he has let things go too far not to comply with the police requests. There may be a mediation of some sort, so police cannot realistically expect unconditional surrender; the ultimate goal is enough compliance to eliminate the public nuisance.

Abandonment

The threat to abandon a property is a weapon available to the individual in the local political arena, especially in cities already afflicted with high numbers of abandoned and derelict properties. It is a more credible threat for the individual property owner who has no other assets in the city, because the loss of capital investment is balanced by the protection from the enforcement. Many of the properties targeted for SMART and RECAP actions, for example, were well below the mean in physical plant, requiring considerable expense to bring fully up to code. Persons owning multiple properties have greater exposure, since liens can be attached to other properties.

Abandoned properties are a matter of considerable concern to municipal agencies. While they stand, they present a negative aspect to the community: eyesores at best, they can become havens for derelicts, drug markets and shooting galleries, hiding and escape routes for criminals, hiding spaces for the street prostitution trade, fire hazards, unregulated dumping grounds, breeding grounds for vermin and any number of other problems. In addition to the loss of tax revenues while they stand fallow, the cost of reclaiming abandoned properties represents a considerable expense to cities and towns involving: legal fees for quick-take claims to transfer ownership to the municipality; public works costs to board, fence, and otherwise secure the properties; potential liability for injuries even to illegal trespassers; demolition costs; and the collateral costs of marketing the properties to obtain as fair a price as possible while transferring responsibility to a new owner as quickly as possible.

Like embarrassment, the threat of abandonment is most effective as a potential weapon. Walking away from a capital investment is not easily done, particularly by the individual investors. The threat is actually a negotiating tool — an attempt to create, for those without real influence, a sympathetic hearing like that provided by influence. Because it is limited in its effective application to out-of-jurisdiction (usually out-of-state) owners and the truly desperate, the threat of abandonment is not often successful.

In certain cases, the abandonment gambit can be neutralized if the police can demonstrate that the owner has already abandoned the property for all intents and purposes, and that the city and the neighborhood would be better off with a boarded-up building. This can be particularly true in cities that have either a strong private-sector economy (a wealth of prospective responsible buyers), and/or a strong nonprofit presence specializing in rehabilitating derelict properties for low-income private ownership[12] and a good potential for quick turnover and reclamation.

Cooptation

Cooptation is a special entrepreneurial adaptation to third-party policing efforts that turns the police initiative into a slumlord's tool. Usually functioning at the low end of the housing stock market, it does not have a broad applicability but nevertheless represents a potentially important unintended consequence. In specific markets, the initial police complaint about the property can be used to justify raising rents or evicting tenants for non-criminal reasons.

Many properties become problematic when the owners stop treating them as long-term investments and begin treating them as short-term income generators. The physical plant is neglected, with repairs made sporadically and then only under order. Tenant screening comes to an end, replaced by the practice of accepting anyone with the rent money in hand (usually Section 8 clients, drug dealers or both). A full building takes priority over a safe and orderly building. A steady inflow of cash and a minimum of hassles replaces the normal duties of property management: it is not unusual for slumlords to be absent from their properties for years on end, employing marginally qualified "managers" who do little more than collect the rent and change light bulbs in the hall in exchange for a reduced rent (Buerger, 1992).

When such properties come under police scrutiny, some landlords turn the situation to their advantage, blaming the police as the bad guys who are "making me do this." When police calls are a part of the targeting process, for instance (as was the case in the RECAP experiment), the owner or manager may take action against the tenants placing the calls, threatening them with eviction because "they" are the cause of the problem. Often, the tenants who call the police about conditions created by other tenants are the same ones who complain about the physical plant, withhold rent and are otherwise burdensome to the landlord. Drug dealers, on the other hand, rarely complain about the conditions in their crackhouse, and they always have the month's rent on time — in cash, which can be an added incentive to the unscrupulous landlord who wishes to keep some income off the books. By evicting the tenants who are trying to maintain the property at a higher level, the landlord reduces the call levels, buying time with the police (unless complaints also come from the surrounding neighbors) and making way for tenants who are less troublesome to the landlord.

Eviction is not necessarily the only option; raising the rent can be an equally effective way of convincing tenants to move. In addition, in some cases landlords can temporarily defeat the police scrutiny by playing "musical tenants": one RECAP landlord who had been given notice about a drug-dealing tenant in one of his buildings obligingly evicted the tenant — by relocating him to another of the landlord's buildings in another section of the city. The relocated tenant promptly resumed his drug sales from the new address, transplanting the problems into a new neighborhood.

Collective Resistance

Not all resistance is individual in nature. Like other forms of employment, property owners and managers form professional associations and relationships to advance their interests in the larger political process. They actively monitor pending legislation, as well as trends in other industries which may affect their livelihoods, and take collective action to defend their interests. Other less formal groups and associations coalesce locally, and may work covertly, in collusion with each other, to resist or neutralize the adverse impact of police attention.

Collusion

Under certain market conditions, the most effective way to rid oneself of police pressure about a property is to sell it. Ostensibly, the sale of a property to a new owner represents a gain for the community: there is a presumption that the new owner will treat it as a long-term investment, improving the conditions and being a good neighbor. That presumption requires the police to suspend the focused pressure brought on the former owner, and return to a more cooperative mode until the new owner demonstrates that he or she is unworthy of that approach. There are several collateral problems that can arise in the process.

A landlord wishing to sell a residential property may fill it with tenants without any regard to their social graces or source of income. At first blush, a fully occupied building is a desirable property: it means immediate maximum-income levels with minimal effort on the part of the new landlord. Since sales may be conducted through intermediaries, a new owner may never actually see the property he or she has purchased and may not be aware of the problems until formally notified by the police. First-time owners may have no experience whatever in the particular market they have entered, and become hapless sponsors of all sorts of unsavory activities, which they have no idea how to stop. (The naive owner tends to be most appreciative of police assistance, and correspondingly cooperative, but the problems caused by the place still take time to correct.)

Legitimate buyers may be in short supply, however, and good-faith negotiations take time. Selling the property to another owner of like mind, and then buying a new property from a third, is an effective dodge used by certain landlords. This technique is more applicable to rental property than to businesses like bars and saunas that require constant management, but the tactic is available across the board. Each sale of the property wins a reprieve for the old owner, and the new owner has a grace period — an informal exemption — during which time he or she is expected to bring the property up to code and correct the conditions that fostered the previous behavioral problems. Even a pending sale is sufficient to forestall action by some regulatory agencies: the municipality's interest is in a thriving, viable property or business under the care of an interested, involved owner.

Each new sale represents the possibility of rescuing a derelict property from the hands of an uncaring owner or manager, but that individual can use the uncertainty of the sale to his or her advantage. "The sale will be quashed if there are liens or other actions against the building," the owner argues, truthfully, in requesting that actions be held in abeyance. This liminal state may last for several months, during which time the owner or manager continues to reap what profits there are, while putting no capital and little effort back into the building. In Minneapolis, RECAP officers discovered that a number of bad properties were routinely sold among a small group of individual landlords who had no formal association, but always seemed to be associated with troublesome properties. One of the most difficult residential properties during the RECAP experiment changed hands four times in the course of a year, each time requiring the officer to start negotiations afresh, as conditions steadily deteriorated and the number of calls continued to rise. At the conclusion of the experiment, the building was sold for the fourth time, to the same individual who had owned it when RECAP began (Buerger, 1992).[13]

The "pending sale" has limits, of course: the existence of the prospective buyer can be checked, and there is always a possibility that the owner/manager will milk it too long and incur the police and regulatory actions anyway. For the pending-sale dodge to work effectively, the sale has to be timely and hence, certain.

The apparently informal collusion encountered in Minneapolis was partly the result of a change in the laws that provided tax incentives for real estate investment (probably a further reward for selling a property rather than working to improve it). Whether it was a planned association or just a fortuitous coincidence is not known. Such situations represent a potential future development in third-party policing: the tracing of ownership patterns of troubled properties.

Informal collusions are at best a localized dodge — in some respects, an avoidance of the larger political arena. It is the formal associations, operating openly in the political arena, that pose the greatest threat to third-party policing. Even though the police bring pressure to bear on illegitimate practices, the expanded government control that third-party policing represents is a potential threat to all business owners. The extent and limits of the new controls are not known beforehand, and it is perhaps natural to assume the worst. Formal, collective responses will not only take place at the local level, seeking wider exemptions, but if necessary also at the state level, in judicial and legislative arenas.

Overturn

Still in its formative stages as a public doctrine, third-party policing is most vulnerable to being struck down in the judicial process. Like all untested police initiatives, third-party policing may function unobstructed until it is brought under judicial scrutiny. At that time, the entire premise can come under formal consideration by the courts, in a manner similar to the way the pat-down frisk came under judicial scrutiny in Terry v. Ohio (1968). Depending on the nature of the case that brings third-party policing to the attention of the courts, the policy may be considered on narrow procedural (due process) grounds or as a broad-based consideration of the entire doctrine.

Cases may come before the judiciary either on appeal of adverse judgments in lower (municipal) courts, or as pleas for an injunction against third-party policing interventions. Well-funded individuals may conduct their own appeals, of course, but it is equally likely that landlord associations will fund individual or class-action suits against initiatives they deem harmful to their mutual business practices. An outside player is the burgeoning property rights movement, which resists a broad range of what it deems government intrusions into private concerns — from zoning and other land use restrictions to eminent domain seizures. The formative nature of third-party policing makes it a potential target for exemplary action by property rights activists.

One of the factors that may limit the use of the appellate process may be the fact that the case will be civil in nature. Even though the police put pressure on place managers and landlords to control criminal conduct, the sanctions actually levied against third parties are entirely civil: housing court penalties, alcohol beverage control actions (fines or license suspensions, etc.), repair orders and health condemnation closings. Civil cases move much more slowly than criminal cases, unless there is a compelling reason for a higher court to extend jurisdiction over a case. Because third-party policing articulates a new variation on the civil/criminal law distinctions, however, there is a potential for much faster movement through the courts.

The questions raised by third-party policing are likely to focus on whether it is an unwarranted intrusion upon individual liberty. Unlike the land takings that have given rise to the loose coalition of the property rights movement, third-party policing intervenes in commerce, which is subject to government regulation despite the nominally private interaction between willing seller and willing buyer. The issue will not be one of separation of powers, nor of the appropriateness of using the civil law for a law enforcement purpose: both police and regulatory functions lie within the executive branch of government, and civil penalties ranging from padlocking to forfeiture have long been applied against public nuisance properties.

The central issue of third-party policing will most likely be the reasonableness of the remedy demanded by the state, as it is imposed by the police. The grounds for forfeiture are well-determined in the legal arena: the documentation of illegal conduct occurring on the premises, notice of same being given to the property owner and failure of the owner to take steps to correct the situation. The middle ground of third-party policing is less well-defined, as it reaches to the future conduct of persons unknown in the absence of demonstrable illegal activity. The legal shift is away from a requirement to correct actual conditions and toward a new requirement to prevent potential, unspecified conditions.

How well the concept of third-party policing will fare under such a review will depend upon several factors: the precision with which a doctrine of public duty is articulated; the fact-pattern of the individual case (including both the municipal support and the actions of the individual officers involved); the reasonableness of the relationship between the prescribed remedy and the results sought; and the level of organization and funding behind the appeal.

The Oakland SMART initiative is one example of a program with a greater chance to withstand appellate challenge. It clearly articulates the expectations of the owners and managers of a commercial place, vetted through the existing political process (participation by various levels of elected and appointed officials, with public hearings and perhaps public referendum; proceeding upon legal advice from corporate counsel, etc.). The vulnerable cases are those in which third-party policing proceeds haphazardly, guided only by the intuitions of one or a handful of individuals in the police department, with little or no mooring in the surrounding legal and political environment.

Acts that shock or offend the conscience of the court (the Rochin v. California [1952] threshold) are the most vulnerable to judicial overturn. One exceptional case that takes the concept of third-party policing to its extreme (the regulatory equivalent of forced stomach pumping) may provide the grist for judicial review, and the fact-pattern of the individual case is critical. The entire use of third-party policing as a strategy could fail because a single officer used the instruments of third-party policing for the wrong reason, or against the wrong individual. Using the threat of civil inspection and sanctions as a means of settling a personal vendetta, demanding the eviction of an individual on mere suspicion of illegal activity (unsupported by articulable evidence), trying to shut down a bar or other commercial establishment in order to further the interests of a competitor and other scenarios provide an opening to examine whether a doctrine like third-party policing is a reasonable tool to provide government agents.

Even cases that are clear abrogations of existing law enforcement standards (involving the actions of rogue or "loose cannon" officers), and thus might ordinarily be decided on their own fact-pattern, open the door to greater scrutiny. Professional associations (landlords, bar owners, etc.) keep a close watch over court dockets for cases that have particular application to their membership, and the prospect of amicus briefs inserting constitutional issues above and beyond the fact pattern is a real one.

Repeal

Legislative action — a single law or group of laws that curtail or block the ability of the police to implement third-party policing — is one of the less likely threats, but one that cannot be discounted. A legislative approach may be undertaken either independently or in conjunction with a judicial appeal or even before third-party policing is applied in a jurisdiction. Use of the legislative option available to either side is also a recourse against an adverse judicial decision. If the judiciary strikes down a third-party policing approach because it lies outside the formal structures of the law, the legislative process may be used to establish it as part of the legal structure. (Similar initiatives undertaken recently have been the constitutional amend-ments proposed to "protect" the flag from burning as a form of social protest, and the Religious Freedom Restoration Act.)

In the current political climate, it is unlikely that any elected official would propose a measure that could be portrayed as "forcing the police to allow drug markets to flourish" or "allowing slumlords to destroy a neighborhood," but it is equally unlikely that a bill would be that direct in its language. The legislative process is rife with opportunities to make subtler changes, in areas not immediately identified with crime control, that can have significant changes for the practice. For example, new legal protections for landlords and place managers can be inserted as riders on bills that are completely unrelated to property management. Procedures that protect landlords can be inserted in bills titled "Tenants' Rights;" while innocuous-sounding phrases like "good faith" can be given definitions so broad that they provide a powerful shield against punitive actions. In Minneapolis, hiring an on-site property manager was considered "good faith" enough to suspend all adverse actions, even though some landlords hired property managers who were incompetent or mentally handicapped (Buerger 1992). It is not necessary to say publicly: "We will not allow the imposition of third-party policing because it offends important political supporters"; the concept can be eviscerated by a series of small stumbling blocks, exemptions and procedural stalling points.

"Money talks" is a catchphrase of those who hold politics in disrepute, and it is a fact of life that political contributions buy influence. Like influence at the personal level, however, influence in the legislative process can be defined — and limited — by external constraints. A well-orchestrated initiative against a problem property or a larger scale "problem" common to many properties, complete with publicity (or the potential for it), creates a better backdrop for sustaining the concept of third-party policing. Such a cry is heard more distinctly if it comes from the citizens rather than the police, and creating such an outcry is an inherently political process. The influence of a local politician (especially one within a legislature's own party) can also carry clout, though it can be mediated by party considerations.

Once third-party policing moves into the legislative realm, it is no longer assured a favorable reception on its own terms. "Lip service" is not the exclusive province of recalcitrant landlords, and third-party policing can be embraced by politicians in theory without receiving any substantive backing. In the turbulent world of competing agendas, priorities can change rapidly. A promising political initiative can be sacrificed on behalf of another gain, either fully or by delay. A bill unfavorable to third-party policing, like the recent welfare bill, may secure grudging acceptance, because the "return vote" is needed for an agenda considered more pressing. Unless third-party policing arrives at the legislatures with a high profile, it is at risk of changing from favored policy to expendable pawn overnight.

Neither judicial overturn nor legislative rebuff will necessarily spell the end of third-party policing, especially if local municipalities consider it a necessary tool for nurturing and maintaining order. As was the case with the overturning of the death penalty, judicial remand may carry the message to refine and narrow the scope of the application in the interests of fairness. What is expendable in the current legislature may be championed in the next, depending upon the political climate and the response of third-party policing advocates to the initial rebuff.

CONCLUSION

It is not enough to put forth a new idea, proclaim it a good thing, and sit back to await the accolades of others. In all cases — be it the initial demand for officially sanctioned legitimacy, or an attempt to rescue the concept from an adverse decision — any new public policy needs public allies who will remain constant throughout a long, up-and-down process. Marshaling such allies is inherently political, and requires a process outside the normal hortatory public relations work police departments engage in. Building a coalition is a different function than maintaining one, but there are several common features. The initiative needs to be properly identified (or "strategically positioned," in market terms); opposition must be anticipated from a variety of fronts; and carefully crafted responses to potential objections must be worked out in advance.

Positioning third-party policing as a prevention measure is perhaps the most logical approach to coalition building. Preventing crime and disorder is intuitively more attractive than reacting to undesirable conditions: it minimizes harm and provides the least possible drains on public resources. Third-party policing also makes tangible the concept of "coproduction" (shared responsibility for crime prevention), although the burden falls disproportionately on a select few.

However, "prevention" has heretofore been a voluntary activity usually subsumed under the heading of "good business practice." Making future prevention an obligation rests in most cases on past behavior, specifically, bad business practices, and there are interesting speculative elements that attach in that regard. These points comprise some of the bases for potential objections to the doctrine, and are components of the third-party policing doctrine that should be worked out in advance of challenges.

What are the workable thresholds of expected order, for instance? Can we reasonably expect a hole-in-the-wall dive to become a Hilton Hotel or a Bull & Finch Pub overnight? Do occasional loud parties or domestic disputes impinge upon the peace of the neighbors to a degree comparable to a crackhouse or the operation of a brothel? Can the police apply the same expectations to illegal activities such as passing bad checks, which does not generate place-based disorder and is generally unrelated to house rules? What are the dimensions of "reasonable" expectations in bringing a derelict property up to code, particularly in those cases where the need exceeds the owner's available resources?

There is an economic reality of even the borderline cases, where the money available for repairs (through rental income or a building account) is far outstripped by the cost of the work needed. Mortgage companies do not allow landlords to skip payments in order to evacuate a building (evict all tenants) for rehabilitation purposes, or to change the population group. Police can be quite cynical about the "crying poverty" dodge, believing that experienced slumlords have ways of hiding the money from scrutiny. However, the issue can be very important to the small independent landlord, whose support may be crucial in both city politics and the private deliberations of the professional associations, and who are most likely to evaluate things from the perspective of "there but for the grace of God go I."

Third-party policing cannot afford the hard-line approach that sometimes attends police initiatives. Part of the process of positioning the initiative must include the equivalent of the sliding scale for enforcement, including workable definitions of what constitutes "good faith" remediation under standard circumstances, as well as the process for working out an equitable formula in unusual cases. It will be the responsibility of the authors (in this case, the police and their allies in city government) to present a well-developed plan that encompasses fairness as well as effectiveness; having such a plan is also helpful when responding to court challenges.

Another important component is how robustly the police information systems can distinguish between (1) problems generated at or by a premises, and (2) problems generated by the immediate neighborhood and attributed to the premises. This can be crucial when calls-for-service data is a part of target selection, as it was for RECAP. Consider the neighborhood bar that is unpopular because of the hubbub its patrons create as they leave the premises in the early morning hours. Local residents also complain of a public urination problem that they attribute to the bar's clientele, even though the neighborhood borders an area inhabited by homeless squatters and many of the public urination complaints occur during a period when the bar is closed. Whether the bar should be "held accountable" for other disorderly conditions is a valid question under these circumstances, and the role of the police will be a difficult one. If they distinguish the urination condition from that of the closing-time mayhem, they may win the cooperation of the management for quieting departing customers but forfeit the support of the neighborhood for not pushing the public urination issue. Should they treat the neighborhood complaints as valid across the board, they may still be able to coerce a grudging compliance on the closing-time issue, but generate deep strains of distrust (invisible to the police) based on the unreliability of the call data and the unfair interpretation of it.

At what point are property managers, having served their time in terms of maintaining good order at an establishment, entitled to a fresh start on the order-maintenance continuum, free from regulatory oversight? The question is linked to the original targeting threshold in most cases, but it also speaks to the degree of control and the limited purpose of third-party intervention. The SMART program had a formal threshold for considering a problem to be "abated" (Green 1996), while RECAP developed a set of ad hoc criteria for moving an address from "active pressure" to "monitor" status. Formal mechanisms may have to stand against the long-held grudges of the neighborhood residents, who see the initial sanctions only as a prelude to shutting down a particular property: at some point the police may have to tell their former allies that the residual problems of the property are not severe enough to warrant continued special sanctions, and be prepared to suffer whatever loss of support ensues.

Having an articulable, relatively neutral threshold for "success" comes full circle, back to the issue of realistic goals. It is an important factor in distinguishing a reasonable, focused public policy from an unchecked police weapon. That, in turn, will be an important element in "selling" third-party policing initiatives to the broader polity, who do not have an immediate stake in it and can weigh its positive and negative points in more abstract terms. The policy must be reasonably focused in terms of outcomes and process, in order to satisfy the "there but for the grace of God go I" test of those who foresee or imagine the policy being applied against them.

Selling the program is the business of politics. Establishing a broad-based coalition of individuals and interest groups who agree upon the need for third-party policing, and who support the nature of the police solutions, is a political process. It requires more than just articulating the project or the doctrine from the viewpoint of its utility to the police. To be successful, the proposed doctrine and responsibilities must embrace as many stakeholders as possible, and speak in conceptual terms meaningful to them as well as to the police. Because third-party policing imposes a new form of public duty, the dimensions, limits and rationale of that duty must be clearly understood across all points of the political spectrum.

Address correspondence to: Michael E. Buerger, College of Criminal Justice, 407 Churchill Hall, 360 Huntington Avenue, Boston, MA 02115. E-mail: <m.buerger@nunet.neu.edu>.

REFERENCES

Buerger, M.E. (ed.) (1992). *The Crime Prevention Casebook: Securing High Crime Locations*. Washington, DC: Crime Control Institute.

—— (1994). "The Problems of Problem-Solving: Resistance, Interdependencies, and Conflicting Interests." *American Journal of Police* 13:1-36.

—— and L.G. Mazerolle (1998). "Third-Party Policing: A Theoretical Analysis of an Emerging Trend." *Justice Quarterly* 15(2):301-327.

Eck, J.E. (1994). "Place Managers." Doctoral dissertation, University of Maryland, College Park.

—— and W. Spelman (1987). *Problem Solving: Problem-Oriented Policing in Newport News*. Police Executive Research Forum. Washington, DC: U.S. National Institute of Justice.

Figlio, R.M., S. Hakim and G.F. Rengert (eds.) (1986). *Metropolitan Crime Patterns*. Monsey, NY: Criminal Justice Press.

Gilsinan, J.F. (1989). "They Is Clowning Tough: 911 and the Social Construction of Reality." *Criminology* 27:329-344.

Goldstein, H. (1979). "Improving Policing: A Problem-Oriented Approach." *Crime & Delinquency* 25:236-258.

—— (1990). *Problem-Oriented Policing*. Philadelphia, PA: Temple University Press.

Green, L.A. (1996). *Policing Places With Drug Problems*. Thousand Oaks, CA: Sage.

Kennedy, D.M. (1993). *Closing the Market: Controlling the Drug Trade in Tampa, Florida,*. NIJ Program Focus Series. Washington, DC: U.S. National Institute of Justice.

Newman, O. (1972). *Defensible Space: Crime Prevention Through Urban Design*. New York, NY: Macmillan.

Pierce, G.L., S.A. Spaar and L.R. Briggs, IV (1984). *The Character of Police Work: Implications for Service Delivery*. Boston, MA: Center for Applied Social Research, Northeastern University.

Poyner, B. (1983). *Design Against Crime: Beyond Defensible* Space. London, UK: Butterworths.

Reiss, A.J., Jr. (1971). *The Police and the Public*. New Haven, CT: Yale University Press.

—— (1984). "Consequences of Compliance and Deterrence Models of Law Enforcement for the Exercise of Police Discretion." *Law and Contemporary Problems* 47:83-122.

Rochin v. California (1952). 343 U.S. 165.

Sherman, L.W. (1987). Repeat Calls to Police in Minneapolis. Washington, DC: Crime Control Institute.

—— (1990). "Police Crackdowns: Initial and Residual Deterrence." In M. Tonry and N. Morris (eds.), *Crime and Justice: A Review of Research*, vol.12. Chicago, IL: University of Chicago Press.

—— P.R. Gartin, and M.E. Buerger (1989). "Hot Spots of Predatory Crime: Routine Activities and the Criminology of Place." *Criminology* 27:27-55.

Terry v. Ohio (1968). 392 U.S. 1, 88 S.CT. 1868.

Wilson, J.Q. and G.L. Kelling (1982). "Broken Windows: The Police and Neighborhood Safety." *Atlantic Monthly* (March):29-38.

NOTES

1. Pierce et al. (1984) analyzed burglary patterns in Boston, while Figlio et al. (1986) examined metropolitan crime patterns. Shortly thereafter, Sherman (1987) conducted a comprehensive analysis of all calls for police service in Minneapolis. DMAP, the Drug Market Analysis Project, was the first large-scale initiative by the National Institute of Justice to integrate police records into useable real-time information via computers, focusing on drug market activity defined by physical places. Since that time, the market for crime-mapping programs has expanded dramatically, and more and more departments are adopting place-based analysis.

2. These databases identify to police dispatchers the location of each call's origin (e.g., Sherman et al. 1989; Gilsinan, 1989), in order to verify information obtained verbally and to cope with the phenomena of 911 hangups and inarticulate callers.

3. In New York City, beat officers had been directed to ignore low-level street dealing as an anti-corruption measure.

4. Police resources include, and can even be limited to, public announcements of a crackdown without any corresponding personnel deployments (Sherman, 1990).

5. Such as a summary of police calls, the results of criminal investigations, or crime maps and a summary of neighbor complaints about a property, etc.

6. CPTED covers a wide range of physical and psychosocial approaches to limit the opportunities for crime. The concept combines Newman's "Defensible Space" concepts (1972) with Barry Poyner's (1983) "Design Against Crime" ones. A parallel concept is Clarke's "Situational Crime Prevention."

7. Hereafter, these individuals will collectively be referred to as "place managers," although this use of the term is broader than Eck's (1994) original definition.

8. In this usage, the "third parties" are persons affected by, but not directly party to, the dispute or the spillover effects of the economic relationship: the occupants of the adjacent apartment whose peace and quiet is disturbed by the domestic dispute in the first instance, and neighbors whose peace (and sometimes safety) is diminished by the spillover from the problem property.

9. This can also occur within police agencies themselves. When the RECAP unit attempted to persuade Minneapolis Public Library officials to enforce certain conduct codes in a branch library, library officials approached the district commander of that area to have a beat officer stop in periodically as an alternative to RECAP's suggestions. Officials effectively "pulled rank" on the RECAP officer, by going to a higher authority within the police department and securing an action that required nothing of them and that (they claimed) made the further scrutiny of RECAP unnecessary.

10. Police officers tend to treat this act contemptuously, as "Phase 6 of the project": that is, "Praise and honors for the non-combatants." It is, however, a fairly cheap price to pay for future support for other initiatives, including budget requests.

11. Once the initial cooperative overtures are rebuffed, closing the premises often becomes the ideal outcome in the minds of the police, but that hope is often tempered by other realities.

12. Nationally, Habitat for Humanity represents one such venture. In Minneapolis in the late 1980s, Catholic Charities and the local Project for Pride in Living were extensively involved in property rehabilitations in neighborhoods targeted by RECAP.

13. The recognition of the pattern of changing ownership came late in the experiment, and the RECAP Unit's role changed shortly thereafter, before the officers had a chance to devise a counter strategy.

CURTAILING YOUTH: A CRITIQUE OF COERCIVE CRIME PREVENTION

by

Robert White
University of Melbourne

Abstract: *This paper provides a critical review of crime prevention measures involving coercive control over the activities, behaviors and public visibility of young people. Drawing on examples and trends in the U.S., Australia and the U.K., the paper reviews four major areas of coercive intervention in youthful activity: reconstructing of public space in ways that basically exclude and/or contain the young in particular ways; extending police powers in regulating the street life of young people; making use of youth curfews; and emphasizing the need for parents to police their offspring. It is argued that adoption of a developmental crime prevention strategy is both possible, and more desirable, than reliance on coercive measures.*

INTRODUCTION

Juvenile crime is big news. Throughout the advanced industrialized countries today, the media are saturated with accounts of youthful wrongdoing and the threats posed to the social order by unruly, antisocial young people. Media hype has been more than matched by tough-talking politicians who have seized upon the "law-and-order" agenda in efforts to enhance their electoral standing. While the problem of juvenile crime has often been exaggerated well out of proportion to actual crime trends and actual levels of social harm, this has not prevented legislators and criminal justice officials from introducing strong measures to combat the perceived juvenile crime wave.

The intention of this paper is to review some of the measures currently in vogue or being mooted for introduction in various jurisdictions in the U.S., Australia and the United Kingdom. More specifically, the concern is to outline and critique those measures that can be described as predominantly coercive in nature, constituting generally repressive forms of control over the activities, behaviors and public visibility of young people. They include: attempts to reconstruct public space in ways that basically exclude and/or contain the young in particular ways; the extension of private and public police powers in regulating the street life of young people; the use of youth curfews; and greater emphasis being placed on parents to police their offspring. I wish to counterpose to these types of interventions a different approach to youth crime prevention — one that focuses on young people as legitimate rights-holders in society and that stresses the developmental rather than coercive in institutional relations with young people.

Crime prevention can be conceptualized in a number of different ways, and in its wide definition can include almost any sort of measure directed at deterring crime. For the purposes of this paper, the term will be used in a much more circumscribed way to refer mainly to those types of interventions that attempt to stop juvenile offending before it begins. This can involve a wide range of intervention measures, including changes to the physical environment, multi-agency service provision and various citizen-participation programs.

Our concern, however, is with those actions that involve coercion as a central element. In this context, coercion refers to elements of compulsion that are generally imposed upon a particular population group (e.g., young people and their parents) from the top-down, with little consideration given to social consequences or to the participation of these groups in the decision-making process. At the heart of coercive approaches is the use or threat of force as the key means of citizen protection or crime prevention. Coercion does not equal the application of criminal law. However, the interventions associated with coercive approaches do constitute a form of criminalization insofar as certain activities and people are continually subject to the scrutiny of the criminal justice system, and remedies are sought that attempt to severely restrict the behavior and presence of young people generally.

In some cases, the crime prevention measures adopted may not be specific to young people (as with some "zero tolerance" policing strategies). However, because of their disenfranchised social position, public visibility and tendency to hang around together in groups, teenagers are especially vulnerable to the disproportionate enforcement of such measures. In other cases, crime prevention is explicitly constructed in youth-specific terms (as with youth curfews). Generally speaking, however, the framework of intervention is very similar, as are the effects. The context for the adoption of crime prevention measures is discussed in the next section.

REGULATING SPACE

Making city streets safer has involved attempts to directly repress so-called undesirable elements from the public domain; it has also involved reconfiguring public space in a manner that excludes certain groups of people. This involves a combination of both street policing, and new architectural and urban planning strategies. Here issues of crime prevention are constructed as part of a technical problem that can be dealt with by recourse to new urban planning techniques, the adoption of sophisticated surveillance technology and the innovative use of legislative mechanisms.

One measure associated with this type of approach is to consciously construct designated zones of safety and public security. In the U.S., the building of urban fortresses and gated suburbs and the drift to rural sanctuaries are illustrations of attempts to purchase security by creating private exclusion areas. Exclusive entry and restricted access are the hallmarks of this type of crime prevention strategy. They are often linked to the privatization of what might previously have been open publicly owned and publicly accessible community space (White, 1996a).

At the local level, the answer to crime for some is to establish security checkpoints as a means to dissuade potential offenders from entering an area. For example, in Rosemont, IL, the local government passed an ordinance mandating police checkpoints at the two entrances to the village's largest residential area. All drivers who pass through checkpoints are stopped and questioned (National Crime Prevention Council, 1996). The emphasis is on deterring would-be offenders by having restricted access to potential targets, and by having a highly visible anti-crime presence. In a similar vein, many towns and cities in the U.S., Australia and Britain now have an extensive array of closed-circuit television cameras in inner-city business districts.

Such strategies appear to be based on "opportunity reduction" theories, which argue that the solution to crime is to increase the cost and reduce the opportunities for the commission of crime and to increase the likelihood of detection. This is commonly linked to both "situational crime prevention" and "Crime Prevention Through Environmental Design" (see, for examples Clarke, 1992, and Felson, 1994). It is generally argued that crime is basically a matter of choice and opportunity, and therefore open for anyone to pursue given the right circumstances. The prevention of juvenile crime, in this framework, is thus premised on increasing surveillance in the public domain (e.g., through stepped-up police patrols) and ensuring better protection of businesses, homes and persons by innovative, locally based design and community initiatives (e.g., neighborhood watch schemes). The message is one of heightened awareness of strangers, and of preemptive action to reduce the presence of potential offenders in particular city locales.

In practice, the creation of private exclusion zones (generally for the wealthy and better-off) is sometimes accompanied by concerted efforts to set up "containment" zones for the dispossessed and economically marginalized. Davis (1994), for example, describes how a "homeless containment zone" has been created in downtown Los Angeles — an overcrowded Skid Row area known as Central City East — into which the poorest and most disadvantaged are literally herded by the Los Angeles Police Department, with the approval of the city.

The strategy of containment, according to Davis (1994), is part of a larger picture based upon "the ecology of fear." Within this framework operate a multitude of overlapping crime control measures that both heighten the fear of crime as they simultaneously appear to offer solutions to it at a local level. The crime control map in this case consists of everything from restricted entry suburbs, to gang-free parks, to narcotics and prostitution abatement zones. The focus on local solutions to issues of crime and crime prevention has spawned a wide array of measures that are now currently in use across the U.S. (see National Crime Prevention Council, 1996). However, as Davis (1994) alerts us, the overall consequence of these kinds of local interventions is to create an intricate web of security and social exclusion that is redefining and reshaping the urban landscape.

Not only is this a matter of concern from the point of view of basic social justice and human rights (e.g., to freedom of movement), but the effects of situational or locally based crime prevention strategies premised upon social exclusion and extensive surveillance may be socially detrimental or, at the extreme, explosive, in their own right. Fundamentally, such strategies generally ignore the basic socioeconomic causes of crime by concentrating on issues of crime control. The imposition of ever-restrictive and, in some cases, harsher, measures to reduce opportunities for crime generates pressures for the displacement of crime in terms of times, places and offenses. It also ignores the creative ways in which people will adapt to and adjust their activity in response to attempts to control their movements, behaviors and appearances. Crime prevention measures of this kind thus lend themselves to the adoption of more subterranean ways to circumvent surveillance and containment (e.g., use of secret hand signals in the case of gang membership).

More generally, the widespread commodification of protective and surveillance devices — and the ability to buy security in regard to both a single residence and whole neighborhood areas — is not a socially neutral process; it emerges from and reflects massive economic and social differences in the general population. The social polarization apparent in the U.S., Britain and Australia is translating into varying forms of spatial apartheid, with some sections of the city or community able to secure a modicum of apparent safety while others are relegated to life in increasingly divisive and hostile environments. Economic exclusivity is not a good basis for meaningful and just crime prevention. And, as the Los Angeles riots in 1992 remind us, the potential for explosive situations is heightened by the combination of the overpolicing and underresourcing of high-rental, low-income neighborhoods.

Attempting to design crime out by introducing new architectural and civic design measures (e.g., thinking about how, or whether, to provide public toilets or comfortable seating in high-transit areas), or by introducing proactive "anti-gang" measures (e.g., via the use of civil injunctions against alleged gang members that ban their use of parks or the wearing of certain types of clothes), often begs the larger question of who the targets of crime prevention actually are and why they are singled out for attention. While such prevention measures may appear to be neutral in application (i.e., the law is to apply to everyone the same way), the technical exercise of reducing opportunities for crime does have major social and political consequences. Invariably, the most vulnerable and marginalized sections of the population benefit the least from such strategies and are, in essence, further penalized and ostracized — not because they are necessarily "criminal", but because they are poor.

To make this observation about unequal applications and outcomes is not, however, to argue that opportunity reduction and situational crime prevention programs and techniques are inherently class-biased. Indeed, as argued by Sutton (1996), such approaches can have significant value in helping to expose social inequities and unmasking power relations. The possibility certainly exists for a more politicized understanding of such approaches, for example, their application as part of the social empowerment of more powerless and vulnerable groups and communities (White, 1996b). There is some merit to the idea of engaging people in disadvantaged areas in discussions of how best to adapt specific crime prevention technologies and techniques to their own needs. But there are limits to how far we might wish to go, and what direction we see crime prevention taking.

For instance, it is arguable whether or not stepped-up surveillance and preventive measures — at their extreme involving the fingerprinting and photographing of all local children (see Davis, 1994) — are particularly helpful or healthy for any society. As expressed elsewhere (White, 1996b), it may well be the case that, at least theoretically, it is possible to prevent crime given the availability of sufficient tools, resources and powers. But do we really want to create, and live in, a kind of "surveillance state" where we all may be free from crime but prisoners of our own security systems?

In addition to this kind of self-imprisonment, and the emotionally and socially debilitating fearfulness that can envelop parents, children and whole communities — the message we tend to currently send to the poor and unemployed will hardly engender good will across the rich-poor divide. The construction of "us" and "them" is achieved through a constant process of stereotyping, and state-sponsored intimidation and criminalization. Drawing new lines in the urban map, however, does nothing to remedy the basic reasons why some young people congregate where they do, engage in certain kinds of both legal and illegal activities and develop modes of being that bear little resemblance to mainstream definitions or aspirations regarding what is "good and decent." The abrogation of social responsibility for underlying problems of inequality, poverty and social injustice is mirrored in attempts to find selective private or local answers to what appears to be a "law-and-order" problem. A coercive response to youth behavior or criminal offending will not contribute to the creation of a more humane, less fearful society.

POLICING THE STREET

Perhaps the most evident and pervasive form of crime prevention pertaining to juveniles is that of street policing. The main objective here is to target young people on the street (including shopping malls, beaches, train stations, etc.) before they can possibly engage in offending behavior. This type of approach is clearly reliant upon the coercive apparatus of the state — namely, the police — and is sustained by and reinforces the notion that crime prevention is basically about crime control.

At a theoretical level, impetus for the adoption of this kind of intervention has been fostered by arguments such as the "broken window" hypothesis of Wilson and Kelling (1982). Commenting on crime strategies in the U.S., Wilson and Kelling (1982) argue that we must suppress the symptoms of disorder by taking vigorous action to clean up the streets (i.e., act strongly now, as one broken window soon leads to two). In practical terms, this has translated into a high, and highly visible, level of police presence in specifically targeted urban areas.

Street policing effectively sees juvenile crime prevention as a matter of deterrence. Proactive strategies are designed to exclude the young from certain types of activities and from certain parts of the public domain. Such strategies take several different forms (Cunneen and White, 1995). For example, in the Australian jurisdiction of New South Wales, legislation was introduced in 1994 allowing the police even greater scope to remove young people from the streets beyond a certain time. Simultaneously, the police in Western Australia — in this case, drawing on existing welfare legislation as the legal basis upon which to act — were engaged in a campaign called 'Operation Sweep' that was intended to forcibly remove young people from the streets of Perth and Fremantle.

While the legislative basis for action varies from state to state, the general trend around Australia has been for police services to be granted extensive new powers vis-a-vis young people. These range from the casual use of name-checks (e.g., requesting names and addresses), and "move-on" powers (e.g., the right to clear designated areas) to an enhanced ability to obtain the fingerprints and bodily samples of alleged offenders.

In the state of Queensland, this kind of street-policing strategy has been extended to include private security personnel as well. Thus, behavior at the South Bank Parklands in Brisbane is covered by legislation granting security officers the power to stop people, ask for their name and address, and direct them to leave the site for 24 hours if the officer considers that the person is causing a "public nuisance." Further exclusionary powers are available upon written notice, or application to a court if the security officers wish to ban someone for up to one year (White et al., 1996).

The systematic harassment and regulation of young people in public spaces has long been a key aspect of the maintenance of public order as conceived by authority figures. Importantly, no actual wrongdoing or criminal act need have been committed. The emphasis on crime control and public order maintenance precludes any consideration of young people's needs and desires for space of their own. Moreover, in many cases the degree and type of intervention is highly discriminatory and often brutal, with greater scrutiny of the most marginalized, vulnerable groups of young people (see White and Alder, 1994).

One outcome of such campaigns, and indeed of the persistent clashes between young people and the police over the use of public space, is that more youths are vulnerable to the criminalization process than might otherwise be the case. This is because the constant harassment of young people by authority figures can set in motion further conflict (such as youth harassment of law enforcement officials), which periodically surfaces in the courts as "offensive behavior," "resisting arrest" and the like. A consequence of street policing as crime prevention, therefore, is the creation of "criminals."

A recent British study (Loader, 1996) suggests that the police often have an ambivalent attitude toward policing the young: they understand some of the problems experienced by young people in their use of time and space, but they are under organizational pressures to do something about the youth presence. Similar tensions have been noted in the Australian case (Alder et al., 1992; White and Alder, 1994). At least part of the problem stems from the ways in which public-order policing has been construed, both operationally and legislatively, as resting upon notions of coercive intervention. Police contact and intervention in the lives of young people is inevitable; the crucial issue is whether or not that intervention will exacerbate or diminish antisocial behavior and criminal activity.

An assessment of this style and type of street intervention must acknowledge that the principal recipients of police attention tend to be sociologically very distinctive. There is ample evidence to show that street policing is overwhelmingly directed at the least powerful and most vulnerable social groups in society. This kind of intervention thus impacts most negatively on homeless young people, the unemployed, indigenous young people and ethnic minority young people. Very often the intervention involved is characterized by heavy reliance upon force, intimidation and maltreatment. The racist character of street policing is also an issue of much concern to minority groups in the U.S., the U.K. and Australia (see Cook and Hudson, 1993; White, 1996c).

Furthermore, given the lack of economic and social resources available to many of these young people, important questions can be asked regarding where they can find space of their own outside of the family home. Similarly, the social vulnerability of these youths is often matched by a vulnerability to criminal victimization. Yet, ironically, the general trend is for youths who are subject to overpolicing to also suffer underpolicing when it comes to their needs and status as victims of crime (see Loader, 1996; Cunneen, 1992).

YOUTH CURFEWS

Juvenile crime prevention is increasingly being constructed in terms of detailed restrictions on the movement and presence of young people outside of the family home. A key mechanism here is that of the youth curfew. The use of curfews is extensive in the U.S., with curfew ordinances in effect in a majority of the largest American cities (Bilchik, 1996). Support for the imposition of curfews has been highlighted in recent debates and political rhetoric on how best to deal with juvenile crime in both the U.K. (Jeffs and Smith, 1996) and Australia (White, 1996d).

Youth curfews represent yet another method by which to clear the streets of young people — again, regardless of whether or not they have done anything wrong, much less illegal. The nature of specific curfew regulation varies considerably, according to such criteria as:

- age (e.g., under 18, under 16, under 10);
- hours of operation (e.g., midnight to 5 a.m.; 10:30 p.m. to 6:30 a.m.; daytime curfews during school hours);
- location (e.g., self-contained local government areas such as country towns, local council areas within a metropolitan area, citywide or statewide curfews);
- primary rationale (e.g., protection of children; dealing with youth crime);
- implementation (e.g., relying solely on fines and court orders; linked to youth social and community programs); and
- enforcement (e.g., rigorous and systematic police intervention, discretionary use with regard to particular locations and target groups).

The logic of the youth curfew is basically centered on the problem of displacement. This relates to the issue of how best to reduce the street presence of young people, particularly in circumstances where they are relatively free from adult supervision and control, by forcing them into situations of close monitoring and where their activities and movements will be subject to stricter regulation (the parental home or structured youth pursuits such as recreation or social clubs).

The use of youth curfews would in some cases simply formalize and extend what is already occurring via existing state policing practices and private security-guard interventions. As with these approaches, the use of curfews is built upon the idea of, in effect, criminalizing non-criminal behavior and thus also increasing the likelihood of some young people being drawn even further into the criminal justice net.

The legal basis of curfews has been the subject of much discussion, as well as a number of significant court cases in the U.S. Issues of freedom of speech, religion, movement and peaceful assembly, for example, have been weighed in several jurisdictions, with the result that legislation is now often narrowly tailored to address the specific needs enumerated by the jurisdiction by the least restrictive means possible (see Bilchik, 1996; Jeffs and Smith, 1996). In Australia, questions have been raised regarding: the lack of legislative authority for police to enforce curfews of a general nature (rather than those tied to bail or community-service order conditions); and the ability of local councils to introduce curfews without prior legislation at the state government level, which would extinguish existing common-law rights relating to the right to move freely around the community (Simpson and Simpson, 1993).

Measuring the effectiveness of youth curfews is highly contentious. Proponents point to data on youth offending and victimization rates, which appear to demonstrate a decline in social harm associated with the imposition of curfews. Opponents, however, are likewise able to point to data suggesting that little is achieved by such measures (see Jeffs and Smith, 1996). Part of the problem with any quantitative analysis is the considerable variation in the actual implementation of curfews in terms of local conditions, legal parameters, community resources and style of criminal justice intervention.

In global terms, however, two recent U.S. surveys provide important observations regarding the use and effectiveness of curfews. Bilchik (1996) provides an overview of the legal challenges to curfews and presents profiles of jurisdictions with comprehensive curfew enforcement programs. It is observed that "The initial evidence offered by the seven communities profiled in this Bulletin is that community-based curfew programs that offer a range of services are more easily and effectively enforced, enjoy community support, and provide a greater benefit in preventing juvenile delinquency and victimization" [Bilchik, 1996:9].

The important point here is that the "success" of the youth curfews is seen to reside not in their coercive aspects (i.e., aggressive street policing), but in the developmental accompaniments to the imposition of the curfew (i.e., recreation centers, counseling services). The presence or absence of additional community supports for young people in the context of the use of curfews is a central factor in how they are put into operation and perceived by residents and young people themselves.

Another concern is that, if the prime policy concern is with the welfare of the young (e.g., the 12-year-old who is roaming the streets after midnight, the plight of the young homeless person), the use of a curfew as such is inappropriate (being linked directly to the personnel, operation and logic of the criminal justice system). A more suitable strategy is to expand the range and availability of local social welfare services, including the number of community outreach workers, and to provide the police with information and training on where to take young people who need assistance.

From the point of view of crime control, a major study on violent offending in the U.S. (Snyder et al., 1996) points out that crimes will be committed by those young people who simply ignore the curfew. The report comments that curfews appear to have little impact on some crimes, and may even increase the incidence of offenses such as those committed in the home against family members. Furthermore, the research finds that a greater proportion of all violent juvenile crime occurs between 2 p.m. and 6 p.m. on those days when school is in session than occurs during an entire year's curfew period. The frequency of violent juvenile crime is also about four times greater in the after-school period than during curfew hours (Snyder et al., 1996).

Measuring the effectiveness of youth curfews in narrow statistical terms (e.g., crime rates) is not sufficient, however, if we are to gauge adequately the social meaning and impact of such prevention measures. For example, from a youth rights perspective, there are inherent difficulties with measures that arbitrarily and unnecessarily discriminate against young people on the basis of their age (see the United Nations Convention on the Rights of the Child). Regardless of moral panics about youth crime, the fact remains that most youthful offending is trivial and episodic in nature, and hardly worthy of a big-stick approach. Additionally, it is also important to recognize that the operationalization of youth curfews, as with street policing generally, is often characterized by highly selective targeting and discriminatory intervention according to the social background of the young person.

Similarly, dealing with issues of the potential victimization of young people in this manner — that is, in a way that penalizes all young people solely on the basis of their age — is manifestly unjust and misconstrues the actual patterns of victimization (e.g., that which takes place within the context of the family home). Alternatively, if we were to accept that the liberty of potential perpetrators ought to be curtailed, then this would require that all young men under the age 30 be subject to curfew conditions, not teenagers as a group.

CONTROLLING PARENTS

A phenomenon closely associated with youth curfews is that of making parents more responsible for the actions of their offspring. This is seen in terms of both the street presence of young people and the ways in which some jurisdictions are responding to youthful offending that has already occurred.

Youth curfews do not take into account different family and parenting contexts, even though they are intended to reinforce the responsibility of parents to control their children. The concept of childhood varies greatly according to cultural and class norms, however,

and these often involve quite different degrees and types of adult supervision and parental control over children. In Australia, for example, there is a marked difference between Anglo-Australian forms of
parenting (and conceptions of childhood) and that practiced by many
indigenous communities (see Johnston, 1991). In the latter, for example, there is frequently encouragement of self-direction and independent action in a manner quite at odds with conventional middle-
class notions of child rearing. Thus, youth curfews may indirectly
penalize some social groups due to differences in parenting practices
relative to the mainstream ideal.

Differences in social and economic resources at the household
level can also impact on the capacity of some parents to regulate
their offspring's behavior even where this is deemed desirable or warranted. Again, in reference to indigenous people in Australia, it has
been observed that in many instances poor educational background
and social and economic circumstances contribute to poor self-
esteem, and that "against this background, parental authority is undermined as the children observe their parents being placed in an
inferior position" (Johnston, 1991:285).

The poor material circumstances of sizeable proportions of indigenous and ethnic minority communities in the U.S., Britain and Australia, and the particularly disadvantaged position of many sole parents in the class structure, means that the enforcement of a universal rule regarding parental responsibility will necessarily have unequal application. Nevertheless, the threat of fines for parents who do
not "control" their children, together with recent public discussion
about the deteriorating quality of parenting, places the focus of responsibility for youth behavior squarely on the backs of the parent.
The idea here is that crime is essentially a matter of poor parenting
and that ultimately the issue is a moral problem. Attention is therefore directed at making the parent more accountable for their child's
criminal offending or antisocial behavior, even if the parent is not
directly involved in the activity.

In the U.S. for example, there are various parental responsibility
laws which attempt to require parents to control their offspring by
making them liable for any damage caused by their children. The
California Civil Code makes parents liable for damages of up to
$25,000 for each incident in which their child willfully harms prop-
erty. In Silverton, OR, parents can be charged with failing to super-
vise a minor in the event of his or her illegal acts and be fined as well
as directed to undertake a parent effectiveness program (see National
Crime Prevention Council, 1996).

Similar types of legislative provisions are now emerging in the
Australian context, particularly in the state of Queensland. Thus, the

Juvenile Justice Act 1992 in Queensland sets out provisions for parental restitution in cases where willful failure on the part of a parent to exercise proper care of, or supervision over, a child was likely to have substantially contributed to the commission of an offence. It is apparent that across most state jurisdictions, there is a renewed push to make parents responsible for compensation payments and to ensure that their children comply with the law as well as stay off of the streets (see Hil, 1996a, 1996b).

In Britain, a useful summary of the debates over parental responsibility is provided by Slapper (1997a, 1997b). Slapper points out that the rhetoric of the major political parties in that country is replete with references to morally deficient parenting as the cause of crime among young people. The solution, as argued by proponents of this view, is to enhance educational and support services for parents, and to penalize poor parenting through the use of fines.

This type of approach is reminiscent of the control theory put forward by Hirschi (1969) and by Gottfredson and Hirschi (1990), which argues that the central issue in explaining crime is that of self-control. The problem is constructed primarily as one of ineffective childrearing. Such a perspective tends not to analyze the specific social divisions (e.g., class, gender, ethnicity) that frame the parenting process, but to rest upon a conception of human nature that sees all people as driven by essentially the same kind of universal tendency to enhance their own pleasure. In practical terms, this translates into policy that attempts to redress the defective social training that apparently characterizes offenders who have in some way "lost control."

But, as Slapper (1997b) argues, the major socioeconomic problems that generate family difficulties are far too deep and entrenched to be overcome simply by ad hoc parent support and/or parent-penalty types of schemes. As Slapper (1997b) puts it:

Anyone serious about being tough on the causes of crime must not just take one step back from the offender to look at his [sic] domestic upbringing and to berate apparently feckless parents. Another step must be taken to go behind the family to address the deep structural defects in our political economy, for it is problems like chronic unemployment, the lengthening of the working week, and high stress levels at work which are the cause of so much bad parenting [p. 70].

Hence, focusing on parents as the key site of juvenile crime prevention misconstrues the nature of the problem. It places the burden of care and responsibility on the individual, while simultaneously dismissing the impact of the retreat of the state from assisting those families and young people who have been placed in precarious economic and social circumstances. The demise in social responsibility on the part of government (at all levels) has gone hand in hand with the further penalization of those most disadvantaged by broader economic restructuring.

Again, if we are serious about the promotion of "good parenting" then it is essential to take seriously the diverse social, economic and cultural contexts of the task. Arbitrarily punishing the parents or imposing parenting classes in cases where the parents are left to struggle in basically unchanged social circumstances is a stop-gap measure at best. And, as the Australian experience with indigenous people has demonstrated, intervention on the part of the state in attempting to control and modify Aboriginal family relationships has done more damage than good, and led to the further breakdown and fragmentation of these communities (Johnston, 1991). Parent support as a concept certainly deserves close attention. However, how, by whom and under what conditions parents are to receive advice, training and support remain crucial issues that have yet to be satisfactorily answered within a criminal justice framework.

COERCIVE CRIME PREVENTION

The inequalities in application and the negative consequences of coercive crime prevention strategies are worthy of careful consideration and critique. But critique does not mean adoption of a "nothing works" philosophy when it comes to juvenile crime prevention. On the contrary, its importance is in helping to shape the kinds of questions we need to ask in reconstituting crime prevention practices and policies at a grassroots level.

The essence of a critique of coercive crime prevention can be summarized as follows:

- Generally speaking, coercive crime prevention strategies emphasize control and containment of young people, rather than addressing the deep structural causes of youthful offending or antisocial behavior.

- Coercive strategies portray young people generally, and specific groups of disadvantaged young people in particular, as "outsiders," who are perceived as threats to the community and not as part of the community.

- Such strategies undermine, both philosophically and literally, the idea that young people are bona fide rightsholders who, as such, should not be subject to measures that limit their rights and freedoms arbitrarily regardless of whether or not any law has been broken and any wrongdoing engaged in.

- Coercive strategies involve the active criminalization of young people who otherwise may not come into short or long-term contact with the criminal justice system, and furthermore can exacerbate tensions between youths and other members of the community due to youths' perceptions of unfair treatment, excessive restrictions and unnecessary intervention in their daily affairs.

- The discriminatory application of coercive measures, both geographically in terms of protected places for the privileged and socially in terms of which groups are targeted for special attention, entrenches major class and ethnic divides but does little to alleviate core problems of poverty, unemployment and racism.

- Coercive crime prevention tends to be premised upon varying kinds of social exclusion, a process that intrinsically alienates young people from decisionmaking and that can lead to their displacement from selected areas and the adoption of alternative lifestyles, some of which may include deviant and antisocial behavior.

This critique does not advocate a retreat from the use of any coercive measures whatsoever, under any circumstances. Rather, it points out that the general contours of the approach — with its emphasis on coercion, control and containment — is fraught with major problems when it comes to how teenagers are positioned in society. In addition, the critique demonstrates that crime prevention itself is framed in such a way as to be manifestly unjust, unfair and, ultimately, unworkable.

YOUTH-FRIENDLY STRATEGIES

From a theoretical viewpoint, it is useful here to make a distinction between coercive crime prevention and developmental approaches (see Polk, 1997). Description of the former has constituted the main part of this essay. The latter is best characterized as an approach that is directed at enhancing the opportunities of young people through encouraging their participation in activities that reflect their interests and needs. The guiding idea, as Polk (1997:196) explains, is that "young people are given some ownership of solutions to youth problems and that young people, local agency representatives and local community residents work together to advocate for the wider involvement and participation of all youth, including the alienated." In other words, it is important to involve young people themselves in any crime prevention strategy — to see them as part of the community, not as merely threats to it.

This is not the place to discuss the pros and cons of a developmental versus coercive approach to crime prevention. However, in keeping with the substantive focus of much coercive crime control on issues of young people and public space, it is useful to contrast the previous descriptions with an example of a developmental approach to these issues.

Much public and private regulation of young people's lives has been directed at their presence and activities in the public domains of the street, shopping centers and malls. Recent Australian work has highlighted the conflicts associated with these areas, and possible ways in which to intervene in a manner that does not involve coercion and social exclusion. Philosophically, such an approach is premised upon the idea of youth rights. Youth rights in this context refers to, firstly, broad human rights, that are deemed to be intrinsic to the individual and, as such, are non-negotiable. They include the rights to be protected from exploitation, physical and emotional harm, and practices that denigrate youths as human beings. Secondly, youth rights refer to a wide range of prescriptive benchmarks pertaining to the social, educational, cultural and economic development and well-being of children (see United Nations Convention on the Rights of the Child). Thirdly, youth rights also include rights accorded by a nation-state, such as freedom of speech, which imply some kind of reciprocal responsibility on the part of the rightsholder, such as adherence to laws relating to noise and public disturbances.

Youth crime prevention approaches need to take into account these different types of rights and the implications they hold for various program initiatives. It is thus essential to acknowledge the basic human rights of young people, to be sensitive to the special needs of young people and the obligations of society to address these needs in a responsive and responsible manner, and to examine the particular social contexts within which certain rights and responsibilities can best be exercised. Accordingly, it has been argued that it is possible to: "develop crime prevention measures which offer a positive alternative to coercive regulation of youth behavior and to do so via techniques of opportunity reduction (e.g., improved street lighting), opportunity enhancement (e.g., diversionary activities such as basketball and netball) and social empowerment (e.g., incorporating youth into decision-making processes)" (White et al., 1996:15).

Strategically, this approach springs from the idea that young people are important. They ought to be treated with dignity and respect, and their rights, needs, aspirations and opinions need to be taken seriously.

In terms of practice and policy, recent Australian cases illustrate that the creation of youth-friendly public space is not only possible, but that such an approach can have significant positive ramifications when it comes to crime prevention. The best example of this is a shopping center complex in Perth, Western Australia (see White et. al., 1996). The management of this complex had reported that it was experiencing considerable difficulties with large numbers of young people at the shopping center. There were reports of young people hanging around in groups, vandalism, graffiti, damage to staff cars and evidence of drug use in the parking lot. Initially management hired more security guards. However, this only increased the conflicts between young people and others in the center, and the manager observed that it became a "cat and mouse" game in an "us and them" situation.

Management finally approached a local youth organization and together they established a committee with members representing the shopping center, the community, the youth service, local council staff and some young people. As a consequence of discussions and a needs analysis survey, the shopping center jointly funded a youth worker position and allocated an office in the shopping center for the worker. The role of the youth worker has been to link young people to support and information services, and to provide a voice for the young people in identifying current gaps in general community services and their particular needs in relation to the shopping center itself. Some of the young people have been employed part-time collecting trolleys, gardening and doing general maintenance.

The shopping center management has noted a significant change since this approach was adopted in 1989, with a dramatic decrease in vandalism and violence. Notably, while the center has a list of 180 young people it says have caused trouble, these individuals have not been banned. When a situation gets out of hand, the youth worker talks with the young people involved and, if necessary, drives them home. The role of the youth worker is not one of quasi-security guard or to "police" the young people. However, the youth workers have been involved in developing general center policies and in conducting training with security officers so that officers know when to approach young people, when to call the youth worker and when to walk away.

From the point of view of the young people, there was the perception that they were being listened to, and that they now had certain recognized rights to hang out in the shopping center. Their changed behavior and attitudes were built on a foundation of open lines of communication, the provision of appropriate youth support services and greater knowledge of how shopkeepers and older customers felt about their activities. The young people became more aware of other users of the shopping center, and how and why their actions could sometimes be interpreted as rude, thoughtless or threatening. They also began to feel that they were now part of a community that included different groups of people with different needs and interests. What this shows is that young people who are consciously allowed to exercise their rights in a supportive environment can and will act responsibly — it all depends on whether or not they have the voice, resources and knowledge to do so.

Crime prevention in this instance has been constructed around the ideas of youth engagement in decision-making processes, and with an acknowledgement of the importance of certain public spaces in the lives of many young people today. It is an inclusive approach, one that depends upon active participation by members of the local community, including young people themselves. Conflict and crime still occur, of course, although to a much lesser degree. But the general climate of the shopping complex is no longer characterized by customer fear, shop-owner complaint, security guard aggression and young people's resentment.

CONCLUSION

This paper has provided a brief, but critical, examination of coercive crime prevention measures as these affect young people. It has been argued that in many instances such an approach is unnecessary, unduly penalizing of all young people and ultimately socially discriminatory. Coercive measures may need to be used in particular circumstances to protect and defend persons and property from actual instances of criminal behavior. However, as argued here, the adoption of coercion as a strategy and as the main policy plank of juvenile crime prevention carries with it major problems from the point of view of youth rights, the fundamental causes of crime, moral panics about perceived youth "crime waves" and economic and social inequalities.

Juvenile crime prevention is always a complicated issue, characterized by constant debate over the choice of immediate tactics and strategies to reduce offensive behavior in the here and now, and ongoing concern (at least among some criminologists) to link concrete action proposals with consideration of how best to tackle the wider social causes of offending (see, for example, O'Malley and Sutton, 1997). At best, I would argue, crime prevention is but a very limited means by which we might be able to minimize the social fallout arising from the broader inequalities and dislocations of the new world political economic order. Nevertheless, how we engage in crime prevention has real consequences for real people, and it does matter in their lives how the issues are constructed and dealt with by criminal justice officials, politicians and criminologists. In this regard, as I have tried to indicate throughout this chapter, my preference is for a strategic vision that takes into account the rights, dignity and voice of the targets of conventional, coercive crime control measures. For to treat the young with disrespect and fear, and to base policy on the controlling impulse, is to create a social body that relies upon repression rather than liberty as its guiding rationale and lifeblood.

Address correspondence to: Robert White, Department of Criminology, University of Melbourne, Parkville Victoria, AUS 3052. E-mail: <r.white@criminology.unimelb.edu.au>.

REFERENCES

Alder, C., I. O'Connor, K. Warner and R. White (1992). *Perceptions of the Treatment of Juveniles in the Legal System*. Hobart, AUS: National Youth Affairs Research Scheme/ National Clearinghouse for Youth Studies.

Bilchik, S. (1996). *Curfew: An Answer to Juvenile Delinquency and Victimization?* Washington, DC: U.S. Office of Juvenile Justice and Delinquency Prevention.

Clarke, R. (ed.) (1992). *Situational Crime Prevention: Successful Case Studies*. Albany, NY: Harrow and Heston.

Cook, D. and B. Hudson (eds.) (1993). *Racism and Criminology*. London, UK: Sage.

Cunneen, C. (1992). "Policing and Aboriginal Communities: Is the Concept of Over-Policing Useful?" In: C. Cunneen (ed.), *Aboriginal Perspectives on Criminal Justice*. Monograph Series 1. Sydney, AUS: Institute of Criminology

—— and R. White (1995). *Juvenile Justice: An Australian Perspective*. Melbourne, AUS: Oxford University Press.

Davis, M. (1994). *Beyond Bladerunner: Urban Control and the Ecology of Fear*. Open Magazine Pamphlet Series #23. Westfield, NJ: Open Magazine.

Felson, M. (1994). *Crime and Everyday Life: Insights and Implications for Society*. Thousand Oaks, CA: Pine Forge Press.

Gottfredson, M. and T. Hirschi (1990). *A General Theory of Crime.* Stanford, CA: Stanford University Press.

Hil, R. (1996a) *Making Them Pay: A Critical Review of Parental Restitution in Australian Juvenile Justice.* Townsville, AUS: Centre for Social and Welfare Research, James Cook University of North Queensland.

—— (1996b) "Crime by Default: Legislating for Parental Restitution in Queensland." *Alternative Law Journal* 21(6):280-283.

Hirschi, T. (1969). *Causes of Delinquency.* Berkeley and Los Angeles, CA: University of California Press.

Jeffs, T. and M. Smith. (1996). " 'Getting the Dirtbags Off the Streets': Curfews & Other Solutions to Juvenile Crime." *Youth and Policy* 53:1-14.

Johnston, E. (1991). *National Report, Royal Commission into Aboriginal Deaths in Custody,* vol. 2. Canberra, AUS: Australian Government Publishing Service.

Loader, I. (1996). *Youth, Policing and Democracy.* London, UK: Macmillan.

National Crime Prevention Council (1996). *Working with Local Laws to Reduce Crime.* Washington, DC: Author.

O'Malley, P. and A. Sutton (eds.) (1997). *Crime Prevention in Australia: Issues in Policy & Research.* Sydney, AUS: Federation Press.

Polk, K. (1997). "A Community and Youth Development Approach to Youth Crime Prevention." In: P. O'Malley and A. Sutton (eds.), *Crime Prevention in Australia.* Sydney, AUS: Federation Press.

Simpson, B. and C. Simpson (1993). "The Use of Curfews to Control Juvenile Offending in Australia: Managing Crime or Wasting Time?" *Current Issues in Criminal Justice* 5(2):184-199.

Slapper, G. (1997a). "Stepping Behind the Family — 1." *New Law Journal* 10 Jan:11-12.

—— (1997b) "Stepping Behind the Family — 2." *New Law Journal* 17 Jan:68-70.

Snyder, H., M. Sickmund and E. Poe-Yamagata (1996). *Juvenile Offenders and Victims: 1996 Update on Violence.* Washington, DC: U.S. Office of Juvenile Justice and Delinquency Prevention.

Sutton, A. (1996). "Taking Out the Interesting Bits? Problem Solving and Crime Prevention." In: R. Homel (ed.), *The Politics and Practice of Situational Crime Prevention.* Crime Prevention Studies, vol. 5. Monsey, NY: Criminal Justice Press.

White, R. (1996a). "No-Go in the Fortress City: Young People, Inequality and Space." *Urban Policy and Research* 14(1):37-50.

—— (1996b). "Situating Crime Prevention: Models, Methods and Political Perspectives." In: R. Homel (ed.), *The Politics and Practice of Situ-*

ational Crime Prevention. Crime Prevention Studies, vol. 5. Monsey, NY: Criminal Justice Press.

—— (1996c). "Racism, Policing and Ethnic Youth Gangs." *Current Issues in Criminal Justice* 7(3):302-313.

—— (1996d). "10 Arguments Against Youth Curfews." *Youth Studies Australia* 15(4):28-30.

—— and C. Alder (eds.) (1994). *The Police and Young People in Australia.* Melbourne, AUS: Cambridge University Press.

—— G. Murray and N. Robins (1996). *Negotiating Youth-Specific Public Space: A Guide for Youth and Community Workers, Town Planners and Local Councils.* Sydney, AUS: Youth Programs Unit, Department of Training and Education Co-ordination (distributed by the Australian Youth Foundation).

Wilson, J. and G. Kelling (1982). "Broken Windows." *Atlantic Monthly* (Mar):29-38.

Part II: Controlling Drug Problems

CONTROLLING SOCIAL DISORDER USING CIVIL REMEDIES: RESULTS FROM A RANDOMIZED FIELD EXPERIMENT IN OAKLAND, CALIFORNIA

by

Lorraine Green Mazerolle
University of Cincinnati

Jan Roehl
Justice Research Center

and

Colleen Kadleck
University of Cincinnati

Abstract: *This paper reports the results of a randomized field study conducted in Oakland, CA where civil remedies were used to target drug, crime and disorder problems in 50 "experimental" places; and traditional police tactics (surveillance, arrests, field interrogations) were used in 50 "control" places. Oakland's civil remedy program uses citations for building, health, sewer, sidewalk and rodent control code violations, drug nuisance abatement laws, and coercion of third parties (such as property owners, apartment superintendents, and business owners) to clean up blighted and drug nuisance places. On-site observations of social activity on the 100 face blocks in our study were used to measure changes in street behavior as a result of the interventions. Results reveal a decrease in drug dealing and a decline in signs of disorder on the Beat Health-*

targeted face blocks. We conclude that the Beat Health program generally enhanced social conditions in the 50 experimental places.

INTRODUCTION

The use of civil remedies in controlling social disorder has become increasingly more central to police problem-solving efforts in recent years. Indeed, police departments from New York to San Francisco to Chicago are now advocating the restoration of order by targeting quality-of-life problems, by aggressively dealing with disorder problems (such as panhandling, public drinking, vandalism, public urination), and by focusing on reducing fear of crime (Kelling and Coles, 1996).

Oakland CA's Beat Health program is an example of a civil remedy program (see also Eck, 1997). Beat Health seeks to control drug, crime and disorder problems and restore order by focusing on the physical decay conditions of targeted commercial establishments, private homes and rental properties. Police work with teams of city agency representatives to inspect drug nuisance properties, coerce landowners to clean up blighted properties, post "no trespassing" signs, enforce civil law codes and municipal regulatory rules, and initiate court proceedings against property owners who fail to comply with civil law citations. While the ultimate targets of the Beat Health program are offending individuals living or socializing in target "zones," the proximate targets of the program include landlords, business owners and private property owners.

This paper examines the impact of the Beat Health program on the social and physical conditions of street blocks (or target zones) surrounding 50 targeted commercial establishments, businesses, private homes and rental properties. These blocks are compared, under experimental conditions, to 50 similar street blocks targeted by the regular patrol division of the Oakland Police Department. We begin our paper with a description of the operational components of the Beat Health program. We then discuss the evaluation design and study site characteristics, and describe the interventions at the target sites. This is followed by a discussion of the outcome data and the data collection methods used to assess the social and physical conditions of the street blocks in the study. The results are then presented, along with a discussion of their theoretical and policy implications.

OAKLAND AS THE STUDY SITE

Oakland is the eighth largest city in California (California, Department of Finance, 1996). The 1990 census data indicate that there are 372,242 people living within the 53.8 square miles of the city. Oakland lies across the bay to the east of San Francisco. The city is ethnically diverse with about 45% of the population being African American; 35% Hispanic;[1] about 15% white; and a growing Asian community. Since the 1960s the average household size has been steadily dropping, and there is now an average of 2.34 persons per household. The median income for residents of Oakland is about $20,000 per year, and more than 16% of families live below the poverty line. During the early 1980s, Oakland experienced severe levels of unemployment, which reached 12.9% in 1982 (California, Oakland Office of Community Development, 1992).

The city of Oakland has over 140,000 housing units, more than 50% of which are rented. In 1989 the median rent for a one-bedroom apartment was $560 per month, representing a 12% increase since 1985. Most of the housing units in Oakland are single-family homes, reflecting a style of housing common throughout the West Coast. As with other U.S. cities, the city of Oakland experienced a large increase in real estate prices during the mid-1980s. However, by the 1990s the cost of purchasing property had declined and the median sale price of an Oakland home was about $185,000 (California, Oakland Office of Community Development, 1992).

OAKLAND'S BEAT HEALTH PROGRAM

The Oakland Police Department established the Beat Health Program in October 1988. Since its inception, the program has been used at nearly 3,000 places throughout Oakland, targeting an average of 330 cases per year. Five Beat Health teams, each comprising one uniformed officer and a "partner" police service technician (non-sworn), provide services throughout the city. Beat Health police officers, working in conjunction with their partner police service technicians, "open" a case after making a preliminary site visit to a place that has generated emergency calls, a number of narcotics arrests or special requests from community groups for police assistance. Police begin by visiting nuisance locations and establishing working relationships with citizens, apartment superintendents, landlord and business owners living or working both at the target address and in the immediate surroundings. During the early stages of the intervention, police communicate landlords' rights and tenants' responsibilities, provide ideas for simple crime prevention measures and gain the citizens' confidence that the police are supporting them in their efforts to clean up the problem location.

The key element of Oakland's Beat Health program is a site visit by the Specialized Multi-Agency Response Team (SMART). The SMART visits involve a series of coordinated visits to problem locations by a group of city inspectors. Depending on preliminary assessments made by the police, representatives from agencies such as housing, fire, public works, Pacific Gas and Electric, and vector control are invited to inspect a problem location, and, where necessary, to enforce local housing, fire and safety codes. About two-thirds of the cases are cited for at least one code violation from a city inspector. The most common type is a housing code violation (Green, 1996).

The police department also draws on its in-house legal expertise and, as needed, uses a variety of civil laws[2] to bring suit against the owners of properties with drug problems. For example, the Uniform Controlled Substances Act makes every building where drug use occurs a nuisance; it allows the city to use the civil law to eliminate the problem by fining the owner, or by closing or selling the property. About 2% of cases result in formal court action against a property owner (Green, 1996).

Although the Beat Health approach focuses on cleaning up the physical conditions of targeted sites, police also increase the levels of uniformed police presence. During routine drive-bys, Beat Health officers sometimes arrest or stop and talk to people who frequent the location (termed a "field contact" in Oakland).

The Landlord Training Program is another important component of the Beat Health program. Landlords are encouraged to screen prospective renters and are informed about the processes for evicting troublesome tenants. In nearly 40% of Beat Health cases, an eviction notice is served against a tenant. Since three-quarters of the locations are typically rented or leased, Beat Health intervention involves a 50% chance of a tenant eviction at some time during the intervention.

STUDY DESIGN

Our evaluation design built from knowledge about the numbers and types of sites that the Beat Health Unit has targeted since 1988 (see Green, 1996). Importantly, we knew that the Beat Health Unit targeted about 14 residential properties for every one commercial site targeted. Moreover, it had been concluded that "...when commercial places were targeted, significant reductions in drug nuisance activity were achieved within targeted sites and surrounding areas" (Green, 1996:98). To enable closer examination of the impact of Beat Health on residential and commercial properties, we used a blocked randomized experimental design by assigning commercial properties to one block and residential properties to another. We randomized cases in the study within statistical blocks because we believed there were substantial differences between drug dealing activities at commercial and residential properties. Randomized block designs, which allocate cases randomly within pairs or groups, minimize the effects of variability on a study by ensuring that like cases are compared with one another (see Lipsey, 1990; Neter, et al., 1990; Weisburd, et al., 1993).[3]

We sought to include 100 cases in our experiment by selecting 14 commercial sites and 86 residential locations to be randomly allocated to the treatment condition (Beat Health intervention) or to the control condition (uniformed patrol response). Potential Beat Health cases were referred to the Beat Health Unit through several different sources including a narcotics hotline, referrals from other Oakland Police Department officers and community groups, and systematic reviews of "hot spot" arrest locations.[4] Approximately 100 cases (both known drug sites and unknown sites) are typically introduced to the Beat Health Unit each month. These referrals, known as "goldenrods," were recorded on a form each day (or as the case became known to the Beat Health Unit).

All incoming goldenrods from October 15 to December 15 were checked as to their eligibility to be included in the study. Not included for random allocation were existing and old Beat Health locations, locations typically not targeted by the program (e.g., Section 8 housing sites[5] and public housing sites), places that had already been targeted by the patrol division and places that were deemed an "imminent danger" (e.g., child abuse problems evident at the site).

As eligible cases were randomly allocated, new incoming cases had to be mapped. If an incoming goldenrod fell within a 300-foot radius (about one street block) of a case already randomly allocated, the case was withheld and not allocated to either the patrol division or the Beat Health Unit.[6] This case selection criterion allowed for an examination of the effects of the experimental and control treatments, without fear of direct proximal contamination from a nearby site. In effect, this design allowed for an analysis of a catchment area activity (or street block activity) free of some of the confounding problems that arise with overlapping catchment areas and duplicate cases that could potentially bias the evaluation results (for a discussion of these issues see Green, 1995).

Incoming cases were also verified as being either commercial or residential properties. Residential properties were allocated within the "residential block" and commercial properties were randomly allocated to the control or experimental treatment within the commercial block.

Cases randomly allocated to the control condition (uniformed patrol response) were referred to beat officers through an established "beat binder" system. These beat binders were simply folders kept in each patrol car that included places that either community service officers or supervising officers requested beat officers pay attention to. During the intervention phase of our experiment, we added control-allocated cases to the beat binders. By mid-December 1995, the Beat Health Unit was targeting 50 sites (7 commercial and 43 residential), and the patrol division was targeting 50 sites (7 commercial and 43 residential).

CHARACTERISTICS OF THE STUDY LOCATIONS

The study sites came to the attention of the Beat Health Unit in roughly three ways: Nearly half of all cases were "goldenrods" from known individuals in the community (48%); about a quarter were referred anonymously through drug hotline calls, and another quarter were identified through hot-spot searches of places with high numbers of vice and drug arrests over the previous six months. Most of the study sites were rental properties (77%) and twelve of the experimental sites and eleven of the control sites were owner-occupied. Of the dozen owner-occupied experimental sites, ten involved problems with relatives of the owner (see Table 1): the most typical situation was when the children or grandchildren of an elderly owner were involved in drug dealing. In one experimental location the problem was the owner. Ten of the experimental sites and seven of the control sites were completely or partially vacant.

Table 1 also presents the distribution of problems by control and experimental sites (as reported on incoming goldenrods). Drug dealing was reported as a major problem in approximately three-quarters of the locations in both groups. Other problems in the experimental sites included drug use (n=14), blight (n=14), and nuisance problems such as noise and unkempt yards (n=7). Of the control sites, 36 recorded drug dealing problems, followed by blight (n=11), other criminal offenses (n=6), drug use (n=4) and nuisance problems (n=4). Other complaints included rat and roach infestations, prostitution, trespassing, problems with pit bulls and/or other animals, and other health and welfare issues.

Prior to the start of the experiment, the control sites and the experimental sites had similar levels of arrest activity (see Table 2). For example, patrol officers made 65 arrests for disorder problems in the experimental sites and 68 in the control sites. For violent crimes, patrol officers made exactly the same number of arrests in the experimental

Table 1: Characteristics of Study Sites

	Experimental		Control	
	Number	Percent	Number	Percent
Reported by:				
Hotline	8	16	19	38
Vice/drug arrest	17	34	8	16
Individual	14	28	10	20
Community/business group	3	6	4	8
Property owner	4	8	2	4
OPD officer (not BH)	1	2	5	10
Beat Health Unit	3	6	1	2
Other			1	1
Problems reported on goldenrods:				
Drug dealing	38	76	36	72
Drug use	14	28	4	8
Trash, blight	14	28	11	22
Rats, rodents	3	6	1	2
Other health hazards	4	8	3	6
Prostitution	3	6	2	4
Trespassing	3	6	1	2
Other criminal offenses	4	8	6	12
Dogs/animals	5	10	3	6
Human welfare	2	4	1	2
Alcohol abuse			2	4
Nuisance	7	14	4	8
Problem involves relatives of owner	10	20	1	2
Problem is owner:	1	2		

Table 2: Pre-Intervention Arrests

Type of Offense	Experimental	Control
Property	54	64
Violent	79	79
Weapons	15	17
Drugs	205	169
Vice	26	21
Disorder	65	68
Total	**444**	**418**

and control sites during the nine and a half months prior to the start of the experiment (n=79). For drug violations, patrol officers made 169 arrests in the control catchment zones, and 205 arrests in the experimental catchment zones prior to the start of the experiment.

EXPERIMENTAL AND CONTROL INTERVENTIONS

Beat Health officers personally visited all but two of the experimental sites. The initial visit was made to confirm the nature of the problem at the target site. The officers checked out the condition of the property from the outside, particularly if trash, blight, hazards or animal problems were reported. Contact was also made with tenants, neighbors and owners/managers to discuss problems or to put tenants on alert that reports had been made. In 35 of the 50 experimental locations, the officers talked to the property owner in person or by telephone. Of the two properties not visited, one was owned by an individual that the Beat Health officers identified as "reputable," and contact was made by a warning letter and telephone calls. The other property was not visited but the owner was sent a warning letter.

Other formal actions taken by officers against the experimental sites included SMART inspections (n=23), general warning letters (n=9), "11570" (drug-related) warning letters (n=13), beat orders (n=9), evictions (n=19) and property clean-ups (n=3). During the 23 SMART inspections instigated against experimental target sites, city inspectors issued nine housing and safety citations, six vector control violations, two sidewalk citations and one sewer violation. The city attorney's office did not file suit against any of the experimental site owners during the period of our experimental tracking (one year).

The nine general warning letters sent by Beat Health officers informed the owners that complaints of problem activities (e.g., drug dealing) had been reported on their property. These letters also advised the owners of steps that they might want to take to prevent or minimize the problems, and offered assistance in resolving the problem. These general warning letters differed from the 11570 letters, which made specific reference to Section 11570 of the California Health and Safety Code (also known as the Drug Nuisance Abatement Act) that holds owners and managers responsible for knowingly allowing illicit drug activity to occur on their property.[7] These 11570 letters also make reference to Section 11366.5(a), stating that criminal actions may be also taken. The 11570 letters serve as official notice of drug activity and a copy is forwarded to the city attorney. The owner is encouraged to call the Beat Health officer in charge of the case for assistance in eliminating the problem.

In most cases the warning letters (both general and 11570), coupled with assistance and pressure from the Beat Health officers, resulted in solving the problem. A primary "solution" to the problem was eviction. In 19 of the 50 experimental sites, problem tenants were evicted from the property. In several other cases, the problem was resolved when the tenants moved out without eviction orders. The Beat Health Unit cannot order or request that tenants be evicted, but they support eviction as a problem-solving strategy.

Beat Orders were issued in at least nine of the experimental sites. These orders officially notified the patrol division of the problems at a specific locations and requested its cooperation in solving the problem. Beat Health officers then worked in partnership with the patrol division to solve the problem. The patrol division provided extra coverage of the experimental sites by stopping suspicious people loitering in the target area, conducting warrant checks and driving by the target site more frequently. Problems related to liquor stores and bars were referred to the Alcohol Beverage Action Team (n=2). Other intervention efforts included property clean-ups and referrals. At one site a property clean-up was conducted by city agencies (who then billed the owner for the work). Referrals to other agencies were also made in some cases, including referrals to Legal Assistance for Seniors and subsidized loan programs for rehabilitation work.

During the five-month intervention period (October 15, 1995 through March 15, 1996), patrol officers continued to make about the same number of arrests in both the control and experimental catchment zones (with n=271, 51% of arrests occurring in the control zones). In total, patrol officers made 247 arrests for drug violations, 85 arrests for property offenses, 85 arrests for violent crime offenses, 65 arrests for disorder violations, 31 arrests for vice offenses and 18 arrests for weapons offenses in the 300-foot catchment areas immediately surrounding the 100 targeted properties (total of N=531 arrests).

OUTCOME DATA AND METHODS

One way to measure social activity on a street block is through on-site field observations of street activity (see, for example, Perkins and Taylor, 1996; Taylor 1995a; 1997b; 1996; 1995b). On-site assessments tend to measure the actual conditions of a location, while surveys of residents tend to capture the actual conditions of a location filtered through the various psychological attributes and psychological processes of residents (see Perkins and Taylor, 1996; Taylor, 1995a; 1995b; 1996; 1997b). One study by Taylor (1995c) finds that up to 90% of the variation in residents' perceptions of ecological conditions may be psychological rather than ecological.

The outcome data reported in this paper draw from on-site observations of the social and physical conditions of the 100 street blocks in the present study.[8] The study supports and extends prior research that uses on-site ratings by trained researchers to capture the "ecological" changes in the neighborhood or street. We do not argue against the use of surveys that focus on residents' perceptions of their street (indeed, see Mazerolle, et al., 1998). Rather, ours is an argument suggesting that residents may not be the most objective lens through which to view the physical changes on a street.

We conducted two on-site observations of each street block as these cases were randomly allocated to either the experimental or control group (before). We then conducted an additional two observations of each street block five months later (after). Structured observations were made of each face block surrounding the 100 problem locations during two of four randomly selected time periods (11 a.m. to 2 p.m., 2 p.m. to 5 p.m., 5 p.m. to 8 p.m. and 8 p.m. and 11 p.m.) . Attention is focused on routine licit activity (e.g., pedestrians, children playing, people coming in and out of businesses), illicit activity (e.g., drug dealing, loitering, urinating in public), litter, graffiti, trash, traffic and the presence of law enforcement and security personnel.

As Table 3 shows, trained observers made 400 on-site visits to the experimental and control sites (200 before and 200 after). The randomization process generated a fairly even distribution of observations across the four time periods, across experimental and control sites, as well as across the before-and after-intervention test periods.

Our decision to conduct two observations per street block per period derived from the understanding that street blocks have standing patterns of behavior, or rhythms of recurring behavior and activity, that are somewhat predictable and routine (Taylor, 1988; Taylor 1997a). Felson (1995) also suggests that activities occur in fairly predictable rhythms where patterns of behavior are dictated by a host of factors, including individual people's working hours, sleeping times and recreational times.

On-site observations of social activity can be conducted for either a sample of a street's activity rhythms or a "census of the total population of activity rhythms." For example, if a street block has a constant standing pattern of behavior (or just one activity rhythm) across all minutes of an hour, across all hours of a day and across all days of a

Table 3: Distributions of Observation Time Periods

	Experimental		Control		Total
	Before	After	Before	After	
11 a.m.-2 p.m.	19	19	28	26	92
2 p.m.-5 p.m.	24	24	19	22	89
5 p.m.-8 p.m.	31	31	25	24	111
8 p.m.-11 p.m.	26	26	28	28	108
Total	100	100	100	100	400

week, then one could reasonably assume that conducting one on-site observation of social activity at any time of the day and on any day of the week would adequately capture the true social activity patterns of that street block. In this extreme case one could argue that consideration of sampling error is not a concern, because one observation would be representative of the population of social activity patterns (n=1) for that street block. Alternatively, if a street block has a varied standing pattern of behavior where, for example, the morning hours are different than the afternoon hours, which are then different from the early evening and the nighttime hours, then one could conclude that there are at least four standing patterns of behavior on that particular street block.[9] In this type of case, the total population of standing patterns of behavior is quite small (N=4), and if one were to draw a sample of time periods of social activity that was quite large (e.g., n=2) relative to the size of the population of time periods of social activity (e.g., N=4), the standard error may not be as problematic as expected (see Blalock, 1979; see also Rosenbaum and Lavrakas, 1995; Weisburd and Green, 1991). Indeed, Rosenbaum and Lavrakas (1995) conclude that the size of the population is not always associated with the stability of estimates (p.296).

We suggest that the reliability and validity of on-site observations increases as the unit of analysis decreases. We propose that street blocks and other small units of analysis (e.g., hot spots, public housing common areas) have fewer and less complex patterns of street activity (or standing patterns of behavior) than neighborhoods, communities or other larger units of analysis that have more complex and varied patterns of social behavior. For example, a street block with an elementary school on the block may have four distinct time periods with four distinct patterns of behavior: (1) the morning hours when children are being dropped off at school; (2) the daytime hours when the children are in school and playing on the school grounds during break times; (3) the afternoon hours when children are being picked up from school and adults are returning home from work; and (4) the evening hours when people are at home with their families. This kind of predictability in the standing patterns of behavior on a street block is rarely present for neighborhoods for a number of reasons: the absolute number of people frequenting a neighborhood makes it more difficult to anticipate standing patterns of behavior; the range of land-use patterns across a neighborhood (businesses, single-family homes, multi-dwellings) creates more complex rhythms of social activity; and the diversity of people living and working in neighborhoods leads to more complex and diverse patterns of social behavior.

The average of the two observations was used as the count of people involved in the various types of activity before and after the intervention. For example, if before the intervention two people were observed selling drugs on a target street block during the time period from 2 p.m. through 5 p.m., and four people were observed selling drugs on the same block during the time period from 8 p.m. to 11 p.m., then we counted three people as selling drugs before the intervention in that particular target street block. The averaged "before" score was regressed onto the raw "after" score to generate a residual gain score (see Bohrnstedt, 1969; Bursik and Webb, 1982; Cronbach and Furby, 1970) and thus enable analysis of the amount of change occurring during the course of the intervention. This procedure allows for identification of changes in a street block activity, such that positive (or greater) scores of a residualized variable indicate more of a particular characteristic (e.g., more drug dealing) than would be expected based on the "before" value and negative (or lower) scores of a residualized variable indicate less of a particular characteristic than would be expected based on the "before" value.

RESULTS

Table 4 presents the mean number of people engaged in a variety of licit activities (e.g., supervised children playing, pedestrians, people at bus stops) and illicit activity (e.g. people selling drugs, people loitering, intoxicated people) both before and after the experiment and in the experimental and control locations. We also present the mean scores (before and after) of observed physical disorder,[10] as well as the presence of police and other security personnel observed on the study blocks before and after the experiment. We display the statistical significance of the differences (using residual gain scores) between the experimental and control conditions, accounting for the block-randomized design of the study.[11]

The key findings from Table 4 show that four conditions (males selling drugs,[12] signs of physical disorder, males at pay phones and males at bus stops) were statistically significant at the .05 level. As the table shows, the mean number of males selling drugs on the experimental street blocks went from .06 (or 3 people) before the intervention to .04 (2 people) after the intervention. For the control street blocks, by contrast, we observed more males selling drugs after the intervention period (22 people) compared to before the intervention (5 people) (p = 0.015).

The differences between the physical disorder conditions of the control and experimental groups are also statistically significant at the .05 level. As Table 4 shows, we find that although the signs of disorder increased slightly for the experimental group (from a score of 8.04 before to 8.46 after), the control group started off with the same score as the experimental group, yet increased to a score of 9.184 by the end of the intervention period (p = 0.020).

Table 4 also shows that the mean amount of prosocial behavior generally increased in both the control and experimental locations. For example, there were more adult males and females stopping to talk to one another on the street, walking up and down a street, and coming in and out of businesses in both the experimental and control sites. We also recorded more police and other security (private, crossing guards) present in both locations after the intervention period.

In terms of antisocial behavior observed after the experiment, there were fewer adult males and females loitering, youths loitering, males with boom boxes, homeless people and people drinking in public in the experimental street blocks after Beat Health intervention than in the control street blocks. These results, however were not statistically significant.

DISCUSSION AND CONCLUSION

The Beat Health program in Oakland, CA is an example of a police-implemented civil remedy program. The Beat Health Unit seeks to clean up the physical conditions of drug dealing places using a number of tactics that rely upon the police working with other city agencies, coercing landowners, building partnerships with business owners and working with people living at the target sites. The civil remedy tactics used by the Beat Health team include police recommendations to landowners to evict troublesome tenants; "SMART" inspections by city

Table 4: Changes in Signs of Physical Disorder and the Mean Number of People (per Street Block) Engaged in Measured Social Activity: Pre- Versus Post-Intervention Periods (by Group)

Dependent Variables	Group				p= (group)**
	Experimental		Control		
	Before Mean	After Mean	Before Mean	After Mean	
Supervised kids playing (private yard, street, school yard)	0.32	0.22	0.26	0.10	0.366
Unsupervised kids playing (private yard, street)	0.02	0.36	0.30	0.26	0.261
Adult males' general activity (stop to talk, pedestrians, in/out businesses)	1.70	2.08	1.68	2.28	0.565
Adult females' general activity (stop to talk, pedestrians, in/out businesses)	0.92	1.44	1.14	1.24	0.202
Males and females on bicycles (adult & youth)	0.36	0.36	0.28	0.28	0.585
Males at bus stops	0.06	0.08	0.04	0.00	0.006*
Females at bus stops	0.06	0.06	0.00	0.06	0.216
Males at pay phones	0.02	0.00	0.04	0.06	0.041*
Adult males loitering (by bars, stores and other places)	1.28	0.40	1.24	0.60	0.281
Adult females loitering (by bars, stores and other places)	0.26	0.16	0.30	0.08	0.299
Male youths loitering (by bars, stores and other places)	0.44	0.40	0.58	0.36	0.815
Female youths loitering (by stores and other places)	0.12	0.04	0.06	0.10	0.210
Males with boom boxes, homeless, or drinking	0.20	0.04	0.14	0.14	0.103
Females drinking	0.08	0.02	0.04	0.00	0.283
Males selling drugs†	0.06	0.04	0.10	0.44	0.015*
Disorder scale (range 4-24) higher values = more disorder	8.04	8.46	8.04	9.18	0.020*
Police/security present	0.00	0.08	0.12	0.16	0.261

*p<0.05

†No females were observed selling drugs.

** Differences in the residual gain scores between control and experimental groups.

housing, sewer, sidewalks and vector control inspectors; and warning letters sent to landowners informing them of the actions that will be taken if the drug dealing, trash and disorder problems are not dealt with.

The results of our randomized field experiment suggest that the Beat Health program decreased the level of drug dealing and improved the physical conditions of street blocks targeted using the Beat Health approach relative to efforts to affect drug dealing and physical decay in the control sites targeted by the uniformed patrol division. In the experimental sites, fewer males were selling drugs and there were fewer signs of physical decay after the intervention relative to the control group sites that were targeted by the patrol division.

Our experiment finds that a civil remedy approach to problem solving adopted by police departments is more effective in resolving problems than traditional police patrols in inflicted neighborhoods. Specifically, our research suggests that the Beat Health approach to solving drug and physical decay problems is effective in decreasing observable problems on target street blocks.

These results have several implications for the development of drug control efforts that aim to target places exhibiting drug and disorder problems. First, unlike other traditional drug enforcement tactics such as arrests, undercover buys, raids and the use of confidential informants, our research shows that a problem-solving approach using civil remedies to clean up the physical conditions of properties can impact the level of drug activity at targeted locations. Second, the use of a civil remedy program like Beat Health illustrates the face value of extending the traditional role of policing (see also Clarke, 1992; 1993; 1994a; 1994b; Goldstein, 1990): the Beat Health program requires the establishment of working relationships with other city agency representatives (such as housing, health and city works) and elicits the support of non-offending third parties (such as landlords and business owners) to bring about a crime control effect.

Address correspondence to: Lorraine Green Mazerolle, Center for Criminal Justice, and Assistant Professor, Division of Criminal Justice, University of Cincinnati, P.O. Box 210389, Cincinnati, OH 45221.

Acknowledgments: This research was supported by grant no. 95-IJ-CX-0039 from the National Institute of Justice. Findings and conclusions are those of the authors and do not necessarily reflect the position or policies of the U.S. Department of Justice.

The authors are indebted to the Oakland (CA) Police Department, with special appreciation to Sergeant Tom Hogenmiller, Daphne Markham, Michael Pellino, Dave Walsh, and the police officers, service technicians and support staff of the Beat Health Unit.

REFERENCES

Blalock, H. M. (1979). *Social Statistics* (3rd ed.). New York, NY: McGraw-Hill.

Brown, B. B. and I. Altman (1981). "Territoriality and Residential Crime: A Conceptual Framework." in P. J. Brantingham and P. L. Brantingham (eds.), *Environmental Criminology*. Prospect Heights, IL: Waveland.

Bohrnstedt, G.W. (1969). "Observations on the Measurement of Change." In E.F. Borgatta (ed.), *Social Methodology*. San Francisco, CA: Jossey-Bass.

Bursik, R.J. and J. Webb (1982). "Community Change and Patterns of Delinquency." *American Journal of Sociology* 88(1):24-42.

California. Department of Finance (1996). "Population Estimates for California Cities and Counties, January 1, 1996 and 1995: Report 96 E-1." Sacramento, CA: author.

California. Oakland Office of Community Development (1992). *Data on the city of Oakland*. Oakland, CA: author.

Clarke, R. (ed.) (1992). *Situational Crime Prevention: Successful Case Studies*. Albany, NY: Harrow & Heston.

—— (ed.) (1993). *Crime Prevention Studies,* vol. 1. Monsey, NY: Criminal Justice Press.

—— (ed.) (1994a). *Crime Prevention Studies,* vol. 2. Monsey, NY: Criminal Justice Press.

—— (ed.) (1994b). *Crime Prevention Studies,* vol. 3. Monsey, NY: Criminal Justice Press.

Cronbach, L.J. and L. Furby (1970). "How Should We Measure 'Change' or Should We?" *Psychological Bulletin* 74:68-80.

Eck, J.E. (1997) "Preventing Crime at Places." In: L.W. Sherman, D. Gottfredson, D. MacKenzie, J.E. Eck, P. Reuter and S. Bushway (eds.), *Preventing Crime: What Works, What Doesn't, What's Promising: A Report to the United States Congress*. Washington, DC: U.S. National Institute of Justice.

Felson, M. (1995). "I Got Rhythms: Crime Rhythms and Routine Activities." Paper presented at the annual meeting of the American Society of Criminology, Boston.

Goldstein, H. (1990). *Problem-Oriented Policing.* New York, NY: McGraw-Hill.

Green, L. (1995). "Cleaning up Drug Hot Spots in Oakland, California: The Displacement and Diffusion Effects." *Justice Quarterly* 12(4):737-754.

—— (1996). *Policing Places with Drug Problems.* Thousand Oaks, CA: Sage.

Kelling, G.L. and C.M. Coles (1996). *Fixing Broken Windows: Restoring Order and Reducing Crime in Our Communities.* New York, NY: Martin Kessler.

Lipsey, M. (1990). *Design Sensitivity: Statistical Power for Experimental Research.* Newbury Park, CA: Sage.

Mazerolle, L.G., C. Kadleck, and J. Roehl (1998). "Controlling Drug and Disorder Problems: The Role of Place Managers." *Criminology* 36(2):402-435.

Neter, J., W. Wasserman and M.H. Kutner (1990). *Applied Linear Statistical Models: Regression, Analysis of Variance, and Experimental Designs* (3rd ed.). Homewood, IL: Irwin.

Perkins, D.D. and R.B. Taylor (1996). "Ecological Assessments of Community Disorder: Their Relationship to Fear of Crime and Theoretical Implications." *American Journal of Community Psychology* 24(1):63-107.

Rosenbaum, D.P. and P.J. Lavrakas (1995). "Self-Reports about Place: The Application of Survey and Interview Methods to the Study of Small Areas." In: J.E. Eck and D. Weisburd (eds.), *Crime and Place.* Crime Prevention Studies, vol. 4. Monsey, NY: Criminal Justice Press.

Taylor, R.B. (1988). *Human Territorial Functioning.* Cambridge, UK: University of Cambridge Press.

—— (1995a). "The Impact of Crime on Communities." *Annals of the American Academy of Political and Social Science* 539:28-45.

—— (1995b). "Responses to Disorder: Relative Impacts of Neighborhood Structure, Crime and Physical Deterioration on Residents and Business Personnel." Final Report for Grant 94-IJ-CX-0018.

—— (1995c). "Crime and Grime: Relative Impacts of Neighborhood Structure, Crime and Physical Deterioration on Residents and Business Personnel." Final Report to the U.S. National Institute of Justice.

—— (1996). "Crime and Grime Over Two Decades: Stability, Decline, and Spatial Inequality in Charm City Neighborhoods." Final Report to the U.S. National Institute of Justice.

—— (1997a). "Social Order and Disorder of Street-Blocks and Neighborhoods: Ecology, Micro-Ecology and the Systemic Model of Social Disorganization." *Journal of Research in Crime and Delinquency* 34(1):113-155.

—— (1997b). "Crime, grime and responses to crime." In: S.P. Lab (ed.), *Crime Prevention at a Crossroads.* Cincinnati, OH: Anderson.

Weisburd, D. and L. Green (1991). *Identifying and Controlling Drug Markets. Technical Report.* Newark, NJ: School of Criminal Justice, Rutgers University.

Weisburd, D. (1993). "Design Sensitivity in Criminal Justice Experiments." *Crime & Justice* 17:337-379.

NOTES

1. The Hispanic category in the census is not mutually exclusive of other racial categories.

2. For example, Section 11570 of the California Health and Safety Code states: "Every building or place used for the purpose of unlawfully selling, serving, storing, keeping, manufacturing, or giving away any controlled substance, precursor or analog specified in this division, and every building or place wherein or upon which those acts take place, is a nuisance which shall be enjoined, abated and prevented, and for which damages may be recovered, whether it is a public or a private nuisance." In addition, Section 11366.5(a) stipulates that persons managing or controlling a building who allow the unlawful manufacturing, storing or distributing of any controlled substance can be imprisoned for up to one year. Some of the local municipal codes that are enforced include obstructions (6-1.09), building constituting a menace to public safety (2-4.09), unnecessary noises (3-1.01), unsecured buildings (2-4.09) and dumping garbage (4-5.12).

3. There are two basic advantages of using a block randomized design: first, computations with randomized block designs are simpler than those with covariance analysis, and, second, randomized block designs are essentially free of assumptions about the nature of the relationship between the blocking variable and the dependent variable, while covariance analysis assumes a definite form of relationship. A drawback of randomized block designs is that somewhat fewer degrees of freedom are available for experimental error than with covariance analysis for a completely randomized design (Neter, et al., 1990).

4. The Beat Health Unit employs a crime analyst (sworn police officer).

5. Section 8 housing sites were excluded because a special unit deals exclusively with problems at these places. Nonetheless, to facilitate coordination and communication the Section 8 Housing Unit sits in on weekly Beat Health Unit meetings.

6. While a larger catchment area radius than 300 feet would have been better (indeed, the larger the uncontaminated catchment area, the better) the realities of withholding cases from intervention raises ethical considerations. By using the 300 foot criteria, we sought to both minimize the ethical problems of withholding cases and maintain our ability to assess the catchment area effects of the interventions without proximal overlap.

7. The penalties under Section 11570 include fines of up to $25,000, closure of the property for up to one year and sale of the property to satisfy city costs.

8. We also conducted a survey of 400 residents living on the 100 street blocks in our study. The results of this survey are reported in Mazerolle, Kadleck, and Roehl (1998).

9. This example would assume constant variation of social activity across days of the week as well as across the four seasons.

10. The physical disorder scale was constructed by adding together a series of ordinal scales of observed physical decay. The scales ranged from 1 (almost none) to 4 (almost everywhere) and included measures of garbage, litter, broken glass, trash, junk, cigarette butts, needles, syringes, empty beer or liquor bottles and graffiti. The alpha reliability score for the scale was .77; and the additive measure could range from 4 (hardly any signs of physical decay) to 24 (extensive signs of physical decay).

11. We used a fixed-model analysis of variance by first taking into account the direct effects of the covariates (block and type), then the main effects of the factors, and then the interactions between block and type to assess statistical significance in our study:

SS (DIFFERENCE) = SS TYPE + SS BLOCK + SS(TYPE X BLOCK)

12. We did not present females selling drugs because no females were observed selling drugs either before or after the experiment.

IMPROVING THE MANAGEMENT OF RENTAL PROPERTIES WITH DRUG PROBLEMS: A RANDOMIZED EXPERIMENT

by

John E. Eck
University of Cincinnati

and

Julie Wartell
San Diego Police Department

Abstract: *Theory and practice point to the link between place management and the likelihood of drug dealing and criminal behavior at places. Theory suggests that drug dealers select places that have weak management. In an experiment conducted in San Diego, CA, 121 rental properties that had already been the target of drug enforcement were randomly assigned to two approximately equal-size treatment groups, or to a control group that received no further police actions. One treatment group received a letter from the police describing the enforcement and offering assistance; the other met with a narcotics detective under threat of nuisance abatement. Results show more evictions of drug offenders for both treatment groups relative to the control group, but more evictions for the meeting group than the letter group. Property owners in the meeting group also had a sizeable reduction in reported crime within six months of the intervention. There is also some evidence in support of a crime reduction effect of the letters, but it is less conclusive. Implications of these findings for theory and practice are discussed.*

This paper describes a test of a crime event theory and an evaluation of a drug sales prevention tactic. The theory is that people who manage places help prevent illicit activities. The tactic is designed to pressure landlords with drug problems on their rental property to improve their management practices. The test and evaluation is a randomized experiment, conducted with the cooperation of the San Diego (CA) Police Department, involving rental places with drug problems.

PLACE MANAGEMENT AND ROUTINE ACTIVITIES

Routine activity theory describes the conditions necessary for crime events to occur and the situations sufficient to prevent crime. Originally, the theory focused on offenders and targets (people and things) coming together in situations without guardians (those present to protect the target [Cohen and Felson, 1979]). Places were settings where offenders, targets and guardians meet — or fail to — but were not an active element in this early version of the theory (Eck, 1995a). In 1986, Felson drew from control theory (Hirschi, 1969) and added handlers to routine activity theory. Handlers are people who have an interest, typically an emotional bond, in keeping potential offenders out of trouble (Felson, 1986). Places became a key element in routine activity theory when Felson (1987) described the "metropolitan reef" and how spaces are increasingly controlled by private organizations.

Guardians may be available to protect some targets of predatory crime, and handlers can sometimes reduce the deviant behavior of the people they care about. But there are many settings where guardians and handlers are not available and where consensual crimes (not predatory) occur. Is there anyone who can control consensual crime, such as drug buying and selling, under these conditions?

Research into the structure of drug markets in San Diego, comparing drug dealing places to places without drug dealing, pointed to the role of property owners and their representatives (place managers) in controlling drug sales (Eck, 1994). Eck (1994) modified routine activity theory to include place managers. This expansion results in a theory with three necessary conditions for crime: a target, an offender, and a common place, as well as controllers — guardians, handlers, and managers — for each of these conditions.

Felson (1995) made the most recent elaboration of routine activity theory when he examined each type of crime controller and divided them into four categories: personal, assigned, diffuse and general. Though these categories apply to all three controllers, we will focus on how they apply to managers. An example of a personal manager is a home owner or store owner. Personal managers have a high stake in the place. Many places are owned by corporations, businesses or governments, where personal managers are seldom present. Assigned managers are people hired and employed to regulate behavior and to ensure the proper functioning of the place. Store clerks, shipping and receiving personnel, janitors, factory workers and foremen, college professors, lifeguards and librarians are examples of assigned managers. Diffuse managers are people who have regular contact with the place but neither own the location nor are employed by the owner. Two examples of diffuse managers are the driver of a food delivery truck who regularly visits convenience stores and the copier service agent who regularly fixes machines in a suite of offices. Finally, general managers are people, such as customers and visitors, who come to and go from places. Picnickers are examples of general managers of a park when they enforce park rules, aid other park users and generally contribute to the functioning of the park. In this paper we will focus on personal and assigned managers of residential apartment complexes. The experiment described is a test of the importance of place management for controlling crime.

Place management has received some attention from policy makers in regard to crime and disorder problems. Efforts to control bar fights and drunk driving have sometimes involved training bartenders and bouncers (assigned managers). Such programs instruct these assigned managers on how to recognize drinkers who have consumed too much alcohol, how to cut off further drinks while minimizing disruptions and how to eject unruly patrons without starting fights (Felson et al., 1997; Homel and Clark, 1994; Homel et al., 1997; Saltz, 1987; Wagenaar and Holder, 1991). Evidence from evaluations of these programs in the U.S. and Australia suggests that they may be effective at preventing assaults and drunk driving (Eck, 1997).

The police and prosecutors have recognized the importance of personal and assigned managers for controlling drug dealing. In their attempts to eliminate drug dealing locations, they have increasingly relied on nuisance abatement statutes (Green, 1996; Davis and Lurigio, 1996) and landlord training programs. Implicit in these programs is a recognition that property owners have the power and responsibility to regulate the behavior of people using their property. Further, the absence of regulation of place user behavior makes places more susceptible to crime.

Nuisance abatement is a civil process by which a government agency, business or private citizen sues the owner of a property that is the source of a public nuisance (for example, drug dealing, prostitution activity, or a public health hazard) to compel the end of the nuisance. Recently, the threat of nuisance abatement has been applied to personal and assigned managers found to have persistent drug dealing on their property. If a property owner does not cooperate with the police in getting rid of drug dealers, then the local government may go to civil court to close the property or gain ownership. This is a time-consuming process that can only be applied to a few very persistent dealing locations.

Landlord training programs are the carrot to the nuisance abatement stick. These training programs are generally directed at small-scale landlords. The programs teach rental property owners and managers how to recognize and eliminate drug dealing through property management procedures. Training programs target many more places than nuisance abatement. However, many of the trainees may not need the training because their properties may not be attractive to drug dealers. In addition, there is often no followup to assure that what was taught was put into practice.

The San Diego Police Department was interested in determining if there was an effective way of preventing and eliminating drug problems at locations susceptible to dealing — an approach that could be widely applied but would be directed at the rental properties that were the greatest problem. To this end, a small program was established that addressed rental properties where police had already conducted some form of drug enforcement. To determine if this program reduced drug dealing and crime, a randomized experiment was designed. This report describes this experiment and its results.

THE PLACES AND THEIR MANAGEMENT

Drug dealing is not randomly spread throughout neighborhoods. Some places are attractive to drug dealers while other places are repellent (Eck, 1994). This suggests that the presence of drug dealers may be a good indicator that the property and the property owner should be targeted for preventive actions to forestall future drug dealing.

From June through November 1993, all residential rental properties that were subject to some form of drug enforcement by the narcotics unit, as well as a number from other uniformed sections, were assigned to this experiment. This yielded 121 locations. Business sites, public places and locations where the drug dealer owned the property were not included in this experiment.[1] The vast majority of these 121 rental drug places (96%) were brought into this study as the result of actions by the Narcotics Unit. One place was entered into the study because of the actions of patrol officers. Four were entered because of the actions of uniformed Neighborhood Policing Teams, special squads in each patrol division that focus on neighborhood concerns.

The enforcement action taken against the drug dealer at the property in over half the cases was a search warrant-based raid (Table 1). Three other tactics were used less frequently. Knock-and-talk actions occur when police officers go to a location, tell the inhabitants that they are police officials and ask to be allowed in to search for drugs. If the inhabitants consent to a search, then the police enter the structure and look for drugs. A buy-bust involves an undercover officer or informant making a controlled buy of drugs followed shortly by the arrest of the seller, usually by other nearby officers. Parole searches and Fourth Amendment waiver actions occur when a suspected drug dealer's condition of parole or probation requires him or her to submit to warrantless searches by officers.

Table 1: Enforcement Actions at the Places (N=121)

	percent
Search warrant	51.2
Knock and talk	16.5
Buy-bust	11.6
Parole search/4th amendment waiver	11.6
Other	3.3
Unknown	5.8
TOTAL	99.9

Drugs were found in all but three locations (97%). At 57% of these places only a single drug was found, while two or more types of drugs were found at over 40% of the places. We see in Table 2 that crack cocaine was found in over a third of the places; powder cocaine and methamphetamine in over a quarter of the places. Though marijuana and heroin are prevalent, these two drugs were more likely to be found with other drugs than alone. Marijuana was associated with methamphetamine, but not other drugs, and heroin was associated with powder cocaine, but not with other drugs.

Table 2: Drugs Found at Places
(N=121)

	percent
Crack cocaine	36.4
Powder cocaine	27.3
Methamphetamine	27.3
Marijuana	30.6
Heroin	20.7
Other	2.5

Several types of data were collected for each place. Police agency records were collected describing the suspects arrested during the first enforcement action. Police records also provided information on crime and drug events at the sites for three months prior to the original enforcement, and for three months subsequent to that effort. Similar data was collected for 30 months following treatment to assess the long-term results of the experiment. A log of police interactions with the owners in the two treatment groups was maintained, and observers collected data on the environmental characteristics of each site. A telephone survey of owners conducted after the experimental period obtained information on their property management practices, characteristics and methods of handling the tenant/drug dealer who precipitated the original enforcement. Owners were identified by property records checks conducted by the police department using city records. Finally, narcotics unit detectives went to each of the sites in the study and attempted to buy drugs as a method of determining if they were still available at the location.

Environmental surveys provided data on the physical structure from which drugs were sold. A visit was made to each property in the experiment, and observations of the physical features, setting and conditions were recorded. Most of the drug places are in apartment buildings (Table 3). Of the remainder, about 20% each are in duplexes and single-family homes. Table 3 also shows that most apartment complexes (in the experiment) with drug dealing are relatively small. Over 48% had fewer than 11 apartment units; about 79% percent had 20 or fewer units. Apartment buildings with over 50 units were rare. Earlier research in San Diego showed that cocaine and heroin dealers seem to prefer smaller apartment buildings over larger complexes (Eck, 1994), a finding consistent with those of the present study.

Table 3: Type of Structure (N=121)

		percent
Apartment buildings		56.2
Number of units	% of apartment buildings	
< 11	48.5	
11-20	30.9	
21-30	8.8	
31-40	5.9	
41-50	2.9	
> 50	2.9	
	99.9	
Duplexes		24.0
Single-family houses		19.8
TOTAL		100.0

The overwhelming majority of these properties (94.9% of 119) were owned by individuals or partnerships (Table 4). Only six properties were owned by corporations or other entities (usually banks); managers of these latter properties are assigned. Because 95% of the managers in this study are personal, we will use the term "manager" to refer to personal managers.

Table 4: Type of Ownership (N=119)

	Percent of owners
Individual	73.9
Partnership	21.0
Corporation	2.5
Other	2.5
TOTAL	99.9

Few of the structures were under 10 years old, though many owners had acquired the property recently (Table 5).

Table 5: Age of Structures and Years Owned

	Percent of Owners	
	Age of Structure (N=115)	Years Owned (N=118)
1 - 5 years	4.3	44.1
6 - 10 years	8.7	23.7
11 - 20 years	11.3	22.0
21 - 30 years	19.1	5.9
30 years	56.5	4.2
TOTAL	99.9	99.9

On average, these properties increased in value from the time of purchase to the interview. The mean purchase price of the structures was $367,712, and owners' estimated current valuation had a mean of $390,114. The mean change in the value of the properties was an increase of $14,618. This change is relatively modest when one considers that the mean change as a percent of purchase price was 7%. Further, almost 57% of the properties (for which this information was provided, n=76) either had not changed or had dropped in value. Almost 83% of the owners had some outstanding debt on the property.[2]

These owners stated that they could afford to spend relatively little on their properties (Table 6). Almost 40% of those who answered this question claimed they could spend nothing to improve their property. Another 23% claimed to be able to afford less than $1,000, while less than 10% of the owners could afford to spend over $5,000.

The reason for this becomes apparent when one considers that 51% (56) of the 110 owners answering the question stated that the rent either just covers costs or that the costs exceed the rental income. Of these 56 owners, 89.3% (50) said that costs were greater than the rent. Further, when asked how important it was for them to have all of the units rented all 12 months of the year (Table 7), 72% indicated that it was "very" or "extremely" important.

The financial constraints owners face may have some influence on their management practices. Slightly over half of the owners said they did not have a property manager (52.1% of 117). Of those with a manager, 58.9% said that the property manager was not located on the property. This implies that 80.3% (of 117) of the properties did not have someone permanently located at the place.

Table 6: Maximum Amount Owner Could Spend To Improve the Property (N=103)

Maximum Dollars	Percent of Owners
$0	37.9
$1 - $1000	23.3
$10001 - $5000	29.1
> $5000	9.7
TOTAL	100.0

Table 7: Importance of Renting All Units All 12 Months to Meet Financial Objectives (N=108)

	Percent of Owners
Not at all	0.0
Not very	5.6
Somewhat	21.3
Very	50.0
Extremely	23.1
TOTAL	100.0

Since property owners and their managers did not live near the property, owners had to make visits to monitor the behavior of tenants. About 45% of the owners visited their properties every week or more (Table 8); a third, monthly; almost a quarter, less frequently than monthly; and a very few, never.

Background checks can help landlords determine whether an applicant for a rental unit will pay his or her rent and maintain the property. Owners were asked whether they checked on the background of the person leasing the unit where the police believed drugs were being sold. Credit and reference checks were the most frequently conducted (see Table 9), followed by employment checks. No local criminal conviction checks were conducted, and in over a quarter of the cases no background check was conducted at all.

Table 8: Frequency of Visits to Property by Owner (N=116)

	Percent of Owners
Weekly or more	44.8
Monthly	31.9
Every other month	11.2
Biannually	6.9
Yearly	3.4
Never	1.7
TOTAL	99.9

Table 9: Background Checks Conducted by Owners

	Respondents Giving Answers (n)	Percent of Respondents
Credit check	110	38.2
Reference check	112	41.1
Bank check	110	1.8
Employment check	110	29.1
Criminal conviction check	110	0.0
No check	110	26.4

THE EXPERIMENT

Randomization was accomplished as follows. Drug enforcement actions by the Narcotics Unit and other sections of the San Diego Police Department were reported to the Crime Analysis Unit daily. The research assistant for the project (Wartell), based in the Crime Analysis Unit, conducted an initial screening to determine if the enforcement had taken place at a residential rental location. If the place met this criteria, it was assigned a control number. The control number and address were faxed to the principle investigator (Eck) in Washington, DC. A computer-generated random number was drawn to determine the treatment assignment and a coded assignment number was faxed back to San Diego. Assignments were confirmed by telephone on the same date.

At a third of the places, following the initial enforcement action, nothing further was done by the police. These places constituted the control group against which places in the two treatment groups were compared. There were 42 places in the control group. By comparing outcomes at these places to outcomes of places in the two treatment groups, the experiment could show whether police follow-up contacts with place managers were superior to drug enforcement alone.

A special unit of the police department, the Drug Abatement Response Team (DART), sent a letter to owners of another third of the places. The letter informed them of the drug activity, and explained that the police would assist them if they needed help to get rid of drug dealers. The letter also warned the owner that under California law, if repeated drug dealing was found the City of San Diego could take the owner to court. If this occurred, the property could be closed for up to one year and the owner fined up to $25,000. The letter was designed to be an inexpensive, informative reminder to property owners. Once the letter was sent, the special unit made no further follow-up with the rental property or its owner, unless the owner requested assistance. The letter group contained 42 places.

DART sent owners of the last third of the places a letter emphasizing the legal action the city could take if the drug problem was not addressed. The letter also stated that the owner should contact DART, or a DART detective would contact the landlord and schedule an interview at the property. The detective then called and scheduled a meeting with the landlord (or a representative) and a member of the city's Code Compliance Department. At the meeting, the detective, code officer and owner inspected the property and began developing a plan for preventing future drug dealing. The detective then worked with the property owner to assure that the changes were made. Thirty-seven places were randomly assigned to the meeting group.

The DART Unit recorded the actions it took on each case on activity logs developed for the project. The DART detective and supervisor wrote short narrative descriptions of activities, by date, for each case they worked on. These were collected by the on-site research assistant. These activity descriptions were then grouped into categories of similar activities. When there were ambiguities in the recorded activities, the on-site research assistant interviewed the detective to clarify the log contents. These logs include actions initiated by DART (e.g., calling owners and making recommendations) and actions initiated by owners (e.g., calling DART or the owner's attorney sending a letter to DART). Table 10 shows the proportion of places in each group that received at least one action or no action. As planned, none of the places in the control group and all of the places in the meeting group received at least one action. The letter group was almost evenly split between action and no action. Though it is possible that some actions were taken that were not recorded, monitoring of cases by the on-site research assistant suggest that this was unlikely.

Table 10: DART Action by Treatment Group

	Percent of Places in Group		
	Control (42)	Letter (42)	Meeting (37)
Action	0.0	52.4	100.0
No action	100.0	47.6	0.0
TOTAL	100.0	100.0	100.0
DART meetings with owners/managers		Letter (22)	Meeting (37)
Unable to inspect property		4.5	5.4
Meeting held with owner or manager		4.5	91.9
Includes building inspector		0.0	81.1

At meeting treatment sites, DART was to meet with property owners or managers; gaining the cooperation of owners and managers for such meetings was relatively easy. DART was unable to arrange a property inspection for only two sites. The bottom panel of Table 10 shows that in over 80% of the meeting places, the DART representative met with the owner or manager and that a representative of the Code Compliance Department was also present. At only one of the letter places did the DART detective meet with the owner or manager, and the code compliance representative never met with the owner or manager.

DART unit activity logs recorded the actions of place managers. We see in Table 11 that place managers in the meeting group expressed greater willingness, as well as greater hesitation, to evict than managers in the letter group. The letter-group managers may have been more ambivalent about evictions than the managers in the meeting group, who faced more intrusive intervention by the police. Offenders were more likely to have left meeting-group places than letter places, according to DART logs. Finally, DART was more likely to recommend management changes to meeting group managers. DART logs show that meeting-group managers were slightly more likely to renovate their property and make recommended management changes. The DART logs noted whether the codes inspector found health and safety code violations; the inspector never reported such infractions.

Table 11: Evictions and Property Improvements

	Percent of Places in Group	
	Letter (22)	Meeting (37)
Owner/manager willing to evict	36.4 (8)	56.8 (21)
Owner/manager hesitant to evict	4.5 (1)	13.5 (5)
Drug offenders have left	27.3 (6)	43.2 (16)
DART recommends management changes	22.7 (5)	51.4 (19)
Owner renovation rental property	0.0 (0)	10.8 (4)
Changes in property management	0.0 (0)	10.8 (4)

Place manager interviews provide another perspective on evictions. Table 12, which compares all three treatment groups, demonstrates that the more intrusive the police intervention the greater the chances that the drug offender was evicted. Though the chi-square statistic is not significant at the .10 level, the correlation between treatment and eviction is significant.

In summary, it appears that compliance with the treatment conditions was high. None of the control-group places had any contact with DART. Though half of the letter group had a phone contact with DART, only one of these cases had a meeting. Finally, all but one of the meeting places had a face-to-face meeting. All but two of the meeting places were inspected by DART, and over 80% of the meeting places were inspected by a representative of the Code Compliance Department. Given this high level of compliance, we will examine the effects of the three groups as they were assigned — control, letter, or meeting — by the experimental design, rather than the way they were implemented.

These treatments appear to have led to some changes in management practices, particularly the evictions of drug offenders. However, the relationship between treatment and managerial changes are moderate at best, and in some cases, weak. Did these changes reduce crime? In the next section we will try to answer this question.

Table 12: Was the Offender Evicted?

	Percent of Places in Group		
	Nothing	Letter	Meeting
No	63.3 (19)	55.2 (16)	34.8 (8)
Yes	36.7 (11)	44.8 (13)	65.2 (15)
TOTAL	100.0 (30)	100.0 (29)	100.0 (23)

	Value	df	T-value	Significance
Chi-square	4.38944	2		.11139
Spearman Correlation	.22154		2.03203	.04547

FINDINGS

The San Diego Police Department's Crime Analysis Unit provided the number of reported crime incidents for each site in the experiment for a 30-month period following treatment. These data, aggregated into five six-month intervals, allow us to describe the long-term effects of the treatments and to determine if effects wear off or remain constant over time. The number of reported crimes at a single place, even a place with multiple residents, is small. To detect a significant reduction in crime it was necessary to aggregate across all felonies reported to have occurred at experimental places.

Table 13 shows the mean number of reported crimes for the places in the three groups, for each of the five six-month periods following treatment. In all five periods, the letter and meeting groups had fewer crimes than the control group. In the first, second and fourth periods, the meeting group had fewer reported crimes than the letter group. Over the entire 30-month post-treatment period, the places in the control group had an average of two more crimes than the meeting group, and one and two-thirds more crimes than the letter group. Note that the control group means drop from period one to period two, and then fluctuate over subsequent periods. Crime in the letter and meeting groups are relatively constant over the five periods insofar as they do not show dramatic period-to-period shifts.

These results suggest that the letter and meeting treatments reduced crime at places relative to the control group. But before we reach this conclusion we should examine the significance tests. This experiment was designed to detect differences at a p value of .10 or less.[3] In other words, if a p value is greater than .10 we will not reject the hypothesis that the findings are due to chance. This will not mean that there is no treatment effect, but that we cannot be confident that the treatments caused the observed results. Further, it implies that even if the treatments caused the observed differences between the control and treatment groups, the substantive effect is small.

Table 13: Mean Number Reported Crimes, by Group and Period (Standard Deviation)

6-Mo. Period	Control (N=42)	Letter (N=42)	Meeting (N=37)
1	1.52 (2.27)	0.74 (1.36)	0.62 (0.89)
2	0.83 (1.41)	0.79 (1.63)	0.76 (1.23)
3	1.02 (1.69)	0.50 (0.80)	0.59 (1.19)
4	0.76 (1.56)	0.76 (1.03)	0.41 (0.76)
5	0.90 (1.39)	0.52 (0.94)	0.65 (1.34)
All	5.05 (6.30)	3.31 (4.18)	3.03 (3.93)

Additionally, we need to account for pre-treatment differences in crime among the places in the three groups. To account for the pre-treatment crime levels, multiple regression models were estimated using the reported crime after treatment as the dependent variables and the reported crime for the three months prior to treatment as independent control variables. Treatment variables were included as dichotomous independent policy variables (0 when absent and 1 when present). The regression models' constants reflect the control group crime levels, adjusting for the number of crimes in the pre-treatment period. The coefficients for the letter and meeting variables show the reduction in crime due to the treatment (again, holding pre-treatment crime constant), relative to the control group. That is, a negative coefficient indicates that the average treatment place has fewer crimes than the average control place. The coefficients for the pre-crime variables reflect the possibility that some places are more crime-prone than others, regardless of the treatment they receive.

Six regression models were estimated, one for each six-month period and one for the entire 30-month period. All of the regression models were significant. The results of these models are shown in the Appendix. Over the entire 30-month period, 40% of the variation in post-treatment reported crime is explained by the treatments and the number of crimes in the three-month pre-treatment period.

176 — John E. Eck and Julie Wartell

Figure 1 summarizes the results for the five six-month period models. It shows how the values of the coefficients for the independent variables fluctuate over the six-month periods. Pre-treatment crime is a significant positive predictor of post-treatment crime in all five periods and for the entire 30-month period, when the treatment is controlled for. These results suggest that there are systematic differences among places that make some properties more susceptible to crime, relative to other places. These differences appear to be stable over time, as the coefficient hovers around 0.4 over the five periods. That is, for every crime occurring at a place during the three months prior to treatment there is, on average, four-tenths of a crime taking place in every six-month period following treatment, or about two crimes in the entire 30-month post-treatment period (see also the estimates for the 30-month model shown in the Appendix).

The control group places, on average, had almost one crime in period 1, when prior crime reports are controlled. Control group crimes dropped in subsequent periods. On average, there were more than three crimes per control group place during the 30-month period, controlling for pre-treatment crimes. The estimates for the control group were significant for all periods.

The letter treatment coefficients are negative for three of the five periods and the entire 30-month period. Despite the fact that during periods 2 and 4 letter places had more crimes than control places, over the entire 30-month period letter places had fewer crimes, taking into account the number of crimes in the pre-treatment period. Over the entire 30-month post-treatment period, the average letter place had .41 fewer crimes than the average control group place. In no period was the coefficient for letter group places significant. Thus, we cannot rule out the possibility that the fewer crimes at the letter places are due to chance.

The meeting treatment coefficients are negative in all six models, indicating that meeting places had less crime in all periods (and over all 30 months) than the control places, once pre-treatment crimes are accounted for. The biggest decline occurs in the first six-month period when the average meeting place had almost .86 fewer crimes than meeting places. Over the entire 30-month follow-up period, the average meeting group place had 1.85 fewer crimes than the average control group place, after pre-treatment crimes are accounted for. In the first period and for all 30 months, these results are significant. We can, therefore, reject the hypothesis that chance created the differences between the control and meeting groups.

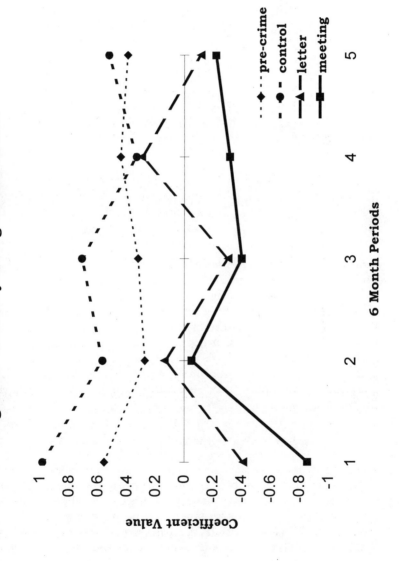

Figure 1: Summary of Regression Results

6 Month Periods

Coefficient Value

pre-crime
control
letter
meeting

177

The crime control effects of the meetings are substantial. The percent reduction in crime,[4] relative to the control group places and taking into account the pre-treatment crime levels, is shown in Figure 2. With pre-treatment crime accounted for, the control group places have about three crimes per place over the entire period. The meeting group places have more than one and a quarter crimes per place over the same period, once pre-treatment crimes are accounted for. This means that there is a 60% reduction in crime in the meeting places relative to the control places over the entire 30-month period.

About 46% of the crime prevention due to meetings occurred in the first six-months following treatment when there were almost 87% fewer crimes at meeting places than at control places. The remaining 64% of the prevention effects of meetings trickled in over the next 24 months. Hence, there is good evidence that the meetings had an effect throughout the 30-month period.

The absence of significant effects during periods 2 through 5 is probably because the effects of meetings deteriorate over time, and the frequency of crime is low. Where the treatment effects were stronger (as measured by coefficient size in period 1 and the entire 30-month period), and where the base rate of crime was higher (the entire 30-month period), we found significant results. In other words, it is likely that similarly designed experiments, with more places in each of the treatment groups, would detect significant reported crime reduction effects for meetings in periods 2 through 5.[5]

We cannot be as certain of the effectiveness of the letter treatment. Still, during period 1 letters may have reduced crime by about 42% and over the entire 30-month period by over 13%. During periods 2 and 4, the letter group places had more crime than the control group places, once pre-treatment crime is accounted for. Letters might have a crime reduction effect but these effects are likely to be weaker than the meeting effects.

IMPLICATIONS

This paper has explored the role of place managers in controlling drug dealing on rental properties, and the consequences of their behavior for crime at these places. We have seen that in San Diego, these managers were not in strong financial positions and were unable or unwilling to regulate the behavior of some of their tenants. The majority of the apartment complexes had less than 20 units. Though most of these places were old, many had been purchased in

Figure 2: Percent Reduction in Crime
Relative To Control Places

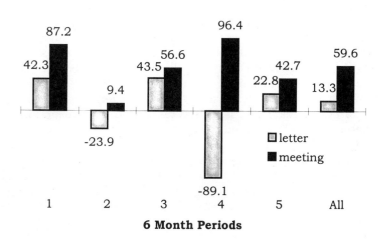

the last 10 years. These observations are consistent with Eck's (1994; 1995b) theory of the geography of retail drug dealing: poor financial positions reduce place management and reduced place management in turn increases the chances of drug dealing on properties. One of the implications of this theory is that improvements in the management of rental places could reduce drug dealing. By curtailing dealing, crime at the location could be reduced. The experiment described in this paper simultaneously tests this theory as well as policies to improve place management.

The experimental findings provide strong support for the policy of having police and code enforcement officials meet with property owners following drug enforcement. These meetings appear to result in large reductions in crime. There is weaker evidence that letters, alone, to property owners may have some effect on crime. We cannot be very certain of this effect, however.

Though we do not have cost figures for either of these treatments, they are not particularly expensive. The DART unit had a single detective conduct the follow-up meetings, and only one city code enforcement officer was involved; letters are even cheaper. When one considers the costs of a drug raid (and the risks to officers, suspects and uninvolved citizens), the marginal costs of either of these follow-up tactics are minimal. Meetings appear to be a cost-effective method of reducing crime, and despite weaker evidence on effectiveness, letters are so inexpensive that they may very well be worth using as well. Though place managers for rental properties with drug problems may have fewer financial resources than rental place managers without drug problems, following drug enforcement it may not take much more effort on the part of the police or major changes on the part of managers to create substantial reductions in crime.

The findings from this experiment are consistent with recent experimental (Mazerolle et al., in this volume) and quasi-experimental evaluations (Green, 1995) conducted in Oakland, CA, and with quasi-experiments in St. Louis, MO (Hope, 1994). All of these evaluations had moderately strong to very strong designs (Eck, 1997), so we can be fairly confident of the results. One evaluation found little evidence that residents' perceptions of drug dealing or personal safety were changed by nuisance abatement, though observations of ten sites indicated that eight of them showed declines in drug dealing (Lurigio et al., 1993; Lurigio et al., this volume). This study employed a particularly weak evaluation design, so we can be much less confident of its results than we can of the results of the other evaluations (Eck, 1997). However, there are other possible explanations for the differences in findings among these studies including state laws, administrative procedures and rental markets.

The collective findings of this experiment and others provide considerable evidence that place management is causally related to crime and drug dealing. This chapter and earlier research (Eck, 1994; Eck and Wartell, 1997) showed how financial considerations influence management, and how economic investment, zoning and land use policies influence the financial viability of properties.

Criminology needs to pay closer attention to the economics of property ownership and the management of places. These concepts may help shed light on the growth of physical and social incivilities in deteriorating communities (Skogan, 1990). Sloan-Howitt and Kelling (1990) illustrate this point in their description of the effects of improved place management on graffiti in the New York City subway system. The economics of place management is also plausible as a rival hypothesis to common theories of community crime patterns. Crime concentration in urban communities may be partially due to economic disinvestment, leading to weak place management and increased crime and disorder, rather than the breakdown in social controls among individuals and families within communities (Shaw and McKay, 1969; Bursik and Grasmick, 1993). Or it is possible that the erosion of place management is part of a larger process that simultaneously undermines guardianship and handling. Clearly, place management is a concept that has substantial implications for crime theory and crime prevention practice.

◆

Address correspondence to: John E. Eck, Division of Criminal Justice, University of Cincinnati, P.O. Box 210389, Cincinnati, OH 45221-0389. E-mail: <JOHN.ECK@UC.EDU>.

Acknowledgments: This research was supported by grant no. 90-IJ-CX-K006 from the U.S. National Institute of Justice to the San Diego Police Department. Points of view are those of the authors and do not necessarily represent the official position of the San Diego Police Department or the National Institute of Justice.

The authors thank Chief Jerry Sanders of the San Diego Police Department for his support of this experiment. We also thank Kimberly Glenn and Patrick Drummy of the Crime Analysis Unit for providing a home for this research, and Lieutenant Guy Swanger and Detective Kathy Healey for their support and hard work. Craig Uchida and Richard Titus have been gracious National Institute of Justice project monitors throughout this endeavor. Finally, we thank Lorraine Mazerolle and Jan Roehl, and two anonymous reviewers, for their comments and suggestions. Though we had many people helping us, all mistakes and misinterpretations in this paper are ours.

REFERENCES

Bursik, R.J. Jr. and H.G. Grasmick (1993). *Neighborhoods and Crime: The Dimensions of Effective Community Control.* New York, NY: Lexington Books.

Cohen, L.E. and M. Felson (1979). "Social Change and Crime Rate Trends: A Routine Activity Approach." *American Sociological Review* 44:588-605.

Davis, R.C. and A.J. Lurigio (1996). *Fighting Back: Neighborhood Anti-drug Strategies.* Thousand Oaks, CA: Sage.

Eck, J.E. (1994). "Drug Markets and Drug Places: A Case-Control Study of the Spatial Structure of Illicit Drug Dealing." Unpublished dissertation, University of Maryland, College Park.

—— (1995a). "Examining Routine Activity Theory: A Review of Two Books." *Justice Quarterly* 12:783-797.

—— (1995b). "A General Model of the Geography of Illicit Retail Marketplaces." In: J.E. Eck and D. Weisburd (eds.), *Crime and Place.* Crime Prevention Studies, vol. 4. Monsey, NY: Criminal Justice Press, pp. 67-94.

—— (1997). "Preventing Crime at Places." In: L. Sherman, D. Gottfredson, D. McKenzie, J. Eck, P. Reuter, and S. Bushway (eds.), *Preventing Crime: What Works, What Doesn't, What's Promising: A Report to the United States Congress.* Washington, DC: U.S. National Institute of Justice.

—— and J. Wartell (1997). "Reducing Crime and Drug Dealing by Improving Place Management: A Randomized Experiment." Report to the U.S. National Institute of Justice. San Diego, CA: San Diego Police Department.

Felson, M. (1986). "Linking Criminal Choices, Routine Activities, Informal Control, and Criminal Outcomes." In: D. Cornish and R. Clarke (eds.), *The Reasoning Criminal: Rational Choice Perspectives on Offending.* New York, NY: Springer-Verlag.

—— (1987). "Routine Activities and Crime Prevention in the Developing Metropolis." *Criminology* 25:911-932.

—— (1995). "Those Who Discourage Crime." In: J.E. Eck and D. Weisburd (eds.), *Crime and Place.* Crime Prevention Studies, vol. 4. Monsey, NY: Criminal Justice Press.

—— R. Berends, B. Richardson and A. Veno (1997). "A Community Policing Initiative to Discourage Abuse of Alcohol." In: R. Homel (ed.), *Policing for Prevention: Reducing Crime, Public Intoxication and Injury.* Crime Prevention Studies, vol. 7. Monsey, NY: Criminal Justice Press.

Green, L. (1995). "Cleaning Up Drug Hotspots in Oakland, California: The Displacement and Diffusion Effects." *Justice Quarterly* 12:737-754.

—— (1996). *Policing Places with Drug Problems.* Thousand Oaks, CA: Sage.

Hirschi, T. (1969). *Causes of Delinquency.* Berkeley: University of California Press.

Homel, R. and J. Clark (1994). "The Prediction and Prevention of Violence in Pubs and Clubs." In: R.V. Clarke (ed.), *Crime Prevention Studies*, vol. 3. Monsey, NY: Criminal Justice Press.

—— M. Hauritz, R. Wortley, G. McIlwain, and R. Carvolth (1997). "Preventing Alcohol-Related Crime Through Community Action: The Surfers Paradise Safety Action Project." In: R.V. Clarke (ed.), *Policing for Prevention: Reducing Crime, Public Intoxication and Injury*. Crime Prevention Studies, vol. 7. Monsey, NY: Criminal Justice Press.

Hope, T. (1994). "Problem-Oriented Policing and Drug Market Locations: Three Case Studies." In: R.V. Clarke (ed.), *Crime Prevention Studies*, vol. 2. Monsey, NY: Criminal Justice Press.

Lurigio, A.J., R.C. Davis, T.A. Regulus, V.E. Gwiasda, S.J. Popkin, M.L. Dantzker, B. Smith and L. Ouellet (1993). *An Evaluation of the Cook County State's Attorney's Office Narcotics Nuisance Abatement Unit.* Chicago, IL: Illinois Criminal Justice Information Authority.

Saltz, R.F. (1987). "The Role of Bars and Restaurants in Preventing Alcohol-Impaired Driving: An Evaluation of Server Education." *Evaluation in Health Professions* 10:5-27.

Shaw, C.R. and H.D. McKay (1969). *Juvenile Delinquency and Urban Areas.* Chicago, IL: University of Chicago.

Skogan, W.G. (1990). *Disorder and Decline: Crime and the Spiral of Decay in American Neighborhoods.* New York, NY: Free Press.

Sloan-Howitt, M. and G.L. Kelling (1990). "Subway Graffiti in New York City: 'Gettin Up' vs. 'Meanin it and Cleaning it.'" *Security Journal* 1:131-36.

Wagenaar, A.C. and H.D. Holder (1991). "Effects of Alcoholic Beverage Server Liability on Traffic Crash Injuries." *Alcoholism: Clinical and Experimental Research* 15:942-947.

APPENDIX: Regression Results

Models for period	Coefficients (standard errors) [p value]				Model Statistics (N=121)		
	constant	letter	meeting	pre-crime	F	R^2	Significance
1	0.981 (0.231) [.0000]*	-0.415 (0.310) [.1836]	-0.855 (0.315) [.0077]*	0.556 (0.084) [.0000]*	14.509	0.271	.0000*
2	0.566 (0.229) [.0148]*	0.135 (0.307) [.6609]	-0.053 (0.312) [.8645]	0.274 (0.083) [.0012]*	3.668	0.086	.0143*
3	0.710 (0.196) [.0004]*	-0.309 (0.264) [.2433]	-0.402 (0.268) [.1365]	0.322 (0.071) [.0000]*	8.342	0.176	.0000*
4	0.331 (0.160) [.0406]*	0.295 (0.215) [.1728]	-0.319 (0.218) [.1463]	0.442 (0.058) [.0000]*	20.570	0.345	.0000*
5	0.522 (0.179) [.0042]*	-0.119 (0.240) [.6206]	-0.223 (0.244) [.3635]	0.392 (0.065) [.0000]*	13.106	0.252	.0000*
All 30 months	3.109 (0.647) [.0000]*	-0.414 (0.870) [.6350]	-1.853 (0.884) [.0383]*	1.986 (0.235) [.0000]*	26.009	0.400	.0000*

* Significant at the .10 level

NOTES

1. Non-residential, non-rental properties were excluded because the experiment was premised on the theory that place management influences crime, and that different types of places require different types of management. Though the generic police intervention might be the same across different places, the specific police intervention would have to vary, and the responses of the place managers might vary. Such divergence could reduce the statistical power of the experiment. Although places owned by drug dealers were also excluded from the experiment, no such place came to the attention of the experimenters during this project.

2. We have no information on how these figures compare to the average rental property in San Diego. However, since the majority of the properties in the experiment were within two low-income neighborhoods, it is likely that these places had smaller increases in value than comparable properties in other parts of the city.

3. A .10 level of significance was used in this experiment for two reasons. First, given the rate at which places were expected to become available for allocation to treatments, the time available to conduct the experiment and the costs of collecting all of the data needed, we established that a .10 significance level would be the most reasonable if we were to examine enough cases to detect a moderate effect in this experiment. Second, the most intrusive intervention in the experiment (the meeting) is much less intrusive than most police interventions (e.g., arrests). Thus, the social and policy costs of a Type I error (reporting a treatment difference that was in fact due to chance) were lower for this type of intervention than for most other police experiments. This justified the use of a lower threshold for significant testing.

4. The mean number of crimes at meeting places is $c+m$, where m is the meeting group coefficient for a period and c is the constant for that period. Thus, $(c+m)/c$ is the proportion of crimes at meeting places relative to control places, and $1-[(c+m)/c]$ is the proportion of crimes prevented. Since $1-[(c+m)/c]=m/c$, $100*m/c$ is the crime prevention effect as a percent. Substituting the letter coefficient for the meeting coefficient yields the percent crime prevention effect of the letter treatment.

5. Of course, the test of this conjecture is a larger scale experiment.

MORE EFFECTIVE PLACE MANAGEMENT: AN EVALUATION OF COOK COUNTY'S NARCOTICS NUISANCE ABATEMENT UNIT

by

Arthur J. Lurigio
Loyola University, Chicago

Robert C. Davis
Victim Services Agency, New York City

Thomas A. Regulus
Southern Illinois University, Edwardsville

Victoria E. Gwiasda
University of Illinois

Susan J. Popkin
Abt Associates

Mark L. Dantzker
Georgia Southern University

Barbara Smith
American Bar Association

and

Lawrence Ovellet
University of Illinois

Crime Prevention Studies, volume 9 (1998), pp. 187-217

Abstract: *This chapter describes an impact evaluation of the Narcotics Nuisance Abatement Unit (NNAU) of the Cook County (Chicago) State's Attorney's Office (CCSAO). A central feature of the program is its emphasis on citizen and police cooperation in identifying properties on which drug sales are occurring. The program began in August 1990 and has become part of a community-based drug control strategy targeting buildings that are sites for drug trafficking or sales of drug paraphernalia. Neighborhood groups, police and other government agencies contact the program to make it aware of such nuisances. The NNAU employs three strategies: voluntary abatement, prosecutorial abatement and community outreach. The current chapter deals with the NNAU's effects on residents' perceptions and on subsequent drug dealing. A survey of residents living on blocks with and without abatement actions produced no evidence that evictions had any impact on citizens' perceptions of drug activity, other signs of disorder or feelings of safety on the block. Follow-up observations found no signs of drug dealing at eight of the ten abated buildings studied or on the blocks on which they were located.*

INTRODUCTION

This chapter describes an impact evaluation of the Narcotics Nuisance Abatement Unit (NNAU) of the Cook County (Chicago) State's Attorney's Office (CCSAO) (Lurigio et al., 1993). The primary objective of the abatement program is to rid neighborhoods of drug activity and drug-related crime through the abatement of drug houses and drug paraphernalia dealing. A central feature of the program is its emphasis on citizen and police cooperation in identifying properties where drug sales are occurring.

The CCSAO created the NNAU in response to the alarming growth of drug arrests in Cook County. The program began in August 1990, and has become part of a community-based drug control strategy targeting buildings that are sites for drug trafficking or sales of drug paraphernalia. Neighborhood groups, police and other government agencies contact the program to make it aware of such nuisances. The NNAU attempts to abate nuisances by employing three strategies: voluntary abatement, prosecutorial abatement and community outreach. As of May 1997, the NNAU received over 10,000 complaints of possible nuisances, leading to over 5,000 voluntary and 200 court-ordered abatements.

Our study of the NNAU was built on earlier research regarding the procedures and outcomes of nuisance abatement programs around the country (see Smith et al., 1992). It examined the program's effects on residents, landlords and drug dealers, and assessed program-related changes in the social character of targeted neighborhoods. Attention focused on signs of disorder such as visible drug dealing, prostitution, graffiti and litter.

The current chapter deals with the NNAU's effects on residents' perceptions and subsequent drug dealing. (For a description of the program's impact on landlords, see Smith and Davis, this volume.) The first section provides an overview of the impact of drugs on communities, of citizen anti-drug initiatives and of drug abatement strategies across the U.S. The second section discusses the NNAU's history, structure and protocol for processing cases. The third section presents the results of our evaluation of the program, involving a survey of residents living on blocks with and without abatement actions and observations of targeted properties and blocks following abatement. The fourth section summarizes the major research findings and draws conclusions about the program's effectiveness.

BACKGROUND

The Impact of Drugs on Communities

Drug sales and the variety of crimes they spawn have affected every major American city. Drugs have had an especially devastating impact on poor communities, and are both a symptom of and a factor in the continued decline of those areas (Johnson et al., 1990). Considerable evidence points to the deterioration of the inner city. Since the 1970s, middle-class residents, businesses and jobs have been fleeing to the suburbs. Among other factors, this exodus has left the poor increasingly isolated and economically disenfranchised (Wilson, 1987). The spread of illicit drug trafficking has aggravated these conditions.

Drugs have contributed to the decline of inner city communities. Johnson et al. (1990) argues that drugs have created a criminal underclass heavily involved in drug distribution, sales and consumption. Members of this underclass often engage in violent and disruptive behaviors that have had a devastating impact on the poor. Scholars have compared the psychological effects of living in underclass neighborhoods to those of living in a war zone (Garbarino et al., 1991). In a 1988 national survey of poor households, 40% of the respondents identified illegal drugs and drug problems as the number one issue facing the nation (Lavrakas, 1988). Similarly, a national survey of law enforcement executives indicated that citizens in their jurisdiction considered drug trafficking the country's principal crime problem (Lavrakas and Rosenbaum, 1989).

Researchers have extensively documented the relationships among drugs, crime and neighborhood disintegration (Clayton, 1981; Gandossy et al., 1980; Inciardi, 1986). Citizens typically perceive visible drug sales and abuse as signs of social disorder and degeneration (Skogan, 1990). When residents become acutely aware of active drug dealers and prospering drug houses, they conclude that citizens and the police have lost control of the streets. Residents soon begin to view their community as an inadequate environment to raise children and establish businesses (Davis and Lurigio, 1996).

Community Initiatives Against Drugs

Criminal justice experts have suggested that perhaps the best hope for curtailing drugs in inner city neighborhoods lies with the cooperation and involvement of local residents (Heinzelmann, 1989; Lavrakas, 1985; Rosenbaum, 1988). Police departments have implemented numerous innovations, including drug hotlines, Crime Stoppers programs (Rosenbaum et al., 1989), and community policing strategies (Eck and Spelman, 1987; Rosenbaum, 1994; Sparrow et al., 1990). Furthermore, the federal government has investigated and promoted grassroots anti-drug projects. In short, law enforcement authorities are acknowledging that the police alone cannot carry out effective anti-drug efforts at the community level. Citizen involvement in the fight to rid neighborhoods of drugs is crucial.

Beginning in the mid-1980s, citizens joined ranks with law enforcement in anti-drug initiatives. Citizen programs to combat drugs have assumed a variety of forms, from visible street patrols to anonymous telephone hotlines. These programs have appeared in hundreds of communities and are endorsed by neighborhood residents. Citizens dissatisfied with governmental responses to the drug problem are now acting in creative ways to "take back the streets" from gangs and drug pushers, and to restore their neighborhoods to places where people can live and work without fear or disruption (Davis and Lurigio, 1996; Rosenbaum et al., 1991).

Drug house-specific municipal ordinances and novel applications of already-existing ordinances and state laws pertaining to "nuisance abatement" or "public safety" are among the newest and potentially most powerful weapons being developed to combat drugs in the private housing sector. Drug house laws vary in content and form (Finn and Hylton, 1994). For example, some involve civil remedies, others, criminal sanctions. Some may be brought by neighborhood residents, whereas others require the intervention of the police or district attorney. The laws are significant because they give property owners a strong incentive to prevent drug sales on their premises. They also afford some protection to property owners who might otherwise be subjected to intimidation or retaliation when they try to evict dealers. However, simply having these laws is not enough. In order for the laws to work, citizen cooperation is extremely important.

National Study of Drug-Abatement Programs

Drug dealers often operate from indoor locations. They may work out of their own homes or apartments; sometimes, they take over entire buildings. In other instances, they seize control over one of the many abandoned buildings in low-income, inner city neighborhoods. The locations frequently become the sites of both drug sales and use: Crack houses and shooting galleries are neighborhood locations where drugs can be bought and used on the premises.

People unfortunate enough to live near drug houses seldom have the luxury of simply escaping the problem. The best solution for most of them is to move to a similar neighborhood in another part of town that probably has the same drug and crime problems as the area they just left. However, in the late 1980s local law enforcement began to discover a promising strategy for getting rid of drug dealers (i.e., drug abatement programs), which involves better place management (Eck and Wartell, 1996). These programs may prove to be among the most effective tools that either police or citizens can use to combat neighborhood drug problems (Green, 1996).

Smith et al., (1992) conducted a national study of drug abatement programs. They investigated the effects of a variety of mechanisms to eliminate drug houses from neighborhoods. The study had three components: a survey of the nation's largest cities to examine existing efforts to eradicate drug houses; a legal analysis of drug house ordinances and laws, and the court challenges abatement efforts have faced; and an in-depth exploration of five drug abatement programs in Alexandria, VA; Milwaukee, WI; Toledo, OH, San Francisco, CA; and Houston, TX.

Smith et al. (1992) found that abatement actions had considerable exposure in their communities. Community awareness was highest in Houston and Toledo, where properties were often visibly closed as a result of abatement actions. It was lowest in Milwaukee, where abatement actions frequently consisted of just a private letter and a quiet eviction. Hence, abatement program methods clearly affected levels of community awareness.

Overall, residents in the sample neighborhoods strongly supported abatement efforts. Across the five cities, 93% of the respondents believed that the specific abatement actions taken in their neighborhoods were warranted and appropriate. Abatement actions were also related to a number of favorable changes in residents' perceptions of their neighborhoods. One in three respondents believed that the actions had reduced drug sales, while one in four believed that the actions had reduced drinking and the number of kids hanging out. The abatement actions had mixed effects on how respondents felt about their neighborhoods. In some instances, abatement actions alerted residents for the first time, to the serious drug problem in the neighborhood, leading them to report that they liked their neighborhoods less and that they were less safe since the abatement action.

PROGRAM HISTORY, STRUCTURE AND CASE PROCESSING

Street-level drug trafficking is an important element of Cook County's illicit drug economy. The strategic use of residential and commercial buildings for drug activities is a critical aspect of this economy. Drug houses have benefits over street-level dealing because they afford traffickers invisibility and other defenses to protect them from law enforcement. The number of such establishments is not precisely known; nonetheless, local law enforcement officials estimate that they are quite common in most areas of Cook County where drug sales and abuse are prevalent.

Program Origins

As shown in Table 1, arrests in drug houses have accounted for a significant percentage of drug arrests in Chicago. Prior to 1990, the Chicago Police Department and other law enforcement agencies in Cook County were primarily responsible for targeting drug houses. However, at that time no systematic or coordinated efforts addressed the problem at the county level. The police department's emphasis on drug house investigations was then sporadic: other drug crimes, other crimes in general and other policy matters were always competing for police resources. Furthermore, targeting drug houses and following through with subsequent arrests did not insure that these properties would remain free of drug activities; drug dealing could, and often did, resume in the property after the police presence diminished.

Table 1: Arrests in Drug Houses — Chicago, 1988-1990

Year	1988	1989	1990
Arrests in properties	5,672	5,704	4,202
Arrests in properties as % of total drug arrests	17%	16%	14%
TOTAL DRUG ARRESTS	33,068	35,662	31,080

Source: (1) Arrests in properties: personal communication from the CPD. (Figures do not represent official reports of that department); (2) Total drug arrests: CPD Annual Reports for 1988, 1989, and 1990.

In the late 1980s, not-for-profit community organizations in Chicago, and to a lesser extent in suburban Cook County, became aggressively involved in combating drug dealing. Drug houses created an eyesore in neighborhoods, threatened to depress property values, and were associated with increased levels of public nuisances (e.g., graffiti, "corner groups" of men and adolescents hanging out on the street) and serious crime. Community groups employed a variety of tactics to discourage drug dealing on these properties, both independent of and in collaboration with law enforcement agencies. The activism of some of these organizations was influential in the decision to initiate a CCSAO narcotics abatement project.

In late 1989 and early 1990, the CCSAO approached the Illinois Criminal Justice Information Authority (ICJIA) to request funds for implementing a pilot drug abatement unit in Cook County. In 1990, the CCSAO submitted a grant proposal to the ICJIA and funding was approved. The NNAU was established on August 1, 1990 and completed its first 15 months of operation on October 31, 1991. Funding of the initial 15 months of the project totaled approximately $900,000, including an ICJIA award of $650,000 and a one-fourth matching-funds allocation by the CCSAO. The ICJIA subsequently funded the program for a second (November 1, 1991 to October 31, 1992) and a third (November 1, 1992 to October 31, 1993) year. The program now operates with county and state funding.

Narcotics Nuisance Abatement Legislation

Statutory provisions for the abatement of drug houses existed prior to the NNAU's creation. In 1915, the state legislature adopted the Lewdness Public Nuisance Act, Chapter 100½, sec.1-13, Illinois Revised Statutes. Although this legislation did not specifically address drug houses, it provided the statutory impetus for civil and criminal abatement of public nuisances. In the amendments added to this statute in 1957, and in the enactment of the Illinois Criminal Code of 1961, Chapter 38, sec. 1, provisions for the abatement of drug houses were specifically mentioned for the first time in Illinois law. Subsequent amendments to these statutes and to the Cannabis Control Act, Chapter 56½, sec. 701-719 and the Controlled Substance Act, Chapter 56½, sec. 1100-1603, advanced the possibility of nuisance abatement as a means for reducing drug houses.

This early legislation neither conformed to current definitions and methods of abatement nor clearly provided for circumstances in which property owners had no knowledge of the nuisances. Hence, provisions in the earlier statutes existed only for voluntary owner abatements, subject to penalties if alleviation of the nuisance did not occur; but all of this was directed at property owners who knew of the nuisances. Furthermore, no clear provisions were available for forfeiture of properties gained through illicit drug and drug paraphernalia profits.

In 1982, the legislature adopted the Narcotics Forfeiture Act, Chapter 56½, sec. 1651-1660, which outlined forfeiture of real and other properties obtained from the receipts of illicit drug profits. The Drug Paraphernalia Act Chapter 56½, sec. 2101-2107 took effect in 1983 and applied forfeiture of illegal drug paraphernalia but not of real property. Amendments in 1990 and 1992 to Chapter 100½ provided greater statutory clarification for both the abatement of drug houses and the encouragement of voluntary abatement by property owners subject to civil prosecution. Also clarified was the definition of a drug house: any property where two arrests for illicit drug activity have occurred within a 12-month period. The elements of the 1990 and 1992 amendments were defined and implemented in large measure by Cook County State's Attorneys Cecil Partee and Jack O'Malley, with the assistance of administrators of the CCSAO's Narcotics Division.

Narcotics Nuisance Abatement Unit

The CCSAO specified for the county two general objectives of the NNAU: the eradication of drug houses, and the elimination of drug paraphernalia dealers. The NNAU executes up to four stages of activities to abate drug nuisances: identifying potential drug houses; investigating potential drug houses; abating drug houses; and monitoring abated properties.

Identification of Drug Houses

To identify potential drug houses, the unit receives referrals and complaints from a variety of outside sources and agencies, and also accesses internal information from the law enforcement community in the form of existing arrests. The NNAU then screens referrals to select appropriate cases for investigation. Program staff enter the selected cases into the NNAU database for case management and tracking.

The NNAU receives referrals from a variety of sources: law enforcement agencies, community organizations, citizens, federal and municipal government agencies, CCSAO assistant state's attorneys (ASAs) in charge of narcotics case preliminary hearings and other CCSAO units. Referrals and complaints of potential drug houses from citizens or community organizations are registered directly to the NNAU staff by telephone or letter. A publicized 24-hour telephone hotline is available for anonymous referrals. ASAs routinely scrutinize drug cases to identify those that should be referred to the NNAU.

Investigation of Drug Houses

Each case that the NNAU identifies for abatement is assigned to an ASA and an investigator. The team verifies the existence of a drug problem at the referred property, establishes the nature and extent of current and past drug problems at the property, and identifies the alleged offender(s) and the owner(s) or manager(s) of the property. The team uses several sources to retrieve this information, as the NNAU relies a great deal on the records and resources of other agencies. The Chicago Police Department's RAMIS computer system is an important investigative resource for the NNAU. RAMIS (Random Access Management Information System) is a computerized listing of all arrests and offenses occurring in Chicago, including arrestees' names, offense locations, dates and other descriptive information. The NNAU uses the RAMIS system to determine whether drug arrests have been made at properties alleged to be drug houses in Chicago, and, if so, to verify the number of arrests at the properties and the names of offenders who have been arrested for drug sales or use at those addresses.

The unit also: searches for potential abatement cases through direct contacts with local police officials; reviews records and documents of local housing and health departments, the Chicago Housing Court, and municipal corporate counsels; and interviews neighborhood residents and tenants of the targeted property. If the individual who made the complaint is known and available, he or she is then interviewed. The investigators then surveil the property to discern whether drug activity is occurring at the site. In addition, the NNAU unit scrutinizes the records of the county Recorder of Deeds, the Tax Assessor's Office and the Treasurer's Office to determine property ownership and management.

Abatement of Properties

The ASA assigned to the case and the NNAU's supervisor review the information obtained during the investigation of the targeted property. Together, they decide how to proceed with the case by considering the following guidelines: (1) If recent arrests for illicit drug activities have occurred on a property, the unit initiates proceedings by sending a letter to the property owner requesting that he or she voluntarily abate the problem. (2) If a past history of arrest(s) exists at the property, but two arrests have not occurred in the last 12 months and/or visible signs of current drug or other illegal activity in and around the property are apparent, the NNAU monitors the property. Under some circumstances, it informs the property owner of the monitoring. In addition, the unit informs relevant law enforcement officials about the complaint, and asks agencies having other means of investigatory authority (health and building code violations) to monitor and report drug activities on the property. (3) If visible signs of potential drug trafficking or other illegal activity are apparent in and around the property, but no current or past records of arrests exist, the unit initiates the above monitoring procedures. (4) If neither a history of drug arrests nor visible signs of drug activity are apparent at the property, the case remains open and the unit monitors it for a period of time. Furthermore, the unit retains records of the referral in the event that a subsequent complaint is made about the property.

In cases identified as drug houses, the unit tries to determine if the property owner is involved in the illicit drug activity, which could provide sufficient grounds for criminal prosecution. In those cases in which the owner is not believed to be a party to the drug activities, the unit initiates a formal process to encourage voluntary abatement of the problem. This encouragement is always backed up by the potential of a civil suit for non-compliance.

Post-Abatement Monitoring

The NNAU monitors abated properties to ascertain whether they remain free of illicit drug activities. The NNAU's post-abatement monitoring includes a periodic review of police arrest records, direct communications from police and community organizations, and periodic visits to abated properties. When the NNAU is advised by a landlord that a problem individual has been evicted, an investigator is dispatched after 180 days to verify that the individual in question is no longer on the premises. Because the program had only five investigators to cover the entire county, its use of the Chicago Police Department's RAMIS database was one of the most effective ways of becoming apprised of whether abated properties remained free of drug-selling activities. Although investigators may determine that a narcotics problem has been resolved, the property is still monitored to insure that the unit is aware of any reoccurrence of the previously existing nuisance.

Linkages with Outside Agencies

Linkages with local police officials, government agencies, community organizations, private citizens and, to a lesser extent, federal law enforcement agencies involved in drug control, are critical to the design and success of the NNAU. The NNAU is primarily a reactive unit and depends on these agencies and groups in two basic ways. First, the NNAU generally does not initiate the identification of drug houses. Instead, it relies on referrals from these other agencies and groups. Second, these agencies and groups are the primary sources of information the NNAU uses to investigate targeted units, decide on abatement proceedings and monitor abated properties. The NNAU also relies on the CCSAO's ongoing relationship with law enforcement agencies for assistance with drug house investigations, referrals of cases, follow-ups on NNAU referrals, and access to computer information and intelligence. These cooperative working relationships are mostly voluntary.

The NNAU has created similar linkages with other governmental agencies at the federal, county and municipal levels through formal communications and discussions with their respective administrators. Other agencies include the Chicago Health and Housing Departments, the Corporate Counsel of the City of Chicago, the Chicago Housing Court, the Cook County Recorder of Deeds, the Cook County Tax Assessor's Office, the Cook County Treasurer's Office, the Chicago Housing Authority, and similar departments in other municipalities. The nature of the NNAU's relationships with other agencies is determined by the needs and responsibilities of each.

The role of community organizations in advancing the unit's goals was designed to be twofold: the NNAU would enlist citizen support to mobilize the community regarding its concerns about drug houses and to encourage citizens to report suspected drug houses in their neighborhoods; and the NNAU would develop collaborative and supportive relationships with community groups to obtain useful investigative, prosecutorial and monitoring information in abatement cases. In addition, the NNAU would establish an Advisory Council consisting of ten local community organizations that would attend regular meetings with program staff.

Case Processing

To examine the processing of typical NNAU cases, we selected a random sample of 300 cases and documented the actions and dispositions noted in each of their files.

Types of Cases Targeted

The majority of NNAU cases originated from CCSAO drug prosecutions. A total of 58%, (n=165) of the cases we sampled out of NNAU files were from the CCSAO, 33% (n=95) resulted from referrals from the police and only 7% (n=20) from community groups or private citizens. The overwhelming majority of targeted properties were located in Chicago: 95% (n=284) of the cases involved properties within the city limits, compared with just 5% (n=15) from suburban communities. Within the city, the NNAU targeted properties over a wide range of police districts. The highest concentration of targeted properties occurred in the 11th district (11%, n=30), the 7th district (9% , n=24), and the 15th district (8%, n=23). Most of the NNAU targeted properties were apartments in multi-family buildings. Seven in 10 (n=195) cases sampled from NNAU files involved multiple family buildings, 20% (n=56), single-family homes, 7% (n=18), commercial properties, and 4%, (n=10) abandoned buildings.

Actions Taken by the NNAU and Property Owners

The most common action taken by the NNAU was to send a letter to the property owners advising them that a nuisance existed and warning them of the consequences if the situation was not corrected. Letters were sent in all but 14% (n=259) of the sampled cases. In 22% (n=63), multiple letters were sent. Telephone calls were made to the owners of targeted properties in 59% (n=176) of the cases. Slightly more than one-fifth (21%, n=64) of the owners received more than one call from program attorneys. Face-to-face meetings between program attorneys and owners was an infrequent NNAU action (4% of the sampled cases, n=12).

In 29% (n=87) of the cases, the owner responded to the NNAU's actions by evicting the problem tenants. In 20% (n=61) of the cases, the problem had been resolved prior to any action by the unit. In a small percentage of cases (n=5) the owner refused to cooperate with the NNAU. However, in more than one-third of cases (39%, n=116), no indication in the paper case file was given regarding the owner's action.

Case Outcomes

The first action the NNAU takes when a case is opened involves a visit to the property by an investigator. During the visit, the investigator gathers information on the owner's name and address, and attempts to verify that a current nuisance does, in fact, exist at the location. The initial investigation frequently finds that no current problem is apparent at the property. In one in five cases, the investigator's report stated that the problem had resolved itself. Most often, this happened because the individual causing the problem moved or was evicted prior to the investigator's arrival: Of the 61 sampled cases already resolved at the investigator's arrival, 58 were resolved because the tenant had moved, 2 because the building was vacant and boarded, and 1 because the building had burned. Cessation of the nuisance prior to the NNAU investigator's arrival was least likely in cases arising from citizen complaints. Just 8% (n=8) of cases stemming from citizen complaints had already been resolved, compared to 19% (n=18) of cases from the police and 22% (n=37) of cases from CCSAO drug prosecutions. Instances in which problems already had been resolved prior to the NNAU's involvement still resulted in the opening of a case file; these cases were maintained as active, allowing the NNAU to monitor the situation for future drug-related developments.

According to the NNAU's computer database, 32% (n=95) of the 300 cases in our sample resulted in abatements, with no new drug activity being reported at the location. More than 60% (64%, n=192) were listed as pending or continuing under investigation, and 3% (n=9) were catalogued as experiencing continuing or renewed drug sales. These case outcome statistics are questionable for two reasons. First, they include, as abated, the 61 cases in which NNAU investigators reported the drug problem was already resolved prior to the program's involvement. If these cases are removed from the "abatement" category, the percentage of abated cases in our sample is reduced by more than half, from 32 to 14% (n=34 out of 239 cases). Second, the NNAU's standard operating procedure is to request from the police a list of any new arrests at targeted locations 60 days after a case is opened. However, no indication was given in the file that a follow-up check was requested in 56% (n=165) of the cases. Further, in another 13% (n=39) of cases no follow-up police information could be located in the file, although it apparently had been requested. Thus, it appears from the paper files that the NNAU could not have known of any continuing or renewed drug activity in nearly 7 out of 10 sampled cases.[1]

PROGRAM IMPACT ON RESIDENTS AND NEIGHBORHOODS

Resident Survey

The NNAU targets properties throughout the Chicago metropolitan area. Therefore, we could not assess program impact by simply comparing data from neighborhoods served by the program with data from neighborhoods not served by the program. Instead, we examined the perceptions of residents living near properties that were the targets of abatement efforts. We asked residents on blocks where abatements had occurred to report changes in levels of crime, drugs and other signs of social and physical disorder since an abatement action had taken place on their blocks. In addition, we selected a comparison sample of residents from blocks where no abatements had occurred. The comparison blocks were located nearby and were similar to targeted blocks in appearance and demographics.

Methodology

From the original 300-case sample drawn from NNAU files, we randomly sampled 10% (n=30) of the cases to examine the impact of the program on neighborhood residents' perceptions of crime, drugs and disorder. These 30 target locations were matched with 30 nearby blocks where the NNAU had not targeted properties. The comparison blocks were chosen through visual inspection by research staff, who used selection criteria such as proximity to the targeted block, housing stock and demographics. The comparison blocks were used to determine whether residents' perceptions improved as a result of the NNAU's actions. Using this design, we hoped to eliminate plausible rival explanations of program effects, including the possibility that residents' perceptions of drugs, crime and disorder were generally improving in Cook County during the time of these abatement efforts.

For each of the 30 targeted and 30 comparison blocks chosen, we defined the sample area as both sides of the street on each block. Within each of the 60 sample areas, we attempted telephone interviews with an average of ten residents. Northwestern University's Survey Laboratory

(NUSL) conducted the interviews. The NUSL used a Coles directory (i.e., reverse telephone directory) to identify residents within the 60 predefined areas. Different sample areas yielded varying numbers of residential units ranging from a low of 1 to a high of 31. In all, 1,061 potential households were identified. NUSL staff attempted to interview, by phone, one member of each household 18 years of age or older who had been living in their present neighborhood for a minimum of one year.

Interviews were successfully completed with 614 respondents for an overall completion rate of 79% and a response rate of 95% (see Table 2). The number of interviews completed in each sampling area ranged from 0 to 22. However, the majority of sampling areas (80%) had between 5 and 15 completions. Interviews were evenly divided between targeted areas (n=307) and comparison areas (n=308).

Table 2: Resident Household Sampling Pool Disposition

	Frequency	Percentage
Completed interview	614	58
Ineligible	124	11
No contact/respondent never available	139	12
Non-working/unlisted number	123	12
Refusal	34	3
Non-English, non-Spanish speaking respondent	15	1
Physical/mental disability	12	1
Non-residential number	6	<1
Miscellaneous	4	<1
TOTAL	1,061	100

The interview schedule was adapted from the one used by Smith et al. (1992). Residents in targeted and comparison areas were asked about their knowledge of the NNAU, their use of the NNAU hotline and their participation in community meetings. The interview also queried respondents about current and past levels of drug activity, other signs of social and physical disorder (e.g., crime, kids hanging out, public drinking, graffiti, litter, etc.), and their perceptions of safety on their blocks.

Table 3: Description of Respondents

	Frequency	Percentage
Years Living in Neighborhood		
3 or less years	154	25
4-10	159	26
11-20	162	27
21 or more	135	22
N=610		
Respondent Age		
18-30	83	14
31-40	115	20
41-60	236	41
61 and over	148	25
N=582		
Race/Ethnicity		
African American	430	71
White	113	19
Hispanic	37	6
Other	24	4
N=604		
Education		
Less than high school	157	26
High school graduate	186	31
Some college	138	23
College graduate or more	122	20
N=603		
Income		
Under $10,000	159	30
$10,000-19,999	137	26
$20,000-40,000	143	27
Over $40,000	86	17
N=525		

Note: Does not include "don't know" responses or refusals.

Description of Respondents

The neighborhoods sampled for this study were relatively stable. The average respondent had lived in his or her neighborhood for about ten years (see Table 3); less than one in four (n=154) had resided in their home for three years or less.[2] The average age of the respondents was 43. Only 14% (n=83) of the sample was 30 years of age or under, while 25% (n=148) was over age 60. A large majority of the sample (71%, n=430) was African American, 19% (n=113) were white (not of Hispanic origin) and just 6% (n=37) were Hispanic. Nearly three in four respondents (n=446) were high school graduates, and 43% (n=260) had completed some college. However, three in ten respondents (30%, n=159) reported earning less than $10,000 per year, and just 17% (n=86) had earned in excess of $40,000 per year.

Resident Knowledge of and Participation in the NNAU

We asked residents a series of questions to explore the depth of NNAU program efforts. Respondents were asked whether they knew of the nuisance abatement program, and whether they had participated in the unit's efforts by calling the state's attorney's hotline or by attending NNAU-sponsored meetings. More than one-quarter of respondents (28%) had heard of the program. By far, the most common source of their knowledge about the NNAU was the media (49%, n=85), followed by community and church organizations (16%, n=27) and neighbors (15%, n=25). Only 4% (n=7) of those who knew of the NNAU had heard about the program through the police.

Although a relatively large number of respondents (n=173) knew about the NNAU, many were very confused about what it actually did. Less than 7% (n=8) of interviewees aware of the program knew that it dealt with the abatement of drug activity, the eviction of drug dealers and the closure of problem buildings due to drug-related activities. Nearly three out of four (n=113) respondents who had heard of the NNAU knew nothing at all about its purpose or believed that it had to do with getting more police on the street.

A surprisingly high proportion of respondents overall (42%, n=258) were aware that the state's attorney's office had a drug hotline; the hotline seemed to be more successfully publicized than the unit itself. However, very few residents (about 3%, n=20) reported that they had called the hotline. A more common form of anti-drug activism involved attending anti-drug meetings: one in four subjects in our sample had done so at least once.

We expected some differences between targeted and comparison blocks with respect to their participation in anti-drug activities. However, our expectation was not confirmed. Targeted and comparison blocks were statistically indistinguishable in terms of having heard of the NNAU (30%, n=91 vs. 27%, n=86); knowing of the state's attorney's drug hotline (42%, n=129 vs. 42%, n=129); calling the hotline (4%, n=12 vs. 3%, n=8); and attending anti-drug meetings (27%, n=83 vs. 23%, n=72).

Perceptions of Drugs and Disorder

We asked respondents a series of questions about levels of drug dealing and other signs of disorder in their neighborhoods. Data showed that 37% (n=224) were not sure if any drug sellers were operating on their block, while 39% (n=237) were sure that no sales were occurring on their block. One-fourth (n=153) of those queried knew for sure that drug dealers were active on their block. Because all of the targeted blocks had at least some drug dealing during the past year, and most likely some portion of the comparison blocks also did, these findings suggest that residents were often not aware of drug activity in their neighborhood. Nearly nine in ten residents (87%, n=138) who were aware of drug sales said that they had found out through personal observation. The fact that only a quarter of the sample was definitely aware of drug dealing on their block indicates that it is unlikely that the NNAU's activity would affect residents' perceptions of drugs on blocks where houses had been targeted. However, it is still possible that the program would have an effect on residents' perceptions of signs of disorder (e.g., graffiti, kids hanging out, etc.) associated with drugs without their being aware of the drug activity *per se.*

Table 4 compares changes in residents' perceptions of conditions on their blocks during the past year — the time period during which the NNAU had taken action against properties in our sample. A slight difference was found between targeted and comparison blocks in the proportion of respondents who believed that drug activity had decreased over time: 27% (n=81) of residents on targeted blocks reported a decrease, compared with 22% (n=69) on comparison blocks. However, an even larger proportion of residents reported *increases* in drug activity on both targeted (35%, n=108) and comparison blocks (37%, n=113). Perceptions of gang activity were also similar on targeted and comparison blocks. On targeted blocks, 24% (n=74) of respondents perceived a decrease over time, compared with 22% (n=68) on comparison blocks. Again, a larger number of people perceived *increases* — about 30% each on targeted (n=90) and comparison blocks (n=91). A similar pattern emerged for perceptions of kids hanging out on the block. On targeted blocks, 35% (n=106) of respondents perceived decreases whereas 34% (n=104) perceived increases. On comparison blocks, the results were 27% (n=84) and 32% (n=98), respectively.

Table 4: Residents' Perceptions of Drugs and Disorder — Comparisons Between Blocks With and Without Properties Targeted by the NNAU

	More		No Change		Less		Tau's C
Drug Dealing and Using							
Targeted	35%	(n=108)	38%	(n=117)	27%	(n=81)	-.04
Non-targeted	37%	(n=113)	41%	(n=126)	22%	(n=69)	
Gang Activity							
Targeted	30%	(n=90)	47%	(n=143)	24%	(n=74)	-.02
Non-targeted	30%	(n=91)	48%	(n=149)	22%	(n=68)	
Kids Hanging Out							
Targeted	34%	(n=104)	32%	(n=97)	35%	(n=106)	-.03
Non-targeted	32%	(n=98)	41%	(n=126)	27%	(n=84)	
Street Robberies							
Targeted	16%	(n=50)	63%	(n=192)	21%	(n=65)	.00
Non-targeted	16%	(n=50)	63%	(n=194)	21%	(n=64)	
Home Burglaries							
Targeted	13%	(n=40)	62%	(n=191)	25%	(n=76)	-.04
Non-targeted	16%	(n=50)	60%	(n=186)	23%	(n=72)	
Vandalism or Graffiti							
Targeted	19%	(n=59)	50%	(n=153)	31%	(n=95)	-.05
Non-targeted	21%	(n=65)	52%	(n=161)	27%	(n=82)	
Public Drinking							
Targeted	20%	(n=62)	54%	(n=166)	26%	(n=79)	-.01
Non-targeted	20%	(n=62)	56%	(n=172)	24%	(n=74)	
Victimization Odds							
Targeted	36%	(n=111)	37%	(n=114)	27%	(n=81)	.01
Non-targeted	37%	(n=114)	34%	(n=104)	29%	(n=90)	
Safety on Block							
Targeted	28%	(n=86)	32%	(n=98)	40%	(n=123)	.05
Non-targeted	19%	(n=59)	42%	(n=128)	39%	(n=121)	

Note: Tau's C is a measure of association used for categorical variables. Its values range from 0 to ±1 with larger values indicating stronger relationships.

Perceptions of crime — both robbery and burglary — did show reductions over time but the reductions were virtually identical on targeted and comparison blocks. On targeted blocks, 21% (n=65) of the respondents noted a decline in robberies and 25% (n=76) noted a decline in burglaries; 16% (n=50) perceived an increase in robberies and 13% (n=40) in burglaries. On comparison blocks, 21% (n=64) believed that robberies had decreased and 23% (n=72) believed that burglaries had decreased; 16% (n=50) thought that robberies had increased and the same proportion thought that burglaries had gone up.

The same pattern of data appeared with regard to other forms of disorder. On targeted blocks, we found a net decline (calculated by the percentage of respondents who thought the problem had decreased minus those who thought it had increased) of 12% (n=16) in perceptions of graffiti and 6% (n=17) in public drinking. On comparison blocks, the net declines were 6% for graffiti (n=17) and 4% for public drinking (n=12).

We asked respondents about changes in feelings of safety over time. No significant differences emerged between targeted and comparison blocks; and on both types of blocks, beliefs in the likelihood of victimization increased over time. Among persons who lived on blocks with a targeted property, 36% (n=111) reported that the chances of becoming a victim were greater now than one year ago, while 27% (n=81) reported that their chances now were less. Among respondents on comparison blocks, 37% (n=114) believed victimization to be more likely currently, while 29% (n=90) believed their chances now were less. The same pattern was evident in response to an additional question about safety — 28% (n=86) of residents on targeted blocks reported feeling more safe than in the past, while 40% (n=123) reported feeling less safe. On comparison blocks, 19% (n=59) reported feeling safer and 39% (n=121) less safe.

A significant difference did appear between targeted and comparison blocks on a question asking whether the respondent knew if anyone on the block had been evicted: 18% (n=56) of respondents on targeted blocks knew of an eviction, compared with only 9% (n=26) of those on comparison blocks. Finally, we were interested in knowing whether the NNAU's abatement actions resulted in buildings being boarded-up and remaining vacant. Responses were virtually identical on targeted and comparison blocks: 16% (n=50) of residents who lived on targeted blocks reported boarded-up buildings on their block compared with 14% (n=44) of those on comparison blocks.

Qualitative Neighborhood Study

A specific objective of the NNAU is to reduce the likelihood that drug dealing will resume in abated properties, and to identify properties for further abatement action if drug selling continues. The NNAU attempts to achieve this objective through the monitoring of abated properties. A larger objective of the program is to improve the quality of life for citizens by eliminating residential drug selling, which may reduce other signs of incivility and crime that are often associated with drug dealing. Although we obtained information on NNAU's impact from surveys of neighborhood residents and property owners, we believed that it was important to study neighborhood effects directly by visiting and observing a small sample of abated properties. Hence, to evaluate the NNAU's impact on illicit drug activity and other indicators of physical and social disorder within targeted neighborhoods, we examined ten abated properties and their corresponding neighborhoods over a period of four months. Two experienced ethnographers conducted and coordinated this component of our evaluation. Observations at these sites generated data on the post-abatement quality of life on residential blocks.

Methodology

We randomly selected a sample of ten abated properties from the 30 properties originally selected for the resident survey. Table 5 summarizes the abated properties and their neighborhood characteristics. Four to six visits were made to each property at different times of the day and on different days of the week between February 1993 and May 1993. Observations were made with regard to the physical appearance and maintenance of the sites, signs of drug dealing, presence of gangs and the character of social life at each of the abated properties and its block. The population and income status characteristics of each site block were also noted.

Physical Description of Targeted Structures and Blocks

Five of the abated properties were two or three flat buildings, two were multiple-unit apartment buildings and three were single-family residential structures. All were located on residential blocks. Although the Washington property — a large multiple unit apartment building — was located in a residential block, this street was a busy thoroughfare with a bus route and heavy traffic. Many of the other target blocks were crossed at one end by moderate to very busy commercial streets. Five of the blocks were in African-American neighborhoods (Ada, Lockwood, Ohio, Washington and Winchester), three were in Puerto Rican neighborhoods (Campbell, Rockwell and Sawyer), and two were in predomi-

Table 5: Target Blocks in Qualitative Study of Nuisance Abatement

Block Location	Police District	Chicago Location	Quality of Life, Race and SES	Case Opened	Factors
Ada	7	Southside	Black/Poverty & Low Income	3/24/92	Drug Dealing Graffiti
Winchester	7	Southside	Black/Poverty & Low Income	3/11/92	Drug Dealing Graffiti
Rockwell	13	Near NW Side	Puerto Rican/Poverty & Low Income	11/18/92	Gangs & Graffiti
Sawyer	14	Northwest Side	Working Class/ Puerto Rican	3/16/92	Gang Graffiti
Campbell	14	Near NW Side	Puerto Rican/Poverty & Low Income	4/14/92	Gangs & Graffiti
Ohio	15	Far West Side	Black/Low Income	3/12/92	Gangs
Washington	15	Far West Side	Black/Low Income & Working Class	11/1/91	Gang Graffiti
Lockwood	15	Far West Side	Black/Working & Middle Class	4/16/91	Gang Graffiti
Knox	17	Northwest Side	White/Middle Class	4/18/91	Quiet, But Some Graffiti
Springfield	17	Northwest Side	White/Middle Class	3/5/92	Quiet, But Some Graffiti

nantly white neighborhoods (Springfield and Knox). The Ada, Campbell, Rockwell and Winchester blocks were in low-income, declining neighborhoods. Physical structures were in poor-to-fair condition, and population density was high. The Sawyer location was primarily low-income but had undergone some physical improvements through gentrification. Signs of efforts to reverse decline in the neighborhood were apparent, such as external rehabilitation of several buildings in the Washington block. Still, this location had the potential for rapid decline because of the high concentration of large multiple-unit apartment buildings, the high density of very low-income and working-class residents, and the extensive decline in surrounding blocks. The Knox, Lockwood, Ohio and

Springfield locations appeared to be economically stable, working or middle class neighborhoods.

Drug Activity

Drug dealing was obvious during the first two visits at the two southside locations (Ada and Winchester). The drug dealing was organized and included lookouts and curbside, drive-up service. On the third visit, drug dealing was no longer apparent at the Ada location but remained at Winchester. Winchester had several residences that appeared to be hangouts for "gangbangers" and locations for drug dealing. Furthermore, in relation to neighboring blocks, this one was perhaps the most blighted, having the greatest number of physical and social incivilities. On the final visits, signs of drug dealing were still absent at the Ada location though it was not clear whether they were apparent at the Winchester location.

No visible signs of drug dealing were observed at any of the other sites observed on the first or subsequent visits. At several sites (Campbell, Lockwood, Ohio, Rockwell and Washington), youths and young adults were congregating at various locations on the blocks but their activities did not obviously involve the selling or exchange of drugs. The Knox, Springfield and Sawyer blocks were usually quiet with few people on the street.

Overall Climate of Targeted Neighborhoods

Five of the abated structures and surrounding blocks were quiet and orderly in terms of social activities during most or all of our observations. The Knox, Lockwood, Springfield and Sawyer blocks were very quiet, with little street activity beyond the ordinary comings and goings of residents. Although signs of drug dealing were apparent during the first visit to Ada, it was quiet and peaceful on subsequent visits. A sign in the Ada neighborhood was posted that warned against public drinking, drug dealing and rowdiness, which suggests that the neighborhood was at least somewhat organized in fighting for control of the block. How successful this neighborhood will be is unclear, as the Ada block was embedded in a community with high levels of drug dealing and gang activity; drug dealing was also apparent on neighboring blocks.

On the Campbell, Rockwell, Ohio and Winchester blocks a number of social incivilities were noted during some of the observations. On the Campbell, Rockwell and Ohio blocks, groups of youths and young adults were congregating or otherwise occupying the streets and were involved in verbal banter, jousting and drinking (Ohio). On Winchester, in addition to drug dealing, the youths were particularly rowdy and threatening. Some adults appeared to go out of their way to avoid these young people. In addition, adults on Rockwell and Campbell seemed to be wary of youths.

Signs of moderate-to-high levels of gang activity in most neighborhoods were evidenced by graffiti and/or youths wearing gang colors (i.e., Kings on Campbell and Rockwell, Vice Lords on Ohio, and Black P Stone nation on Winchester). Graffiti evidence of gangs was also visible in most of the other communities — Knox, Springfield, Sawyer and Ada.

Comparison of Observations to Residents' Perceptions

We compared our observations about the impact of drug house abatement on these blocks with the perceptions of residents, which were recorded in our resident survey. Table 6 shows the percentages of surveyed residents living on each of the observed blocks who felt that, since the targeted property on the block had been abated, a reduction had occurred in each of the following: people hanging out; gang activity; drug use and drug dealing; number of drug dealers; and burglary and robbery. Also shown are the percentages of surveyed residents on each block who felt more safe and who felt that the likelihood of being a crime victim had decreased over time or did not exist. Resident opinions are reported for only nine of the ten blocks in which observations were conducted, because no surveys were obtained from residents of the Lockwood block.

Table 6 also shows the rankings assigned to each of these blocks based on our observations about drugs and other problems. The Ada and Winchester blocks are ranked "1," indicating that they exhibited the most problems in terms of drug trafficking, gang activity and signs of other social problems. The Knox, Lockwood and Springfield blocks are ranked "5," indicating they exhibited the fewest visible problems overall. Rankings of 2, 3 and 4 are reported for the other blocks.

Among blocks we rated as having the greatest number of problems (blocks ranked 1 and 2), compared with blocks we judged as having fewer overall problems, surveyed residents were slightly more likely to report reductions in people hanging out but less likely to report reductions in gang activity, drug use and dealing, and the presence of drug dealers. On the other hand, for blocks we judged as having the most problems, larger percentages of residents reported reductions in burglaries and robberies and feeling safer with respect to criminal victimization.

Table 6: Percentage of Residents Reporting Improvements and Ethnographic Ranking for 10 Abatement Blocks[a]

Street	HNG OUT Less & None	GNG ACT Less & None	DRG SAFE More	DRG VCTM Less	DL/USE Less & None	DLERS None	CRME Less & None	Rank
Rockwell (n=5)	100%	80%	60%	20%	60%	40%	80%	2
Sawyer (n=7)	43	61	29	43	57	57	57	4
Knox (n=6)	33	17	33	0	67	83	17	5
Campbell (n=8)	63	38	38	38	63	75	63	2
Springfield (n=14)	21	21	36	14	21	36	50	5
Ohio (n=10)	60	40	50	50	60	60	40	3
Winchester (n=6)	33	17	50	17	33	33	67	1
Washington (n=8)	50	50	25	38	50	50	63	4
Ada (n=7)	0	14	14	43	0	14	43	1
Lockwood (n=0)	--	--	--	--	--	--	--	4
TOTAL (N=71)	42	37	37	30	44	49	52	

[a]Resident survey responses in ethnographic study neighborhoods. No respondents in Lockwood block.

HNGOUT--percentage reporting no hanging out on block or less than before abatement.

GNGACT--percentage reporting no gang activity on block or less than before abatement.

SAFE--percentage reporting feeling safer than before abatement.

VCTM--percentage reporting less likely to be crime victim on block than before abatement.

DRG DL/USE--percentage reporting no drug use and dealing on block or less than before abatement.

DRG DLERS--percentage reporting no drug dealer on block after abatement.

CRME--percentage reporting no crime on block or less than before abatement.

RANK--estimate problem rank on block based on ethnographic observation.

"1" blocks with greatest problems; "5" blocks with fewest problems.

211

Caution must be used when interpreting these results because our rankings were based on impressionistic observations; furthermore, the number of surveyed residents, when broken down by block, is very small (5 to 14). Notwithstanding these caveats, slight (people hanging out) to modest (drug use and dealing) agreement emerged between our ranking of drug and gang problems and residents' opinions about the impact of drug house abatement on these blocks. The fact that residents of blocks with the most problems were more likely to report reductions in crime and to feel safer seems inconsistent with the serious extent of the apparent signs of drug, gang and crime problems in their neighborhoods. However, in these neighborhoods, the smaller impact of drug house intervention on overall neighborhood problems may have a larger perceived effect on safety and crime reduction than occurs on blocks that initially experienced fewer overall problems with drugs and gangs. The difference is not that drug house abatement matters less in socially better-off communities; it may be that perceptions of the impact of drug house abatement differ in degree because of differences in the pre-existing scope of drugs and other social problems in these neighborhoods.

Displacement of Drug Sales

The Smith et al. (1992) study of abatement programs strongly indicates that these efforts are effective, at a very modest cost, in getting rid of drug nuisances from particular locations. But are the drug dealers' activities stopped or slowed as a result of the abatement? Or, do they just set up shop in a nearby location and continue doing business as usual? One Milwaukee, WI criminal attorney likened abatement programs to "scattering rats in a woodpile." He argued that it was better for authorities to keep drug dealers stable and concentrated in particular blocks where they could readily be monitored. Abatement programs ultimately made the job of the police harder because the evicted dealers were dispersed over broad areas of a city.

The question of what evicted drug sellers do when they relocate is the single most important question about abatement programs. Is the Milwaukee attorney's theory correct (i.e., do evicted dealers continue selling as before but from a new place)? Or does the abatement reduce their sales by making them more circumspect or by separating them temporarily or permanently from their customer base?

We attempted to address this question in our evaluation. Using the sample of 300 cases drawn from NNAU files, we selected a subsample of cases in which an eviction had occurred. We tracked evicted dealers through the Cook County Adult Probation Department because probation records contained current addresses on offenders. Hence, our subsample was further limited to those individuals currently or formerly on probation whose criminal identification number was available in the NNAU's files (so that we could access their criminal histories through the city and state bureaus of identification).

The size of the subsample of cases meeting these multiple criteria was small, and it was made smaller still by the fact that some of the "evictees" were presently living at the same addresses according to the probation department records. (We did not know if the evictions simply never took place or if the probation department's addresses were out-of-date.) Of the 300 cases in the overall sample, 13 met all of our criteria.

We asked the police to run a check of arrests at the 13 addresses where the sellers had moved. According to the RAMIS computer database, no arrests had been made at any of the 13 addresses since the time that the sellers had moved there. We also went to four of the locations, accompanied by a NNAU investigator. At two, neighbors' reports clearly indicated that drug sales were taking place at the locations in question. At one address, neighbors' reports clearly indicated that no selling was taking place. At the fourth location, we were uncertain from our conversations with neighbors whether selling was occurring.

SUMMARY AND CONCLUSIONS

More residents were aware of evictions on blocks where the NNAU had targeted a property for abatement than on comparison blocks. But no evidence was found suggesting that the evictions had any impact on perceptions of drug activity, other signs of disorder or feelings of safety on the block. Although at first glance these findings are not very positive, they need to be understood in a larger context. The Smith et al. (1992) study found that abatement programs similar to the NNAU, which work by sending letters to landlords and launching quiet evictions, had less impact on residents' perceptions than more visible programs. Specifically, programs that closed problem buildings immediately with a large and public display of force, often accompanied by the press, had the greatest effect on perceptions of drugs and disorder. However, these highly visible programs were able to target only a handful of properties per year, not the hundreds that the NNAU targeted. Also, it is probable that NNAU-targeted properties were on blocks that had the most serious drug problems. On blocks with multiple sellers, the closing of one sales location is more likely to go relatively unnoticed by neighbors. Nonetheless, recognition of the state's attorney's drug hotline was quite high among the residents surveyed. This recognition gives the program a solid base to work from in soliciting community support.

No signs of drug dealing were visible at eight of the ten abated buildings or on the blocks on which they were located. Indications of drug dealing were apparent at the Ada location during the initial observation, but these were not obvious by the end of the observation period. Drug dealing was consistently observed during all but the last observations on Winchester. Although drug dealing was not observed at eight locations, three had significant numbers of gang youths, and a general atmosphere of neighborhood uneasiness and anxiousness surrounded these youths. In addition, these same three blocks were in a state of physical decline and disrepair, which added to the climate of apprehension.

The elimination of drug houses in five locations did appear to contribute to the preservation of quiet and orderly environments. In three other locations, abatement had eliminated, displaced or driven drug dealing underground. Because we had no pre-abatement data, we do not know precisely if the nuisance abatements have had any effects on the gang activity and other social disorders prominent in these neighborhoods. However, residents of these blocks also reported reductions of varying degrees in such problems after the abatements.

Drug house abatement on Ada had not completely eliminated the problem, as drug dealing continued sporadically. Nonetheless, observations suggested that this block may have been able to sustain some control over the problem through citizen action. Abatement had not reduced drug dealing at the Winchester location, a multiple-apartment-unit block where drug dealing, gang activity and possibly other unconventional activities were prevalent. Other interventions, in addition to nuisance abatement, were apparently needed at this location. Although drug activity was not visibly obvious, highly visible gang activity and the general climates of these blocks left the impression that drug dealing and use were probably in close proximity to each other.

Based on these limited observations, drug house abatement appears to be most effective in otherwise stable or slowly declining communities, and to facilitate a degree of order in these communities when citizens actively participate in problem control. In the most drug-plagued neighborhoods, drug house abatement has the capability of improving residents' perceptions of change. However, without community mobilization and sustained, official drug intervention, residents' perceptions of positive change may be short-lived.

Our findings indicated that continued drug activity by evicted sellers is not universal, although clearly some individuals continue to sell.

Abatement, in some cases at least, may slow drug sales by targeted individuals or even stop it altogether. Because of the small sample, our conclusions are tentative. More research with larger numbers of cases is needed to quantify the deterrent effects of abatement programs.

Address correspondence to: Arthur J. Lurigio, Department of Criminal Justice, Loyola University Chicago, 820 N. Michigan Ave., Chicago, IL 60611.

Acknowledgments: This project was supported by grant no. 90-DB-CX-0017 from the Bureau of Justice Assistance. Points of view or opinions contained within this document are those of the author and do not necessarily represent the official position or policies of the U.S. Department of Justice.

REFERENCES

Clayton, R.R. (1981). "Federal Drugs-Crime Research: Setting the Agenda." In: J. Inciardi (ed.), *The Drugs-Crime Connection.* Newbury Park, CA: Sage.

Davis, R.C. and A.J. Lurigio (1996). *Fighting Back: Neighborhood Antidrug Strategies.* Thousand Oaks, CA: Sage.

Eck, J.E. and W. Spelman (1987). *Problem Solving: Problem-Oriented Policing in Newport News.* Washington, DC: Police Executive Research Forum.

Eck, J.E. and J. Wartell (1996). *Reducing Crime and Drug Dealing by Improving Place Management: A Randomized Experiment.* Washington, DC: U.S. Department of Justice.

Finn, P. and M. Hylton (1994). *Using Civil Remedies for Criminal Behavior: Rationale, Case Studies, and Constitutional Issues.* Washington, DC: U.S. Department of Justice.

Gandossy, R.P., J.R. Williams, J. Cohen and H. J. Harwood (1980). *Drugs and Crime: A Survey and Analysis of the Literature.* Washington, DC: U.S. National Institute of Justice.

Garbarino, J., K. Kostenly and N. Dubrow (1991). *No Place to Be a Child: Growing Up in a War Zone.* Lexington, MA: Lexington Books.

Green, L. (1996). *Policing Places with Drug Problems.* Thousand Oaks, CA: Sage.

Heinzelmann, F. (1989). "The Federal Role in Supporting Research and Demonstration Efforts in Crime Prevention and Control." Paper presented at the Annual Meeting of the Academy of Criminal Justice Sciences, Washington, DC.

Inciardi, J. (1986). *The War on Drugs: Heroin, Cocaine, Crime, and Public Policy.* Palo Alto, CA: Mayfield.

Johnson, B.D., T. Williams, K.A. Dei and H. Sanabria (1990). "Drug Abuse in the Inner City: Impact on Hard-Drug Users and the Community." In: M. Tonry and J. Q. Wilson (eds.), *Drugs and Crime.* Chicago: University of Chicago Press.

Lavrakas, P.J. (1985). "Citizen Self-Help and Neighborhood Crime Prevention Policy." In: L. A. Curtis (ed.), *American Violence and Public Policy.* New Haven, CT: Yale University Press.

—— (1988). *Richard Clark and Associates 1988 Survey of Black Americans.* Evanston, IL: Northwestern University Survey Laboratory.

—— and D. P. Rosenbaum (1989). *Crime Prevention Beliefs, Policies, and Practices of Chief Law Enforcement Executives: Results of a National Survey.* Evanston, IL: Northwestern University Survey Laboratory.

Lurigio, A.J., R.C. Davis, T.A. Regulus, V.E. Gwiasda, S.J. Popkin, M.L. Dantzker, B.E. Smith and L. Ovellet (1993). *An Evaluation of the Cook County State's Attorney's Office Narcotics Nuisance Abatement Unit.* Chicago: Illinois Criminal Justice Information Authority.

Rosenbaum, D.P. (1988). "Community Crime Prevention: A Review and Synthesis of the Literature." *Justice Quarterly* 5:323-395.

—— (ed.). (1994). *The Challenge of Community Policing: Testing the Promises.* Thousand Oaks, CA: Sage.

—— S. Bennett, B. Lindsay, B. Davis, C. Taranowski and P.J. Lavrakas (1991). *Community Responses to the Drug Abuse National Demonstration Program: A Formative and Process Evaluation.* Final report to the U.S. National Institute of Justice. Washington, DC.

—— A.J. Lurigio and P.J. Lavrakas (1989). "Enhancing Citizen Participation and Solving Serious Crime: A National Evaluation of Crime Stoppers Programs." *Crime & Delinquency* 35:401-420.

Skogan, W.G. (1990). *Disorder and Decline.* New York, NY: Free Press.

Smith, B.E., S.W. Hillenbrand, R.C. Davis and S.R. Goretsky (1992). *Ridding Neighborhoods of Drug Houses in the Private Sector.* Washington, DC: American Bar Association.

Sparrow, M.K., M.H. Moore and D.M. Kennedy (1990). *Beyond 911*. New York, NY: Basic Books.

Wilson, J.W. (1987). *The Truly Disadvantaged*. Chicago: University of Chicago Press.

NOTES

1. Our interpretation of case outcomes was based primarily on an analysis of information contained in paper files. Hence, the discrepancy between computer-based and case file statistics, and the absence of follow-up statistics in the case files, may not necessarily demonstrate a problem in program operations or practices. Instead, it may indicate a failure to cross-reference between computer and case files.

2. A total of 124 respondents (12% of the initial sample) were determined to be ineligible for this study because they had not lived in their present neighborhood for a minimum of one year. If we included these respondents in our analysis, the character of the neighborhoods may have appeared to be less stable.

THE COST-EFFECTIVENESS OF CIVIL REMEDIES: THE CASE OF DRUG CONTROL INTERVENTIONS

by

Jonathan P. Caulkins

Carnegie Mellon University
and
Drug Policy Research Center, RAND

Abstract: *Civil remedies allow an individual to coerce a third party into taking action against offenders who are imposing hardship on the individual initiating the remedy. Thus, there is a disjunction between the individual who initiates and benefits from a civil remedy and the entity that bears most of the cost of implementing the remedy. At their best, civil remedies can make negligent organizations responsive to the needs of the citizenry. At their worst, civil remedies allow individuals to hijack the resources of well-run and well-meaning organizations and force those resources to be used for private but not necessarily public benefit. This paper discusses the cost-effectiveness of civil remedies for drug control interventions. Given the paucity of evaluation data, it is not possible to provide a point estimate as to their average cost-effectiveness. However, a conceptual framework for understanding cost-effectiveness and rough rules of thumb for assessing the effectiveness of individual interventions are provided.*

INTRODUCTION

There is an emerging literature on the cost-effectiveness of drug control strategies such as source country control, interdiction, domestic enforcement, mandatory minimum sentences, treatment and prevention. This literature draws conclusions such as: seven dollars in social cost are averted for every dollar spent treating heavy cocaine users (Rydell and Everingham, 1994; Gerstein et al., 1994), and about 23 serious crimes are averted per million dollars spent on federal mandatory minimum drug sentences (Caulkins et al., 1997).

It would be desirable to obtain parallel, quantitative estimates of the cost-effectiveness of civil remedies for drug problems. Unfortunately, there are at least three reasons why this is not possible.

First, there do not exist sufficient evaluation data to support such calculations.

Second, civil remedies are a heterogeneous class of interventions, and there is no such thing as a prototypical or representative program. Nor is there a database cataloguing all such interventions that would allow one to compute the characteristics of an "average" program.

Third, even if one could produce an estimate that, on average, X kilograms of cocaine consumption could be averted per million dollars spent on civil remedies for drug control, that result would not be terribly meaningful. Some people who initiate civil remedies do not make decisions about how to allocate drug control resources across different drug control programs. Indeed, sometimes civil remedies are the only alternative available to the people who pursue them. Furthermore, those pursuing civil remedies are typically not interested in reducing drug consumption in total but rather in ameliorating a more local problem.

Nevertheless, thinking about what it would require for civil remedies to be cost-effective generates interesting insights that are relevant for policy makers contemplating rule changes that would facilitate or deter the pursuit of civil remedies. This paper pursues such an exercise in five sections. The first seeks to clarify from whose perspective the cost-effectiveness calculation should be conducted, and, in the process, identifies two key conditions civil remedies must meet to be cost-effective — whether they seek to control drug problems or other problems. The second section presents a simple conceptual framework for analyzing the cost-effectiveness of drug control programs. The third and fourth sections discuss how likely it is that drug control-oriented civil remedies meet the two key conditions. The final section offers some conclusions.

CIVIL REMEDIES: COST-EFFECTIVE FOR WHOM?

An axiom of cost-benefit analysis is that one must explicitly define who the decision maker is and what perspective the analysis is taking. For most of the literature on the cost-effectiveness of drug control interventions, the decision maker is implicitly a "benevolent dictator" seeking to advance the interests of American "society" in general. Reifying the complex processes of governmental decision making in this manner is a dubious proposition, but on a fundamental level the government in a democratic society is at least theoretically supposed to serve the interests of the population as a whole. Such simplistic aggregation cannot be justified for civil remedies because of their very nature. This volume defines civil remedies as a tool with which the individual initiating the remedy can coerce non-offending "third parties" into taking some action that helps control the actions of others (the offenders). (For ease of exposition, the individual(s) making the decision to initiate a civil remedy will sometimes be referred to in this chapter as "the plaintiff," even though not all civil remedies are achieved through civil suits.)

This definition underscores the disjunction between the decision maker (plaintiff) who initiates and benefits from a civil remedy intervention, and the individuals or group (the third parties) who bear the burden of implementing the intervention that affects the offenders. This disjunction between the decision maker and the actor responsible for the intervention has important ramifications for any analysis of cost-effectiveness. In particular, it creates the possibility that a civil remedy might be cost-effective for the decision maker who initiates the action, but not for society generally.

Ideally, the third parties have some special power over the offenders that makes it easy for them to take action, and the only reason the third parties have not already acted is that it was not in their selfish interest to do so. In that scenario, the civil remedy can be seen as a way of aligning the interests of the entity empowered to effect change (namely, the "third party") with the interests of society. By solving that incentive incompatibility problem, the civil remedy can bring about an outcome that is better for society generally. The third party is, presumably, less well-off than before. (If taking the action would have improved the third party's welfare, it would have been taken voluntarily and there would be no reason to apply additional pressure.) However, the loss of welfare to the third party may be more than offset by the gain to the individual or group initiating the civil remedy.

The happy ending in this ideal scenario depends on two key assumptions. First, it assumes that the third party has an efficient way of controlling the offender. Second, it assumes that the decision maker's interests are well-aligned with those of society. It is worth considering what could happen if either of these two assumptions is violated.

First, suppose that the third party can only achieve the conditions the decision maker demands by expending an enormous amount of resources, resources that from society's perspective might better be spent elsewhere. Those initiating the civil remedy have little selfish interest in how wisely those resources are spent, because they are just one or a few of a very large number of citizens or taxpayers. Hence, there may be instances in which it is in the decision maker's interest to compel actions that are not cost-effective from society's perspective. The basic problem is that the decision maker is buying something (relief from the actions of the offender) with someone else's money (the resources of the third parties). Both economics and common sense suggest that such a situation can lead to an inefficient or even irresponsible allocation of resources.

The second necessary condition for the ideal scenario to pertain is that the decision maker's interests are well-aligned with those of society more generally. This is not a singular concern when the decision maker initiating the action is part of an official agency, such as the police or a state attorney's office. That is not to say that such agencies would never pursue a civil remedy that is not in the public interest, but merely that such concerns are no more severe with respect to civil remedies than they are for more familiar agency actions. However, this second condition may be more problematic when the decision maker initiating the action is a private citizen or group of citizens who are interested in ameliorating a very local problem, and who have no direct interest in what happens to people outside their immediate community. If the third party's intervention merely displaces the nuisance to another location, society as a whole may not benefit even though that outcome may be highly valued by the plaintiff(s).

A variant on this problem can occur if there are a large number of different individuals who can apply the civil remedy tool to a given third party. For example, there might be one plaintiff for each neighborhood. The common third party might be a city agency that has limited resources that can be spent providing services or responding to civil litigation. Every plaintiff may be better off initiating a civil action than not doing so, even though civil actions reduce the resources the agency can devote to providing services, because the plaintiff's neighborhood may receive a greater share of the agency's limited resources. However, if every neighborhood initiates a suit, their efforts to grab a greater proportion of the pie may be offset, leaving every neighborhood with the same proportion of a smaller pie. Such a situation would be a classic example of a tragedy of the commons.

To summarize, civil remedies are basically a lever with which someone can coerce another entity into spending that entity's resources to accomplish something for the plaintiff. Thus, one can think of civil remedies as comprising two distinct components: a coercive confrontation between the plaintiff and the third party, and the action taken by the third parties against the offender(s). Both are costly to society, but only the second directly generates benefits; the first guides the nature of the benefits but does not generate benefits itself. Hence, (1) if the action(s) taken by the third parties against the offender(s) are not cost-effective, the civil remedy as a whole cannot be cost-effective. Likewise, (2) if what the plaintiff demands is not good for society, the civil remedy will not be cost-effective for society. Hence, whether civil remedies are cost-effective for society depends on, among other things, whether these two key conditions are satisfied.

The remainder of this paper explores the extent to which these two conditions are likely to be satisfied in the case of drug control interventions. The next section lays the groundwork by describing a simple conceptual framework for understanding the cost-effectiveness of drug control programs. The subsequent section considers the ability of third-party interventions to control drug use; the final section considers the alignment of plaintiff's and society's interests.

FRAMEWORK FOR UNDERSTANDING DRUG CONTROL PROGRAMS' EFFECTIVENESS

We wish to explore the extent to which tactics that third parties commonly employ in response to a plaintiff's civil pressure are likely to be cost-effective. One framework for understanding drug control interventions envisions actions taken to control drug problems as operating in one of three ways: 1) reducing the quantity of drugs consumed; 2) reducing the magnitude of "the drug problem" per kilogram consumed; or 3) displacing the problem from one location, time, population, etc. to another.

It is possible to reduce the magnitude of the drug problem per unit consumed (#2), because quantity consumed is only a surrogate or proxy for the magnitude of the drug problem (Reuter and Caulkins, 1995). The magnitude of the drug problem is some agglomeration of intoxication-based functional impairment, numbers of overdoses, amounts of drug-related crime and violence, etc. There is no physical

224 — Jonathan P. Caulkins

law that mandates a constant ratio among these different elements of the drug problem or between them and consumption. For example, the number of drug-related homicides per kilogram consumed may vary depending on the involvement of gangs in retail sales, marketing trends, and the nature and intensity of police enforcement.

One intervention can generate more than one type of outcome. For example, when police shut down an outdoor street market, there might be some reduction in selling and use (#1), some displacement of the selling to another location (#3) and some displacement to more covert forms of dealing that impose fewer harms on neighbors per gram sold (#2) (Caulkins, 1992).

Typically, when one thinks about the effectiveness of drug control interventions, one begins by estimating their impact on use (#1) and then considers (sometimes less quantitatively) their impact on harm per unit use and displacement. This division is useful here, because it turns out that the second and third ways in which drug control actions work are most conveniently considered in conjunction with how well plaintiffs' interests are aligned with those of society.

Drug control interventions can reduce consumption by reducing demand, constraining supply, or driving a wedge between supply and demand. Demand can be suppressed by treating current users or preventing people from initiating or escalating use in the first place. The mechanisms through which these interventions operate are easy to understand, so there is no need to elaborate.

Analyzing the effect of interventions on supply and their ability to drive a wedge between supply and demand requires more explanation. Enforcement against suppliers can reduce consumption by driving up the dollar price of drugs, and/or by driving up the non-dollar costs users pay in order to obtain drugs. The first is captured in "risks and prices" calculations of the sort pioneered by Reuter and Kleiman (1986). The second considers user sanctions and the impact on "search time" of interventions that make it difficult for retail sellers and customers to find each other and complete a transaction (Moore, 1973; Kleiman and Smith, 1990).

The "risks and prices" paradigm recognizes that increasing enforcement risks for dealers raises their cost of doing business. Dealers could simply absorb those costs, but presumably prefer — at least in the long run — to pass increased costs along to users in the form of higher retail prices. Drug users, like consumers of other goods, respond to higher prices by reducing consumption (van Ours, 1995; Saffer and Chaloupka, 1995; Grossman et al., 1996).

The "search time" argument recognizes that the costs drug users pay to obtain and consume drugs are not limited to the dollar price paid to the dealer. Users also must expend time and effort in order to locate a dealer and complete a transaction. To the extent that this activity is unpleasant and/or the users could have done something else valuable with the time they spent obtaining drugs, this time and inconvenience represent a true cost of using drugs. Raising these costs would presumably discourage use to some extent, even though the costs are not paid for in dollars.

Finally, enforcement against users can also raise non-dollar costs associated with drug use. These costs include the risk of arrest and sanction from the criminal justice system, as well as social approbation and reductions in future licit labor market earnings that are sometimes associated with such an arrest. These costs are perhaps the least well-studied or quantified; they are also the least relevant for this paper because civil remedies rarely seek to apply sanctions to drug users.

Source country control, border interdiction and domestic enforcement against high-level dealers operate primarily through the "risks and prices" mechanism, because they do not affect retail sellers or users directly and it is rare for high-level interventions to create physical scarcity (as opposed to higher prices) for mass market drugs such as marijuana, cocaine and, to an increasing extent, heroin.[1] In contrast, although retail enforcement certainly imposes costs on suppliers ("risks and prices"), it can also force retail sellers to be more discreet (raising "search time") and sometimes involves user sanctions. Furthermore, local enforcement can affect harm per unit use and displacement more directly than can higher level interventions.

This framework for understanding drug control interventions is summarized in Figure 1. With this framework in mind, we turn to the question of whether the actions coerced by civil remedies are likely to be cost-effective ways of controlling drug use.

THIRD PARTIES' ABILITY TO CONTROL DRUG USE COST-EFFECTIVELY

Civil remedies span a range of scenarios and interventions. We focus on two: individual demands for greater drug control efforts on the part of a government agency, and interventions that shut down particular dealing locations. This focus should not be construed as an endorsement of these two forms or a statement that they are the most promising. Rather, they seem to be the two most common types of interventions, and they are two about which some cost-effectiveness calculations can be performed. We also briefly mention a third, treating drug users, as a foil. The calculations focus on cocaine because it has been the subject of the most prior analysis.

Figure 1: Framework for Understanding Drug Control Programs' Effectiveness

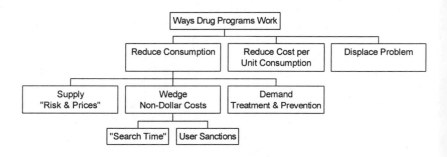

Stimulating Local Drug Enforcement

Sometimes the plaintiffs are individuals demanding greater drug control efforts from government agencies, typically the police. For the moment, we will set aside the problem that greater resources for one neighborhood might be obtained by reducing services elsewhere. Suppose the civil remedies stimulate greater total expenditures of resources on local drug enforcement. How cost-effective are such efforts likely to be? This question is worth answering both for its own sake and because it lays the groundwork for evaluating civil remedies that impose costs on drug sellers, for example, by evicting them from apartments.

Domestic enforcement in general has been found to be substantially more cost-effective than supply-side interventions further upstream (such as source country control and border interdiction), but less effective than treating heavy users in terms of kilograms of consumption averted per million program dollars spent (see, e.g., Rydell and Everingham, 1994). In particular, risk and price calculations estimate that domestic enforcement against cocaine suppliers averts an average of 27.5 kilograms of consumption per million dollars spent (Caulkins et al., 1997, updating Rydell and Everingham, 1994).

The 27.5 kilogram per million dollar figure represents an average over all types of enforcement against suppliers pursued within U.S. borders, including state, local and federal efforts. However, the actions arising from citizen complaints are usually directed at street markets occupied by retail dealers, and, from a risks and prices perspective, higher level domestic enforcement is more efficacious than is retail enforcement. For example, local enforcement can arrest, prosecute and incarcerate 120 typical retail cocaine dealers at a cost to the taxpayer of 1 million dollars, thereby averting 9.1 kilograms of cocaine consumption.[2]

Hence, risk and price calculations suggest that greater local enforcement stimulated by civil remedies would not be very cost-effective. Before accepting that conclusion, however, one should augment these estimates with estimates of the consumption reduction that can be achieved by driving up search times. The literature does not contain such estimates and relevant data are sparse, so the best we can do is make some very rough calculations using data from heroin users.

Rocheleau and Boyum (1994) interviewed experienced heroin users about their purchasing patterns. The heroin users took an average of 35 minutes to make a purchase and spent an average of $26 per purchase. If these users valued their time at $7 per hour, this suggests that non-dollar search-time costs represent 14% of the combined search time plus the dollar cost of obtaining heroin.[3] If the elasticity of demand for heroin is around -1, which is a plausible estimate of the elasticity of demand for cocaine (Caulkins et al., 1997), this implies that any program that doubles the average search time for heroin users could reduce consumption by about 14%.

Suppose, for the sake of argument, that arresting a user's primary supplier imposes an additional search time cost on the user of 100 hours. This additional search time includes both the time taken to locate an alternative dealer and an ongoing increment in search time associated with protective measures dealers take in response to the increased risk of arrest. This 100-hour estimate may be optimistic given that just 4% of the study subjects reported knowing only one or two dealers, and more than half reported being approached by dealers on a regular basis. Nevertheless, to the best of my knowledge, there is absolutely no empirical basis for the magnitude of such a number. I invite the reader to pick one that he or she feels is reasonable and follow through the calculations with that number. If the reader believes this number should be 200 hours, the reader will want to double my estimate of the search-time component of retail enforcement's ability to reduce consumption. If the reader believes this number should be 50 hours, he or she should halve my estimate.

Rocheleau and Boyum (1994) found that users made an average of 13 purchases per week, implying a total annual search time of 13 times/week * 52 weeks/year * (35/60) hours/search = 394 hours. Thus, given the assumption above, arresting a user's dealer would raise his or her annual search-time cost by about 100/394 = 25%, leading to a 25% * 14% = 3.5% reduction in consumption.[4]

If these heroin figures are applied to the cocaine market, then arresting every retail cocaine seller one more time per year would reduce cocaine consumption by 3.5% of the national total of about 291 metric tons, or about 10,185 kilograms. How much would it cost to arrest every retail cocaine seller? There are on the order of 1 million retail cocaine sellers,[5] so if 120 such sellers can be arrested per million dollars, the total cost would be about $8,333 million. Thus, subject to the rather heroic assumptions made, the search-time impact of retail enforcement might increase the efficacy of retail enforcement by about 1.2 kilograms per million dollars spent, from 9.1 to 10.3 kilograms per million dollars — an amount that is still well below the cost-effectiveness of domestic enforcement generally or of treatment.

Thus, to the extent that civil remedies simply stimulate additional local drug enforcement, they are not likely to be a cost-effective way of reducing drug use. If such stimulation of local enforcement is to be cost-effective, it must be so by virtue of its ability to reduce the harm per unit of drugs sold and consumed.

Forcing Dealers to Move

Many civil remedies involve forcing dealers to change location by evicting them; boarding up abandoned buildings that have become selling locations; or purchasing, renovating and selling units to stable tenants. The plaintiffs can be private citizens or government agencies. Shutting down a dealing location does not reduce dealing and use by an amount equal to the volume that was transacted at that location, because the dealers can often relocate and/or the users can find other dealers. Nevertheless, shutting down a dealing location can reduce dealing and use, not just move it, to the extent that moving is costly for dealers and users. Inconvenience to users was discussed earlier. If adding 100 hours of search time reduced use by 3.5%, then since an average heavy cocaine user consumes about 120 grams per year, that suggests that a rough rule of thumb is 1gram of consumption averted for every 25 hours of additional search time generated for users.

Risk and price models provide a similar rule of thumb for costs imposed on dealers. On average one must impose $71,000 in costs on cocaine dealers in order to drive up prices enough to reduce consumption by one kilogram (Caulkins et al., 1997). Hence, if an intervention can impose two dollars in cost on dealers for every dollar of resources expended on the intervention, that intervention would be, on average, as cost-effective as domestic enforcement.

Shutting down a dealing location can impose both costs on dealers and inconvenience on users, and the benefits of doing so are cumulative. If it cost the dealers $2,000 to relocate and the 20 users who frequented the location an average of 25 hours of inconvenience time each, a point estimate of the associated consumption reduction would be about 48 grams, or over 40% of a year's consumption for a typical heavy user.[6] If a civil remedy could shut down such a dealing location for $1,750 or less, it would be on average as cost-effective as domestic enforcement. If it cost $450 or less, the civil remedy would be as cost-effective as treating heavy users.

It is not clear whether an intervention such as coercing a landlord to evict a drug-dealing tenant meets this criterion. Anecdotal reports suggest that pursuing civil remedies can be a lengthy and time-consuming process for individuals (e.g., Meyers, 1995; Schmitz, 1995). State attorney's offices and police can often coerce landlords into action with a simple letter or a phone call (Mazerolle et al., this volume; Lurigio et al., this volume; Eck and Wartell, this volume), but one must also include the costs to the landlord, which can easily exceed $1,750 (Smith and Davis, this volume).

The empirical work has not been done to estimate how disruptive it is for dealers and users to have a location shut down, so it is unknown whether the estimates of $2,000 in cost to dealers and 25 hours per user for 20 users are reasonable. However, rules of thumb for converting such costs into consumption reductions are useful guides, even if they are highly imprecise.

Treatment

Even if civil remedies for drug control are not very cost-effective in an absolute sense, they might still be worth pursuing if no better alternative strategies were available. That may be the case for individuals, but is not so for the government. It is well-established that treating heavy users can be a cost-effective way of reducing drug use (Rydell and Everingham, 1994; Gerstein et al., 1994), averting on the order of 100 kilograms per million dollars spent. [7] It is also well-established that people who are coerced into treatment do as well, in general, as people who enter treatment voluntarily (Anglin and Hser, 1990). Hence, local resources could profitably be devoted to expanding treatment, either in traditional forms or in conjunction with the criminal justice system as in TASC, drug courts or coerced abstinence programs.

Note that civil commitment to treatment is a viable drug control option, but, despite its name, it does not fit the civil remedy model considered here. Civil commitment is an action taken directly against the offender (the user), not a third party (unless the plaintiff brought suit against a user's guardian, seeking to compel the guardian to commit the user to treatment).

Summary

The range of third-party actions that civil remedies induce is broad. Certainly some are likely to be cost-effective. However, it is not obvious that the most common tactics civil remedies coerce third parties to employ (local drug enforcement and shutting down dealing locations) are cost-effective at reducing drug use either in an absolute sense or relative to alternatives available to government agencies (e.g., conventional domestic enforcement and treating heavy users).

DECISION MAKERS' INTERESTS VERSUS THOSE OF SOCIETY

A belief that civil remedies are not cost-effective for controlling drug *use* does not imply that they are not cost-effective for controlling drug *problems*. It is possible to reduce the magnitude of the drug problem per unit of consumption or use. For example, interventions might target particularly problematic selling or use and displace those activities into less damaging locations or forms. Such a belief would mean, though, that it is necessary to achieve such targeting if civil remedies are to be cost-effective ways of controlling drug problems. This is related to the question of whether the interests of the plaintiffs who initiate civil remedies are well-aligned with those of society. In particular, are they better aligned than is typical of actions taken under drug control programs that do not involve civil remedies?

The potential for such alignment is great because of civil remedies' grassroots character. Dealers who sell without generating many obvious negative externalities (e.g., do not intimidate neighbors, carry a gun, employ children as lookouts, etc.) are not likely to be the focus of a civil remedy. Conversely, particularly heinous offenders are the most likely to attract the wrath (and energy) of the citizenry. That enmity can manifest in a civil action filed by a private citizen, or in the form of complaints that direct the actions of official agencies pursuing civil remedies.

Of course official agencies operating through conventional procedures also try to prioritize their actions in response to perceived and reported problems. However, agency decision makers are one step removed from the citizens who are experiencing the problems. Civil remedies empower individuals and communities to direct action at the dealers, users and street markets that cause them the greatest problems. Hence, one might expect them to be well-aligned with society's interests. There are, however, reasons why this expectation might be overly optimistic. Two were discussed above. Plaintiffs may be satisfied with improving their lot at the expense of others, and civil actions allow plaintiffs to buy relief with someone else's resources. These are concerns with respect to all forms of civil remedies, but the fluid nature of drug markets makes them particularly problematic in this context.

Drug markets are notorious for their ability to adapt to assaults of various forms. Sometimes they adapt in ways that reduce the overall level of the drug problem, as when a flagrant market is pushed underground. It is not uncommon, though, for the adaptation to take the form of simple physical displacement, in which case the intervention's principal effect may be to move the problem, not reduce it. To the extent that this happens, societal resources are expended (specifically, the third party's resources), making some people better off (including the plaintiff) and other people worse off (those living around locations to which the activity is displaced), with perhaps no net reduction in the magnitude of the drug problem. The fact that the people who benefit are readily identifiable and those who are hurt are diffuse may make the benefits easier to see than the costs, but it does not make the costs any less real or important.

An implication is that rules governing civil remedies should be designed in a way that discourages plaintiffs with parochial interests from demanding interventions that have a reasonable likelihood of leading to physical displacement. Unfortunately, at least at present, there does not exist a set of interventions against particular drug markets with which no reasonable chance of displacement is associated. This suggests that civil remedies should be made available only to those who are likely to care about the welfare not only of residents surrounding the current market, but also of those who might suffer from displacement if it were to occur.

The implications of possible displacement are the most significant qualification to the optimistic view that civil remedy plaintiffs will tend to pursue actions that further societal interests, but two others will be discussed briefly.

Will Civil Remedies Be Applied Where the Need is Greatest?

All citizens are entitled to equal protection under the law, yet some classes of citizens suffer vastly more at the hands of drug-law violators than do others. Residents of poor, urban areas plagued by flagrant retail drug markets are famously ill-served by conventional drug control in this respect. Civil remedies are available to all citizens and so they offer the promise of helping to rectify the disparity in damage done by drug dealing.

In practice, however, it takes resources and a certain amount of sophistication to pursue civil remedies. Such remedies initiated by neighborhood groups require ongoing attention over an extended period. Although programs have been successfully launched in poor neighborhoods, residents of highly transient neighborhoods may have difficulty banding together quickly or persistently enough to carry through a suit successfully.

Attorneys are not required to bring a civil suit (Weingart, 1993), and are financially prohibitive for some. Even when an attorney is not used, better educated plaintiffs may, on average, be more successful at winning their day in court. A brief and informal survey of cases reported in the press and academic literature suggests that civil remedies are initiated by professionals living in neighborhoods of mixed socioeconomic status more often than they are by members of the underclass (although there may be a selection bias affecting which cases are reported).

To those who view neighborhoods of mixed socioeconomic status as singularly important to the health of cities, the possibility that a program might not help the neighborhoods in greatest need is not an argument against supporting that program. To others, though, civil remedies might seem less appealing to the extent that they help the affluent, the educated and the well-connected further protect their neighborhoods at the expense of residents with fewer resources who already suffer a greater burden, on average, of the problems associated with drug markets.

Do Civil Remedies Ever Punish Bad Outcomes Instead of Bad Intentions?

Civil remedies are premised on the third party's dereliction of duty, as evidenced by the existence of a nuisance that aggrieves the plaintiff. For example, a landlord is held responsible because a tenant in one of his or her buildings is selling drugs.

An axiom of decision analysis is that good decisions can lead to bad outcomes and vice versa. A corollary in this context is that good intentions and faithful execution of a customary level of care do not guarantee the absence of a nuisance on one's property. Hence, punishing for the existence of a nuisance can result in punishing not just the irresponsible but also the unlucky. For example, even a landlord who screens potential tenants carefully may not be able to detect and reject everyone who might at some point sell drugs from their apartment. If and when such selling occurs, the landlord may view him or herself as the victim and consider the police to be at fault for failing to deter the crime. Yet, through civil remedies, the landlord can be forced to bear both the personal risk of confronting and evicting the dealer and the associated financial costs.

If most landlords welcomed drug dealers as tenants or willfully turned a blind eye toward such activity, the proportion of sanctioned landlords who were irresponsible rather than unlucky would likely be modest. But many landlords claim they were not aware of the drug nuisance on their property (Lurigio et al., this volume), and landlords already have incentives — besides the risk of civil remedies — for not renting to drug dealers (Hayes, 1994; Smith and Davis, this volume).

What can happen once to an individual through bad luck can happen several times, albeit with lower probability. As the number of civil remedies pursued increases, the expected number of such occurrences grows as well. If a landlord were unlucky enough to have two or three tenants sell drugs within a certain period of time, the plaintiff might construe that as evidence of willful lack of cooperation and respond by seeking a more punitive remedy. In Oakland, CA, the Uniformed Controlled Substances Act (which declares a building to be a nuisance if it is the site of drug use, not just dealing) gives the city the power to fine the owner and close or sell the property (Maze-rolle et al., this volume). Such actions have been taken in some juris-dictions (George, 1997). Shutting down a property is not an insignifi-cant punishment, particularly given that many landlords are small businesspeople of modest means, not large corporations with deep pockets (Eck and Wartell, this volume; Lurigio et al., this volume). Criminal law interventions can also inadvertently punish "innocent" people, but the low burden of proof and broad powers of forfeiture associated with civil cases make this concern more salient (Cheh, this volume).

CONCLUSION

The policy question pertaining to civil remedies is whether the government should take actions to facilitate or encourage the use of civil procedures for drug control. From the perspective of cost-effectiveness the answer is clearly, "It depends." It is easy to imagine civil remedies that are sufficiently beneficial for society to be actively encouraged. Likewise, it is easy to imagine civil remedies that are sufficiently ineffective, or even outright harmful, to not be encouraged or facilitated. Unfortunately, it is generally not obvious what policies or rules would encourage only the "right" kinds of civil interventions. One possible exception pertains to who initiates the action. Since a key concern is whether the plaintiff's interests are well-aligned with broader societal interests, it would seem less risky to encourage gov-ernment agencies to seek civil remedies than to have private citizens do so.

It remains an open question whether in practice the preponder-ance of civil remedies are cost-effective. In theory one could collect information about a range of civil interventions, characterize them according to how beneficial they were, and design policies that en-courage those that are beneficial and discourage those that are not. Practically, this would be a formidable task. The best that can be done at present is to provide a framework for understanding and dis-cussing the issues.

Address correspondence to: Jonathan P. Caulkins, Carnegie Mellon University, H. John Heinz III School of Public Policy and Management, 5000 Forbes Ave., Pittsburgh, PA 15213-3890.

REFERENCES

Anglin, M.D. and Y. Hser (1990). "Treatment of Drug Abuse" In: James Q. Wilson and M. Tonry (eds.), *Crime and Justice: An Annual Review of Research,* vol. 13. Chicago, IL: The University of Chicago Press.

Caulkins, J.P. (1992). "Thinking About Displacement in Drug Markets: Why Observing Change of Venue Isn't Enough." *Journal of Drug Issues* 22:17-30.

—— C.P. Rydell, W.L. Schwabe and J. Chiesa (1997. *Mandatory Minimum Drug Sentences: Throwing Away the Key or the Taxpayers' Money?* Santa Monica, CA: Rand.

George, D.E. (1997). "Is There Another Way to Stop Drug Trafficking?" *The NarcOfficer* (January/February):36.

Gerstein, D.R., R.A. Johnson, H.J. Harwood, D. Fountain, N. Suter and K. Malloy (1994). *Evaluating Recovery Services: The California Drug and Alcohol Treatment Assessment (CALDATA).* Sacramento, CA: California Department of Alcohol and Drug Programs.

Grossman, M., F.J. Chaloupka and C.C. Brown (1996). *The Demand for Cocaine by Young Adults: A Rational Addiction Approach.* Working Paper 5713. Cambridge, MA: National Bureau of Economic Research.

Hayes, L. (1994). "Creating a Drug-Resistant Property." *Journal of Property Management* 59:28-31.

Kleiman, M.A.R. and K.D. Smith (1990). "State and Local Drug Enforcement: In Search of a Strategy." In: Norval Morris and Michael Tonry (eds.), *Crime and Justice: An Annual Review of Research.* Chicago, IL: University of Chicago Press.

Meyers, L. (1995). "The Home Rangers." *LA Magazine* (40)2:80-87.

Moore, M.H. (1973). "Achieving Discrimination on the Effective Price of Heroin." *American Economic Review* 63:270-277.

Office of National Drug Control Policy (1996). *The National Drug Control Strategy: 1996.* Washington, DC: author.

Reuter, P. and J.P. Caulkins (1995). "Redefining the Goals of Drug Policy: Report of a Working Group." *American Journal of Public Health* 85:1059-1063.

Reuter, P. and M.A.R. Kleiman (1986). "Risks and Prices: An Economic Analysis of Drug Enforcement." In: M. Tonry and N. Morris (eds.), *Crime and Justice: An Annual Review of Research*, vol. 7. Chicago, IL: University of Chicago Press.

Reuter, P., R.J. MacCoun and P. Murphy (1990). "Money from Crime: A Study of the Economics of Drug Dealing in Washington, DC." Santa Monica, CA: Rand.

Rocheleau, A.M. and D. Boyum (1994). "Measuring Heroin Availability in Three Cities." Washington, DC: U.S. Office of National Drug Control Policy.

—— and M.A.R. Kleiman (1993). "Measuring Heroin Availability: A Demonstration." Washington, DC: U.S. Office of National Drug Control Policy.

Rydell, C.P. and S.S. Everingham (1994). *Controlling Cocaine: Supply vs. Demand Programs*. Santa Monica, CA: Rand.

Saffer, H. and F. Chaloupka (1995). "The Demand for Illicit Drugs." Working Paper No.5238, Cambridge, MA: National Bureau of Economic Research.

Schmitz, A. (1995). "Who Cares About Frogtown?" *Minneapolis/St. Paul* 23(7):54-57, 121-25.

van Ours, J.C. (1995). "The Price Elasticity of Hard Drugs: The Case of Opium in the Dutch East Indies, 1923-1938." *Journal of Political Economy* 103:261-279.

Weingart, S.N. (1993. "A Typology of Community Responses to Drugs." In: R.C. Davis, A.J. Lurigio and D.P. Rosenbaum (eds.), *Drugs and the Community*. Springfield, IL: Charles C Thomas.

NOTES

1. Since some suppliers are also users, most supply control programs that involve incarceration also incapacitate a certain amount of demand.

2. This assumes that: 70% of those arrested are convicted; 60% of those arrested are incarcerated; the average time of incarceration is 90 days; $750 worth of drugs but no other assets are seized per arrest; no fine is paid; and the disutility of incarceration is equivalent to $25,000 per cell year. Police costs are assumed to be $2,000 per arrest, adjudication costs are $1,262 per arrest plus $3,884 per trial (with 15% of those arrested going to trial), and incarceration costs are $24,972 per cell year (Caulkins et al., 1997).

3. 13.6% = ($7*35 minutes/60 minutes per hour)/($7*35/60 + $26). A parallel calculation using the median time to purchase (30 minutes) and purchase value ($20) would suggest that 14.9% of the total cost of obtaining heroin is attributable to search time.

4. Parallel calculations with figures from Rocheleau and Kleiman (1993) yield very similar results.

5. The retail value of the cocaine market was between $30 and $40 billion between 1988 and 1993 (Office of National Drug Control Policy, 1996). Reuter et al. (1990) estimate that a regular (more than once a week) cocaine retailer in Washington, DC sold an average of $4,570 worth of cocaine a month (median was less than $3,600), and that there were 22 dealers for every 14 full-time equivalent dealers. Thus, there are about (22/14) * $35B / ($4,570 * 12 months/yr.) = 1,003,000 retail cocaine dealers.

6. 48 grams = ($2,000/$71,000 per kilogram) * 1,000 grams/kilogram + (20 users * 25 hours/user) / 25 user-hours per gram.

7. In round numbers, according to Rydell and Everingham (1994), about 80% of users do not use during the 0.3 years they are in treatment and otherwise would have consumed at a rate of 120 grams per year. Also, on average, 13% of those entering treatment will not be heavy users after treatment as a result of that treatment. One-third of those cease use altogether, averting a future net present value (NPV) of 1 kilogram of consumption. Two-thirds use at a reduced rate akin to that of a light user, i.e., consuming an NPV of 165 grams, not 1,000 kilograms. Thus, the expected reduction in consumption by the treated individual is about 144 grams. Reducing demand by one person shrinks the market, allowing other interventions to focus on the smaller, residual market and, thereby, become more effective. This effect creates a "market multiplier" for demand interventions of about 1.25, so each treatment leads to a reduction of 145 * 1.25 = 180 grams. Since the average treatment costs $1,740, this implies treatment can avert about 103 kilograms per million dollars spent.

Part III: Community Perspectives

CIVIL REMEDIES FOR CONTROLLING CRIME: THE ROLE OF COMMUNITY ORGANIZATIONS

by

Jan Roehl
Justice Research Center

Abstract: *Over the past decade, community organizations and citizens have increasingly used civil remedies to compel non-offending third parties to take action to prevent or mitigate crime, drug and disorder problems in their neighborhoods. Nuisance and drug abatement ordinances and municipal codes are the most common civil laws employed by community organizations, which may or may not work in concert with law enforcement, prosecutors and other government agencies. While civil remedy strategies are not without problems, community organizations report general success in their use. In this chapter, the history of civil remedies used by community organizations is reviewed and the results of a national survey of community organizations are presented. The results include the characteristics of the respondent organizations, the types and prevalence of civil remedy strategies used, problems encountered and outcomes of the application of strategies.*

INTRODUCTION

Today, preventing and resolving neighborhood crime and disorder problems are the responsibilities of law enforcement professionals and other government authorities — and citizens, acting individually and collectively. These citizens are not experts in crime prevention, drug interventions or neighborhood revitalization. They are everyday people — residents, workers and business owners — working to improve the public safety and quality of life of the neighborhoods in which they work and live. To prevent and resolve neighborhood crime and disorder problems, these everyday people receive training, support, assistance and protection from community organizations and their paid staff. Over time, a number of these people become experts themselves — community activists with the expertise and tenacity to play a central role in turning neighborhoods around. In this heyday of community policing, community organizations and citizens play a crucial role in maintaining order, public safety and the quality of life in our nation's neighborhoods.

In recent years, community organizations and citizens have learned to apply civil remedies, to use civil laws and mechanisms to compel non-offending third parties to take action to prevent or mitigate criminal and other problems. This chapter presents the results of a national survey of community organizations focused on their civil remedy activities. These organizations engage in a variety of civil remedies, alone and in concert with law enforcement and other agencies. As described below, they also fill a unique role that these other agencies cannot.

ROOTS OF CIVIL REMEDIES BY COMMUNITY ORGANIZATIONS

Three decades of rising concern with neighborhood crime, topped by radical changes in the nature of such crime due to drug dealing and the violence that has accompanied it, have been paralleled by increases and changes in collective citizen action. Community crime prevention flourished in the late 1970s and early 1980s, then slowly gave way to community-based anti-drug efforts in the late 1980s and 1990s. Community involvement in civil remedies aimed at crime and drug control emerged with the anti-drug activities of recent years.

The importance of community organizations and citizens in community crime prevention and order maintenance efforts became apparent in the mid-1970s, as concerns about street crime and residential burglaries began to rise and it became obvious that the police alone could not control crime. With the formation and early success of neighborhood and block watch efforts, citizens themselves realized they could do something about the local crime problems that concerned them most. DuBow and Emmons (1981) labeled this the "community hypothesis," stating that neighborhood residents could be mobilized to participate in collective crime prevention, which would get residents to take greater responsibility for local problems, increase social interaction, rebuild informal social control, and reduce crime and fear of crime.

Central community crime prevention strategies of the 1980s included neighborhood and block watches (Cirel et al., 1977), citizen patrols (Yin et al., 1977), surveillance and reporting of suspicious behavior to police

(Bickman et al., 1977), and environmental design changes, commonly referred to as Crime Prevention through Environmental Design (CPTED) (Gardiner, 1978; Fowler et al., 1979; Fowler and Mangione, 1982; Crowe, 1991). Several theoretical models underpin community crime prevention approaches. One school of thought concludes that high crime is found in neighborhoods with substantial social disorganization and a weakened capacity for local institutions and organizations to control the behavior of local residents (Greenberg et al., 1982, 1985). According to this theory of informal social control, community crime prevention involves strengthening or resurrecting traditional agents of social control — families, churches, schools, ethnic solidarity, traditional values — and improving community cohesion. A second theory, opportunity reduction, covers the mainstream community crime prevention approaches such as neighborhood watch and a sizable variety of CPTED principles. Here, crime prevention involves removing or reducing opportunities for crime (Rosenbaum, 1988). A third theoretical model is the "broken windows," or "incivilities," thesis (Greene and Taylor, 1988), most cogently raised by Wilson and Kelling (1982), which posits that physical (graffiti, broken windows, trash, etc.) and social (public drug use, loitering, etc.) incivilities indicate that neither area residents nor municipal authorities care about the neighborhood or can enforce social control. As incivilities become more widespread, neighborhood deterioration and alienation, fear of crime, and victimization increase. In this model, citizen action takes a variety of directions, including neighborhood clean-ups, problem solving and application of civil remedies.

Community organizations ranging from small, barely organized grassroots groups to umbrella organizations serving other community groups and coalitions of block watches have been instrumental in organizing and training citizens in community crime prevention efforts (Roehl and Cook, 1984). Two core elements are common to most community crime prevention efforts. Community organizing, typically leading to the formation of watch programs characterized by looking out for neighbors, reporting suspicious activity, household target hardening and marking valuables (i.e., Operation ID), is the basic building block of community crime prevention. Forming and sustaining collaborative working relationships with local police is also a key component of most community crime prevention efforts, recognized as necessary and valuable by both police and community (Feins, 1983). Citizens have become "the eyes and ears" of police, using the well-accepted tactic of documenting and reporting suspicious behavior to police and looking out for one another's homes. Police officers, for their part, provide community crime prevention groups with information on crime problems in their areas, and on training and education in target hardening and personal safety.

A decade of research on community crime prevention programs has suggested that poor, high-crime, disordered neighborhoods — where the need is greatest — would be the least likely to launch and sustain community-based anti-drug efforts (Skogan and Maxfield, 1981; Lavrakas et al., 1981; Skogan, 1988). Further, successful community crime prevention are rarely located in neighborhoods with the worst crime (Yin, 1986). While there were signs of success in early community crime prevention programs (Cirel et al., 1977; Fowler and Mangione, 1982), other studies found little evidence of their effectiveness in reducing crime (Rosenbaum et al., 1986; Lavrakas et al., 1989).

As the scourge of drug use and dealing came to dominate pockets of neighborhood life, community crime prevention efforts of the 1980s evolved into the community-based anti-drug efforts of the 1990s (Roehl et al., 1995). The anti-drug methods are similar to those of community crime prevention, yet more intense and focused on specific dealers and residential, commercial, and open-air drug markets. Community-based anti-drug efforts also concentrate heavily on prevention strategies (Roehl et al., 1995), grounded in social development and influence models (Hawkins et al., 1992; Pentz et al., 1989; Ellickson and Bell, 1990).

These community anti-drug efforts, while having much in common with community crime prevention efforts, also differ in important ways. New evidence challenges some of the conventional wisdom about community crime prevention (Davis et al., 1993). For example, community anti-drug programs have been successfully launched in poor neighborhoods, especially when given substantial technical assistance and police involvement (Lurigio and Davis, 1992; Skogan and Lurigio, 1992), and these programs have been shown to succeed with the involvement of only small numbers of citizens (Smith and Davis, 1993; Weingart, 1993; Weingart et al., 1993). A national assessment of community-based anti-drug efforts, coupled with the research cited above, found that determined, organized citizens play roles that other institutions cannot, and are effective, valuable partners in anti-drug efforts (Roehl et al., 1995).

The targets of anti-drug efforts, clearly, are different from those of community crime prevention. Rather than protecting neighborhoods against unknown and largely unseen perpetrators, these efforts target drug dealers who are visible and sometimes known by the residents. Partnerships with law enforcement are also integral to community anti-drug efforts, yet the scope of anti-drug partnerships has been expanded by community groups to include schools, businesses, health and social service agencies, and housing and code enforcement agencies. Block watch participants still serve as the eyes and ears of the police, but they are also trained to be intense surveyors and reporters, recording specific information about dealers and buyers (race, physical characteristics, clothing, etc.), their cars (make, color, licenses numbers, etc.), and dealing activities (what drugs are being sold? where are they hidden?). Focusing specifically on drugs has led community organizations and citizens to revise and adapt community crime prevention tactics such as community organizing, environmental design changes, citizen patrols, vigils and marches (Rosenbaum et al., 1994).

During the past three decades, policing has also changed substantially in both method and philosophy. In the 1970s, law enforcement agencies were proud of their "professional policing," which focused on crime control and response time and gave little emphasis to community concerns or roles. As crime rates and community crime prevention efforts grew, *partnerships* between the police and community became the new buzzword — certainly in the rhetoric of policing and crime prevention, and evident in varying degrees in U.S. cities. The drug problems of the mid-1980s, however, were met with a "war" waged by federal, state and local law enforcement officials, with little room for citizen participation. At the local level, these drug enforcement tactics were found to have limited success, effective primarily in the short term and immediate area (Sherman, 1990; Moore and Kleiman, 1989). Slowly over the past decade, community policing, with its emphasis on problem solving —of drug problems in particular as well as those of concern to neighborhood residents — has become the dominant policing model (Skolnick and Bayley, 1986; Pate et al., 1986; Eck and Spelman, 1987; Greene and Mastrofski, 1988; Goldstein, 1990; Rosenbaum, 1994; Skogan and Hartnett, 1997).

The use of civil remedies for controlling neighborhood crime, drug problems and disorder is the newest tool in the community-based anti-drug workshop. The majority of civil remedies are directed toward targets who are neither known dealers nor unknown criminals —usually building owners, landlords and managers who are responsible for a place where crime, drugs and/or disorder are harming the quality of life of a neighborhood. As shown here and elsewhere in this volume, civil remedies are also directed at perpetrators themselves, such as loiterers, panhandlers, and disruptive youths. The remedies are based on civil rather than criminal laws, requiring less of a burden of evidence and capable of being applied by non-criminal justice groups — such as citizens and community organizations. While environmental changes, multi-agency partnerships and community organizing continue to be

part of community crime control efforts using civil remedies, civil litigation, code enforcement and eviction are also critical tools.

THE ROLE OF COMMUNITY ORGANIZATIONS IN
CIVIL REMEDIES

Descriptions of uses of civil remedies by community organizations
began to appear around 1990 through the work of the National Training
and Information Center and the National Crime Prevention Council
(NCPC) (Feldman and Trapp, 1990; NCPC, 1992; Rosenbaum et al.,
1994). Although Davis and Lurigio (1996) cite Portland, OR's Office of
Neighborhood Associations as the leader in community-based civil
remedies in the mid-1980s, the landmark case that set the stage for
future work was *Kellner v. Cappellini*. In 1986, private attorney Douglas
Kellner, acting on behalf of 26 petitioners from the grassroots organization the Westside Crime Prevention Program in Manhattan, used a 125-
year-old New York State statute known as "the bawdy house law" (Real
Property Actions and Proceedings Law 715) to file suit against a "crack
den" (a residence-based drug dealing operation). The court ordered the
residents evicted, the crack house sold and the legal costs of the petitioners paid from the sale of the house. The civil statute invoked in this
first case of the use of civil remedies by a community group to close a
drug house is presently used by the Manhattan District Attorney's Office
in its own Narcotics Eviction Program.

Civil remedies have assumed many forms in the past decade. In
1993, Roehl et al. (1997) launched a national study of the extent, nature
and effectiveness of the use of civil remedies by community members
and groups to reduce neighborhood crime, disorder, drug use and drug
trafficking. The results of the national study are reported below.

Characteristics of Community Organizations Using Civil
Remedies and the Neighborhoods Served

A national search for community organizations actively involved in
applying civil remedies to neighborhood crime, drug and disorder problems resulted in detailed surveys completed by 73 organizations located
from coast to coast, with no regional patterns apparent. The organizations range from very large to very small in terms of staffing, funding
and overall activities, but many of them are well-established groups (see
Table 1). Most organizations reported they had legal assistance readily
available to them.

Table 1: Characteristics of Organizations Using Civil Remedies and the Communities They Serve (N=73)

Organizations		
No. with operating funds	57 (79%)	
Average annual budget (top 5% removed): Range:	$238,762 $50-4,000,000	
Average no. of paid staff: Range:	8 1-60	
Target Communities		
Population (average): Range:	154,492 500-2,000,000	
Income level:		
Middle to upper income	3	(3%)
Middle income	9	(12%)
Lower income, working class	28	(38%)
Lower income, public assistance	13	(18%)
Areas include all SES groups	20	(27%)
Ethnicity:		
White	34%	
African-American	43%	
Hispanic	14%	
Asian	6%	
Other	3%	

The large majority of the organizations serve urban areas, with half targeting inner city areas. Sixty percent concentrated their civil remedy strategies in specific neighborhoods; these neighborhoods contain sizable proportions of lower income and minority populations. Drug dealing (typically crack or heroin), property crime, violent crime and blight — in that order — were cited as significant problems. Crack and alcohol were reported to be the most serious substance problems in the target communities.

Types and Prevalence of Civil Remedy Strategies

Broadly stated, two strategies were found to be the most common forms of civil remedies used by community organizations: environmental changes and enforcement strategies. Within these strategies, civil remedy tactics take many forms, as listed in Table 2.

Table 2: Percentage of Surveyed Organizations Reporting Various Civil Remedy Tactics (N=73)

Area clean-up, improvements, demolition, board-ups, etc.	93%
Report information to authorities (e.g., license numbers, logs of illegal activity)	86%
Pressure government agencies to enforce building and health codes	85%
Pressure landlords and property owners to deal with a problem	78%
Urge government or appropriate agencies to establish (pass) new or revised ordinances, laws, etc.	74%
Specific environmental changes (e.g., removing pay phones, altering traffic patterns, etc.)	74%
Ask authorities to enforce alcohol and beverage laws and regulations	63%
File formal complaints with prosecution or law enforcement to enforce ordinances, laws, etc.	60%
Appear at hearings regarding the issuance or renewal licenses and permits	52%
Ask authorities to initiate seizure and forfeiture actions	51%
Fix a problem directly (e.g., board a building)	38%
Initial legal action (e.g., small claims court filing, testifying in civil suit, etc.)	36%
Banning of drug-related items (e.g., beepers, paraphernalia, etc.)	29%
Training for landlords and property owners (e.g., writing drug-free leases, tenant screening, etc.)	27%
Other civil remedy strategies not listed above	19%

Environmental Strategies

Neighborhood-based environmental changes are extensions of crime prevention through environmental design (CPTED) approaches and are designed to secure properties, enhance the physical appearance of a neighborhood and indicate the presence of caring, vigilant residents. Traditional forms of environmental changes reported by the surveyed organizations include neighborhood clean-ups, board-ups and demolitions of abandoned property, and beautification efforts, including graffiti eradication. These changes are made by property owners or local agencies, after requests and pressure from community groups and/or organized community members.

The most common environmental change directed specifically against drug dealing, and one that falls more squarely under the civil remedies heading, is the removal of pay phones used by dealers for drug transactions or their alteration, to allow outgoing calls only. Other specific changes include improving street lighting, removing billboards (especially those advertising liquor), installing speed bumps and the like.

Enforcement Strategies

Civil enforcement strategies rely on the use of state statutes, local ordinances, and building and health codes to abate crime, drug, and disorder problems. The laws most frequently used in civil remedies are municipal drug or nuisance abatement ordinances (a few organizations rely on similar county ordinances or state statutes). While all nuisance abatement ordinances do not specifically identify drug activity as a nuisance, their use against such activity has generally been successful. In a 50-state statutory analysis, Smith et al. (1992) found that most abatement ordinances designate public prosecutors as the individuals who may initiate an abatement action, although citizens may do so in at least 16 states. The ordinances typically enable a plaintiff (private citizens, community organizations, city attorneys, etc.) to take legal action against an owner who knowingly allows a crime or nuisance problems to exist at his or her property (Cadwalader et al., 1993). Court-ordered sanctions include imposing fines and penalties, ordering the property closed, allowing the city to take action at the owner's expense, seizing the property and other remedies. Ordinances are also used to abate specific problems such as cigarette machines in areas frequented by youths, motels with hourly rates, graffiti, abandoned vehicles and property maintenance.

Municipal codes specifying safety and health standards for private residential and commercial properties are also used by community groups to force an owner to remedy problems. Owners who ignore violations issued by municipal agencies are subject to the same sanctions listed above. Other laws used in civil remedy strategies include loitering, trespassing and curfew ordinances, which are usually directed at reducing problems with youths and gangs. Zoning changes to establish drug-free zones around schools and neighborhoods are also used, as are state laws and local regulations and ordinances concerning the sale of liquor.

Bars, liquor stores and houses harboring drug dealers are the typical targets of enforcement efforts instigated by community organizations.

Community groups and citizens often approach enforcement in a step-wise fashion. The first step is to document the problem thoroughly, as though evidence is being prepared for legal action (as it may well be). Some organizations then directly approach the offenders (usually tenants in residential or commercial properties); however, most choose to work instead with the landlords and owners responsible for the property. Using threats to enforce ordinances that provide particular remedies, the community organizations and citizen activists pressure tenants, landlords and owners to resolve the problem.

In the face of intransigent owners and in situations where the community organization feels that approaching the owners is unwise, community groups approach public agencies to pressure them to enforce existing ordinances. The public officials worked with most often are, in order, the police, elected officials, building inspectors and prosecutors. Citizens and community groups provide these officials with the information gathered as evidence of the problem(s) and urge them to enforce existing laws by notifying landlords and owners, inspecting and citing for code violations, calling for solutions for unlawful nuisances and criminal behavior, and threatening and taking legal action. Private-sector companies such as mortgage and advertising firms may be approached by community groups as well. A fairly new tactic aims to not only get rid of the problem but to obtain resources for neighborhood improvement at the same time. For example, several community organizations have pushed to have seized and forfeited property and proceeds returned to the community for its own use.

When enforcement tactics short of adjudication fail to result in positive changes in individual properties, community organizations may file lawsuits against property owners or pressure city prosecutors to do so. Another growing form of direct enforcement strategy, which does not require the involvement of police or prosecutors, is the use of small-claims court actions against owners who knowingly allow a nuisance to remain. The tactic of small-claims courts for drug and disorder abatement was pioneered by the Oakland-based Safe Streets Now! community organization, which combines traditional organizing and empowerment strategies with the civil remedy. Safe Streets Now! organizers provide expertise, training and protection to residents in filing small claims actions — one for every man, woman, and child — up to the maximum. In most cases, community pressure and threats to sue — along with media reports of the success of this civil remedy approach — are enough to make landlords resolve the problem. With one exception in which no award was given to the neighborhood, small-claims courts have ruled in favor of community residents (Roehl et al., 1997).

Community organization staff organize the activities of residents and participate in them. They provide needed assistance and support in research, technical areas, and legal proceedings; obtain materials and publicity; and perform specific tasks such as writing letters to property owners and coordinating with city agencies and other community groups. Community organizations also serve an important protection function — they shield the identity of citizens from the targets (drug dealers, angry landlords, etc.) of their efforts. Letters to owners come from the organization, rather than individual residents, and court filings are made by the organization or an attorney operating on their behalf.

Half of the organizations involved in enforcement activities obtained legal advice or assistance in the process, while the other half said no special legal assistance was required. The majority of those receiving assistance obtained it from public attorneys (city, district or state attorneys); others used board members and/or community volunteers. While 12% of the organizations expressed a desire for technical assistance in legal procedures and use of ordinances, often for the residents who work with them, most of the organizations reported no problems with obtaining legal assistance, usually *pro bono.*

Lobbying for Civil Remedies

In some situations, local and state civil laws are not available or adequate for combating drug and other problems. The majority of the surveyed organizations have lobbied for the passage of new ordinances or other regulations useful for enforcement. A small number have taken the lead and written the proposed ordinances themselves, then pushed for passage. Community organization staff and citizens often attend hearings of alcohol beverage control regulators and permit-granting bodies to influence the issuance or renewal of permits and liquor licenses. A third of the organizations have worked to ban drug-related items such as beepers, cigarette machines and drug paraphernalia.

Civil Remedies for Prevention and Neighborhood Improvement

A final category of civil remedies used by community groups are those that are preventive and proactive, aiming, respectively, to reduce opportunities for problems to arise, and to improve and protect the quality of neighborhood life. The most common prevention strategy is to provide training and assistance to landlords and owners in tenant screening and relations, management techniques, and security and crime prevention, similar to the program offered by the Oakland (CA) Police Department's Beat Health Unit (see Mazerolle et al., this volume). The proactive use of civil remedies by community organizations is in an embryonic form. Examples include working to increase alcohol tax revenues and have a larger proportion returned to the community, and turning abandoned property into needed housing for low-income families or other special groups.

Obstacles and Outcomes

The large majority of the community organizations surveyed reported success in their civil remedy strategies. Environmental changes were relatively easy to implement and usually successful in cleaning up the neighborhood and promoting community awareness, pride and commitment. On the down side, several organizations reported the nagging recurrence of trash and graffiti.

Subjective reports of the outcomes of enforcement strategies are similarly positive. The organizations report that in 80 to 90% of the cases, owners take steps to resolve the problems before legal actions are needed. While rare, lawsuits are also generally effective. All but one of eight lawsuits initiated by surveyed organizations were decided in favor of the plaintiffs. Organizations also reported details of success with specific problems, such as evicting a drug dealer and closing a problem bar, and many have an impressive track record of ongoing successes (e.g., closing down 50 crack houses in the past several years). Beyond these resolutions of specific problems, a number of organizations report reductions in crime, loitering and other problems, and increases in community awareness and commitment. Most of the organizations were generally satisfied with the responses of police, prosecutors and housing officials.

In spite of generally positive results, the civil remedy strategies used by community organizations are seldom quick, easy or trouble-free. Agency "red tape" and resistance, legal roadblocks, unyielding landlords and owners, slothful tenants, and the lengthy, often frustrating time required by civil solutions were among the obstacles reported by community organizations. They also reported problems common to community crime prevention efforts, such as difficulty in getting residents involved and keeping them involved, fear of retaliation, and lack of funds and resources. Concerns about retaliation, unfortunately, are well-founded. Nearly a third of the organizations surveyed reported attacks, mostly verbal threats and some vandalism against citizens, believed to be in retaliation for their involvement in anti-drug activities.

The directors of the organizations surveyed expressed concern about the potential of civil remedies to cause harm, such as making false accusations against innocent people or, more typically, instigating the eviction of the mother or child of a drug dealer. Twenty percent of the directors reported receiving complaints about violations of civil rights, mostly from targets of tactics. Constitutional challenges to specific ordinances are discussed in Cadwalader et al., (1993), Smith et al., (1992) and Finn and Hylton (1994).

SUMMARY AND CONCLUSIONS

In the national survey, civil remedies were found to be most common in urban areas, and particularly in inner-city neighborhoods where drug problems and their devastating effects are greatest. The main roles of neighborhood residents in the enforcement of civil remedy strategies are (1) to identify and document the problem, (2) to keep pressure on appropriate authorities to resolve the problem, and (3) to monitor the situation over time. In these roles residents gather information, provide information to authorities, write letters, and appear and present at hearings. Within environmental change strategies, citizens provide the manual labor needed — they paint out the graffiti, haul trash, plant shrubs, etc.

Community organizations active in civil remedies tend to be well-established groups with solid funding and staff support, although fledgling groups of residents have mounted numerous successful efforts. Although money and staff are not *required* for civil remedies, they do require specific expertise, knowledge and tenacity to succeed. Additional funding and technical assistance support would likely increase the intensity and duration of civil intervention efforts.

There may also be a natural maturation process underway in many community organizations. A number of participants in the national survey began with the basic building blocks of community organizing years ago, moved into neighborhood watch and community crime prevention, and then on to anti-drug efforts and civil remedies applied to specific "hot spots." The organizations surveyed reported general success with their civil remedy tactics. In fact, there is emerging evidence in this volume and elsewhere (Finn and Hylton, 1994; Davis and Lurigio, 1996) that civil remedies may be more effective than criminal prosecution in alleviating neighborhood drug problems. This evidence, however, is largely anecdotal, self-reported and focused on the short-term. There has been very limited support for impact evaluations directed toward the work of community organizations to determine what works and what does not.

Perhaps the greatest challenge to community-based civil remedies is the charge that they displace, rather than eliminate, crime and drug problems. Community organizations are concerned about displacement (and particularly the possible harm done to innocent residents); nonetheless, they consider the eviction of a drug dealer a small victory to be combined with others to achieve long-term success. Lurigio et al. (1993), in a limited follow-up study of displaced dealers, also provide tentative hope for positive impacts on displacement as well. Yet the long-term effects of civil remedy outcomes such as evictions need further study, including assessments of their effectiveness in reducing neighborhood problems (Smith et al., 1992), their potential for harming innocent parties (Davis and Lurigio, 1996), and the high level of retaliation against those involved in civil remedies (Roehl et al., 1997). The most tenacious problems faced by community organizations involve properties that are owner-occupied, owned by absentee owners, or no longer financially viable; the slowness of bureaucratic procedures; and the stubborn ability of drug problems to return. This may be due, in part, to the continued failure to address the underlying conditions that contribute to drugs and crime.

Although citizens and community organizations can and do apply civil remedies on their own, they benefit greatly from the clout and support of city agencies, particularly the police, housing officials and public prosecutors. Multi-group partnerships are often necessary to apply effective civil remedies, in the same vein that such cooperation underlies the most effective crime prevention and community policing strategies (Friedman, 1994). Future advancements and acceptance of civil remedies may depend on enhancing mutual problem-solving and information-sharing between citizens and government officials with enforcement responsibilities.

Finally, community organizations have a special and unique role in community-based crime control and neighborhood revitalization. Community organizations cannot always apply civil remedy strategies alone, but they *can* do things for their communities that government agencies cannot or do not. Many of the community groups use civil remedies to mitigate crime, drug and disorder problems, yet aim for a more permanent solution by leaving behind an empowered citizenry that can work toward and then protect a higher quality of life in the neighborhood. If and when crime or disorder reappear, residents are ready and able to tackle them quickly. The preventive and proactive applications of civil remedies by community organizations, such as training landlords and turning seized drug houses and abandoned properties into low-income housing and community centers, also hold much promise for neighborhood improvement and empowerment. Increasing community empowerment is inherent in the majority of civil remedy actions guided by community groups — these actions are accompanied by training and support designed to increase citizens' knowledge, expertise and power.

Address correspondence to: Jan Roehl, Justice Research Center, 591 Lighthouse Avenue, Suite 24, Pacific Grove, CA 93950. E-mail: <jrcpg@redshift.com>.

Acknowledgments: This research was conducted under Cooperative Agreement No. 93-IJ-CX-K010 from the National Institute of Justice, Office of Justice Programs, U.S. Department of Justice. Points of view are those of the author and do not necessarily represent the official position of the Department of Justice.

REFERENCES

Bickman, L., P.J. Lavrakas, and S.K. Green (1977). *National Evaluation Program —— Phase I Summary Report: Citizen Crime Reporting Projects*. Washington, DC: Law Enforcement Assistance Administration, U.S. Department of Justice.

Cadwalader, Wickersham, and Taft, Attorneys at Law (1993). *A Civil War: A Community Legal Guide to Fighting Street Drug Markets*. New York, NY: author.

Cirel, P., P. Evans, D. McGillis, and D. Whitcomb (1977). *An Exemplary Project: Community Crime Prevention Program, Seattle, Washington*. Washington, DC: National Institute of Law Enforcement and Criminal Justice, U.S. Department of Justice.

Crowe, T.D. (1991). *Crime Prevention Through Environmental Design: Applications of Architectural Design and Space Management Concepts*. Boston, MA: Butterworth-Heinemann.

Davis, R.C., A.J. Lurigio, and D.P. Rosenbaum (eds.) (1993). *Drugs and the Community*. Springfield, IL: Charles C. Thomas.

—— and A.J. Lurigio (1996). *Fighting Back: Neighborhood Antidrug Strategies*. Thousand Oaks, CA: Sage.

DuBow, F. and D. Emmons (1981). "The Community Hypothesis." In: D.A. Lewis (ed.), *Reactions to Crime.* Sage Criminal Justice System Annuals, vol. 16. Beverly Hills, CA: Sage.

Eck, J.E. and W. Spelman (1987). *Solving Problems: Problem-oriented Policing in Newport News.* Washington, DC: Police Executive Research Forum.

Ellickson, P.L. and R.M. Bell (1990). *Prospects for Preventing Drug Use Among Young Adolescents.* Santa Monica, CA: Rand.

Feins, J.D. (1983). *Partnerships for Neighborhood Crime Prevention.* Washington, DC: U.S. National Institute of Justice.

Feldman, J. and S. Trapp (1990). *Taking Our Neighborhoods Back.* Chicago, IL: National Training and Information Center.

Finn, P. and M.O. Hylton (1994). *Using Civil Remedies for Criminal Behavior: Rationale, Case Studies, and Constitutional Issues.* Washington, DC: U.S. National Institute of Justice.

Fowler, F.J., Jr. and T.W. Mangione (1982). *Neighborhood Crime, Fear, and Social Control: A Second Look at the Hartford Program (Executive summary).* Washington, DC: National Institute of Justice, U.S. Department of Justice.

—— M.E. McCalla and T.W. Mangione (1979). *Reducing Residential Crime and Fear: The Hartford Neighborhood Crime Prevention Program.* Washington, DC: U.S. Government Printing Office.

Friedman, W. (1994). "The Community Role in Community Policing." In: D.P. Rosenbaum, (ed.), *The Challenge of Community Policing: Testing the Promises.* Thousand Oaks, CA: Sage.

Gardiner, R.A. (1978). *Design for Safe Neighborhoods: The Environmental Security Planning and Design Process.* Washington, DC: National Institute of Law Enforcement and Criminal Justice, U.S. Department of Justice.

Goldstein, H. (1990). *Problem-Oriented Policing.* New York, NY: McGraw Hill.

Greenberg, S.W., W.M. Rohe, and J.R. Williams (1982). *Safe and Secure Neighborhoods: Physical Characteristics and Informal Territorial Control in High and Low Crime Neighborhoods.* Washington, DC: U.S. National Institute of Justice.

—— (1985). *Informal Citizen Action and Crime Prevention at'the Neighborhood Level: Synthesis and Assessment of the Research.* Washington, DC: U.S. National Institute of Justice.

Greene, J.R. and R.B. Taylor (1988). "Community-based Policing and Foot Patrol: Issues of Theory and Evaluation." In: J.R. Greene and S.D.

Mastrofski (eds.), *Community Policing: Rhetoric or Reality.* New York, NY: Praeger.

—— and S.D. Mastrofski, S.D. (eds.) (1988). *Community Policing: Rhetoric or Reality.* New York, NY: Praeger.

Hawkins, J.D., R.F. Catalano, and J.Y. Miller (1992). "Risk and Protective Factors for Alcohol and Other Drug Problems in Adolescence and Early Adulthood: Implications for Substance Abuse Prevention." *Psychological Bulletin* 112:64-105.

Lavrakas, P., J. Normoyle, W.G. Skogan, E.J. Herz, G. Salem, and D.A. Lewis (1981). *Factors Related to Citizen Involvement in Personal, Household, and Neighborhood Anti-Crime Measures (Executive summary).* Washington, DC: U.S. National Institute of Justice.

—— S.F. Bennett, B.S. Fisher, E. Reninger, R.A. Maier, and G. Jobi (1989). *A Process and Impact Evaluation of the 1983-86 Neighborhood Anti-Crime Self-Help Program: Summary Report.* Evanston, IL: Center for Urban Affairs, Northwestern University.

Lurigio A.J., and R.C. Davis (1992). "Taking the War on Drugs to the Streets: The Perceptual Impact of Four Neighborhood Drug Programs." *Crime & Delinquency* 38(4):522-538.

—— R. Davis, T. Regulus, V. Gwisada, S. Popkin, M. Dantzker, B. Smith, and A. Ouellet (1993). *An Evaluation of the Cook County State's Attorney's Office Narcotics Nuisance Abatement Program.* Chicago, IL: Loyola University Department of Criminal Justice.

Moore, M.H. and M.A. Kleiman. (1989). "The Police and Drugs." *Perspectives on Policing, vol. 11.* Washington, DC: U.S. National Institute of Justice.

National Crime Prevention Council (1992). *Creating a Climate of Hope: Ten Neighborhoods Tackle the Drug Crisis.* Washington, DC: National Crime Prevention Council.

Pate, A.M., M.A. Wycoff, W.G. Skogan, and L.W. Sherman (1986). *Reducing Fear of Crime in Houston and Newark: A Summary Report.* Washington, DC: U.S. National Institute of Justice.

Pentz, M.A., J.H. Dwyer, D.P. MacKinnon, B.R. Flay, W.B. Hansen, E.Y. Yang, and C.A. Johnson (1989). "A Multicommunity Trial for Primary Prevention of Adolescent Drug Abuse." *Journal of the American Medical Association* 261(22):3259-3266.

Roehl, J.A. and R.C. Cook (1984). *Evaluation of the Urban Crime Prevention Program: Executive Summary.* Washington, DC: U.S. National Institute of Justice.

—— H. Wong, C. Andrews, R. Huitt and G.E. Capowich (1995). *A National Assessment of Community-based Anti-drug Efforts.* Pacific Grove, CA: Institute for Social Analysis.

—— H. Wong, and C. Andrews (1997). *The Use of Civil Remedies by Community Organizations for Neighborhood Crime and Drug Abatement.* Pacific Grove, CA: Institute for Social Analysis.

Rosenbaum, D.P. (1988). "Community Crime Prevention: A Review and Synthesis of the Literature." *Justice Quarterly* 5(3):323-95.

—— (ed.) (1994). *The Challenge of Community Policing: Testing the Promises.* Thousand Oaks, CA: Sage.

—— S. Bennett, B. Lindsay, and D. Wilkinson (1994). *Community Responses to Drug Abuse: A Program Evaluation.* Washington, DC: U.S. Department of Justice.

—— D.A. Lewis, and J.A. Grant (1986). "Neighborhood-based Crime Prevention: Assessing the Efficacy of Community Organizing in Chicago." In: D.P. Rosenbaum (ed.), *Community Crime Prevention: Does It Work?* Beverly Hills, CA: Sage.

Sherman, L.W. (1990). "Police Crackdowns: Initial and Residual Deterrence." In: M. Tonry and N. Morris (eds.), *Crime and Justice: A Review of Research,* vol. 12. Chicago, IL: University of Chicago Press.

Skogan, W.G. (1988). "Communities, Crime, and Neighborhood Organization." *Crime & Delinquency* 35(3):437-457.

—— and A.J. Lurigio (1992). "The Correlates of Community Antidrug Activism." *Crime & Delinquency* 38(4):510-521.

—— and M.G. Maxfield (1981). *Coping with Crime: Individual and Neighborhood Reactions.* Sage Library of Social Research, vol. 124. Beverly Hills, CA: Sage.

—— and S.M. Hartnett (1997). *Community Policing, Chicago Style.* New York, NY: Oxford University Press.

Skolnick, J.H. and D.H. Bayley (1986). *The New Blue Line: Police Innovation in Six American Cities.* New York, NY: Free Press.

Smith, B.E., R.C. Davis, S.W. Hillenbrand, and S.R. Goretsky (1992). *Ridding Neighborhoods of Drug Houses in the Private Sector.* Washington, DC: American Bar Association.

—— and R.C. Davis (1993). "Successful Community Anticrime Programs: What Makes Them Work?" In: R.C. Davis, A.J. Lurigio, and D.P. Rosenbaum (eds.), *Drugs and the Community: Involving Community Residents in Combating the Sale of Illegal Drugs.* Springfield, IL: Charles C Thomas.

Weingart, S.N. (1993). "A Typology of Community Responses to Drugs." In: R.C. Davis, A.J. Lurigio, and D.P. Rosenbaum (eds.), *Drugs and the Community: Involving Community Residents in Combating the Sale of Illegal Drugs.* Springfield, IL: Charles C Thomas.

—— F.X. Hartmann, and D. Osborne (1993). *Lessons Learned: Case Studies of the Initiation and Maintenance of the Community Response to Drugs.* Cambridge, MA: John F. Kennedy School of Government, Harvard University.

Wilson, J.Q. and Kelling, G.L. (1982). "Broken windows: The Police and Neighborhood Safety." *Atlantic Monthly* (Mar):29-38.

Yin, R. (1986). "Community Crime Prevention: A Synthesis of Eleven Evaluations." In: D.P. Rosenbaum (ed.), *Community Crime Prevention: Does It Work?* Beverly Hills, CA: Sage.

—— M.E. Vogel, and J.M. Chaiken (1977). *National Evaluation Program — Phase I Summary Report: Citizen Patrol Projects.* Washington, DC: Law Enforcement Assistance Administration, U.S. Department of Justice.

A CO-PRODUCTION MODEL OF CODE ENFORCEMENT AND NUISANCE ABATEMENT

by

Anne Blumenberg
Community Law Center

Brenda Bratton Blom
Empowerment Legal Services Program, Inc.

and

Erin Artigiani
Center for Substance Abuse Research
University of Maryland, College Park

Abstract: In Baltimore, MD, communities are reducing "crime and grime" and developing comprehensive strategies for community revitalization and reclamation using principles grounded in "co-production" — the coordinated efforts of residents and government agencies, who share authority and responsibility for success. In the co-production model, community organizations take a very active role in deciding when to initiate legal action to abate a nuisance situation, defining the nature and source of the problems and developing a strategy to address the problems. Solutions typically require the extensive cooperation of local government as a partner in problem solving. In this chapter, the processes and theoretical underpinnings of the co-production model of health and safety code enforcement are compared and contrasted to other service delivery models. Co-production strategies appear to be particularly appropriate in the areas of zoning, day care, local traffic regulation, park and recreation facility maintenance, and law enforcement and public safety. Like other forms of civil remedies, co-production strategies have the potential for both abusing the power the model provides and producing positive effects throughout the community.

INTRODUCTION

In Their Own Words

"We don't have bullet holes anymore. Don't even have gun fire."

"My father, I remember a time when they (drug dealers) went after him for watching them. One of them told me, 'I'll kill him.' But I told him then he better kill me too, 'cause there's no way I'd let him get away with that. Now, my father has cookouts on the street."

"Remember that pop, pop, pop sound? Now, it be [sic] so quiet sometimes I have to go out and see if the street is still there."

(Quotes from members of the Boyd Booth community at their Victory Celebration Supper)

The Community Law Center

Baltimore, MD communities are reducing "crime and grime" and developing comprehensive strategies for community revitalization and reclamation using principles grounded in "co-production" — the coordinated efforts of residents and government agencies, who share authority and responsibility for success. Assisted by the Community Law Center of Baltimore, the community organization takes a very active role in deciding when to use legal action to abate a nuisance situation, i.e., reduce crime and grime, and the appropriate remedy to seek. Additional support and technical services available to the community organization typically include: an organizer and ongoing technical support and training (typically provided by the Citizens' Planning and Housing Association [CPHA]); physical design and community planning services (generally supplied by the Neighborhood Design Center [NDC]); and an entity able to perform or coordinate construction work, e.g., a housing development corporation, a community development corporation or a newly created community service crew. In some communities, a neighborhood contractor may be hired on a per-job basis. In others, the police are an initial and integral part of the effort, and in still others, they are "brought in."

These resources are combined to assist community residents as they define the problems and their immediate sources and causes, and seek a vision of what they want their community to be like. In defining the problem, it is not enough to say that a drug dealer operates out of a certain house. Before that problem can be addressed, one must know who (by name and detailed description) deals what, at what times during the day, to whom and exactly how. This is information best obtained by the residents. The police will need such information before they can get a search and seizure warrant. The lawyer will need to know this information as well as who owns the house, the owner's circumstances and what the community thinks is the appropriate remedy to the situation, before a civil lawsuit can be filed.

The second step is to develop a strategy to address the problems. That strategy will include many components, e.g., community mobilization, defensible space plans, securing and eventually renovating or demolishing vacant houses, removing drug dealers and drug buyers, and starting community-building and youth programs.

An Overview of the Law

In working with communities, the Law Center has developed a body of law built upon common law nuisance. The fundamental premise is that people have a right to the reasonable enjoyment of their property without intrusion from unreasonable activities or conditions emanating from another property. Those unreasonable activities and conditions are a nuisance. Persons negatively affected have the right to seek a court-ordered abatement of the condition or activity causing the nuisance. Abatement is the correction or cessation of the problem.

Translated into everyday English: vacant lots and houses which are a breeding ground for rats, drug users and trash, are a nuisance; commercial signage and billboards without the proper permit in a residential area are a nuisance; open-air drug markets are a nuisance; and shootings, fear and constant police raids are a nuisance. The nuisance and code enforcement laws that form the basis of the Law Center's work in community comprehensive plans are presented in Appendix 2; a glossary of frequently used terms in Appendix 1.

Following are two hypothetical examples of conditions that are nuisances under the common law. Reference will be made to these examples throughout this chapter.

	The Vacant Lot	**The 1300 Illegal Billboards**
The Owner	A little old lady receiving Supplemental Security Income (SSI) has been in a nursing home for 15 years. Her family home used to be on this vacant lot. When the owner went into the nursing home, the house needed a lot of repairs. Once vacant, it was vandalized. Then, drug addicts used it as a shooting gallery. There was a major fire, set by a drug addict trying to keep warm, and the house was destroyed. Finally, the City demolished what was left.	Two related national corporations with small offices in Baltimore own approximately 1,300 "junior" billboards. The zoning code requires a permit to place a billboard or any other commercial signage. The owners only have permits for approximately 75 billboards.
The Problem	The lot is overgrown with weeds and infested with rats and other undesirable creatures. In addition, it is used by drug dealers who stash drugs among the weeds and dump drugs when the police come. Home improvement contractors and others also dump on the lot. Now there are refrigerators, washing machines and old building materials with environmental hazards on the lot.	Many of the billboards advertise alcohol and cigarettes. Most are in low-income residential areas, in which it is highly unlikely a permit would have been granted had the company applied for one. Some billboards have been placed on buildings without the knowledge or consent of the owner of the property.

THE THEORETICAL BASIS: CO-PRODUCTION

Community groups care little about ongoing theoretical debates regarding their role in community change. But to those who study community change, there are many different models by which to trace this change. In the end, what matters to the community is that change has occurred. But, for professionals, the definitions and models can affect how money is allocated, and the way community groups are included or excluded from any process.

Enforcement Models

Many different models have been developed to explain and analyze the effectiveness of the delivery of services through code enforcement. However, there are two basic models. The first is the *deterrence- or rule-oriented enforcement strategy*, which "...seeks to coerce compliance through the maximal detection and sanctioning of violation of legal rules" (Scholz, 1984:179). Discussion of this model, particularly as it applies to housing codes, can most easily be followed in law journals. For example: "The effectiveness of housing code enforcement, however, is a subject of debate among social scientists. While vigorous code enforcement should have a positive effect on housing quality, some articles suggest that vigorous enforcement leads to abandonment, demolition or substantial rent increases, resulting in a decrease in the supply of low-cost housing" (Ramsey and Zolna, 1992:605). Deterrence enforcement, the strict enforcement to the fullest extent of the law, pleases the intended beneficiary of the laws — the consumers of housing and the community residents — so long as costs are not increased beyond their affordability. Those who are the "actors" in deterrence enforcement are generally the government agency professionals and employees hired for enforcement activities.

Law students and professors have analyzed code enforcement activities in particular cities, coming to varying conclusions about the effectiveness of any given code enforcement system (Ramsey and Zolna, 1991). The emphasis in these analyses tends to focus on: (1) whether the "rules" (laws) are fair and constitutional; (2) whether there is an administrative mechanism to enforce the "rules"; (3) whether the mechanism effectively enforces the "rules"; (4) the role of the courts in the enforcement procedure; and (5) the effect on the housing stock. There are a number of stages in deterrence code enforcement, and coordination among agencies is often a problem. As noted by Miller (1983): "It is striking, nationwide, how little communication and cooperation exist among the code agencies, the prosecutors, and the courts" (p.349). It is often in this lack of coordination that deterrence enforcement breaks down.

The second basic code enforcement model is *the cooperative strategy*, which "...emphasizes flexible or selective enforcement that takes into consideration the particular circumstances of an observed violation" (Scholz, 1984:180). For Scholz, cooperation is not an altruistic strategy but a way to "achieve higher utility in the long run by abstaining from temptations to maximize short term gains" (Scholz, 1984:181). He develops a model for a cooperative strategy that grows out of public choice theories. According to Mueller (1979), "public choice can be defined as the economic study of non market decision making...The basic behavioral postulate of public choice, as for economics, is that man is an egoistic, rational, utility maximizer" (p.1). Scholz (1984) used the "repeated prisoner's dilemma" to show that "the advantage of the combined strategy (deterrence and cooperation) over simple deterrence...increases with enforcement tradeoffs that reduce costs for cooperative firms, with diminishing returns that increase the advantages of cooperation, and with the degree to which the sanction structure favors cooperation over evasion" (p.219).

John T. Scholz (1991) implemented this cooperative model in his study of the Occupational Safety and Health Administration. His cooperative model was to challenge the traditional deterrence enforcement models in several ways. The first challenge — to the concept of a natural conflict —suggests that "both firms (that are regulated) and (the enforcement) agency can be better off if the agency forgoes legalistic enforcement of regulations that are inappropriate for a particular firm in return for extralegal efforts on the part of that firm to work toward the policy objective" (Scholz, 1991:115).

Scholz's second challenge was to the two-party formulation. This change is critical for communities involved with code enforcement. Scholz introduced into the policy equation the role of the policy beneficiaries — in this case, the employees of the regulated firm. But, in his study, the policy beneficiaries end up opposing cooperative enforcement strategies because they have no control over the flexibility and deal-making of the government agency: "If beneficiaries always assume that their opponents will soon control the enforcement bureaucracy...it appears unlikely that they would ever trust the bureaucracy with long-term discretion required for effective enforcement" (Scholz 1991:132) This finding is echoed by enforcement officials in cities across America. If they try to adopt a flexible attitude, community residents complain and charge them with failing to do their job appropriately. There is little doubt that the delivery of services — whether code enforcement, crime enforcement or the basic services of garbage collection — has been seen by community residents as ineffective. Code enforcement models must be viewed within the larger perspective of inefficient service delivery.

Problems with Traditional Service Delivery Models

Systems analysis theoreticians and researchers have been attempting to understand the management and structure of cities and their agencies for many years. Rogers (1971) looked at service delivery systems by examining four parameters: "(1) the political setting or environment; (2) the organizational design [both planned and unplanned]; (3) the nature of the transactions among the participants; and (4) the outputs (p.148). " His conclusions about the ability to effectively coordinate all these parameters for the delivery of services were bleak. He looked at the complexity purely from a systems approach.

Sharp (1986) takes a thorough look at the body of literature that points to a time of excessive demand for services and a rising sense of entitlement. This "overload" school suggests that "there is a growing consensus that governments in post industrial societies face heavy demands for solutions to all manner of problems that were not necessarily laid at their doorsteps in the past" and that these rising demands will create a situation in which "governments are stalemated from acting on competing demands or at which government's solutions modifies expectations downward" (Sharp, 1986:163-164).

But Sharp goes on to look at the research examining the ethic of self-reliance that permeates public opinion and action in this country. In our nation's older cities, there are decreasing resources that are totally unable to meet the rising demands. Sharp (1986), however, does not despair but moves on to examine alternatives arising in response to the overload.

Alternative Service Delivery Models

The alternative service delivery models for local governments have included service rationing, privatization and "off-budget enterprises" (Sharp, 1986:182). Local governments are also lessening the provision of direct services through the development of user fees, voucher systems or special use districts.

Co-Production as a Promising Alternative

"Co-production involves a mixing of the productive efforts of regular (a government agency) and consumer producers. This mixing may occur directly, involving coordinated efforts in the same production process, or indirectly through independent, yet related efforts of regular producers and consumer producers" (Parks et al., 1981:1002). Whitaker (1980) explains that "rather than an agent presenting a `finished product' to the citizen, agent and citizen together produce the desired transformation" (p.240). Although much of the research on co-production has been aimed at community safety efforts (Percy, 1978), the concept can apply as well to education, health care and crisis intervention. The Community Law Center's model for nuisance abatement is a clear indication that the co-production model also applies to code enforcement and nuisance abatement issues.

This co-production strategy fundamentally challenges the traditional economic "public choice" model by bringing the policy beneficiaries/consumers — in this case, the community residents of the affected neighborhood — into the equation as co-producers of services. Hence, the enforcement mechanism is transformed: it becomes both more flexible when in the mode of cooperative enforcement, and more effective in a deterrence mode when interests are indeed antagonistic and unresolvable. Scholz's (1991)difficulty with sabotage by the beneficiaries becomes transformed into something more than a consultative relationship or influence groups trying to be heard. As a co-producer of the services necessary for the abatement of nuisances in housing and crime, trust is reinforced, rather than undermined.

Co-Production in a Political Context

Liebmann (1993), a Baltimore attorney, examined the co-production model in the context of effective models of democracy, asserting that "the size of contemporary municipalities is inconsistent with a significant degree of direct civic participation of the town-meeting model" (p.337) He further contends that "decentralization will not achieve the town meeting ideal of participatory democracy unless the community involved is extremely small" (p.339, quoting Yates, [1973]). Liebmann (1993) then examines the kinds of tasks that are prime candidates for use of the co-production model at the block, club or community association level. In his opinion, these include zoning, day care regulation, traffic regulation, schooling at the elementary level, park and recreational facility maintenance, and law enforcement, particularly as to property and nuisance crimes.

Liebmann's (1993) examination places into a theoretical context what the Law Center has seen in a practical context as it serves its clients. The Law Center's work started with the attorney-client relationship and evolved, rather organically, from that point. Co-production is centered on the understanding that the community organization is an equal partner in efforts to maintain and develop safe and secure communities. These organizations are not to be consulted, but are indeed to be an integral part of the planning and implementation of plans for change, enforcement and problem-solving within the boundaries of the community.

CLIENT-DRIVEN REMEDIES

Traditional Role of the Attorney with a Business Client

No rational person undertakes a business enterprise in the U.S. without an attorney. The attorney is paid by the client. Both the attorney and client have a mutual interest in the business succeeding and growing. The first role of the attorney is to know the client's business thoroughly, so that he or she can know the legal issues involved and how best to address them. This is a proactive use of and response to the law to promote the client's interests. The attorney will provide legal counsel enabling the client to develop and go forward with his or her plans and to keep out of trouble. The attorney will represent the client in negotiations with third parties, and prepare legal agreements and contracts. The attorney will represent the client in litigation — both offensively as the plaintiff and defensively as the defendant when sued. When the law is an impediment to the success of the client, the attorney will assist the client in changing the law to promote the client's goals.

Attorney's Role When Serving Nonprofit Community Organizations Established to Promote Community Welfare

The aforementioned attorney's role does not change when the client is a community organization seeking to promote the public welfare. The first requirement is getting to know the client's interests and business — its strengths and weaknesses, goals and resources, and development of realistic plans to obtain those goals. From that point forward, the role of the attorney follows the same pattern as with any business client. The attorney will:

- Help develop a comprehensive plan. This is discussed in detail in the section, "The Community Law Center's Experience in Baltimore."

- Provide legal counsel to enable the client to go forward with its plans and to keep it out of trouble. Community organizations have the same need for legal counsel as any other entity seeking to accomplish a goal. If the client wants to plant a community garden, it will need to establish the legal right to use the land. If the client wants to have a parade, it will need a permit. If the client wants to open a day care center, it will need permits, zoning, state certification and a lease or ownership of a building. If the client wants to block off any alley to stop the escape route of drug dealers, it will need the approval of the local government and any other person with an interest in the land.

- Provide representation in litigation, both as plaintiff to further the client's goals and as defendant in response to possible lawsuits against the client. The client's goal, broadly stated, is the promotion of the welfare of its community. If a condition exists within the community that is detrimental to the community welfare, the client's interest is to have that condition remedied. This may be done by seeking to have the local administrative agency enforce the legal code, or the client may seek direct action on its own behalf. If there is a vacant lot that is repeatedly used as a dumping ground by certain small demolition companies, the community organization may notify the local government agency and request that it enforce the codes that prohibit dumping and maintaining unsanitary lots. Or, it may, after due notice is given to the parties, seek a court order in its own name requiring the owner to clean up the vacant lot and secure it against future dumping, and requiring the "certain small demolition companies" to do the clean-up or to pay for it to be done.

- Seek to change the law when it does not promote the client's interests, through a number of possible approaches. The client may want to prohibit certain behavior that would require a change in the law, e.g., prohibiting billboards in residential areas. Another approach is to expand the rights of the organization to directly use the law to reach its goals, e.g., for the organization itself to have the right to take the owner of the vacant lot to court.

Integrating the Role of the Attorney with the Co-Production Model of Health and Safety Code Enforcement

The promotion of the public welfare through the use of the legal system has become the providence of the local and state government. The standards for what is not acceptable to the community have been embodied in legislative codes enforced by an administrative agency of the government. The ultimate method of enforcement, in Baltimore and many other cities, is through a criminal charge in which the administrative agency seeks a fine against the owner or offender. The underlying theory is that this ultimate enforcement is a deterrence to such behavior.

The enforcement system may be planned and methodical, as in a property-by-property, block-by-block inspection system or an annual inspection of every rental dwelling unit. Given the dwindling resources available to local governments, this is rarely the approach. The enforcement system is more likely to be "complaint-driven," where local inspections and enforcement occur only in response to a complaint. Or, code enforcement may combine these two approaches — methodical inspection as to certain dwelling units, e.g., Section 8 subsidized units for which the U.S. Department of Housing and Urban Development requires an annual inspection, and complaint-driven inspection for all others. In all of these methods, the role of a community organization representing the interests of the residents is at best advisory. The community is at the mercy of the political will, resources and capacity of the local administrative agency. Even in a cooperative situation, community organizations all too often have to rely upon the "squeaky wheel" syndrome to get anything done.

If the community organization client should develop its own plan and strategy for removing and remedying nuisance situations, which typically are in violation of a code or statute, it still must rely upon local government support for implementation. In the vacant lot example, the client could attempt to remedy the problem by taking direct action itself or by seeking to have the local administrative agency enforce the codes. However, to take action in Maryland, , the community organization *must* have a property interest that is directly affected. Individual members who own property may seek a court remedy. But, without a property interest of its own, under Maryland common law the organization will not have standing to do so, unless there is explicit legislation giving it this right. Standing is the right of direct access to the courts and legal system on one's own behalf. If there is legislation granting the community organization standing, then the client may seek code enforcement itself.

Changes Implied by a Co-Production Model

If the client (the community-based organization) has the *right* to seek direct civil enforcement of the law (standing) and the *capacity* to do so (an attorney), then it has more than an advisory role. It has the authority to assume responsibility and develop a strategy that best uses available resources to obtain its goal — the promotion of the community welfare. The question then is, when should or must the client seek to work cooperatively with government agencies?

The general answer to that question is relatively easy. When the community organization does not have the capacity to implement or cause to be implemented *all* of the roles and actions needed to remedy the situation, then it must work cooperatively with other resources to accomplish its ends. Using the vacant lot example, if the owner cannot be made to clean the lot because she is an impoverished, little old lady in a nursing home on SSI and the persons doing the dumping cannot be located, *then* the community organization must have some other means at its disposal for accomplishing the cleaning and securing of the lot. If the organization itself has the capacity to do this, it only needs the authority of the law to effect the remedy. If it does not have this capacity, then it must have available to it some other entity that can pay for the cost of accomplishing the goal.

In the billboard example, enforcement consists of billboard companies not putting alcohol or tobacco ads in residential neighborhoods, or removing any that exist. It is within the capacity of the billboard company to do this. Therefore, the community organization does not need additional resources to accomplish its objective. In some situations, such as seeking to remove open-air drug dealing from the community, the activity is too dangerous for residents to directly take on the responsibility. If the only remedy is criminal enforcement, then the cooperation of the local agency, the police and the State's Attorney's Office is essential.

Traditionally, government agencies have had the responsibility and exclusive authority to enforce public codes. The residents of the community have been the beneficiaries of this service. When a community organization has access to the law and an attorney, co-production then entails a shared authority and responsibility with the local government agencies. Even with its new found authority, if the local governmental agencies do not work cooperatively in the venture, the community organization is, as a practical matter, still limited in what it can do on its own behalf. Acceptance of a co-production model has ramifications for the actions of local government agencies as well as for the communities they are chartered to serve.

If the local governmental agencies *do* work in a co-productive manner, then the "policy beneficiaries," i.e., the residents of the community needing code enforcement, and the traditional "service providers" are working together toward a mutual public policy objective. Moreover, in the experience of the Community Law Center, community residents are very aware of appropriate "selective and policy-oriented" enforcement as being more solution-oriented and preferable. That is to say, if the property owner is the proverbial "little old lady," community residents would be much more familiar with her status than would a distant government employee. Furthermore, they will receive much less criticism for taking a "firm" approach, if that is what is needed.

Developing the Law, Support Structures, Working Relationships and Bureaucratic Systems

Code enforcement is, by its very nature, an interactive process dependent on governmental systems such as inspections, government records, the court system and a system of follow-up to ensure compliance with a court order. This is true whether it is a governmental agency or a community organization seeking enforcement. This necessary coordination is usually lacking even when enforcement is done solely by governmental agencies. The inspectors have difficulty communicating with the prosecutors, who are then removed from the problem and forced to rely upon the written record and the letter of the law. The courts have no relationship with the administrative efforts to enforce the code. When a court order is given, often there is no rational method of follow-through to ensure that it is implemented.

A community organization may be able to fulfill the roles of government agencies — inspection, verification, documentation and record keeping — but it is very difficult. Moreover, a court is much more likely to trust administrative or police records, and may require such records in addition to the well-documented records of community residents. By way of example, a tenant may thoroughly document serious code deficiencies in her dwelling when seeking rent escrow. However, in Baltimore City, a rent escrow will normally not be finally ordered until there is an inspection by a city official confirming those defects. One strength community residents *do* have is the ability to monitor whether the court order is ever actually accomplished. But, in the traditional system, no one ever asks them.

For a system of proactive code enforcement to succeed, all of these functions must be coordinated or there must be a dogged advocate — such as the attorney for the community organization — tracking a case through the system. In either case, a new method of doing the public's business is being developed. Whenever there is a new method, system or process being initiated, each and every step and person along the way must be developed.

Court Orders with No Means to Implement Them — Creating Support Structures

Problem properties typically have problem owners who lack either the will or the ability to correct the problem. Therefore, if there is to be a remedy to the problem, under authority of the law, someone else must do it. With some exceptions, problem properties often do not have the market value to support the cost of code enforcement; this is particularly true of vacant and abandoned properties. For such a property, the cost of code enforcement cannot be covered by a lien on the property as the cost to correct the problem exceeds the market value of the property.

Court orders and the law alone will not solve the problem; someone must implement the remedy and "make things right." Since its inception, the Community Law Center has sought to develop the resources necessary to solve the problem. Consequently, the center created Save A Neighborhood, Inc. (SAN) as a separate legal entity to accomplish this task, and then procured the necessary funding. Once created, SAN took on a life of its own to assist community organizations enforce public codes and abate nuisances. It is the court-appointed receiver in vacant house cases, and maintains a fund and program available to neighborhoods seeking to secure vacant properties from drug dealers. In addition, SAN administers a series of "community service crews" that work on neighborhood clean-ups, graffiti removal and park maintenance. SAN is now preparing to be a court-appointed administrator in rent escrow cases to ensure that the court-ordered repairs are actually done, and to use the escrowed rents to pay for it. In most communities, some entity must fulfill the role of SAN to implement the court-ordered remedy.

Developing the Law and Court Procedures

To seek a legal remedy to abate a nuisance, one must have standing. Normally, to have standing, a person must have a right to the reasonable use and enjoyment of a property — as either an owner or tenant. Situations and conditions that interfere with this right are a nuisance. But, if there is no property interest, under the common law there is no standing to seek abatement of the nuisance. An abatement is the cessation of or solution to the problem; it does *not* seek money damages for injuries or losses caused by the problem.

Most community organizations do not own real estate. Therefore, under Maryland common law, they do not have standing to seek abatement of nuisances. If community organizations are to have this right, it must be gained through legislation. One should first look to the state law to see what rights organizations have as representatives of their members, and whether needed changes should be made on the state or local level.

Which Court Has Jurisdiction?

The attorney's role is to seek the best and most effective way to gain standing for his or her client under existing state and local law and political and administrative circumstances. To fulfill this role, the approach of the Community Law Center has been to change the law as little as necessary, incrementally expand the rights of the community organization and stay in district court whenever possible. District court is the lowest level of court in Maryland. The procedures are simpler and one is able to obtain a hearing in a reasonable amount of time (in weeks), as compared to circuit court, which is the court of general jurisdiction and in which it may take years to get a hearing. The ability to effect a remedy within a reasonable time frame is essential to the community. However, the jurisdiction of the Maryland district court is limited. Except in the case of code enforcement, district court in Maryland does not have equity jurisdiction unless authorized by a specific statute. Abatement of a nuisance is an equity matter. Under Maryland law, any matter concerning the jurisdiction of district court must be statewide. Finally, in Maryland it is much easier for Baltimore City community organizations to deal with the City Council than the state legislature where there is a good deal of animosity toward the city.

As Appendix 2 demonstrates, what now exists is a mixture of state and local law and administrative policies that grant legal authority to community organizations to take legal action under a variety of circumstances. This represents an incremental development of the law. In each case, the Law Center has taken a few test cases to work them through the system and determine what administrative and judicial supports are needed. By way of example, the district court docket system is computerized, but does not have the capacity to register two different types of complaints in one proceeding. Nor, initially, was there a way for the computer system to register vacant house receivership cases; for the first two years these were all added to the docket by hand. To date, most of the Community Law Center's cases do not fit into the normal routine of the district court clerk's office and are handled by assigned clerks who know the process.

In and of themselves, these "nuts and bolts" details seem somewhat tedious. However, for the attorney trying to change the law, system and method of doing business for the public welfare, these details must be considered and can determine one's success.

THE COMMUNITY LAW CENTER'S EXPERIENCE IN BALTIMORE CITY

The Law Center has looked to the principles of co-production to explain the theoretical structure of its work. This approach enables a community-based organization (representing the citizens) to develop comprehensive strategies to meet the neighborhood's needs and work cooperatively with city and state agencies to attain its goals.

The most basic principle of community revitalization is that *neighborhood residents know their neighborhood best*, and, therefore, should be intimately involved in planning and implementing revitalization efforts. They must be in charge of the development and implementation of their community's strategy to inhibit causes of urban decay such as vacant buildings, poorly lit alleys, and trash filled lots, and to control criminal behavior such as dealing or using drugs, displaying illegal billboards, serving alcohol to minors, and violating various city and state codes. To resolve these problems successfully, the community strategy must break the links among the causes of urban decay and crime, the subsequent socialization that fosters criminal behavior, and the processes permitting the criminal behavior to organize in a durable structure. The problems facing urban communities are multi-faceted; so, too, must be the solutions.

Comprehensive Strategies

Co-production is an integral part of a comprehensive strategy. A comprehensive strategy is a method for community problem-solving. It is the continuous process of using a wide range of resources to combat community problems. It involves *action-oriented resource gathering* that provides community organizations with the means to take direct action to address problems, and improve the quality of life, the physical appearance, and the economic viability of their communities.

Comprehensive strategies will vary from neighborhood to neighborhood and will change over time. Each neighborhood's strategy must meet its changing needs. The strategies are solution-oriented. To be successful, they must: be inclusive and access the resources and talents that already exist in the community; be constructive and based on actions designed to revitalize some aspect or part of the community; and preserve the history and reclaim the perceived quality of life of the community they are designed to serve. The role of a comprehensive strategy in a crime control plan is described in Maryland Crime Control and Prevention Strategy, 1998 Edition (see Actions: Target Crime "Hot Spots" with a Comprehensive Strategy).

How a Community Organization Develops a Comprehensive Strategy

The driving force in developing a comprehensive strategy for any neighborhood should be: *Think Big*. Be as inclusive and far reaching as possible. Community residents should be encouraged to make a list of anything and everything they want to see happen in their neighborhood.

Community organizations should work through the basic steps to develop a comprehensive strategy at their own speed. The more initial information-gathering and organizing that is completed, the easier it is to implement and monitor a strategy in the future. The seven basic steps are:

- Set boundaries and geographical target areas.
- Establish a collaborative process and include government agencies.
- Take stock of the resources and talents community members can provide and what needs to be found elsewhere.
- Think big and develop a vision for the future by setting long-range goals.
- Get focused: prioritize goals and objectives, and develop a reasonable and flexible schedule of events to work toward the goals.
- Implement the strategy through task assignment, monitoring, evaluation and feedback
- Evaluate and update: periodically step back and evaluate how the strategy is progressing, and make any changes that the community feels are necessary (U.S. Department of Housing and Urban Development, 1994:2-3).

Finally, after people have developed a vision for their neighborhood, collected as much information as they can and looked at the problem they want to tackle from all angles, they can begin to look for real solutions. The community organization needs to be involved in the remedy they have developed or selected every step of the way.

Baltimore residents have taken on this responsibility and created many successful comprehensive strategies — strategies shaped by collaboration and anchored in block-by-block participation. The sample below illustrates the activities and benchmarks a community might set up to combat an endemic problem — in this case, vacant housing.

Example: Comprehensive Strategy for Four Block Target Area

Priority:　Rehabilitating vacant houses

Actions:　Organize block meetings, code a map to identify vacant properties and their status, recruit developer(s), board the properties, clean the block, locate the owners of the properties, get inspections and conduct code enforcement (receivership) actions

Schedule:

May 1:　Create strategy at community association meeting.

May 2 - May 20:　Organize block meetings for each block and get maps (one map for each block and one for the target area).

May - June　Hold block meetings to bring out residents of each block, code the maps, schedule clean-ups and boardings, and determine need for inspections.

June - June　Conduct initial clean-ups, boardings and meetings with potential developers. (These events could spark interest in other aspects of a comprehensive strategy, such as drug nuisance cases and defensible space plans. Develop additional subcommittees and schedules as needed to initiate work in the target area on these projects as well. Some projects, such as developing a youth program, may need to be postponed until other projects begin to be successful. The area should be made safe before the kids can come out to play.)

June - July :　Work with the community attorney to write contracts, locate property owners, and set up consent agreements.

July:　Begin receivership actions.

October - March:　Schedule court hearings and negotiations with owners.

January - July :   Transfer case to receiver, hold an auction and
                     transfer of title to developer.
August: Begin rehabilitation of property.

Benchmarks:

- Complete block meetings
- Complete map of target area
- Initiate clean-up and boarding
- Hold first greening event (e.g., tree planting, tire garden planting
- Expanding participation, especially to include youths
- Find a developer
- Schedule district court hearings and appointments of receivers
- Hold ground breaking for construction of new homes

The Law Gives Leverage in Conjunction with Other Activities

The services of the Law Center equip community organizations with an array of "legal tools" allowing them to determine the remedies — solutions — and to take direct action to implement those remedies. Remedies are sustainable when civil cases are pursued together with other activities. Activities such as rallies, boardings, clean-ups, marches, and cookouts offer a visual and empowering method of calling attention to and reinforcing civil cases. They are a way for the community organization to make itself known, involve a lot of people in a positive activity, and put the drug dealers and property owners on notice. These activities provide a unified voice and often attract new members to the association. They can contribute to strengthening a sense of community and, ultimately, of hope.

For instance, a series of rallies or cookouts or children's games can be used to take back a drug corner, an alley or even a playground. A community organization does not have to have speakers or even posters. It can just use the space in a positive way. A march can be used to announce the posting of a drug house prior to filing a drug nuisance case, or simply to announce to the neighborhood that drug activity is no longer welcome. Boardings and clean-ups are a powerful way to change the physical appearance of a block or street. They also deprive drug dealers of the space to conduct their trade. Some communities hold regular clean-ups and monitor boarded properties to maintain the new cleaner appearance of their neighborhood. Other activities that can be done in conjunction with boardings and clean-ups are getting children and youths to paint pictures on the boards, weeding the community garden and having a cookout at the end of the event to reward weary workers. The following case studies show how five community organizations created strategies and used civil legal remedies to effect systematic and sustainable change in their neighborhoods.

Southeast Baltimore: Butcher's Hill

The members of the Butcher's Hill Community Association established that they had the right to board property themselves *and* get a judgment against the property owner for the cost of boarding the property. The problem that Butcher's Hill faced is common in many Baltimore neighborhoods. A vacant and abandoned house had become a base of operations for drug users and drug dealers. It acted as a magnet for criminal activity, drawing a steady stream of drug dealers and users to the block from a wide radius.

The Butcher's Hill residents notified the owner of the vacant drug property that community residents would board the property, if he did not. When the owner failed to respond, the community boarded the property using construction techniques specifically developed to keep the building secure from the drug crowd. "We cinder blocked the basement entrance, and boarded all the doors and windows with plywood anchored to a frame of 2 x 4's," explained a community resident. "We also cleaned the backyard and sealed the door to the backyard. This kept the property secure for months and helped get rid of most of the drug dealing from the corners."

The Butchers' Hill Association plans to use this tool to deal with other vacant drug houses in their neighborhood. "We know now that we don't have to sit by and plead with someone else to keep the property secure," said one community resident. "We can do it ourselves, and we plan to do so."

The success of the Butcher's Hill strategy captured the attention of the Southeastern Police District and surrounding neighborhoods. Five more neighborhoods are implementing comprehensive strategies. Two communities worked to raise money to fund a Law Center staff attorney and paralegal, and the police department appointed a community services officer to collect police evidence for civil actions. That is co-production. There is joint planning, joint sharing of task allocation and joint responsibility for implementing the action plan.

West Baltimore: Carrollton Avenue

One of the first drug nuisance cases in Baltimore City was under-taken by the Carrollton Association. The property in question was being used by the local drug trade as a location to purchase and use drugs. The association and its community attorney met with the Western District police. Community residents began collecting detailed evidence for the police to do a search-and-seizure — or "drug raid" — at the properties. The actual drug nuisance abatement cases filed on behalf of the community association were built upon the police evidence in the search-and-seizure warrants. After the cases were filed, the association held a march. They were joined by the mayor, various police officials and the press as they traversed their neighborhood chanting and sing-ing. The event culminated in the posting of the property by the mayor and the community attorney.

Shortly after this event, the Carrollton Association and its attorney entered into negotiations with the owner of the property. At the hearing, a consent order was entered in which the owner promised to evict the tenants involved with the drug activity. One of the tenants agreed to enter a drug treatment program. The association has been monitoring the property, which has been vacant but quiet ever since.

The success of this case prompted the Carrollton Association to get more involved in drug nuisance cases. Members began keeping obser-vation logs and communicating regularly with the police. They decided to target a block on the main street in their neighborhood. Police search-and-seizure warrants indicated that three houses in this block were used by the same drug crew. All three drug nuisance cases were filed simultaneously to increase the impact of the strategy. Consent orders were entered into with the owners of all three properties, and the tenants involved in the drug activity were evicted. The association monitors the properties and reboards them when necessary to make sure that they remain secure.

The drug nuisance properties on Carrollton Avenue have remained vacant. There is still a major drug apartment building. Theirs is a continuing story.

West Baltimore: Franklin Square

The Franklin Square Community Association was one of the first or-ganizations to develop a comprehensive strategy. The focus of its strat-egy was to stop the open-air drug dealing and set up regular community activities for neighborhood residents. Violent crimes decreased by 44%

282 — Anne Blumenberg et al.

over the last four years. The association has set up a senior center, a recreation center, a community center and a summer youth program.

Residents noticed that one corporation owned many problem properties in their neighborhood. Consequently, when they filed suit for a drug nuisance at one property, their attorney also developed a very broad consent order requiring that improvements be performed at all of the properties owned by the corporation, and that representatives of the corporation attend community meetings and support community events.

The Franklin Square Community Association also pioneered the block-by-block approach. They selected a six block target area, held block meetings, and developed coded maps for each block that included their anti-crime, housing, lighting and greening strategies. They then prioritized the blocks and have been working block by block pursuing drug nuisance cases, planting gardens, planning playgrounds, boarding vacants and developing youth programs. The Franklin Square Community Association has been forging a co-productive relationship with the city and with the Western District police station.

Southwest Baltimore: Boyd Booth

Like Franklin Square, the small neighborhood of Boyd Booth was one of the first to implement a comprehensive strategy. In the early 1990s, this community seemed to be disintegrating under the pressure of an open-air drug market. The local press described Boyd Booth as a battleground, and the neighborhood social worker described the lives of the children as hopeless. Boyd Booth's residents, however, proved that they are far from powerless or hopeless. Over the last three years, this neighborhood has been the scene of a dramatically effective community-based effort to reduce drug-related violent crime. Violent crime has dropped 55% in Boyd booth since 1992, and narcotics-related calls for police service and arrests each have dropped over 90%.

These statistics only hint at the overall improvement in the quality of life in Boyd Booth. The local press now lists it as one of Baltimore's safest neighborhoods. Moreover, at a recent community party the residents spoke of their sense of power and how much safer they feel. To create this amazing change, the people of Boyd Booth pooled their resources. They worked with a part-time organizer, a community attorney, a community paralegal, the Southwestern Police Drug Enforcement Unit, a task force of city agencies and surrounding community associations established by the mayor, the Victory Outreach drug abuse treatment program, the largest employer in the community (a hospital), and several local funders.

To deny drug dealers the space to operate their open-air market, the community association conducted self-help boardings of vacant properties, drug nuisance abatement cases, clean-ups and a defensible space program. The defensible space program involved putting up lights, fencing off foot alleyways and vacant lots, and removing public telephones. The members of the association also communicated intolerance for drug dealing by holding vigils: on 17 consecutive Friday nights they put up signs and held community events in public spaces. Most recently, they have established a youth program and set up a Youth Council with the surrounding neighborhoods.

Southwest Baltimore: Forest Heights

The Forest Heights Tenants Council faced a more unique problem than the preceding neighborhoods. Their low-income townhouse development had become a thriving drive-through drug market. Research on cars seen in the area revealed that people were coming from across the state to purchase drugs in Forest Heights. The apartment complex is just two blocks from a major interstate highway. The Tenant Council developed a comprehensive strategy to tackle this problem. It decided to focus on the primary drug site — the main road that winds in a "U" shape through their neighborhood.

The Tenant Council recruited new members and started inviting the development manager and a Community Law Center attorney to their meetings. The council also extended open invitations to nearby shop owners. As the collaborative process developed, members of the council began to specialize: one worked on youth programs, another led rallies and vigils, others distributed fliers.

After its capacity was established, the council set four goals. First, make the community drug-free. Second, hold regular meetings and community events. Third, create a youth center and programs for neighborhood youths. Fourth, plant a community garden.

To make the community drug-free, the Tenant Council scheduled regular community meetings, established a drug subcommittee, and planned several rallies and vigils. The council worked with the police to collect information about raids conducted in the area and with the management company to evict tenants involved in the drug trade. As the rallies and vigils were held, residents of the community became more mobilized. The management company hired private security guards and agreed to evict tenants involved in drug-related activities. If they had not, the Law Center attorney would have brought legal action to force them to do so. The subcommittee kept observation logs and shared information regularly with Southwestern District Police, who raided the key problem properties. The President of the City Council's Office started a letter-writing campaign directed at the registered owners of cars seen in the area based on license plate numbers received from the Tenant Council.

As a result of these activities, drug dealing went down in Forest Heights 90% in a year and a half. Today, private security still patrols the development and the Tenant Council is developing new ways to work together with the police to catch the remaining dealers. An annual flea market, community day, back-to-school event and holiday party are held in the neighborhood. Funds were also raised to plant a community garden.

CONCLUSION AND IMPLICATIONS

What Issues Are Co-Production Code Enforcement Friendly?

Not every problem that troubles a community can be solved either by direct citizen action or through a co-production strategy. However, communities are pushing the limits of their abilities. Those areas that seem particularly appropriate for a co-production approach include: zoning; day care; local traffic regulation and street closing; park and recreation facility maintenance; and law enforcement or public safety.

Traffic regulation is closely tied to the comprehensive plan for combating open-air drug markets and drive-through drug traffic. The Neighborhood Design Center works closely with many communities, the Law Center, and the Citizens Planning and Housing Association to help communities understand "defensible space" and how traffic flow, pedestrian traffic, and green/open space affect crime and grime in their communities. This planning is being implemented in many communities as part of a comprehensive strategy. These communities are then seeking grants for implementation of their plans.

The maintenance of parks and recreation facilities is one of the biggest challenges facing communities in cities with a declining tax base. It is often one of the first areas to receive cuts. The effect on the day-to-day quality of life is immediate and dramatic. Youth programs close, forcing more young people out on the street and into a criminal lifestyle. Many communities are organizing regular clean-ups of open spaces, working with nonprofit organizations to plant and maintain urban gardens and to create youth programs. This work is very volunteer-intensive, but also very rewarding. The impact is also immediate.

The role of community groups in law enforcement has been discussed in many books and articles. There is a growing movement of citizen-based groups participating in organized activity to extend the eyes and ears of the police, and to maintain a presence on their neighborhood streets. In Baltimore, these are known as "Citizens on Patrol" or "Peace Patrols." Similarly, people are being trained to collect and transmit evidence regarding the use and distribution of drugs in their community.

The experience in Baltimore shows that when a problem affects the quality of life of residents and is, by its very nature, destroying the fabric of the community, it is an issue that the residents are most qualified to address. However, many of these problems require a co-productive response involving residents and government agencies.

Private Enforcement of the Public Welfare: The Down Side — Potential Abuse and Vigilantism

Once community organizations have power, will they abuse it? Will the petty vendetta or the "not in my back yard" syndrome be the guiding force? With any type of authority, this may happen. However, it has not been the experience of the Community Law Center.

There are a number of checks that discourage the petty complaints. The very first hurdle is the requirement of a group decision to go forward. In the experience of the Law Center, there is a great deal of discussion on the remedy — or solution — to the problem. For example, in cases where there is drug dealing out of a house, the question is, how can we get the 22 year old, drug dealing son out of the house but not force the mother and four-year-old grandchild to move? These questions involve real people and do not have easy answers. In low income neighborhoods that are not transient, residents have known each other for years.

The second check is the court. Courts dismiss complaints that do not have merit. If the case is filed in district court, pretrial activities and costs are very limited. If it is a case without merit, the burden on the defendant is minimal and it will be dismissed quickly.

The third check is the attorney. In Maryland, all corporations, including community associations, must be represented in court by an attorney. These are not cases for money damages. Rarely can a community organization pay a normal attorney's fee. Attorneys will not take questionable cases for free. And, should they do so, there are sanctions that can be imposed against them for filing frivolous litigation.

Community Enforcement of the Public Welfare: The Up Side of Code Enforcement and More In Low-Income Communities

Neighborhood residents, participating through their community organizations in a co-production model of code enforcement and nuisance abatement, produce a very positive ripple effect. Not only are problems remedied, but the ancillary effects for the community can be profound. Decisions are made. Action is taken. There is a result. It is an occasion for community-building, empowerment and celebration. People march together, cook out together, and laugh and cry together. It is community- building.

Change occurs in the monthly meetings held by the residents with the community police officer, city inspectors, and community lawyer to evaluate implementation of the community's plan. If it works well, local government is viewed as a partner in problem-solving. If it does not work well, the community has explicit documentation and can go up the chain of command for accountability. If it still does not work well, the community can at least get on with its business and do what it can; it is not powerless and totally dependent.

There is also a change in people's view of the law. Residents of low-income neighborhoods typically see the law in a very cynical way. Rarely is it seen as a positive force to improve the quality of life in their neighborhood. Rather, the law is something used against the individuals, as in non-payment of rent or a debt or criminal violation. Alternatively, it is something to which one may resort for a windfall when in a car accident or because of a work-related injury. Or, in the case of public nuisances, the law often is not enforced in their neighborhood, e.g., in the form of illegally placed billboards or dumping of trash; in these cases the law is just ignored. However, when community organizations have the authority and capacity to use the law to further the welfare of their community, people's perception of the law is profoundly changed.

For those of us who live and have lived in the neighborhoods of Baltimore, it is not a huge surprise that co-production is evolving and being tested in our neighborhoods. Baltimore's citizens are fiercely loyal to their neighborhoods. Generations grow up and live in the same neighborhood — sometimes on the same block. But, over the last 30 years, the sense that they can control and determine the quality of life in these communities has ebbed to a desperately low level.

Like many older cities, Baltimore has lost a significant portion of its population in the last 40 years. However, for those who have stayed — who have either had no alternative or whose loyalty has outweighed fear — there is renewed determination to recreate our communities. And this creativity is being linked with resources. It is a time for new models. Co-production is one model that fits in this community, and that will offer lessons for us all.

Address correspondence to: Anne Blumenberg, Community Law Center, 2500 Maryland Avenue, Baltimore, MD 21218.

REFERENCES

Liebmann, G.W. (1993). "Devolution of Power to Community and Block Associations." *The Urban Lawyer* 25:335.

Miller, H.C. (1983). "Code Enforcement: An Overview." *University of Detroit Journal of Urban Law* 60:349-371.

Mueller, D.C. (1979). *Public Choice.* Cambridge, MA: Cambridge University Press.

Parks, R., P.C. Baker, L. Kiser, R. Oakerson, E. Ostrom, V. Ostrom, S.L. Percy, M.B. Vandivort, G.P. Whitaker and R. Wilson (1981). "Consumers as Co-producers of Public Services: Some Economic and Institutional Considerations." *Policy Studies Journal* (Summer):999-1011.

Percy, S.L. (1978). "Conceptualizing and Measuring Citizen Co-Production of Community Safety." *Policy Studies Journal* 7:486-493.

Ramsey, S.H., and F. Zolna. (1991). "A Piece in the Puzzle of Providing Adequate Housing: Court Effectiveness in Code Enforcement." *Fordham Urban Law Journal* 18:605-54.

Rogers, D. (1971). *The Management of Big Cities.* Beverly Hills, CA: Sage.

Scholz, J.T. (1984). "Cooperation, Deterrence, and the Ecology of Regulatory Enforcement." *Law & Society Review* 18:179-224.

—— (1991). "Cooperative Regulatory Enforcement and the Politics of Administrative Effectiveness." *American Political Science Review* 85:115-136.

Sharp, E. B. (1986). *Citizen Demand-Making in the Urban Context.* University, AL: University of Alabama Press.

U.S. Department of Housing and Urban Development, Office of Community Planning and Development (1994). *Guidebook: Strategic Planning, Building Communities Together.* Washington, DC: author.

Whitaker, Gordon P. (1980). "Coproduction: Citizen Participation in Service Delivery." *Public Administration Review* 40:240.

APPENDIX 1: GLOSSARY

Abatement of a nuisance: the cessation or correction of a nuisance. For example, the abatement of the vacant lot nuisance could include one or all of the following: cleaning the lot, fencing or otherwise securing the lot so it cannot be used as a dump or by drug dealers, and ceasing dumping on the lot.

Equity: justice administered according to fairness in a particular situation as opposed to strictly formulated rules. Equity applies only to civil law cases and the judge must follow general principles, but it affords a great deal of discretion as to the remedy granted.

Jurisdiction: the scope of authority and power granted to a court to hear and decide cases, including: subject matter limitations, proper parties, geographic limitations and remedies that may be granted

Nuisance: an offensive, annoying, unpleasant, or obnoxious thing or practice; a cause or source of annoyance, especially a continuing or repeated invasion or disturbance of another's right, or anything that works to hurt, inconvenience or damage. (*Rankin v. Harvey Aluminum*, 226 F. Supp. 169, 175.

Standing: also know as the "*standing to sue doctrine,*" means that a party has a sufficient stake in an otherwise justiciable controversy to obtain judicial resolution to that controversy. That "stake" *must already be recognized or granted* by the law or rules of procedure of the court at the time the law suit is filed.

Appendix 2

SUMMARY OF CIVIL LEGAL REMEDIES

Law	Plaintiff	Defendant	Requirements
Common Law Nuisance Seeking court order for abatement of nuisance	Person or entity negatively affected and with a property interest	Property owner and possibly the person causing the nuisance	• Common law, common sense notice to defendant and attempts to remedy without litigation • Plan for abating the nuisance and monitoring the property for compliance
Self Help Nuisance Abatement A common law nuisance abatement used to secure vacant properties and lots	Neighboring property owner with standing, or community association	Property owner	• Plaintiff's property must be adversely affected by the nuisance • Reasonable — at least two weeks, notice to owner by regular and certified mail • Abatement without damage to property. • Records and receipts
Drug Nuisance Abatement Any drug-related nuisance at any type of property; the remedy can be very broad (Md. Ann. Code, RP sec.14-120.)	Community association, local prosecutor or civil attorney for the political subdivision	Property owner, tenants and occupants causing the nuisance. Occupants may be limited to the drug dealers at the plaintiff's option.	• Police evidence or detailed observation logs maintained by neighbors • Statutory prior notice to defendants • Plan for abating nuisance and monitoring property for compliance • Witnesses - police and/or community residents

Law	Plaintiff	Defendant	Requirements
Vacant House Receivership Case Code enforcement to rehabilitate vacant property with out-standing violations notices from the city. (Baltimore City Building Code, 1994 edition, sec.123.6 et seq.)	Community association	Property owner, tax sale certificate holder or any other parties with property interest	• City Department of Housing and Community Development has "designated" community organization to stand in its shoes • Developer with financing and commitment to renovate the property • Receiver - almost always, Save A Neighborhood, Inc. • Vacant building notice and violation from the Dept of Housing • Ten day notice to owner of intent to file a Show Cause Order for appointment of a receiver
Community Bill of Rights Abatement of a nuisance on private property that is a violation of a city code. (Md. Ann. Code, RP sec.14-123)	Incorporated, tax-exempt community association	Property owner (and possibly the person causing the nuisance)	• Community association with geographic boundaries, with 40 households, composed of at least 25% of adult residents who pay dues and in existence for two years. • 60-day notice to owner and appropriate city agency • Community residents must build the case

WHAT DO LANDLORDS THINK ABOUT DRUG ABATEMENT LAWS?

by

Barbara E. Smith
Consultant, American Bar Association
Criminal Justice Section

and

Robert C. Davis
Victim Services Agency, New York City

Abstract: *Across the country, drug house abatement statutes have become a popular tool for reducing drug activities in targeted neighborhoods. These statutes vary in content; in the types of civil or criminal penalties that apply; and in the type of administrative/court proceedings and appeals available. Despite differences among the statutes, they share a common goal of ameliorating drug activity and holding landlords responsible for ridding their properties of drug dealers and customers. Rather than target drug sellers directly, drug house abatement programs target property owners in order to curb the activities of residents. In this chapter, we focus on the reactions of property owners to abatement actions, drawing data from interviews conducted in two major studies of drug house abatement efforts. Property owners favor the goals of abatement programs, but resent being targeted by authorities. We conclude that efforts are needed by local officials to enlist property owners to work cooperatively with them in order to solve common problems.*

INTRODUCTION

Across the country, drug house abatement statutes have become a popular tool for reducing drug activities in targeted neighborhoods. These statutes vary in content, in the types of civil or criminal penalties that apply, and in the type of administrative/court proceedings and appeals available. Despite differences among the statutes, they share a common goal of ameliorating drug activity and holding landlords responsible for ridding their properties of drug dealers and customers.

We have been involved in two major studies of drug house abatement efforts: one multi-city investigation (Smith et al., 1992) and one single-site study (Lurigio et al., 1993). Both studies provided evidence that abatement actions are effective in cleaning up problem buildings and reducing signs of disorder in the vicinity of targeted properties. Moreover, our work suggests that the drug problems tend not to return any time soon and may not be displaced to other locations. Recent work reported in this volume by Eck and Wartell and by Mazerolle et al. using true experimental designs has also found abatement programs to be effective.

Our work (see also, Eck and Wartell in this volume) has also found that abatement efforts are very cost-effective relative to other law enforcement approaches to drug sales. Many cities conduct drug nuisance abatement actions with funds from existing municipal budgets. In a large majority of properties targeted, abatement of the nuisance is achieved through a single letter to the property owner. Similar to other local anti-drug initiatives, abatement actions are popular with residents of neighborhoods where drug dealing is extensive (Rosenbaum, 1993).

Drug nuisance abatement actions target property owners rather than the drug dealers themselves, and their success is dependent upon the cooperation of the owners. How do landlords respond to abatement notices, and what consequences do they suffer at the hands of tenants who are evicted because of the notice? Do the actions taken by the landlords reduce drug activities at their properties? How costly is the process for landlords? What do property owners/managers think of the use of the abatement laws? What management changes are undertaken by landlords to avoid abatement notices in the future? Do landlords think abatement laws are fair? These questions are the focus of this chapter. The answers have important implications for the success of drug abatement programs that rely so heavily on landlords cleaning up drug-infested properties.

STUDY SITES

Study 1

We obtained the landlords' perspective as part of two different studies. The first was a 1992 study funded by the National Institute of

Justice that assessed drug abatement programs in five sites: Alexandria, VA; Houston, TX; Milwaukee, WI; San Francisco, CA and Toledo, OH. To provide a sense of the abatement efforts studied, we will briefly describe each site's program as it was operating at the time of our 1992 study.

Alexandria

Alexandria is using a long-standing nuisance statute designed to rid neighborhoods of prostitution and massage parlors. The 1950 civil statute was revised in 1990 to add drug sales and use to the list of nuisance violations. The Commonwealth's Attorney works in close coordination with the police department to identify problem houses, and to warn landlords to stop the drug dealing from their property. Once the police notify the Commonwealth's Attorney that drugs have been found in a residence, the prosecutor's office sends a letter to the landlord alerting him or her that drugs are being sold on the property. The landlord is warned to take action to stop future drug sales or risk prosecution or civil action to confiscate their property. Once the letter is delivered to the landlord, it is up to the police to monitor the situation to determine if the he or she has taken appropriate action and drug dealing has ceased. The prosecutor will not take further action *unless* alerted by the police that dealing is continuing in the house. If another arrest is made in the house — or the police learn of subsequent drug dealing from informants or through surveillance — the police will report the case back to the prosecutor's office.

Houston

Houston's drug house abatement team is a cooperative venture between the offices of the Houston City Attorney and the Harris County Attorney. The program's actions are based on an old bawdy house ordinance that permits closure of properties defined as a common and/or public nuisance. The statute was updated in 1987 to include narcotics in the scope of what it defines as a nuisance. By the time the abatement team receives a case from the police, the police have already made attempts to reduce the drug activity through traditional law enforcement methods. If the team believes action is warranted, it has a number of options. If the building is vacant, the case may be referred to the city's neighborhood protection team. This program razes buildings that are deemed structurally unsafe. A second option is to refer a case to the County Attorney's Office for a forfeiture action. The final option available is to file a civil suit in district court seeking injunctive relief.

Milwaukee

Milwaukee's drug abatement law is an updated version of an older bawdy house law that allows the city to file a civil suit in order to have a property declared a public nuisance. If the circuit court finds that a property is being used to facilitate the delivery or manufacture of drugs, it may issue injunctive relief. An order to close can follow and, eventually, an order to sell, with the owner getting nothing from the sale. Property owners can submit a petition to the court to attempt to stop the process. If the court does close a property, the structure must remain closed until any building code violations are cleared. Properties are targeted by the drug abatement team following complaints from community residents or tips from police informants. Once a drug sales location is reported to the police department, the police attempt to make an undercover buy. If drugs are discovered in the search and/or arrests are made, the case is referred to the law enforcement drug abatement team. The team sends the property owner an abatement letter in which he or she is given five days to stop the activity at the property. If drug sales persist, a second letter is sent. If this letter fails to abate the nuisance, a suit is filed in civil court that may eventually result in closure and/or sale of the property.

San Francisco

The district attorney's office focuses on the prosecution of drug dealers and a multi-agency task force focuses on improving the quality of housing stock by removing drug dealers and eradicating unsafe and run-down housing. At task force meetings, problem buildings are identified and monitored and enforcement strategies are jointly planned. The task force makes specific recommendations to owners as to strategies they might undertake to stop drug dealing in their buildings. Many landlords cooperate and follow through on those recommendations. For uncooperative landlords, possible sanctions include closures, property liens and administrative fines.

When civil actions fail, the case is referred to the district attorneys' office for action. The district attorney may undertake several progressively more punitive steps to insure that drug activity stops, including: (1) filing a lawsuit, (2) seeking temporary injunctive relief and closure, and (3) seeking a permanent abatement order to close the property and collect damages.

Toledo

By Ohio statute, premises where felony violations of controlled substances laws occur are nuisances subject to abatement. Where a nuisance exists, the prosecuting attorney may bring an action in equity asking the court to order the premises closed and padlocked for up to a year. The Toledo Police Department's Vice-Metro Section targets drug houses for potential closure. Evidence of both "recent" and "continuing" illegal activity is necessary for a padlock order. Upon a recommendation from Vice-Metro, the prosecutor's office prepares a complaint and a motion for a temporary restraining order (TRO). The former details evidence that a particular property is a "nuisance" subject to abatement; the latter seeks a court order to close and padlock the premises immediately, pending a hearing for a preliminary or permanent injunction to close the premises for a year.

The TRO is obtained and executed on the same day. A contingent of approximately 25 persons appears at the targeted premises, armed with a battering ram. An "entry team" of five or six members of the police department SWAT team secures the premises, serves search warrants and makes arrests if required. The sheriff's office, responsible for executing the TRO, sends eight to 10 deputies to serve the summons and complaint, videotape the entry, make a videotaped inventory of the premises, and oversee the padlocking and, if necessary, the boarding up of the premises. Within two weeks of the execution of the TRO a hearing is held on the prosecutor's request for a preliminary and/or permanent injunction.

Study 2

The second study in which we examined the perspectives of landlords was a 1993 evaluation, funded by the Bureau of Justice Assistance of the Cook County (Chicago, IL) State's Attorney's Office's Narcotics Nuisance Abatement Unit.

Cook County

The program employs three strategies: (a) voluntary abatement, (b) prosecutorial abatement and (c) community outreach. To identify potential drug houses for targeting, the program receives referrals and complaints from community organizations and the police, and also accesses internal information from current prosecutions of the state's attorney's office. Next, the program screens referrals to select appropriate cases for investigation. Each case that the program identifies for abatement is assigned to an assistant state's attorney and an investigator. The team verifies the existence of a drug problem at the referred property, establishes the nature and extent of current and/or past drug problems at the property, and identifies the alleged offender(s) and the owners or managers of the property. If investigation confirms a current nuisance, the program informs the property owner by letter that a drug nuisance exists on his or her property and requests a meeting between the owner and the program to resolve the problem. Thirty to 60 days are usually allowed for voluntary compliance with the abatement plan arrived at during the meeting. If the owner fails to cooperate with the program, the assigned attorney initiates action in the civil courts. If the case is brought to civil court, the property may be closed for a period of one year. The program also has the option of filing criminal charges if an owner does not comply with the voluntary abatement, or if the owner refuses to cooperate and a new drug arrest occurs on his or her property.

STUDY SAMPLES

In the 1992 study, we randomly selected four to five landlords/property managers in each of the five study sites and were successful in completing a total of 22 interviews by telephone. All but one of the respondents were investment owners/managers; one was the attorney for a man whose live-in grandchildren were the alleged dealers/users. In some cases the actual property owner was unavailable, and therefore we interviewed the property manager familiar with the abatement action.

In the 1993 Cook County study, a randomly selected sample of the drug abatement program files was used to obtain the names and phone numbers of landlords. A total of 230 interviews were completed with property owners, a completion rate of 64% of all those tried. The interviewed property owners were quite diverse. Their ages ranged from 24 to 94. Sixteen percent (n=35) had less than a high-school education, 17% (n=38) had completed high school, 25% (n=55) had some college education and 42% (n=91) were college graduates or more. Over half (52%, n=111) were African-American; 36% (n=76) were white; and 4% (n=8) were Asian. Just under 10% (n=21) identified themselves as Hispanic. Nearly 14% (n=30) of the landlords reported incomes under $10,000 per year; 15% (n=33) reported incomes between $10,000 and $19,999; 19% (n=42) reported incomes between $20,000 and $40,000; and 38% (n=82) more than $40,000. Twenty percent (n=46) of the landlords reported living at the address of the drug nuisance. Eighty-eight percent (n=203) said they rented units at that address. Nearly two-thirds (60%, n=136) of the property owners said that they owned or managed other units.

Although the 1992 sample was quite small, the findings were remarkably similar to the larger 1993 Cook County study and, combined, present an interesting picture of how landlords feel about drug abatement laws.

ACTIONS BY LANDLORDS IN RESPONSE TO NOTIFICATION OF THE PROBLEM AND TENANT RESPONSE

In the 1992 study, the property owners we interviewed reported being just as desirous of eliminating drug dealing from their property as were city officials. In fact, we were quite surprised that half of the property owners we spoke to said that they has been the ones to alert the authorities about drug dealing on their premises. Several expressed concern that the wording of abatement notices made it seem as if they were culpable and/or were somehow profiting from knowingly allowing drug sales to take place.

In the 1992 study, all of the landlords interviewed evicted one or more tenants as a result of the abatement notification. A majority of tenants did not resist abatement actions, and only one landlord reported a tenant fighting the eviction in court. Although there were no retaliatory actions by tenants in three-quarters of the cases, one property manager reported receiving threats against her personally as well as threats against the building, and one property owner said his property manager was beaten up and shots were fired at a window in one of his buildings.

There is concern in some quarters that in the process of evicting drug dealers innocent family members may be put out as well. In the 1992 survey, close to half of the respondents reported that innocent people had to move out as a result of the eviction. In most cases, this involved children or other family members of the alleged drug dealer, although in one case the entire rooming house was shut down, and everyone had to vacate. For those landlords who reported receiving feedback from other tenants about the eviction in the 1992 sample, most said the other tenants were supportive and "very happy. " One property owner, however, said other tenants moved out due to fear that the problem would recur.

In the 1993 Cook County study, the most common action landlords took after being notified of the drug nuisance was to evict the offending tenants. Sixty-two percent (n=142) reported that they had evicted tenants. Twenty-eight percent (n=64) reported that the problem tenants had left by the time the state's attorney contacted them, and 13% (n=30) said that they had taken no particular action, either because the problem was abated without their efforts or it was being ignored. Nine percent (n=21) reported asking non-legal tenants to leave, and only 3% (n=8) said they had improved security (Table 1).

The 1992 study found that a few retaliatory actions had been taken by evicted tenants. The 1993 Cook County study uncovered a bigger problem with retaliation against landlords. Among the respondents in the 1993 study who said they had attempted to evict legal tenants, 35% (n=49) reported that the tenants had tried to resist the eviction. Of those who reported resistance, half (n=25) said the tenants had refused to move. Slightly over one-third (36%; n=18) reported that the tenant had appealed the eviction to the courts. More seriously, 18% (n=9) reported being threatened and two property owners reported that the tenants had damaged their property (Table 1).

Table 1: Survey Results from Cook County Sample

Actions Taken by Landlords Following Abatement Notice*	
Evicted tenants	62%
Tenants had already vacated	28%
Took no action	13%
Required non-legal tenants to vacate	9%
Improved security	3%
Actions Taken by Tenants Against Landlords Following Eviction Notice*	
Tenants refused to move	50%
Tenants appealed eviction	36%
Tenants threatened landlord	18%
Tenants damaged landlord's property	8%

* Numbers do not total 100% because the landlord may have taken more than one action
** Numbers do not total 100% because the tenant may have taken more than one action against the landlord

ASSESSMENT OF THE IMPACT OF ACTIONS TAKEN

In the 1992 study, 59% of the respondents said the eviction had reduced drug problems at the property, 53% said that loitering had decreased subsequent to the eviction, and 47% noted a decrease in vandalism and graffiti. In the 1993 Cook County study, the majority of property owners also felt that drug problems and related signs of disorder improved as a result of their involvement in the abatement process. Eighty percent (n=168) of owners reported that their actions had reduced overall drug problems in their building and 62% (n=130) said that loitering in and around their property had been reduced. Forty-five percent said that vandalism and graffiti were also reduced as a result of their efforts to abate the drug nuisance.

COSTS INCURRED BY THE LANDLORDS

According to the 1992 study, the abatement process was costly to some landlords. Expenses were broken down into (a) legal fees relating to the actual eviction, (b) other legal fees, (c) lost rent and (d) miscellaneous expenses. Twelve of the 22 respondents reported no legal fees with respect to the actual eviction, and several said there were no subsequent costs, either. Others were not so fortunate, and legal fees for these evictions ranged from $14 to $5,000. "Other" legal fees ranged from $100 all the way to $70,000 (to contest the loss of a rooming house license). The two most costly categories were in lost rent and miscellaneous expenses. Income from rental properties was curtailed for several months up to a year — both non-payment of rent and closure of property for renovation — costing landlords from $900 to $45,000 (thus far). Significant costs, enumerated under the "miscellaneous " category, included hiring security guards and paying money for renovations, cleaning and maintenance. Some jurisdictions also required the posting of a bond to ensure against further drug activity on the premises. For example, in one jurisdiction the bond amount is $5,000, and is returnable after one year. In another jurisdiction, a landlord had to put up the value of the property for one year. This landlord characterized the bond as "putting the house on probation."

In the 1993 Cook County study, slightly over one-third (34%, n=78) of the property owners reported having contacted a lawyer or tried to take their case to court. Nearly two-thirds (63%; n=141) said that dealing with the drug problem had cost them money in the form of either legal fees or lost rent.

MANAGEMENT CHANGES UNDERTAKEN TO AVOID
FUTURE PROBLEMS

In the 1992 study, we asked property owners/managers if they had initiated any changes in the way they do business as a result of their experience with the abatement process. Close to half said they had made changes with respect to screening and management, and half said they had not. In some ways this result can be attributed to the fact that for some of the property owners, the problem came with the property. Four of the landlords came into possession of properties in which the drug dealer already resided. In another case, the landlord had rented to a tenant who in turn had sublet the apartment without the owner's knowledge; this person turned out to be a drug dealer. One case involved a man's live-in grandchildren. With respect to any changes made in the way they screen prospective tenants (for those who had this in their control), most landlords said they would "be more careful" and conduct more thorough background checks. One landlord took himself off the low-income property roll, however. He felt this was an unfortunate side effect of the problem but he did not want to face the possibility of being targeted for abatement efforts in the future.

When asked about any changes in management style, the most common answer among property owners in the 1992 study was that they will be more careful, more visible around the property and "nosier." A couple have hired security guards and guard dogs; one off-site owner has a neighbor reporting to her and another has changed the lease to specifically cite drug use as grounds for eviction.

Similar to the 1992 study, the 1993 Cook County study also found that the abatement process caused landlords to alter the way they do business. In the 1993 study, over half (53%; n=110) of the landlords reported that their experience with the drug problem in their building changed how they screen new tenants. Among those who reported a change, 38% (n=38) said they now ask tenants for references; 32% (n=32) said they interview tenants' previous landlords; 12% conduct an employment check (n=12); 12% check the tenants' criminal records (n=12); 10% inform new tenants of drug laws (n=9); and 9% (n=9) have added a credit check (Table 2). Further, 41% (n=156) of the respondents said they were less likely to own or manage rental properties in the future because of their experience with the drug nuisance.

Table 2: Survey Results from Cook County Sample

Impact of Abatement on How Landlords Conduct Their Business	
Ask new tenants for reference	38%
Interview new tenants' previous landlords	32%
Conduct an employment check on new tenants	12%
Check new tenants' criminal record	12%
Inform new tenants of drug laws	10%
Conduct credit check on new tenants	41%

* Numbers do not total 100% because landlords may have initiated more than one change in how they conduct business

ARE ABATEMENT LAWS A GOOD IDEA?

Two-fifths of the landlords in the 1992 survey thought abatement laws were a good idea, one-third thought they were a bad idea and one-quarter were unsure. For those who believed the law was a good idea, most acknowledged its effectiveness at getting rid of a problem — the fact that "it works." For those who did not agree that the law is a good idea, the majority felt that it makes landlords responsible for something they did not do. Some made the point that unless they are on the property themselves every day, watching, they are unlikely to be aware of such activity.

In the 1992 study, several landlords said they would have felt better about the process if they had been informed and prepared. Many did not know in advance that they could be held accountable for drug use/sale on their property, and were surprised and often embarrassed by the abatement notice, saying *they* felt like the criminal. Others said they would have liked to have been informed earlier in the process of drug sales on their property, rather than finding out after several raids or buys.

In the 1993 study, we again asked the respondents whether they thought holding landlords responsible for tenants who deal drugs is a good idea. Even more often than in the 1992 study, the answer was a resounding no: the majority of the property owners (75%; n=156) said it was not a good idea. Among the reasons were: (a) landlords are unaware of tenants' activities (n=64); (b) landlords cannot control tenants (n=13); (c) the police and state's attorney's office should be responsible for dealing with drug nuisances (n=10); (d) landlords should not be held responsible if they cooperate with authorities (n=10); and (e) landlords become victims of the abatement process (n=9). Respondents who said that they thought the nuisance abatement law was a good idea offered only qualified support. More than half of those providing a reason (n=30) suggested that it was positive only if landlords were aware of the problem, and a few (n=6) thought it was only a good idea if the landlord gets cooperation from outside agencies such as the state's attorney or the police.

CONCLUSIONS

In an effort to close down drug houses, authorities are reinstituting old "bawdy house " laws and other Prohibition-era statutes and applying them to drug activity occurring at privately owned properties. Certainly, there are advantages for the criminal justice system (lower standard of proof, use of non-criminal justice resources), but the onus is placed primarily on property owners to clean up drug buildings. The landlords we interviewed had some positive things to say about abatement laws. Most notably, over half thought abatement efforts directed at their property helped reduce drug and disorder problems. However, the vast majority believed the laws are unfair to property owners.

While abatement programs have shown promise in controlling drug sales at particular locations, serious legal and ethical concerns have been raised about their reckless application (see Cheh, this volume). Because abatement strategies hold property owners accountable for tenants' behaviors, these statutes may infringe on owners' rights to use and enjoy property (Smith et al., 1992). Furthermore, statutes that permit authorities to close properties without notifying owners may infringe upon due process rights. Improperly applied abatement laws can injure innocent family members who are evicted along with drug dealers, as well as other tenants who are forced out with the closure of entire buildings.

Ultimately, the success of abatement programs depends on landlords cooperating with city officials to remove drug dealers. If most landlords continue to see the laws as unfair, they may drop out of the real estate market (increasing already high numbers of abandoned inner city properties), or take steps to circumvent the law (reducing compliance). In either case, this does not bode well for the future of abatement programs. City officials should consider ways to positively involve property owners in abatement efforts, and to reduce the overwhelming perception that abatements laws are unfair to owners. Opening the doors of communication through seminars, workshops or town meetings with government attorneys, law enforcement officials and interested property owners could be valuable and could provide the opportunity to make suggestions to owners on how to screen prospective tenants, provide security, and use abatement laws to their best advantage. This might lead to an atmosphere of cooperation between abatement program staff and property owners, and turn around some of the resentment felt by many owners.

Address correspondence to: Barbara E. Smith, American Bar Association, 740 15th Street, NW, Washington, DC 20005.

REFERENCES

Lurigio, A., R. Davis, T. Regulus, V. Gwisada, S. Popkin, M. Dantzker, B. Smith and A. Ouellet (1993). *An Evaluation of the Cook County State's Attorney's Office Narcotics Nuisance Abatement Program*. Chicago, IL: Department of Criminal Justice, Loyola University.

Rosenbaum, D.P. (1993). "Civil Liberties and Aggressive Enforcement: Balancing the Rights of Individuals and Society in the Drug War. " In: R.C. Davis, A.J. Lurigio and D.P. Rosenbaum (eds.), *Drugs and the Community*. Springfield, IL: Charles C Thomas.

Smith, B.E., R.C. Davis, S.W. Hillenbrand, and S.R. Goretsky (1992). *Ridding Neighborhoods of Drug Houses in the Private Sector*. Washington, DC: American Bar Association.

Part IV: Civil Remedies in Public Housing

GETTING EVICTED FROM PUBLIC HOUSING: AN ANALYSIS OF THE FACTORS INFLUENCING EVICTION DECISIONS IN SIX PUBLIC HOUSING SITES

by

Justin Ready
Rutgers University

Lorraine Green Mazerolle
University of Cincinnati

and

Elyse Revere
Rutgers University

Abstract: *Evictions, perhaps more than other civil remedies for controlling crime and disorder in public housing, have seized the attention of policy makers and housing directors during the 1990s. Nonetheless, public housing authorities have been slow to enforce the federal "one strike" policy, which grants site managers the authority to evict suspected offenders after an administrative hearing, without having to wait for a criminal conviction. This paper examines the effects of criminal and lease-violating behavior on evictions among residents living in six public housing developments in Jersey City, NJ after controlling for family characteristics. We examine, first, the structural and violation characteristics of a sample of households evicted in 1994 and 1995; second, whether evicted households differ significantly on various social dimensions using a random sample of households taken from the same population; and third, the relative importance of family, economic and lease-violating factors in predicting whether an eviction will result. The implications, based on a logistic regression model, point to the discretionary use of administrative* *and policy violation notices as a promising tool for dealing with problem apartments in public housing communities.*

INTRODUCTION

For many years, public housing developments across the U.S. have served as testing grounds for a broad range of crime prevention strategies. Early research efforts, most notably by Oscar Newman, found that accessibility and physical layout were key determinants of crime, fear and transience in urban housing populations (Newman, 1973; Newman and Franck, 1980). Newman and his colleagues subsequently advocated changes to the design of public housing to create "defensible space." Rainwater (1970) found that residents of the Pruitt-Igoe housing development in St. Louis felt endangered and socially isolated because of the poor security and extreme disrepair of their surroundings. These findings spawned extensive efforts to clean up the physical appearances of public housing sites, and highlighted the importance of social programs for public housing residents.

In recent years, many local police departments and public housing police agencies have taken a problem-solving approach to control crime and disorder problems in public housing sites (see Dunworth and Saiger, 1994; Giacomazzi et al., 1995; Mazerolle and Terrill, 1997; Weisel, 1990). Problem-oriented policing typically extends the responsibility for crime control beyond the police and relies on third parties such as property owners, citizen groups and municipal agencies, to solve crime and disorder problems (see Buerger and Mazerolle, 1998; Eck and Spelman, 1987; Goldstein, 1990). In addition to collaboration, the problem-solving approach requires police departments and partnership agencies to develop an understanding of how criminal incidents form patterns across targeted areas so that this knowledge can be used to implement long-term solutions.

Since traditional policing activities involve mostly arrests and prosecution, it is easy to forget that the police and municipal agencies can initiate a number of other legal actions to deal with recurring problems in public housing. For example, problem-solving programs can make use of city licensing, zoning laws, forfeitures, tenant lease policies and other civil remedies to gain compliance from residents and outsiders who are responsible for creating, or exacerbating, problems (see Goldstein, 1990). Problem-solving teams, working in selected housing developments of Philadelphia and Jersey City, for instance, have aggressively enforced health codes and city ordinances to alleviate drugs and inci-vilities (Weisel, 1990; Mazerolle and Terrill, 1997). Anti-drug efforts initiated by the U.S. Department of Housing and Urban Development (HUD) have also relied on civil measures, such as leasehold forfeitures and restraining orders, to solve public nuisance and drug problems (Popkin et al., 1995; Weisel, 1990).

The proliferation of alternatives to traditional policing methods is largely representative of a paradigm shift in policing that assumes that the police cannot effectively deal with crime on their own (see also Skogan and Annan, 1994). It is within this context that we examine the factors that influence eviction decisions in six public housing develop-ments in Jersey City, NJ. We begin our paper with a summary of the legal basis for evicting public housing residents. We then discuss our research methods and data and conclude with a discussion of the role of evictions as an alternative means to resolve problems in public housing sites.

LEGAL BASIS TO EVICT RESIDENTS FROM PUBLIC HOUSING

Evictions, perhaps more than other civil remedies, have seized the attention of policy makers and public housing directors during the 1990s. Many commentators suggest that the legal authority to evict a resident who sells narcotics out of his or her apartment can provide an effective response to problems in public housing sites. The Anti-Drug Abuse Act of 1988 (Public Law 100-690) explicitly states that criminal activity, including drug use, is cause for termination of tenancy. None-theless, housing authorities have been slow to enforce this policy, partly because of the tedious administrative hearings that accompany evic-tions for misconduct. In addition, site managers are not always able to obtain reliable information that will stand up in court, and, in some cases, they do not realize the scope of their legal authority. This is understandable, considering the vague guidelines that HUD provides for implementing drug-related evictions: "The decision whether to initiate proceedings to terminate tenancy in a particular case remains a matter of good judgement by the Public Housing Authority (PHA) based on the factual situation" (Anti-Drug Abuse Act of 1988).

Under the guidance of the federal "one strike" policy, and in accor-dance with the Housing Opportunity Program Extension Act of 1996, public housing managers have recently been given the authority to evict suspected offenders after an administrative hearing, without having to wait for a criminal conviction. Police officers and resident leaders may provide arrest reports and personal testimony during the tenancy hearings. The lease amendment specifies that proof of criminal activity by a "preponderance of evidence" is sufficient to establish that there has been a violation. Housing directors largely support the new policy, which could potentially streamline a process that often takes years to complete (Cazenave, 1990). At the same time, many feel that the new policy fails to address a number of real-world issues. Specifically, local courts have been reluctant to fully embrace zero-tolerance eviction programs as a method of crime control. Judges acknowledge that public housing is a last resort for severely disadvantaged households with special difficulties locating adequate, affordable housing in the private market, particularly families experiencing single parenthood, discrimination and long-term poverty (President's Commission on Housing, 1982; see also Holzman, 1996). Indeed, the crime-reducing benefits gained by evicting a tenant must be measured against the considerable human and monetary costs of homelessness that may result (Weil, 1991).

To date, few criminologists have empirically examined the use of evictions to control crime in public housing, or the characteristics of households evicted for lease-violating behavior. Studies that incorporate measures of evictions usually rely on anecdotal information provided by housing authorities, much of which is reported in case studies and interviews with local officials (Dunworth and Saiger, 1993). For example, Harold Lucas, executive director of the Newark Housing Authority, reported 20 eviction cases resulting from criminal activity from 1992 through 1995 (*Sunday Star-Ledger*, 1996). The Jersey City Housing Authority (JCHA), the second largest of New Jersey's 81 agencies, chronicled only six criminal tenancy cases that led to evictions in 1995. These low numbers illustrate that crime- and drug-related evictions are relatively uncommon, despite the fact that over 900 felony arrests are made in both Jersey City and Newark housing developments annually (Center for Crime Prevention Studies, 1995).

This paper examines the effects of criminal and lease-violating behavior on evictions among residents living in six public housing developments in Jersey City, NJ after controlling for economic and family characteristics. We examine, first, the structural and violation characteristics of a sample of households evicted in 1994 and 1995; second, whether evicted households differ significantly on various social dimensions from a random sample of households taken from the same population; and, third, the relative importance of family, economic and lease-violating factors in predicting whether an eviction will result. We are particularly interested in examining the relative influences of criminal

violations compared to rent delinquency and other non-criminal violations in determining a manager's use of the civil law to deal with problem households.

Public Housing Residents of Jersey City

Jersey City resembles other densely populated, industrial cities in
the northeast U.S. Located in the New York City metropolitan area,
Jersey City sustains concentrated areas of low-income housing, jobless-
ness and crime. Three out of ten Jersey City residents are foreign born
— a higher proportion than is found in any other metropolis except
Miami, FL. Encompassing 41% of the population of Hudson County, the
city is best characterized as a blue-collar, urban center. The 1990
census shows an overall unemployment rate of 11%, and indicates that
18% of the total population (229,000) and 35% of all female-headed
households live in poverty. A substantial number of these impoverished
families reside in the 11 public housing developments managed by the
JCHA.

Rates of violent crime and disorder are generally higher in other
public housing than other inner-city locations. Comparative research
using census tract and block-level data shows that, after controlling for
economic and housing characteristics, public housing generates more
index crimes of all types (Brill and Associates, 1977; Roncek, et al.,
1981). Dunworth and Saiger (1993) found that housing developments
in Phoenix, AZ; Los Angeles, CA; and Washington D.C. produced significantly higher levels of violent and drug-related activity compared to citywide and nearby neighborhood crime rates. Consistent with past research, public housing in Jersey City has been designated a "High
Intensity Drug Trafficking Area," pursuant to Section 1005 of the Anti-
Drug Abuse Act of 1988.

Weisburd and Green (1995) used mapping software to plot arrest
and criminal investigation data against street addresses, and found that
six public housing developments in Jersey City ranked among the top
ten drug market and violent crime locations in the city. Drawing from
a citywide analysis of narcotics and violent crime data, six developments
emerged as experiencing severe and persistent crime problems: Duncan
Apartments, Curries Woods Apartments, Montgomery Gardens,
Lafayette Gardens, Booker T. Apartments and Marion Gardens (Weisburd and Green, 1995).

Table 1 profiles the six public housing developments included in this
study. Each development was built during the 1950s and houses between 243 and 649 families.[1] Overall, the housing developments com-

prise a total of 2,640 discrete units. The percentage of elderly house-holds ranges from 5% in one study site (Duncan Apartments) to 22% in another (Booker T. Apartments), with most sites falling well below the city (25%) and national (35%) averages (Holzman, 1996).[2] Approximately one-third of all leaseholders living within the six public housing sites works at least part-time, while 37% receive Aid to Families with De-pendent Children (AFDC).

Table 1: Profile of Targeted Public Housing Developments in Jersey City, NJ

Development	Style	Units	% One Adult	% AFDC	% Employed	% Elderly
Duncan	High-rise	645	60	51	27	5
Curries Woods	High-rise	524	52	38	30	15
Montgomery	High-rise	440	51	34	40	10
Lafayette	Walk-up	487	47	30	32	18
Booker T.	Walk-up	314	42	32	35	22
Marion	Walk-up	230	45	35	24	18

Source: Jersey City Housing Authority lease records and internal files

PUBLIC HOUSING LEASE RECORDS AND STUDY METHODS

Measuring the criminal and lease-violating conduct of public hous-ing residents is a menacing task. Police department records are impre-cise because they are affected by variations in citizen reporting and police deployment across neighborhoods (Dunworth and Saiger, 1993; Eck and Spelman, 1987). Although official data sources comprise de-tailed information on offense types and locations, they do not keep household-level information on public housing populations. Since this paper examines both criminal and noncriminal behavior, and circum-stances that influence a manager's decision to evict a household, back-ground factors that are not routinely collected through police reports must be incorporated as control variables. Furthermore, since many incidents that are known to and recorded by the police are never brought to the attention of housing officials (thus cannot be considered during the decision-making process that precedes tenancy hearings), it makes methodological sense to use data that are internal to public housing authorities, preferably data upon which tenancy decisions are based.

As part of HUD's record-keeping system, housing authorities are required to maintain a lease file on each household. In addition to providing a unit-by-unit list of addresses within each site, the files include details on lease violations and the circumstances surrounding each event. The JCHA's data files are supplemented with arrest reports, treatment referrals and narratives furnished by police officers and social service providers. The exact procedure followed by individual agencies in documenting lease data varies, depending on the size and administrative style of the PHA (Holzman, 1996). In general, agencies update household records yearly and register violations with written "notices to cease" or "notices of nonpayment," depending on the nature of the infraction.

Lease records from 352 households across six public housing developments were examined in the spring of 1996. The sampling procedure involved the selection of two distinct samples. The first included lease records from 85 households that were evicted in 1994 and 1995. With the exception of three files that were either missing or being used in court, field researchers retrieved archival data on all leases terminated within the study period.[3] The second sample included lease records for 267 randomly selected non-evicted households, stratified by housing development.[4] For analytic purposes, a probability sample was used approximating household characteristics (i.e., employment status, number of minors, age of leaseholder) of the larger public housing communities. In total, we examined the lease records for 352 public housing households in Jersey City.

Study Variables

The dependent variable used in this study was the eviction status of each household, measured as "evicted" or "not evicted." The variable of eviction, then, is a dichotomous variable: households that were not evicted in either 1994 or 1995 received a score of zero, while those that were evicted received a score of 1. A total of 88 households were evicted during the study period.

The stated cause for eviction in most cases was habitual non-payment of rent. The tenant lease agreement stipulates that legal action for non-payment may be instituted one month after a second written notice is issued (one notice is mailed out after each month a leaseholder fails to pay rent), allowing managers wide discretion in deciding when to initiate proceedings. Indeed, the average number of non-payment notices issued to non-evicted households was 2.9, more than the minimum requirement for legal action, suggesting that legal action is largely a function of a manager's control over the eviction process. As Keyes (1992) explains: "Many managers use nonpayment as a means of getting an eviction for what is actually a drug situation. When managers should go for a drug-related eviction and when they should go for nonpayment is a critical strategy decision, because the courts will not allow the conversion of one tactic to the other" (p.182). Since New Jersey state law prevents PHAs from displacing juvenile offenders and residents who are in court-ordered drug treatment programs, eviction for non-payment may be seen as a tool for getting around legal obstacles.

The effects of criminal and lease-violating activity on evictions are examined using three primary independent variables: criminal lease violations, noncriminal policy violations and administrative complaints. These are interval-level variables indicating the number of violations of a specific type incurred by a household in 1994 and 1995. Since habitual non-payment of rent is the expressed cause for termination in most cases, high numbers of non-payment notices are naturally expected to increase the probability of eviction. However, we hypothesize that the presence of other forms of lease-violating behavior, particularly criminal activity, will increase the odds of eviction to a greater degree than non-payment. Violations unrelated to payment history, serving as latent predictors of eviction, are suspected to be an underlying cause for legal action in many situations, whereas rent-based proceedings mask their influence. This hypothesis will be tested statistically in the ensuing analysis by examining the odds ratios for latent predictors, which reflect the average change in the probability of eviction for every additional lease violation, holding all other independent variables constant.

Table 2 displays the composition of the three types of lease violations examined in this study. The first category of lease violations comprises crimes reported to and cleared by the police and later recorded by managers as household violations involving illegal activity. Over three-fourths of these criminal violations were recorded directly from arrest reports provided by Jersey City public housing officers. Assaults, drug-related crimes and disputes between intimates account for more than half of all arrests that eventually result in written violation notices. The second category of lease violations includes infractions that violate public housing policy, but that are generally less serious in nature and do not involve a criminal justice system response. Most of the infractions in this category are social incivilities related to household cleaning habits, everyday interactions with neighbors and treatment of the premises. The third and last category of lease violations includes administrative complaints issued when a leaseholder habitually fails to file occupancy forms, attend meetings or follow procedures set forth by the management.

Table 2: Categories of Public Housing Lease Violations

Criminal Violations	Policy Violations	Administrative Complaints
Drug crimes	Occupancy violation (boarders)	Failure to file occupancy forms
Disorderly conduct	Throwing objects from window	Inspection noncompliance
Larceny-theft	Unsanitary conditions	Failure to attend meetings
Aggravated assault	Littering/dumping	
Restraining-order violation	Graffiti in halls	
Receipt of stolen property	Dog ownership	
Vandalism/arson	Unruly behavior (minors)	
Public drunkenness		
Open warrant		

(a) *Source:* Jersey City Housing Authority lease records and internal files.
(b) Field researchers occasionally found a criminal and administrative violation on a single notice to cease. These violations were coded individually as if they were on separate notices.

Housing authorities are required to issue a preliminary notice to cease for any of these activities if they threaten the health, safety or right to peaceful enjoyment of the premises of other residents. It is only when such noncriminal activities continue that a manager has a cause for eviction.

Six control variables were included in the analysis, representing the structural and financial characteristics of the individual households in the study sample: (1) the age of the leaseholder; (2) the number of minors in the family; (3) one-adult household (yes/no); (4) the number of years living in public housing; (5) the monthly rent (dollars amount); and (6) the number of non-payment-of-rent slips issued. One-adult household is a binary variable indicating whether a household has one or more adult family members (18 years or older) on the lease. This measure should be interpreted with caution because of the regularity of adult males living "off the record" with a spouse or relatives. Like the violation types shown in 2, non-payment of rent slips issued is a continuous variable denoting the number of rent violations a household accumulated in 1994 and 1995, with 24 being the maximum number of issuances possible. In sum, the household variables selected here are moderately correlated with violation types (see Appendix), and, according to interviews with the site managers (n=6), are reasonably well-established factors influencing PHA decisions regarding eviction proceedings.

RESEARCH RESULTS

The analytic strategy used in this study involves a number of statistical tests. First, the average numbers of infractions committed by evicted and non-evicted households are compared. Second, using independent sample t-tests, the differences in family characteristics between the two samples are examined. Finally, a multiple logistic regression model is used to control for the effects of the household structural characteristics, allowing for an examination of the isolated effects of violation types on public housing evictions. Table 3 compares the characteristics of evicted and non-evicted households from the six public housing developments.

Table 3 presents eviction and non-eviction group percentages that reveal several noteworthy differences in earning potential and violation characteristics. A substantially higher percentage of non-evicted households (38%) than evicted households (24%) reported at least part-time employment in 1994 and 1995. Twenty percent more of the evicted households than the non-evicted households received AFDC or general assistance as their main source of income. The gap in earning potential is magnified after taking into account the proportion of working-age leaseholders in each of the samples: nearly 20% of non-evicted leaseholders were retired and receiving social security or pension benefits compared to just 6% of leaseholders in the eviction group. The higher percentage of rent violations incurred by evicted households than non-evicted households, shown at the bottom of Table 3, may be the result of different employment circumstances.

Table 3: Characteristics of Evicted and Non-Evicted Households from Public Housing Developments in Jersey City, NJ (1994-95)

Household Characteristics	Evicted (N=85)	Not Evicted (N=267)
Female leaseholders	89%	85%
One adult households	47%	39%
African-American families	91%	89%
Part-time (or more)employees	24%	38%
AFDC/general assistance recipients	58%	38%
One or more criminal violations	52%	12%
One or more drug-related violations	32%	5%
Four or more non-payment slips	67%	32%

Source: Jersey City Housing Authority lease records and internal files.

Table 3 also indicates that more than twice as many evicted households than non-evicted households incurred one or more drug-related violations, even though the eviction sample is much smaller than the non-evicted sample. Measuring the extent to which drug and alcohol addiction precipitates rent delinquency is not the focus here, but it is reasonable to speculate that long-term addiction detracts from a resident's ability to make payments on time and comply with management policies.

A striking result presented in Table 3 shows that over half (52%) of those evicted from public housing incurred one or more violation notices for illegal activity in their last two years of residence, compared with 12% of households in the non-evicted sample. Only a handful of the active lease files (4%) contained more than one violation resulting in arrest, while 15% of the terminated files produced a string of three or more criminal violations. Family composition factors remained relatively stable across these groups. Female leaseholders were predominant in both samples. Just under half of the households contained one adult family member, and, on average, three residents occupied each of the units.

While Table 3 illustrates important differences between the evicted and non-evicted samples, statistical tests of the differences in family characteristics between the two samples are provided in Table 4.

Table 4: Independent Sample t-tests for Evicted and Non-Evicted Public Housing Households in Jersey City, NJ (1994-95)

Household Characteristics	Mean Value Evicted	Mean Value Not Evicted	t	Sig. (2-tailed)
Age of leaseholder	40.6	46.7	-3.367	.001
Family size	3.1	2.9	.903	.368
Number of minors in family	1.8	1.3	2.148	.034
Years as resident	12.0	16.9	-3.527	.000
Total annual income	9217.5	NA	NA	NA
Monthly rent	197.1	240.9	-2.240	.027
Nonpayment notices	6.2	2.9	6.091	.000
Criminal violations	1.0	0.2	7.373	.000
Policy violations	0.7	0.2	6.326	.000
Administrative complaints	1.6	0.3	8.754	.000
Total lease violations	3.3	0.6	11.493	.000

(a) *Source:* Jersey City Housing Authority lease records and internal files
(b) Levene's Test for Equality of Variance was used to determine whether equal sample variances could be assumed for the above variables. Pooled variance scores were adjusted accordingly.
(c) *Total lease violations* is the sum of all lease violation types, excluding non-payment of rent.
(d) NA indicates data not available.

As Table 4 shows, the evicted households and non-evicted households are significantly different across a number of family and violation characteristics. Evicted household leaseholders tend to be younger (40.6 years) than non-evicted leaseholders (46.7 years); evicted households have significantly more children in their care (1.8 children) than non-evicted households (1.3 children); evicted households have lived in public housing for a shorter time (12 years) than their non-evicted counterparts (16.9 years); evicted households pay significantly less monthly rent ($197) than the non-evicted households ($241); and evicted households have far more lease violations (3.3) than non-evicted households (0.6).

Table 5 below presents the results from a multiple logistic regression model that is used to control for the effects of household structural characteristics, in order to examine the isolated effects of violation types on whether a household is likely to be evicted or not.[5] The odds ratios and p-values for predictor variables are presented in Table 5. In general, the coefficient β_i in the logistic model estimates the average change in the log-odds of eviction when x_i is increased by one unit, holding all other independent variables fixed. The antilog of the coefficient, e^β, then estimates the odds ratio

$$\frac{\pi_{x+1} / (1-\pi_{x+1})}{\pi_x / (1-\pi_x)}$$

where π_x is the value of $P(y=1)$ for a fixed value x (Mendenhall and Sincich, 1996). Column 4 of Table 5 lists the computed values of $(e^\beta)-1$, which is an estimate of the percent change in the odds of eviction $\pi = P(y=1) / P(y=0)$ resulting from every one-unit increase in x_i. The odds ratio for criminal lease violations, for example, estimates the percentage increase in the odds that a household will be evicted from public housing for every unit increase in criminal violations, holding all other socioeconomic and violation variables fixed. The Wald chi-square ratio (Column 3), like the t-ratio for ordinary least squares regression, provides a statistic for testing the contribution of each variable to the model.

Table 5 shows that for each additional criminal violation incurred by a public housing household in this study, the odds of eviction increase by 51%.[6] Administrative complaints show a stronger effect than other violation types, increasing the likelihood of eviction by 68% for each infraction. Policy violations are also a significant predictor of whether or not a household is evicted (p=.035): for each additional policy violation, the odds of eviction increase by 41%.

Socioeconomic factors were quite limited in their predictive power of whether or not a household was evicted. Important exceptions were years as resident and monthly rent, both of which showed small, inverse effects. That is, as the number of years living in public housing and the monthly rent payments increase, the probability of eviction decreases.

Interestingly, non-payment slips issued was not significant at the p < .05 level when criminal violations and, in particular, administrative complaints were added to the model. This finding suggests that non-payment of rent will only lead to eviction when more serious conduct violations (i.e., criminal and administrative violations) are also present. The chi-square test of overall model adequacy is given in the lower portion of Table 5 as χ^2= 133.207, with an observed significance level p < .000.

Table 5: Multiple Logistic Regression Model Predicting for Public Housing Evictions in Jersey City, NJ

Tenant Characteristics	B	S.E.	Wald	Odds Ratio	Sig.
Family Structure Factors					
Age of leaseholder	-.006	.016	.123	-.006	.726
Number of minors in family	.039	.115	.113	.038	.737
One adult household	.348	.383	.826	.294	.364
Years as resident	-.058	.020	8.329	-.059	.004*
Economic Factors					
Monthly rent	-.002	.001	4.070	-.002	.044*
Nonpayment slips	.055	.037	2.238	.054	.135
Lease Violation Factors					
Criminal violations	.720	.182	15.671	.513	.000*
Policy violations	.528	.251	4.425	.410	.035*
Administrative complaints	1.136	.196	33.710	.679	.000*

Total N = 352
Dependent Variable = Eviction
Model Chi-Square = 133.207 p < .000

Source: Jersey City Housing Authority lease records and internal files.
* p<.05

DISCUSSION AND CONCLUSION

This paper explored the factors that contribute to families being evicted from public housing. In particular, we examined the structural and violation characteristics of a sample of households evicted in 1994 and 1995, whether evicted households differed from non-evicted households on various social dimensions, and the importance of family, economic, and lease-violating factors in predicting whether or not a household would be evicted. We were particularly interested in examining the relative influences of criminal violations compared to rent delinquency and other non-criminal violations in determining a manager's use of the civil law to deal with problem households. We began our paper by hypothesizing that the presence of lease-violating behavior, particularly criminal activity, would increase the odds of eviction to a greater degree than non-payment of rent. We also suspected that violations unrelated to payment history, serving as latent predictors of eviction, would be an underlying cause for legal action in many situations.

The results indicate that non-payment of rent plays a smaller role in eviction decisionmaking than once expected. After statistically controlling for noncriminal policy violations and household characteristics, rent delinquency failed to predict the occurrence of public housing evictions at the .05 level of significance. Moreover, although arrests are an important factor that managers considered in eviction hearings, administrative complaints (violations for behaviors that are unrelated to criminal activity or non-payment of rent) are the most important predictor of whether or not a household is evicted. Administrative complaints are recorded as "notices to cease" and are typically used by public housing managers for "lack of behavior" rather than for involvement in illegal activities or delinquent rent payments. For example, when residents are perceived by public housing administrators as being uncooperative — when they refuse to file or deliberately lie on occupancy forms, or when they fail to attend inspections and tenancy meetings — then a "notice to cease" may be issued. Site managers have considerable discretion in issuing "notices to cease," and many observers comment that the administrative complaint mechanism, and to a lesser degree policy violations, provide site managers with a capacity to build a case against residents who they see as being troublesome.

Within the broader context of civil remedies, notices to cease appear to be an important and direct tool used by site managers to control the activities of public housing residents. The vagueness of an "administrative complaint" allows site managers wide discretion in their decision to invoke this particular type of civil remedy in a range of different situations. On one hand, administrative and policy violation notices are social control tools that give site managers the means for controlling the behavior of law-abiding public housing residents. This type of civil remedy is inappropriate if site managers overuse administrative complaints and violations, or use them to unfairly target particular public housing residents. On the other hand, the administrative complaint and policy violation options provide managers with a method for systematically targeting criminally active public housing residents who pay their rent on time and avoid arrest. In these situations, public housing managers can use the administrative and policy violation mechanisms as a means to initiate eviction proceedings and deal with persistent problems in public housing settings.

The key to fair play in the use of administrative and policy violations in the public housing eviction process appears to be in controlling the unfettered discretionary use of a tool that has the potential for abuse. This is a specific challenge that is reflective of a broader challenge in the general use of civil remedies for crime control purposes. Given that a household that has been evicted from public housing is no longer eligible for federally subsidized housing, we suggest that the discretionary use of administrative complaints and policy violation notices as a strategy to control the misconduct of public housing residents should be carefully monitored, and guidelines be developed to eliminate disparities in eviction decision-making processes. One direction PHAs could take is to standardize the eviction process, whereby households would incur a varying number of points for administrative, policy and rent violations. Public housing directors could set an annual point threshold, at which point an eviction hearing may be scheduled. Such guidelines would regulate site managers' discretion over the eviction process, at the same time allowing them to use a widely accessible civil remedy for controlling crime and incivilities in public housing communities across the U.S.

Address correspondence to: Justin Ready, Rutgers University, Center for Crime Prevention Studies, School of Criminal Justice, S.I. Newhouse Center for Law and Justice, 15 Washington Street, Newark, NJ 07102.

Acknowledgments: This research was supported by grant no. 94-IJ-CX-0063 from the National Institute of Justice. Points of view or opinions expressed in the paper do not necessarily represent the official positions or policies of the National Institute of Justice or the U.S. Department of Justice. We would like to thank Bill Terrill, Elin Waring, Deputy Chief Frank Gajewski, Lieutenant Charles Bellucci, Sergeant Brian McDonough and the members of the six public housing problem-solving teams for their help in this project.

REFERENCES

Brill, W. and Associates (1977). *Victimization, Fear of Crime, and Altered Behavior: A Profile of the Crime Problem in Capper Dwellings, Washington, D.C.* Washington, DC: U.S. Department of Housing and Urban Development.

Buerger, M. and L.G. Mazerolle (1998). "Third-Party Policing: A Theoretical Analysis of an Emerging Trend." *Justice Quarterly* 15(2):301-328.

Cazenave, D.P. (1990). "Congress Steps Up War on Drugs in Public Housing — Has It Gone One Step Too Far?" *Loyola Law Review* 36:137-157.

Center for Crime Prevention Studies (1995). "Jersey City Problem-Oriented Policing Public Housing Program." Unpublished Internal Memos, Rutgers University, Newark, NJ.

Dunworth, T. and A. Saiger (1993). *Drugs and Crime in Public Housing: A Three-City Analysis.* Santa Monica, CA: Rand.

Eck J.E. and W. Spelman (1987). "Who Ya Gonna Call? The Police as Problem-Busters." *Crime & Delinquency* 33:31-52.

Giacomazzi, A.L., E.F. McGarrell and Q.C. Thurman (1995). "Community Crime Prevention and Public Housing: A Preliminary Assessment of a Multi-Level, Collaborative Drug-Crime Elimination Strategy." Paper presented at the annual meeting of the American Society of Criminology, Boston, MA.

Goldstein, H. (1990). *Problem-Oriented Policing.* New York, NY: McGraw-Hill, Inc.

Holzman, H.R. (1996). "Criminological Research on Public Housing: Toward a Better Understanding of People, Places, and Spaces." *Crime & Delinquency* 42:361-378.

Keyes, L.C. (1992). *Strategies and Saints: Fighting Drugs in Subsidized Housing.* Washington, DC: Urban Institute Press.

Mazerolle, L.G. and W. Terrill (1997). "Problem-Oriented Policing in Public Housing: Identifying the Distribution of Problem Places." *Policing: An International Journal of Police Strategies & Management* 20(2):235-255.

Newman, O. (1973). Defensible Space: *Crime Prevention Through Urban Design.* New York, NY: Macmillan.

—— and K.A. Franck (1980). *Factors Influencing Crime and Instability in Urban Housing Developments.* Washington, DC: U.S. National Institute of Justice.

Popkin, S.J., L.M. Olson, A.J. Lurigio, V.E. Gwiasda and R.G. Carter (1995). "Sweeping Out Drugs and Crime: Residents' Views of the Chicago

Housing Authority's Public Housing Drug Elimination Program." *Crime & Delinquency* 41:73-99.

Rainwater, L. (1970). *Behind Ghetto Walls: Black Families in a Federal Slum.* Chicago, IL: Aldine.

Roncek, D.W., R. Bell and J. Francik (1981). "Housing Projects and Crime." *Social Problems* 29:151-66.

Skogan, W.G. and S.O. Annan (1994). "Drugs in Public Housing: Toward an Effective Police Response." In: D.L. MacKenzie and C.D. Uchida (eds.), *Drugs and Crime: Evaluating Public Police Initiatives.* Thousand Oaks, CA: Sage.

Roberts, R. (1996)., "Zero Tolerance: Public Housing Directors Applaud Federal Law Allowing Their Agencies to Evict Crime Suspects." *Sunday Star-Ledger* May 5, p.29.

U.S. President's Commission on Housing (1982). *The Report of the President's Commission on Housing.* Washington, DC: U.S. Government Printing Office.

Weil, L. (1991). "Drug-Related Evictions in Public Housing: Congress' Addiction to a Quick Fix." *Yale Law and Policy Review* 161(9).

Weisburd, D. and L. Green (1995). "Policing Drug Hot Spots: The Jersey City DMA Experiment." *Justice Quarterly* 12:711-736.

Weisel, D.L. (1990). *Tackling Drug Problems in Public Housing: A Guide for Police.* Washington, DC: Police Executive Research Forum.

Appendix: Correlation Matrix of Household Factors Influencing Public Housing Evictions

	1	2	3	4	5	6	7	8	9	10
1. Age of leaseholder	1.00									
2. Family size	**-.21**	1.00								
3. Number of minors	**-.39**	**.87**	1.00							
4. Years as resident	**.53**	-.03	**-.20**	1.00						
5. Monthly rent	**.22**	.10	-.10	**.25**	1.00					
6. Non-payment slips	**-.25**	.02	.07	-.09	.02	1.00				
7. Criminal violations	**-.11**	**.19**	**.20**	-.02	-.09	**.22**	1.00			
8. Policy violations	**-.11**	**.18**	**.22**	-.08	-.04	**.29**	**.33**	1.00		
9. Administrative complaints	-.09	.04	.07	-.03	.09	**.35**	**.18**	**.38**	1.00	
10. Total violations	**-.14**	**.17**	**.21**	-.05	.00	**.40**	**.66**	**.70**	**.80**	1.00

(a) **Boldface** signifies p < .05.

325

NOTES

1. Many households have second generation families (e.g., a mother, daughter and daughter's children) living in the same unit. Variations in how extended families are grouped account for the discrepancy between the number of families residing in the six housing developments and the number of units reported in Table 1.

2. Elderly households include a primary leaseholder who is 62 years or older.

3. Records were designated "skipouts" when a family violated the lease agreement (usually through non-payment of rent), then moved from the housing development before eviction proceedings could run their course. Because this paper is only concerned with lockouts, and because it is impossible to determine which skipouts would have resulted in evictions had the families remained in public housing, these records were excluded from the sample.

4. Originally, 50 occupied units were randomly selected from each of the developments, totaling 300 households. Because JCHA lease records are not computerized and frequently change offices (i.e., management office, legal office), 33 records could not be coded. Background checks were made here to ensure that bias was not introduced into the sample.

5. The logistic analysis was built from the ground up by running a series of independent sample t-tests on household variables, then placing key predictors in the final model based on whether or not mean sample values differed significantly at the $p < .01$ level. Contextual information gathered during management interviews aided the selection process. Nine predictors were obtained, most of which are listed in Table 4 along with their respective t-values. Each independent variable was regressed on the remaining ones to test for multicollinearity; consequently, total lease violations and *family size* were discarded. One adult household was added to obtain a rough measure of the impact of adult guardianship on the odds of eviction.

6. The reasoning behind the model specified in Table 4 and the methods that guided this specification, are exploratory and not capable of ruling out alternative models for estimating PHA lockouts. Many factors retained here yield significant parameter estimates and the model chi-square test indicates that the data fit the model. But it is important to note that the tenant population and bureaucratic style of the JCHA are unique from those of other PHAs. Samples from high-crime developments in Jersey City, for example, may be disproportionately composed of tenants who have higher vulnerability to arrest, higher levels of nonpayment stemming from eco-

nomic hardship or more violation notices because of less tolerant management policies. These regional circumstances warrant caution in the generalizations that can be drawn.

A CASE FOR PARTNERSHIP: THE LOCAL AUTHORITY LANDLORD AND THE LOCAL POLICE

by

Sheridan Morris
**formerly with Police Research Group,
U.K. Home Office**

Abstract: *The partnership approach to crime reduction and antisocial behavior is now well-established in the academic literature and the operational reality of many agencies. A more recent, and still developing aspect of such initiatives in the U.K., is the use of civil statutes alongside criminal law to tackle criminal and nuisance behavior. This paper features two case studies that describe the use of two civil instruments, injunctions and evictions, and the joint police-housing department operations that utilized them. The creation of a housing Tenancy Enforcement Team in Gateshead, Newcastle, represented an innovative approach to the enforcement of housing department tenancy agreements. An initiative by the local police and Hackney Housing department in London involved a criminal investigation and the test use of local council legal powers. The development, process and impact of both initiatives are discussed. The cases suggest that the partnership approach can strengthen both criminal and civil actions through the exchange of information and mutual enforcement support.*

This paper will discuss initiatives undertaken by what are known in the U.K. as local authority housing departments. Local authority is a term for the city or area council (e.g., Newcastle City Council), led by elected officials, that provides local (non-federal) governments with essential services such as education and housing. Such a body spends its budget and — as a legal entity — is able to instigate legal proceedings as its elected leaders and professional staff deem fit. Funding for such services, including the housing department that builds and manages the housing stock, is provided by a local property tax. The housing officers discussed in the two case studies in this chapter are employees of the local authority and are therefore public sector workers, though not central government civil servants. Unlike cities such as New York, those in the U.K. do not have dedicated housing police. The police units discussed comprise locally based officers who belong to the police force that covers the local region, county or city (e.g. the Metropolitan Police in Hackney, London and the Northumbria Police in Gateshead, Newcastle).

INTRODUCTION

In recent years, local authority housing departments in the U.K. have stepped up their efforts at tackling nuisance and criminal behavior on the housing estates where they are the sole or major landlord (Department of the Environment, 1990). The departments are increasingly addressing the security and safety concerns of residents not only through design measures but by adopting a tough stance against antisocial behavior by tenants. This approach involves the use of civil instruments such as tenancy agreements and local authority powers, which may ultimately lead to an eviction and/or an injunction, the latter a court-issued restraining-type order. In addition to problem behavior of a civil nature, housing departments are increasingly initiating civil actions to tackle criminal behavior in instances where the police have been unable to effect a successful outcome. Though such civil proceedings can be run independent of any criminal action, this paper will seek to illustrate how such civil remedies may run parallel to, and be facilitated by, related police actions.

The civil interventions adopted by the two local authority housing departments discussed here draw upon national civil statute and local authority administrative regulations. The government has recently strengthened the use of civil statute in this area by simplifying the eviction process and attaching greater police powers of arrest to civil injunctions. Local authorities have strengthened their ability to pursue administrative remedies by re-drafting their tenancy agreements. Both these developments are indicative of the growing reliance upon such forms of intervention in the face of the inability of the police to tackle adequately many problems in local authority housing areas.

Civil Mechanisms and Sanctions

Traditionally, local authorities have relied upon general nuisance clauses of tenancy agreements to deal with antisocial or criminal tenants. The past ten years have seen the strengthening of such agreements by the inclusion of more detailed clauses in agreements to address harassment, nuisance and crime. An example would be the London Borough of Hammersmith and Fulham's tenancy agreement clause specifically relating to domestic violence or violence toward others. The clause states: "It shall be a breach of these tenancy obligations for the tenant, unlawfully to commit, cause or threaten any violence against a member of the household, or unlawfully to force another person to leave the dwelling because of violence or threatened violence." An unpublished survey by the Association of Metropolitan Authorities (1994) indicated that almost half of the respondent local authorities were revising tenancy contracts to include breaches concerning nuisance, harassment or crime. Another 79% reported that tenancy agreements were being reviewed to improve the success of enforcement.

Eviction has been viewed as a last resort by councils because it has been a slow and expensive procedure, requiring the obtaining of two separate court orders. As evidence of the government's support for the use of civil remedies by local authorities, the 1996 Housing Act shortened this procedure to a single court application. In addition to evictions that are considered a measure of final resort, authorities are increasingly exploring the use of injunctions. An injunction is a court order that, in the U.K., can be used to require an individual, group or organization to carry out or refrain from specified actions. Such actions may include damaging property, the forbidding of breaking specified tenancy clauses, or entering a stated property or defined locale (e.g., exclusion order). Rather than making a formal judgment, a judge often asks the parties to agree to an "undertaking" by the defendant to refrain from a specified action. As with evictions, the 1996 Housing Act has strengthened injunctions by allowing police powers of arrest to be used in their enforcement. Previously, such breaches were generally seen as being in contempt of court and required further court proceedings; as such they were non-arrestable offenses and could not be immediately enforced by the police. This bolstering of such measures is again, indicative of the government's support for their increased use.

The use of civil remedies such as evictions or injunctions may serve a number of means. First, they provide civil enforcement where the criminal process is not available. Much nuisance behavior may only be resolved via the civil courts as no criminal law is being broken. Until a civil solution is achieved the police may be called to repeatedly attend incidents to which they can offer no viable solution, a concern echoed by Skogan (1988) in his examination of the role of community decline in the rise in crime and incivilities in residential areas. Second, such remedies may provide civil enforcement where the criminal process is not effective. Evidential requirements under the criminal process are such that the viability of prosecution may limit effective police and prosecution intervention. Such requirements may not inhibit a local authority from taking action however, as civil injunctions are not required to prove intent and require a significantly lower burden of proof "the balance of probability" rather than the criminal "beyond reasonable doubt." Also, where a criminal action has failed, a local authority may attempt civil proceedings utilizing, by prior agreement, the statements and information gathered previously by the police. Third, such measures represent a potentially powerful sanction. Partial exclusion from one's immediate social group, by an injunction barring entry to a residential area, may serve as a strong deterrent and penalty compared to a fine or suspended sentence in the criminal court. Finally, injunctions can help in countering witness intimidation. In the absence of the suspects being held on remand during a criminal case (or to prevent interference during a civil case), a civil injunction may be the only instrument available to deter intimidation. Such an injunction can forbid contact or proximity between the accused and the witness.

The civil tools in these case studies have targeted both offenders and non-offending parties who are deemed to bear a legal responsibility for the actions of others. The parent(s) of offenders are increasingly liable under the terms of their tenancy agreement for the behavior of persons residing in their home, e.g.. their dependents, adult or otherwise. The potential for parents or other guardian figures to influence the behavior of juvenile offenders is highlighted by Felson (1986, 1995). Felson (1995) argues that the parent, or any other person with proximity to and knowledge of a juvenile offender's behavior, can become an instrument of informal social control. Thus, the parent or another relative who is the contractual tenant of a local authority residence where the offender is living is in a position to act as a "handler" — capable of exercising a level of personal responsibility for the actions of their charge. Such control can be in the form of "discouragement," described as a reminder to cease any given behavior. If this level of informal social control fails, then coercion may be used by the handler to restrain inappropriate behavior. The premise that underlies this perspective however, is that those with whom an offender resides, are in fact willing or capable of taking on the role of "personal handler." A local authority will not undertake the legal expense of a court action lightly, and such a move will only be initiated once numerous contacts with tenant parents — probably also involving the police — have failed. Thus, the enforced personal handler role, the result of a civil action, may represent a new category for Felson's (1995) model.

The Hackney Council Housing Department, the subject of the second case study, has taken this approach when dealing with juveniles (aged 17 or younger) that visit one of its residential housing estates and engage in criminal and antisocial behavior. The use of injunctions to exclude these individuals from the area has encountered resistance from the courts. As a court order is only as effective as its enforcement, the courts have been reluctant to issue an order against young offenders who, in the likelihood of breaching an injunction, are unable to pay a fine and are too young to receive a custodial sentence for contempt of court as a result of the non-payment. For such juveniles, the housing department feels that the only viable option is to request an injunction against their tenant-guardians, generally their parents, requiring that they restrain their children from the proscribed actions. Such legal actions are currently ongoing.

A Remedial Strategy

Any remedial approach should consider both multi-agency strategy and operational tactics. Figure 1 illustrates the scope of civil and criminal initiatives found in the two case studies discussed in this report. Preventive measures are found in the collaborative approach to risk management, expressed in these cases by the joint identification of problem areas and multi-agency working groups. This cooperation is also evidenced by a mutual support for the investigation and prosecution process, and, ultimately, support from the police in enforcing injunctions and their application. This proactive approach by civil housing departments raises a number of issues regarding the development of civil enforcement actions, and is discussed in the final section of the paper, following a consideration of the case studies themselves.

Figure 1: Multi-Agency Compliance and Enforcement Approaches

Point of Intervention	Police and Criminal Process Support
Risk Management	• Joint mapping of problem "hotspots" • Joint strategic working group
Investigation	• Intelligence sharing • Police criminal investigations
Prosecution	• Criminal charges • Provision of criminal evidence for civil process
Enforcement	• Policing of injunctions • Enforcing of evictions • Notification of police-related incidents

CIVIL AND CRIMINAL PARTNERSHIPS

Gateshead Metropolitan Borough Council Tenancy Enforcement Team and Northumbria Police

In early 1994, the Housing Committee of Gateshead Metropolitan Borough Council in Newcastle decided to establish a Tenancy Enforcement Team (TET) to tackle growing criminal and anti-social behavior on council housing estates. The authority's concern was that although eviction was possible under the nuisance clause of their residents' tenancy agreement, it was very time-consuming (albeit less so now). More importantly, very few actions had been able to proceed "because of the real fears of reprisal felt [by resident witnesses and victims] despite assistance and encouragement from [housing] officers" (Gateshead Metropolitan Borough Council, 1993). In addition to centralizing housing department actions regarding problem tenants, the provision of a dedicated team distanced enforcement actions from local housing staff (often located on the estate concerned), who were increasingly subject to threatening behavior while dealing with complaints.

The Tenancy Enforcement Team

The TET has a comprehensive remit to contact victims of criminal and/or antisocial behavior on council estates and liaise with the relevant agencies and council departments so as to develop swift and effective problem-resolving strategies. This frequently involves gathering suitable evidence, including witness statements, and assisting in the preparation of legal notices (where appropriate) and attending court hearings.

Such is the commitment to a vigorous civil remedy approach that the team has recently increased from three to five council housing officers and has increased its responsibility from a handful of estates to the whole borough, covering approximately 30,000 properties. In addition to other council departments, external agencies drawn upon include the Northumbria Police, the North East Mediation Service, the Department of Social Security fraud investigators and Victim Support. Specific assistance includes training for officers in mediation skills from the North East Mediation Service and in static surveillance techniques from the police.

The housing team originally targeted problem residents referred by local housing offices. It has now combined this follow-up procedure with a more aggressive "blitzing" of targeted council estates, sometimes accompanied by a "pulse" policing operation. Such operations rely upon the unexpected deployment of large numbers of council and police personnel and hope to make more of an impact on crime and incivilities than a less intense but more sustained initiative. In conducting interviews when investigating complaints, housing officers will meet individuals at any place and at any time and may attend people's homes disguised as workmen. Such an approach is essential to prevent and overcome the fear of intimidation felt by victims and witnesses. When gathering evidence of nuisance behavior housing officers may undertake covert observation of target individuals and residences using video time-lapse recording systems. An anonymous phoneline for complaints and information regarding antisocial or criminal behavior by tenants is also maintained. The team maintain a central registry of all complaints, referrals and operations. This allows problem areas or tenants to be identified and monitored, supporting early intervention and later legal action. This registry is the source of much of the intelligence that the local authority housing department is able to provide to the police and other civic agencies, such as the Benefit Agency fraud investigators. The registry also holds intelligence received from other parties.

Police Cooperation

Day-to-day liaison with the police occurs via a liaison inspector or contact officer in the Intelligence Unit, although meetings may involve the superintendent divisional commander if required. Police assistance includes identifying problem residents, supplying information to support local authority civil actions and warning problem tenants of possible council action.

With the establishment of the enforcement team, the housing department and the local police commander together identified the ten most problematic families on the estate, so as to "concentrate on the most criminal and anti-social households rather than diffusing the effort" (Clarke, 1994:18-19). Having assisted in drawing a target list of ten families, the police then disclosed information that assisted council intervention, e.g., an injunction or eviction. Such information includes incident calls, arrests, charges, pending proceedings and convictions. This exchange of information has recently been enhanced by the flagging of problem residents or premises on the local police incident computer. As coverage of the team has increased, only individuals targeted during an estate-specific blitz are flagged. Any police incident that involves an individual or address on the problem resident list is automatically brought to the attention of the liaison inspector. A vetting process occurs at this stage, and information considered non-sensitive and relevant to the TET remit is passed on. Two of the housing team's officers are charged with liaising with the police and other agencies on a daily basis and collating information to build up the evidence needed to support civil actions.

The mutually supportive nature of this joint criminal and civil enforcement approach is illustrated in the protocol the housing department and the police have developed regarding the issuing of warnings to tenants following an incident requiring police attendance. The police may inform the TET of their attendance at an incident (subject to vetting), while also providing the tenant involved with written communication stating that the housing department has been informed of an incident and that he or she may be in breach of their tenancy agreement. The TET also informs the tenant that an incident has been brought to its attention and that the incident may be investigated. An aspect of such an intervention stressed by both parties is that action against problem behavior is swift. A tenant could receive two formal warning letters within a week of a criminal or antisocial incident. In practice however, a more informal approach has been adopted to date, with verbal warnings from officers.

Tenancy Enforcement Team Operations

Operational information relating to the team was provided by the housing department. Of the original ten target families or individuals, seven left the estate voluntarily, two ceased their antisocial behavior and one individual — a child dependent — was taken into care. In the first eight months of operation, the Gateshead team recorded 27 incidents of problem non-tenant residents leaving the estate following formal warnings from the housing department. The majority of these were adult dependents of estate tenants. The specific activity of the team and its use of the civil remedies of injunction and eviction is detailed in Table 1 below.

Since the team's inception, approximately 150 notices of seeking possession have been granted by the courts as of September 1996. However, as indicated, until February 1997 this was a drawn out two-stage process and only two possession orders had been granted by the court.

Table 1: Operational Activity of the Tenancy Enforcement Team

Cases Undertaken, July 1994-March 1996	No.
Enquiries re: the TET Registry	1807
Cases referred for TET action	498
Interviews and information received	1334
Formal cautions to tenants (verbal and written)	139
Results of Cases, April 1996-September 1996	
Notice of seeking possession served	43
Notice of seeking possession still active*	59
Injunctions granted	1
Possessions orders granted	2

* Court orders are valid for 12 months, and these are notices from the previous recording period that are still active.

Another example of the use of specialist housing officers to vigorously draw upon civil powers in tackling problem residents of high-crime housing areas is found in London, and is discussed below. The problems faced here were predominantly the crimes of robbery and burglary, committed by a small number of the dependents of tenants. The following case again highlights the relation between the use of civil tools and the criminal powers of the police.

Hackney Housing Department, London and the Metropolitan Police

The Housing Department of the Hackney Borough Council in London experienced major problems with one of its housing estates, before initiating a number of civil measures. The Kingsmead Estate is a 17-acre estate of 1,084 dwellings in the Borough of Hackney, east London. The estate, built in 1936, is made up of 16 five-story walk-up buildings, the eight largest occupying the central part of the estate and the remaining smaller buildings arranged along the perimeter. In 1993 a high number of iron shutters and doors, a product of the high burglary and void (empty property) rates, visually blighted the area. Just under half of the approximate 3,000 residents are Afro-Caribbeans, Africans, Greeks, Turks, Asians and Vietnamese. Unemployment on the estate is one of the worst in London, with about 80% of residents receiving state benefits and a large number of unemployed 16 to 21 year olds.

The key criminal and disorder problems as reported to the police and council investigators were burglary, robbery and related witness intimidation. In 1992, according to local detectives and council housing officers, almost all of these problems stemmed from a hard core of approximately ten juveniles, three of whom were brothers. Such was the fear of reprisals that many victims and witnesses did not report offenses. The true level of offending on the estate was only uncovered by an initial audit of the estate by the housing department investigative team, whose figures revealed a dramatic escalation of crime in during 1992. As the confidence of the offenders increased, the crime situation spiralled and residents' confidence in the police and the local authority plummeted. The following excerpt from a collective statement by a group of residents, illustrates the extreme intimidation felt by victims and witnesses that hampered police intervention: "The Kingsmead Estate and Sherry's Wharf are suffering from a reign of terror by a youth gang who [sic] appear to be led by X and his brothers. There are numerous break-ins to property by the youth gang who appear to have little fear of arrest. Tenants are intimidated and harassed to such a degree that the gang members are rarely identified to the police following robberies" (Hackney Housing Department, 1993).

In December 1992, a joint "Think Tank Team," comprising senior housing and police officers, was established. An ensuing police investigation reviewed all burglaries and robberies committed on the estate over the previous six months, and undertook a surveillance operation (Operation Boston) against the family of key offenders. These individuals, the sons of the registered tenant, were later arrested and charged.

Running in parallel to the police operation, a special housing team (discussed below) was preparing a civil course of action. Following the criminal convictions, of three individuals convicted for robbery, burglary and drug offenses, police evidence was made available for the housing department eviction proceedings. Injunctions (in the form of exclusion orders) were served in May 1993 against five defendants, four of them from the problem family, on the grounds of abusing their tenancy agreement through criminal actions.

Hackney Housing Department Housing Inspectorate Team

The Housing Inspectorate Team (HIT), formerly known as the Tenancy Audit Team was established in the autumn of 1991. This team quickly became involved with the Kingsmead Estate project and was able to offer a detailed knowledge of the area's residents. During the investigations of the team, which ran parallel to the police operation, they were often able to obtain information not given to the detective team because of their non-police status and broader concerns regarding the estate and its residents. The team operates out of an anonymous council property, providing discretion important in overcoming the fear of intimidation, and encouraging individuals to attend meetings and give statements (to HIT and the police) if they do not wish to be visited at home on the estate. As stated by a victim to housing investigation officers in December 1992, "The general feeling on the estate is that the police are not discreet and people reporting crimes become known to the gang who retaliate later." Following the serving of the injunctions in May 1993, the housing team also monitored the estate for evidence of the orders being breached. As in the previous case study, these specialist housing officers undertook video surveillance and engaged in clandestine meetings with victims and witnesses.

The Hackney housing team has developed a computer system that is able to search through numerous local authority databases (council tenancies, council tax payees, housing benefit recipients). The system can identify individuals via personal information (vehicle index, date of birth, telephone number) provided on almost any council form. The use of basic crime pattern analysis techniques allows the identification of potential problem "hot spots" e.g., if 40% of a council residential block is void (empty) this may indicate (or give rise to) problems in the block. In addition, the system is used to detect benefit frauds by claimants and multiple accommodation applications or tenancies. Further, it provides a tracking ability and may be used by the housing investigation team in locating individuals, a facility sometimes extended to the police. Frequently tenants may reside at more than one address in the locale due to an extended family network, and the HIT officers can often provide an address for individuals sought by the police if they are in the borough. This cooperation helps the authorities deal with serious problems and criminal tenants, and engenders a positive relationship between the police and the local authority. Information on the location or actions of problem individuals is also received from other residents. Residents are invited to discuss problems, and over a number of meetings they establish relationships with the housing officer. If suitable, and with their permission, the officer may then introduce the resident to a local police detective who may develop an independent relationship with that individual.

Injunctions were sought to provide interim relief from antisocial and criminal behavior, and to try and counter witness and victim intimidation on the Kingsmead Estate. The injunctions were undertaken under Section 222 of the Local Government Act 1972, which provides local authorities with very broad powers to prosecute "...where a local authority consider(s) it expedient for the promotion or protection of the interests of the inhabitants of their area." Once served in May 1993, the injunctions specifically prohibited named individuals from entering designated properties on the estate and causing damage to council property, and from assaulting or threatening council employees or estate residents. Affidavits can be used in applying for injunctions, though if challenged (and here they were, funded by legal aid) witness cross-examination may be required. In an attempt to minimize potential intimidation, witnesses who had since moved off the estate were able, with the permission of the judge, to keep their addresses confidential. The importance of any measure that encourages residents to make statements by deterring intimidation could not be over-emphasized by the team.

Police Cooperation

The key police initiatives were the re-investigation of previous cases and Operation Boston. In conducting these and subsequent operations, a close relationship developed between the investigating housing department officers and the police. As indicated, the police passed to the housing team evidence and statements, following the criminal prosecution, so as to assist in obtaining injunctions and evictions. Once the injunctions were served, the local patrol officer played an important role in enforcing the injunction by reporting any breach of the order to the housing department, e.g., if an individual under notice was seen on the estate.

The cooperation between the local authority and the police following the operations on the Kingsmead Estate has been sustained by the creation of a joint Crime on Estates Working Group in January 1995. This forum seeks to identify problem areas throughout the borough and coordinate multiagency action. Issues discussed include pirate radio stations, prostitution and the mutual monitoring of crime and nuisance on the estates in the area. This collective approach to the controlling of problems on the estate was further enhanced in 1997 by the establishment of a shared computer data mapping format. This allows for enhanced crime pattern analysis and the identification of police and council hot spots, be they for recorded criminal or antisocial incidents. Such an exchange provides an operational platform for the support of civil remedies with police resources, and vice-versa.

Improvements on the Estate

The crime-recorded rate for the estate is illustrated by the bar chart in the figures below. The wider trend for the Hackney and Shoreditch police sectors, the East London area in which the Kingsmead Estate is found, is shown by the data line. Figure 2 below details the changes in burglary on the estate. Following the arrests in January 1993, domestic burglaries for the year fell 69% compared to 1992, five times the reduction experienced by the surrounding East London area (14%). Incidents rose in 1994, followed by a continued decline in burglary to 25 (from 139) incidents in 1996. This represents an 82% reduction over the 1992-96 period, compared to a 45% reduction for the local area.

As depicted in Figure 3, robberies on the Kingsmead fell 21% in 1993, compared to a 16% rise locally. Robbery on the estate continued to fall to five incidents in 1996, a 79% decrease compared to

1992 levels, in marked contrast to an overall rise of 24% in the surrounding areas.

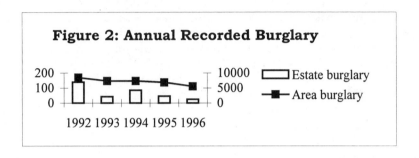

Figure 2: Annual Recorded Burglary

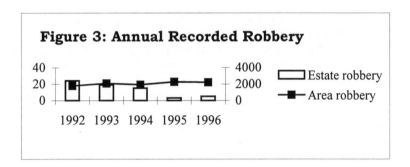

Figure 3: Annual Recorded Robbery

Vehicle crime (including theft of and from vehicles also fell dramatically, with a one year interruption, recording a reduction of 55%
(from 45 to 20). This contrasts with an overall fall in the east London
area of 13%, as shown in Figure 4.

A partial explanation put forward by local police and the HIT officers for the rise in burglaries and vehicle crime during 1994 was that
another large criminal family living on the estate had become active
in the area following the removal of the initial family of offenders. By
this time also however, some of the original group of offenders had
also been released from detention and were known to visit the estate.

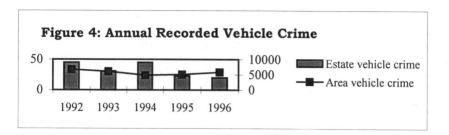

Figure 4: Annual Recorded Vehicle Crime

Another indicator of turnaround for the estate was the level of empty (void) properties, a result of residents leaving the estate and the reluctance of new tenants to accept accommodation on the Kingsmead estate. Following the high-profile crime crackdown in February 1993, coupled with an intense estate management approach of services on the estate (such as maintenance), the number of void properties dropped significantly. Void levels fell from 262 in April 1993 to 56 in January 1997, a drop of 78%. The block where the key offenders lived, along with the block opposite where they frequently offended, had void levels of 45%. With the removal of the problem family (who occupied but one apartment), the void level in the two blocks dropped to 12% by May 1995. The execution of an injunction against another problem tenant who had driven out neighbors through abuse and intimidation led to a drop in void levels of more than 50% (from 12 to 5) by the following year. Although anecdotal, a final indicator of improvement on the estate regarding the fear of intimidation from offenders is the offering by residents of their homes as observation sites to the housing team; in 1992 residents were reluctant even to talk to the team.

CONCLUSIONS

The increasingly vigorous use of civil remedies to tackle problems of crime and anti-social behavior in both residential and non-residential settings has, as illustrated by the case studies, entailed a number of related developments. These include the growth in civil intelligence gathering to support the use of civil instruments, as well as the strengthening of the instruments themselves. A number of issues regarding the changing nature of compliance enforcement in central and local government have been identified by Sparrow (1994). A shift from an individual "incident" to a broader "risk" orientation by civil enforcement departments is illustrated by the adoption of joint mapping of problem areas, targeting priority offenders with the police and the setting up of strategic fora such as the Hackney Crime on Estates Working Group. Risks may be identified in terms of offense category (e.g., robbery) or geographically (e.g., the Gateshead estate "blitzes"). The monitoring of related problems by different agency mechanisms — police-recorded crime and housing department resident complaints — may identify different offenders and problem areas. New information may be gleaned by both parties in drawing up a joint priority list. This proactive, intelligence-oriented approach, now common in the criminal law enforcement arena, serves to facilitate the 'strategic selection of enforcement targets' (Sparrow, 1994: xxvi).

Both the Gateshead Tenancy Enforcement Team and the Hackney Housing Inspectorate Team acknowledge that resource as well as strategic factors influence their points of intervention, i.e., who they investigate and for what they prosecute. "Enforcement agencies face up to the fact that there are not, and never will be, sufficient resources to support successful prosecution of all offenders. They also accept that prosecuting every offender...would be destructive of their relationship with the public" (Sparrow, 1994: xxv). The move to a broader, more preventive "unit of work" involves the judicious selection of targets and a need to assess risk and prioritize complaints. The police and housing departments in both studies deliberately adopted a pro-media policy in the hope that high profile prosecutions would serve to deter problem behavior by other tenants.

With the growth in civil enforcement by housing departments, there is a danger that officials may come to view estate residents as a population to be regulated — as part of the problem rather than the solution. Such a perspective would displace the "client" and "partner" ethos that has started taking hold in much local government provision, as tenants are increasingly being seen as active consumers rather than passive recipients of municipal services. In regard to tackling problems in Hackney, London, tenants' associations are involved in devising strategies to tackle crime and fear of crime on their estates by an involvement in multi-agency working groups. On a more operational level, as victims or witnesses, the cooperation of residents is needed to report incidents and give evidence, be it a police statement or a civil affidavit. Without this support from residents, no serious attempt can be made at tackling problems. Both housing department teams also receive information from residents in various forms, such as anonymous phone calls or letters. The cooperation of tenants is especially needed for the provision of observation points during the surveillance of problem dwellings and residents.

In the U.K., the call from central government for local authorities to tackle problem tenants found the civil process of evictions and injunctions to be wanting. Hackney and Gateshead housing officials indicated that their enforcement activity would be facilitated by the recent simplification of the eviction procedure and the ability to enforce injunctions with police assistance. However, increased activity for such teams brings with it increased costs, despite the adoption of a priority approach. Housing departments may find it difficult to fund such enforcement when resources are already over-allocated for primary housing provision. Such problems echo the experiences of other civil enforcement activity, such as the Inland Revenue Service and Environmental Protection Agency in the U.S., where the adoption of a more vigorous compliance policy has revealed shortcomings in the enforcement capability of those charged with tackling newly prioritized problems (Sparrow, 1994).

An underlying theme of the enforcement initiatives undertaken by both local authorities discussed here is the relationship with other government agencies, primarily the police service. Although each case study has looked at differing mechanisms of cooperation, the outcome is that civil intervention can be reinforced by the criminal process and police resources at key stages. Although communications between local authorities and local police may generally exist at a senior level, actions by the two bodies are frequently uncoordinated. This is understandable given the distinct legal and administrative processes under which the two operate. As the use of civil mechanisms to tackle antisocial — and increasingly criminal, behavior — flourishes, inter-agency discussion forums will need to be supplemented by a partnership format that allows for the exchange of information according to daily operational requirements rather than timetabled monthly meetings. Such an approach will enable a corresponding and supportive police response to the development of municipal agency enforcement teams that increasingly utilize civil remedies, with an aggression previously found in the criminal process.

◆

Address correspondence to: Sheridan Morris, c/o U.K. Home Office, Police Research Group, 50 Queen Anne's Gate, London SW1H 9AT United Kingdom.

REFERENCES

Association of Metropolitan Authorities (1994). Unpublished survey from the seminar "Managing Neighbour Disputes, Nuisance and Crime on Council Estates; the Social Landlord."

Clarke, M. (1994). "Tyneside's Least Wanted." *Police Review* 11:18-19.

Department of the Environment (1990). *Crime Prevention on Council Estates*. London, UK: Her Majesty's Stationery Office.

Felson, M. (1986). "Routine Activities, Social Controls, Rational Decisions, and Criminal Outcomes." In: D. Cornish and R. Clarke (eds.), *The Reasoning Criminal*. New York, NY: Springer-Verlag.

—— (1995). "Those Who Discourage Crime." In: J.E. Eck and D. Weisburd (eds.), *Crime and Place*. Crime Prevention Studies, vol. 4. Monsey, NY: Criminal Justice Press.

Gateshead Metropolitan Borough Council (1993). Unpublished minutes of the Housing Committee, November 1994.

Hackney Housing Department (1993). Personal communication to the Tenancy Audit Team officers from local tenants.

Skogan, W. G. (1988). "Disorder, Crime and Community." In: T. Hope and M. Shaw (eds.), *Communities and Crime Reduction*. London, UK: Her Majesty's Stationery Office.

Sparrow, M. K. (1994). *Imposing Duties: Government's Changing Approach to Compliance*. Westport, CT: Praeger.